SpringerBriefs in Economics

More information about this series at http://www.springer.com/series/8876

Arup Mitra · Aya Okada

Labour Market Participation in India

A Region- and Gender-Specific Study

Springer

Arup Mitra
National Institute of Labour Economics Research and Development, Institute of Economic Growth
New Delhi
India

Aya Okada
Graduate School of International Development
Nagoya University
Nagoya
Japan

ISSN 2191-5504 ISSN 2191-5512 (electronic)
SpringerBriefs in Economics
ISBN 978-981-10-7142-3 ISBN 978-981-10-7143-0 (eBook)
https://doi.org/10.1007/978-981-10-7143-0

Library of Congress Control Number: 2017958568

Printed on acid-free paper

This Springer imprint is published by Springer Nature
The registered company is Springer Nature Singapore Pte Ltd.
The registered company address is: 152 Beach Road, #21-01/04 Gateway East, Singapore 189721, Singapore

Contents

About the Authors

Arup Mitra is Professor of Economics at the Institute of Economic Growth, New Delhi, India. He is currently serving as Director General, National Institute of Labour Economics Research and Development (NILERD), New Delhi. His research interests include development economics, urban development, labour and welfare, industrial productivity growth and employment, services sector growth and trade in services, and gender studies. He has published in a number of international and national journals. He worked as a Senior Researcher at the International Labour Organization, Geneva, was offered a Visiting Fellowship at the Institute of Developing Economies, Tokyo, has held the Indian Economy Chair at Sciences Po, Paris, and was a Visting Professor at the Graduate School of International Development, Nagoya University, Japan. The Indian Econometric Society awarded him the Mahalanobis Memorial Gold Medal for his outstanding contributions in the field of quantitative economics. His work has been cited in the *Handbook of Regional and Urban Economics* (Elsevier, 2004), and he has also contributed to the *Encyclopaedia of Life Support Systems* (EOLSS), *Mathematical Models in Economics* (Ed. Zhang, W.), developed under the auspices of UNESCO, and to the *Encyclopaedia of Sustainability*, Great Barrington, MA: Berkshire Publishing.

Aya Okada is Vice Trustee for International Cooperation and Professor of Political Economy at the Graduate School of International Development (GSID), Nagoya University. She holds an M.Phil. in Development Studies from the University of Sussex and a Ph.D. in Economic Development from Massachusetts Institute of Technology (MIT). Her research interests include economic and social development, regional planning, education and skills development, and gender and development. Her publications include books such as *Industrial Skills Development: Globalization and Human Resource Development in Developing Countries* (co-edited, 2008, in Japanese) and numerous chapters and articles in international journals such as *World Development*. She was Research Fellow at

MIT's Industrial Performance Center (IPC) from 1997 to 1998. She was a Visiting Scholar at MIT and Visiting Professor at Jawaharlal Nehru University, India, both as an Abe Fellow awarded by the Social Science Research Council. More recently, she has also played consulting/advisory roles in development projects sponsored by JICA, UNESCO and the Japanese government.

Labour Market Participation in India: A Region- and Gender-Specific Study

Abstract This study in the Indian context focuses on the gender-specific labour force participation across regions and makes an attempt to identify the important determinants. Before turning to the Indian situation, the participation rates are examined for various countries in the Asia-Pacific region. In India like many other countries, the female participation rate is significantly lower than that among the males. The rural–urban differentials are more pronounced, and the interstate variations are sizable in the case of females than males. Even in the large cities the female labour market participation is lower than that in the rural areas despite higher levels of education. However, in terms of inter-spatial (rural/urban/city) variations, the impact of infrastructure, education, health and urbanization on labour force participation of both the gender is quite distinct. With improved infrastructure, the quantum of investment is expected to shoot up and the accessibility to growth centres offering better livelihood opportunities can perk up. While industrialization and growth in services show a positive effect on participation, economic growth unravels a positive impact on urban males only. Also, there is evidence on poverty-induced participation in agricultural activities, suggesting clearly the importance of rural diversification for creation of productive employment. Women's participation improves child health significantly. Access of mothers to resources enhances the health status of the children as their nutritional status and access to curative health care get better. On the whole, women participation in productive activities has a double effect: first, it raises the household income; second, it contributes to the well-being of the household. These findings are important from policy point of view because different infrastructure variables are seen to improve both participation and labour productivity. Infrastructure (social, physical and financial) can to certain extent break the social and cultural barriers and help women join the labour market, thus enabling them to make productive contribution to the growth process. Though the level of urbanization raises the urban participation rate in an inter-spatial sense, a similar pattern is not evident in the context of rural females (at least at the state level). How urbanization can be

This study was carried out during Arup Mitra's visit (November 2016–March 2017) at the Graduate School of International Development, Nagoya University, Nagoya, Japan

A. Mitra and A. Okada, *Labour Market Participation in India*, SpringerBriefs in Economics, https://doi.org/10.1007/978-981-10-7143-0_1

made more generative with positive spillover effects in the rural neighbourhood is an important policy concern because increased urbanization ushering in greater concentration of non-farm activities holds the potentiality to create employment prospects and at the same time result in productivity gains.

1 Analytical Frame

Labour force participation rate is an important indicator of development. With increased human capital formation, people are able to participate in productive activities which result in higher levels of value addition. Without human capital formation, a high level of labour market participation is also evident, but in that case, it is associated with low levels of labour productivity. How labour market participation can improve with rising labour productivity is, therefore, an important research and policy question. Particularly in societies experiencing rise in life expectancy, population must be engaged in productive activities so that for future years (for old age), they are able to save enough. India has witnessed considerable decline in fertility rate with an increase in the percentage of population in the working age brackets, which is seen to be the source of demographic dividend. But such benefits can materialize and enhance economic growth only when from supply point of view there is skilled and highly employable labour force and from demand side there are enough opportunities to absorb them productively. The new technology is skill intensive, and as the study by Okada (2004) reveals, the dynamic industrial transformations in the 1990s significantly changed the nature, content and extent of skill development as far as the domestic suppliers are concerned. However, in India, a large majority of young people still continue to have limited access to education and training because the dropout rates are high despite an expansion in the capacity of educational institutions and enrolments (Okada 2012). The skill mismatch index is huge, indicating poor employability of a large percentage of the available labour force (Mitra 2013a). Dreze and Gandhi-Kingdon present evidence to suggest that school participation, especially among girls, responds to a wide range of variables, including parental education and motivation, social background, dependency ratios, work opportunities, village development, teacher postings, teacher regularity, midday meals and also school quality.

One of the important drivers of socio-economic transformations is urbanization. There is an economic reason to justify this view. Large human settlements emerge from concentration of activities. Large volume of investments, indivisibilities in infrastructure and other assets and large expenditure incurred by the state naturally give rise to several external economies of scale attracting firms and business to concentrate. The agglomeration economies in other words motivate growth centres to expand which in turn attract labour from other areas as job search cost tends to decline sizably. Thus, population growth takes place and cities grow in size. The external economies of scale result in higher total factor productivity growth which gets translated in terms of higher real wages. Many development indicators such as literacy and social capital formation are likely to improve significantly, as urbanization draws larger government resources for human capital formation. On the whole, it envisages upward mobility for all, both the migrants and the natives.

The received theory suggests that urbanization follows as a concomitant of industrialization and, at a later stage, it is related to growth in services. In other words, with urbanization, the decline in the share of agriculture or any other primary activity is strongly associated. Since productivity levels in the non-primary sectors, particularly in the industrial sector due to the agglomeration benefits, are higher, wage differentials also rise rapidly, which in turn raise the participation rate, particularly in the context of the developing countries. Higher levels of income per person may result in a higher dependency ratio, but the counterargument can also be put forth to suggest that at higher levels of development, each individual is conscious of his/her own identity; hence, urbanization, productivity growth and wage growth may all coincide with increased participation rate. From a different angle, if urbanization occurs in response to rapid outflow of rural population who are in economically active age brackets, then naturally the participation rate is expected to pick up.

Ideally speaking, urbanization is unlikely to pursue the traditional caste-based occupations which are more prevalent in the rural areas. It also envisages upward mobility for the socially backward classes. Quite opposite results may follow if the modern growth process involves the highly skilled labour force only. Since the low-caste population did not have access to higher levels of education, their absorption in the modern sector is less probable. Thus, dualism in development is not an unexpected outcome—the urban areas remain populated by the advantaged classes, while their disadvantaged counterparts remain engaged in petty and low-productivity jobs even after migrating to the urban areas in the face of a tight rural labour market. However, jobs in the informal sector also attract migrants and the rural job seekers respond positively (Banerjee 1984) instead of searching jobs exclusively in the large-scale industrial sector, as many of the theoretical models made us believe (Harris and Todaro 1970). The reservation system followed in the formal sector (particularly in the government sector) for the scheduled caste and scheduled tribe population encourages their migration to the urban areas, which is expected to result in an enhanced participation rate. The private job placement cells have been recruiting many tribal women from the rural areas and engaging them in home care and other related services (Mitra 2013b).

Among various supply- and demand-side factors which impinge on women labour force participation rate, economic growth is seen to have a nonlinear relationship (see Mathur 1994): initially, growth is found to have a negative impact on labour force participation rate, but at higher levels of growth, it tends to increase, thus giving rise to a U-shaped relationship. Cagatay and Ozler (1995) also suggest the possibility of a U-shaped relationship between long-term development and women's share of the labour force. Even the historical record of the developed countries indicates such a relationship between economic development and women's labour force participation rate (Goldin 1994).[1] With urbanization and industrialization, female-dominated home-based production is expected to decline, as it would be largely replaced by male-dominated factory production (Boserup 1970). This falling part of the U-shaped curve corroborates Boserup's analysis of women's contribution. However, with further economic development, women's labour force participation rate is expected to increase as enhanced urbanization and industrialization, more education for women, commodification of domestic labour and falling fertility rates help women workers participate in the labour market more explicitly (Oppenheimer 1970; Boserup 1970). Also, as per the neoclassical approach with economic growth, gender inequalities in terms of access to employment opportunities, work conditions, nature of work and earnings tend to decline (Forsythe et al. 2000). This implies an increase in women's labour participation rate since discouraged dropouts tend to decline: with improved and equal status in the job market, women get encouraged to participate in the labour market (Mitra 2005).

Some of the recent evidence also supports that higher human development index (HDI), let alone growth, does not necessarily ensure gender equality measured in terms of gender development index (GDI): in the Asia-Pacific context, Japan and Korea have the highest HDI-GDI gap, while Thailand and China whose HDI and GDI are both lower in absolute terms than Japan and Korea demonstrate lower gender gaps (Murayama 2005). Gender norms and systems vary widely across cultures, but they shape people's lives and interactions in all societies (Hayase 2005). In general, as women's educational-level improves, gender inequality declines (UN 2001). In other words, with improved levels of education, labour market participation of women in high-income jobs is expected to rise (Murayama 2005; Pradhan et al. 2015), though in India many educated women remain outside the labour market, implying that the education level of women non-workers is more than that of women workers. Keeping in view a long-term perspective, the 'Gender Kuznets Curve' and the U-shaped relationship between women labour participation rate and development are mutually consistent.

A variety of other factors have been considered as determinants of female labour force participation rate. These include opportunities for informal employment which tend to decline with development (Bharadwaj 1989), technological and structural change (Sen 1981),[2] the conflict between housework (including child-care) and earning opportunities in the labour market, and spouse's income resulting in withdrawal from the labour market (rationalizing the backward sloping supply curve of female labour). While education of various types may become instrumental to labour market participation, income levels also matter. For example, activities with very low wages with a low elasticity with respect to labour productivity attract

[1]Goldin (1994) found this association for women aged 45–59 for cross section of countries using GDP per capita as an index of development.

[2]Sen (1981) in the case of Indian agriculture showed that women withdraw from the labour market as male income increases.

less labour. Many of the women workers are subjected to this phenomenon of 'discouraged dropouts' from the labour market. The neoclassical principle of marginal productivity-based pricing of the factor of production is not necessarily realistic as many women workers are seen to be engaged in intense work with meagre earnings because of their docility and poor bargaining power, inability to commute and limited access to diversified social network (Mitra 2005).

Among various socio-economic factors, fertility, cross-regional cultural norms, attitude towards manual work, the relative incidence of low caste and tribal population, the size of the agricultural sector, cultivation techniques, crop patterns, poverty and technology are some of the determinants of female work participation rate (see Agarwal 1988). Fertility and age and marriage are inter-woven, and they both influence the decision to participate in the labour market. Usually, a higher fertility rate and a lower age at marriage reduce women's labour market participation. However, in the rural context, some of the socially backward classes such as scheduled tribes exhibit a higher labour participation rate among females in spite of a higher fertility rate, as the matrilineal traits are more prevalent among them. Also, there can be a positive association between labour participation rate and the percentage of workers engaged in the tertiary sector as activities in this sector provide greater employment opportunities for women and teenage workers. However, low-productivity activities are mostly concentrated in the tertiary sector, and hence, as the share of the tertiary sector in total employment increases, dropouts from the labour market are also expected to be high, thus reducing the labour participation rate.

Rapid economic growth is definitely a determinant of employment though it is not a sufficient condition. Mechanization of agriculture, for example, may raise production without any impact on employment. The composition of agricultural production also impinges on participation, particularly in the case of women. In rice cultivation, for example, a number of activities are to be carried out by labour for which the domestic supplies involving women are tapped. Many of the folklores, particularly in rice-cultivating areas in India, are therefore pro-women, indicating clearly that even in a prevailing patriarchal milieu women's participation in the agricultural process has contributed to enhancing their status. In rice-cultivating areas, women have a major role to perform at every stage of the production process in so much so that with non-cooperation of women there can be a steady drop in agricultural produce (Mohanty 2008).

Similarly in the context of the non-farm sector, industrialization and faster growth in the services are likely to generate employment opportunities on a large scale which in turn could raise the labour force participation rate by augmenting labour demand. However, the adoption of capital- and skill-intensive technology is seen to reduce the pace of the industrialization of work force. With such technology, economic growth can be stepped up but with no dent on employment; rather, it may prompt a withdrawal from the labour market and/or lead to a residual absorption of labour in low-productivity informal sector activities. On the same vein, the high-productivity services which are capital and skill intensive can raise the economic growth but cannot generate large-scale employment for the unskilled and semi-skilled variety of the work force except nominally through secondary effects. From the point of view of workers' preference, it is noted that women, particularly the urban-based educated ones, have a natural urge to work in the services sector (Nord 1989). This means that female labour force participation rate and growth in the services sector are expected to go hand in hand.

Relating to labour regulations, it is believed that they tend to reduce the pace of employment generation. Besley and Burgess (2004) showed that Indian states which amended the Industrial Disputes Act in a pro-worker direction experienced lowered output, employment, investment and productivity in the organized manufacturing. Bhattacharjea (2006) on the other hand criticized the widely used index of state-level labour regulation devised by Besley and Burgess (2004), and the econometric methodology they used to demonstrate the dampening effect of excessively pro-worker regulation on performance in Indian manufacturing. On the whole, while there may be a case for removing labour market rigidities by discouraging the political patronization of the unions and relaxing the strict labour laws that prohibit employment growth, attention also needs to be given to the labour welfare issues.

Notwithstanding these concerns expressed by ILO, the Indian labour market has been experiencing rapid contractualization. In order to keep the labour cost low, it is being followed both in the rural and in the urban labour markets. Both agriculture and other activities in the rural areas such as construction involve a great deal of contractual labour who migrated from other areas with the help of the labour-contracting firms. Similarly in the urban context, manufacturing and services both in the formal sector are hiring contract labour on a large scale in order to avoid the labour market regulations. Often, it is seen that the employers prefer female workers as they have a lesser bargaining strength and their wages are fixed at a level substantially lower than the male wage on a false belief that female workers are less productive. This has resulted in feminization in the labour market reflected in the rising female-to-male workers ratio in a number of activities (Banerjee 1997). In fact, like contractualization, feminization is an arrangement pursued to reduce labour cost sizably. The other new change which is perceived in the recent years is the practice of business subcontracting from the formal to the informal sector. Though it creates work opportunities in the informal sector, the business contractors follow the payment practice based on piece rate, holding the key to reduce the remuneration of the workers. As many of the home-based workers are women, they are the ones who are worst hit (Patrick 2001).

Poor health conditions hamper labour force participation rate, particularly in developing countries where many prime age adults are undernourished and are in poor health (Currie and Madrian 1999). In ageing societies, more individuals keep reaching age brackets where health has the greatest impact on labour market participation (Currie and Madrian 1999). In general, poor health reduces the capacity to work and productivity levels which in turn reduce wages. The cost of accommodating a worker in poor health is passed on in the form of lower wages. Low wages dampen participation. Both from supply and demand sides, poor health can reduce participation. Particularly in the case of women, those burdened with high fertility rate and poor maternal and child health are unable to participate in the labour market. Even many educated women in India let alone their uneducated counterparts are outside the labour market partly because of the social norms, reinforcing the division of labour along the lines of gender and partly because of poor health conditions. A mere increase in literacy is not able to counter the cultural practices and the social outlook which perceives women participation in the labour market as a low-status phenomenon. Even among the educated lot this mindset is widely prevalent, forcing many of them, particularly if married, to withdraw from the job market (Jalan 2000; Schultz 1990). Household activities and domestic responsibilities involving children and the elderly are given higher priority over participation (Hirway 2010). As the IFC report observed globally, while women's education levels have increased and educated women earn more than their uneducated peers, gender gaps in labour market participation and wage levels persist. In the rural areas even among the poor households, the labour force participation rate remains modest possibly because of poor health conditions and healthcare facilities. Long and frequent absence from work can discourage employers to engage workers, while poor health reduces the supply of labour hours per individual. Workers in poor health are constantly discriminated against, as the efficiency wage hypothesis would posit.

Relating to physical and financial infrastructure, it has been noted extensively that the potential entrants to the labour market respond to these facilities positively. In particular, women are severely constrained by physical, financial and poor sanitation facilities. With slightest support, they are eager to explore earning opportunities which augment family income (Cook et al. 2005). The microcredit provision, for example, is seen to have provided earning possibilities across regions despite the serious limitations associated with this option (ICDF 2002). Many rural children with better connectivity and support for acquiring reading materials have shown greater enrolment ratio. The accessibility to road and sanitation has encouraged educational enrolment, particularly in the case of girl children. As Dreze and Khera (2015) write, the child development index fared better in the states of Kerala, Tamil Nadu and Himachal Pradesh. Part of this improvement was expansion in elementary education, while part of it is attributed to the constructive role of the state in providing a wide range of facilities ranging from health care and clean water to social security and basic infrastructure. All this has a future bearing on the labour market participation as childhood conditions (heath and education) have profound effects on future outcomes (Grossman 1975; Wadsworth 1986).

The rural employment guarantee act (MGNREGA) in order to enhance the livelihood security of the rural population offers hundred days of employment in a year to every household whose adult members volunteer to do unskilled jobs (Dreze and Khera 2009). In response to this programme, it has been observed that women participation has gone up extensively. Males being the primary bread earners possibly look for jobs with longer duration and, hence, they may not be seeking work under MGNREGA, while women, who are mainly homemakers and/or seasonal workers in the agriculture sector or pursue economic activities as subsidiary status workers, may take the opportunity of participating in MGNREGA as it enables them to access cash income. Also, as the male members migrate out from the rural areas in search of better jobs, women from the rural households remain as the primary job seekers under MGNREGA. However, the number of days of work per household being only one hundred it is unlikely to raise the women labour force participation rate as per the usual principal status which considers one hundred and eighty days as the benchmark.

Keeping in view this perspective, the present study proposes to examine the labour force participation rates across regions (rural and urban) and sexes in India. It is largely a cross-sectional study as the time dimensionality is highly limited. Hence, the main task is to examine the long-term changes in the participation rate and the factors which influence the participation rate in the long run with cross-sectional data. We may, therefore, propose to take the view that differences across regions can be considered as reflection of long-run changes as regions are unevenly developed and laggard regions would follow the path of more developed regions in labour market participation pattern.

The unit of analysis is both state and district. Further, we consider the participation rates at the level of cities in order to capture the impact of urbanism which can possibly be felt only in large cities. The database of the study is drawn from population census (2011) as well as the annual surveys of labour force conducted by the Ministry of Labour and Employment (Labour Bureau) for the years 2009–10, 2011–12, 2012–13, 2013–14 and 2014–15. Different correlates are taken from the population census data as well as other sources mentioned in the appendix. Since the population census does not report figures on labour force (working persons and unemployed), rather on working persons only, we consider the work participation rates. Further, we focus only on the main workers leaving out those who are working on subsidiary basis known as marginal workers. However, the Labour Bureau's estimates are wide which consider the main or principal status workers, the marginal or subsidiary status workers and also those who are not working but seeking or available for work—all adding up to labour force. The rest of the paper is organized as follows. The following section examines certain labour market indicators in the Asia-Pacific context. The country-specific figures are considered to delineate systematic patterns, if any. In Sect. 3, we turn to the Indian labour market situation, highlighting the regional variations and, more importantly, the gender differentials. It argues that the lower participation rates of women are instrumental to gender subjugation and suggests that empowerment can be attained through improvement in women participation rates. Section 4 based on the inter-spatial variations in gender- and region-specific participation rates makes an attempt to identify the determinants and their differential impact in rural and urban areas (and cities). Section 5 turns to issues related to productivity and women participation rate. Finally, Sect. 6 concludes with policy directives.

2 Asia-Pacific Perspective[3]

Before turning to the Indian situation, it may be desirable to examine the participation rates across countries, at least in the Asia-Pacific context. Most of these countries still belong to the developing world, and several have witnessed structural reforms and pursued industrialization and liberalization policies vigorously in the recent past. The Asia-Pacific region has made good progress in reducing gender discrimination, but appalling disparities remain (United Nations 2007). Besides, the diversity of the Asian experience is not limited to rates and patterns of economic growth only. Initial conditions, ongoing experience with government plans and policies, and governmental and non-governmental programmes, differences in the political environment, differences in commitment to poverty alleviation and gender equity within each country, traditional gender hierarchies and their impact on women's participation in work outside the home, the sexual division of labour, migration and control over income all tend to vary across countries and within a country, across regions. In response to globalization, some of these aspects are also undergoing changes and new patterns are emerging. It becomes necessary to assess whether participation rates tend to be similar if the level of economic development is the same or can they still be different because of the social factors.

The study by ILO (2000) on Asia-Pacific countries argued that women's labour force participation was universally lower than that of men's in 1996. Level of development did not appear to be an important determinant of women's labour force participation, while sociocultural context was. Further, it pointed out that the male–female differential in labour force participation was smallest in the transition economies and largest in South Asian and Pacific countries. The differential in the fast-growing economies of East and Southeast Asia and in the advanced industrialized countries was somewhere in between the two extremes, and among the advanced industrialized countries, it was largest in Japan. The share of females in total labour force ranged from 26 to 42% in South Asia, from 37 to 46% in East and Southeast Asia, from 41 to 44% in the advanced industrialized countries and from 45 to 53% in transition economies. At the same time, women predominated in those categories of the labour force that were not officially recorded in most countries, e.g. subsistence agriculture (ILO 2000). Our analysis based on the KILM data set of ILO shows that the female labour participation rate has considerable variations across countries (Mitra 2010). At two time points, for example 1980 and 2006, there are countries such as India, Pakistan and Sri Lanka that show a participation rate of less than 35%, while in countries such as Cambodia, China, Papua New Guinea, Thailand and Vietnam, the rate has been nearly 70% or more. These wide variations are reflected in the coefficient of variations pertaining to the female labour force participation rate. The role of factors such as education, attitude

[3]This part is drawn from Mitra (2013b).

towards female work and other socio-economic conditions which influence the female work participation rate cannot be ruled out in the context of these cross-country variations.

However, what is interesting to note is that over time these variations are declining, indicating that some of the countries are experiencing a rise while some others experience a decline with an overall decline in the cross-country differences (Table A.1 in the Appendix). Though at this stage it is incorrect to suggest that there can be a unique participation rate around which many countries may tend to converge, the decline in the cross-country variations is a matter that needs further investigation. As regards variation within a sub-region, we note that countries within show wide variations with respect to female labour force participation rate. For example, within Northeast Asia, the Democratic People's Republic of Korea reported a figure of only 48%, while Cambodia peaked as high as 75%. These variations are expected to result in variations in other socio-economic profiles of women including human capital formation.

In contrast to female labour force participation rate, the male LFPR shows less variation across countries (Table A.2 in the Appendix). The ratio of female-to-male participation rate also shows wide variations: while the female–male differences are extremely high in the case of India, Pakistan and Sri Lanka, countries such as Vietnam, Vanuatu and Papua New Guinea, Macau, China (SAR), and Thailand show minimal differences between the sexes. The variations in the ratio of female-to male participation seem to have declined over time. Since the variation in male labour force participation rate is not high and since the magnitude has not undergone any major change over time, the variations and the change in the variations in the female–male differences (measured in terms of the ratio of female-to-male participation rate) are largely caused by the variations and the change in the variations in the female labour force participation rates, respectively.

The differences between the female and male participation rates captured in terms of the ratio of female LFPR to male LFPR varies within a wide range (Table A.3 in the Appendix)—from 0.45 to 0.92—implying that in some of the countries the women labour participation rate is less than half of its male counterpart, while in certain others it is as high as that of males. In fact, the extent of correlation between the female and male labour force participation is very low (0.18 for 2005), though positive. Secondly higher is the male labour force participation rate lower is the female to male participation ratio and also higher is the female labour force participation rate lower is the female to male participation ratio though the degree of association is extremely weak (−0.17 and −0.20, respectively, for 2005). This would again tend to suggest that female and male participation rates have a positive association between them possibly, indicating that as opportunities grow both male and female labour supplies respond positively. In other words, the substitutability hypothesis between male and female labour does not seem to be consistently valid. However, the complementary relation is not too strong as the co-movement takes place only marginally. Hence, policy interventions will be required for women's strategic needs to be met instead of leaving it to the market forces and waiting for demand to grow and bridge the gender gap. The other point relates to the change in the labour participation rate of women over time. Countries which experienced a decline in the female labour force participation rate between 1980 and 1990 to the extent of around three percentage points include Timor-Leste, Fiji, Maldives and the Philippines. Countries that experienced a decline in the labour force participation rate between 1990 and 2006 are Bangladesh, Sri Lanka, Thailand, China, the Democratic People's Republic of Korea and Cambodia.

On the other hand, countries such as the Solomon Islands, French Polynesia, the Republic of Korea, Macau, China (SAR), Singapore, Sri Lanka, Guam, Indonesia and Brunei Darussalam experienced more than three percentage points increase in the labour force participation rates between 1980 and 1990. And, the following countries registered an increase of more than three percentage point in the female labour force participation rate between 1990 and 2006: the Republic of Korea, Pakistan, Timor-Leste, Hong Kong, China (SAR), Tonga, the Philippines, Bhutan, Macau, China (SAR) and Maldives.

Why these countries have shown such large changes in women labour participation rates over time is an important issue. Whether the countries that recorded an increase in the female labour participation rate also witnessed improvements in human capital and whether a drop in the female labour participation rate in certain other countries was largely due to shrinkage in job opportunities leading to discouraged dropouts are some of the interesting angles for further exploration. Like labour force participation rate, work force participation rate also seems to have large cross-sectional variations in the case of females compared to the males. The other interesting point related to the female work participation rate is the extent of the recent rise (2000–2006), which is greater than that during the period 1995–2000 (Table A.4 in the Appendix). The youth and adult illiteracy rate among females is high though it does not appear to be abnormally high in comparison with males (Table A.5 in the Appendix). In some of the countries for which information is available for two time points, the rate seems to have declined considerably.

The school enrolment ratio is not impressive in many countries particularly at the primary level, but it has improved over time (Table A.6 in the Appendix). Table A.6 shows that expenditure per student particularly at the tertiary level is quite high and there is a strong possibility that after women complete higher levels of education, they tend to participate in the job market. All this would presumably support the view that education has played a crucial role in enhancing the work force participation rate of females, which in turn is contributing to human capital formation among the younger girl children. In the process of growth, the women work participation rate may decline as women may not be required to participate in the job market. However, Behrman and Zhang (1995) noted that in Asia, the labour force participation rate of females aged 15–64 did not show a U-shaped relationship with respect to per capita income, which Goldin (1994) posited in the process of development. They noted that in some of the Asian countries, it increased over time (Pakistan, Malaysia and Singapore), but in others, it remained basically stable (Hong Kong, China (SAR) and Japan) or fallen (Sri Lanka, Thailand and Turkey). Above the regression line, they found countries such as Bangladesh, China and Thailand, thus arguing that these countries utilized their adult females in a much better way, in contrast to and most other countries in Asia. The plot of female work force participation rate (2006) against GDP per capita (2005, US$ adjusted for purchasing power parity) does not suggest any specific pattern. The regression of the ratio of female-to-male work participation rate on per capita GDP does not show any significant relationship, suggesting that growth alone cannot result in a reduction in inequality in the labour market by generating human capital formation for the disadvantaged sex. Explicit policy interventions would be required to curb inequality in the labour market and make growth more equitable and pro-women.

Employment Elasticity

The next issue relates to the employment sensitivity of economic growth or the employment generating capacity of economic growth. Since most of the developing countries (and even some of the developed countries like Japan where sluggish employment growth has become a serious issue) are not merely interested in the magnitude of economic growth, but rather the employable capacity of growth, particularly keeping in view the issue of productive absorption of the unskilled and semi-skilled work force, this paper focuses on the summary measure of employment elasticity. However, most of the studies have looked at this index in aggregative terms and not gender wise. We, therefore, in this paper pose the question how employment and gender-sensitive economic growth has been in countries in the Asia-Pacific region. In doing this, it has not however been possible to decompose value added in terms of contribution made by female and male workers separately. We merely define it as the ratio of employment growth of female (male) workers to aggregate GDP growth.

1993–97

Female employment elasticity defined as the ratio of female employment growth to aggregate value-added growth appears to be quite low in South and West Asia with a few exceptions such as Maldives and Nepal (Table A.7 in the Appendix). In Southeast Asia, with the exception of Brunei and the Philippines, the elasticity is again on the low side. In Northeast Asia, Hong Kong, China (SAR), is an exception with female employment elasticity of 0.7, while in China, it is pitiably low at 0.12 —in fact, lowest among all the 29 countries in the Asia-Pacific region. All three Pacific countries on the other hand seem to have a relatively higher estimate of elasticity of female employment.

1997–01

While most of the South and West Asian countries in Table A.7 experienced a rise in the elasticity of female employment during 1997–2001 in comparison with that in 1992–97, Nepal observed a major decline from 0.82 to 0.39 over the same period. In Southeast Asia, Indonesia reported a negative figure during this period, while in other countries, the magnitude improved relative to the preceding period. (Though Brunei witnessed a mild decline, it still persisted at a very high level.) The bright picture of the Pacific as observed between 1992 and 1997 seems to have undergone deterioration: the elasticity declined in Fiji became negative in Solomon, and only in Papua New Guinea, it improved further. In countries in the Northeast region, the elasticity by and large improved though the magnitude of the rise in China was only nominal (from 0.09 to 0.12).

2001–05

The Northeast Asian countries, however, experienced a decline in the female employment elasticity, and some of them, in fact, became worse relative to the estimates for 1993–97. All three Pacific countries witnessed improvement relative to the preceding period, and two, relative to the first sub-period as well. Although in four of the six countries in Southeast Asia the elasticity declined, the estimates are quite diverse in this region. Interestingly, in South and West Asia, four of the seven countries show an estimate of unity or more than that, while Bangladesh, India and Sri Lanka have lagged behind—in fact a marked deterioration in the case of Bangladesh and India while Sri Lanka has been dwindling at a low level. Too high an employment growth rate (or employment elasticity going beyond unity) may imply sluggish labour productivity growth. Therefore, the interpretations drawn on the basis of employment elasticity need to be viewed carefully. Since employment elasticity is a ratio, we need to examine separately the employment growth rates. In spite of a high employment growth rate, employment elasticity can turn out to be low if the value-added growth rate exceeds the employment growth rate substantially. On the other hand, the employment elasticity may turn out to be high, despite the fact that both employment growth and value-added growth are unimpressive if the former exceeds the latter. In fact, Papua New Guinea in the Pacific sub-region is a good example of this situation; that is, with a sluggish female employment growth rate (less than two per cent per annum), it could record high female employment elasticity between 1993–97 and 1997–01. Other countries that recorded a sluggish female employment growth rate (irrespective of the magnitude of employment elasticity) between 1993 and 1997 are China, Fiji, Thailand, Bangladesh, Bhutan, India, Pakistan and Sri Lanka. Between 1997 and 2001 while only India and Nepal from South and West Asia registered sluggish female employment growth rate, a considerable number of countries from other sub-regions joined this set: China, Hong Kong, China (SAR), the Republic of Korea, Mongolia, Fiji, Papua New Guinea, Brunei, Indonesia, Malaysia, Singapore and Thailand. Between 2001 and 2005, again several countries continued to experience sluggish female employment growth: China, Republic of Korea, Fiji, Brunei, Indonesia, Singapore, Bangladesh, India and Sri Lanka. Besides, it may be noted that in many countries, the female employment elasticity has been lower than its male counterpart, implying that the female employment has been growing at a slower pace than the male employment even when both the growth rates are quite low (e.g. China). All this can be taken to conclude that while globalization has affected employment adversely in many countries, the female workers are possibly the worst sufferers. The growth process and technological progress seem to have become increasingly more capital and skill intensive, implying that employment opportunities for unskilled and semi-skilled workers are pitiably meagre. Given the relatively low skill base of a large number of women workers, they seem to be deprived more than males from accessing the benefits of productive employment opportunities. And this is obviously indicative of sluggish human capital formation among women relative to males, which aggravates gender inequality, thus reinforcing the need for policy interventions to meet women's strategic needs.

Unemployment Rate

One indicator of deprivation is the unemployment rate. However, the open unemployment rate, i.e. those remaining without work and searching for a job for a long time as a percentage of labour force, is not expected to be very high in the developing countries (for, not too many can afford open unemployment for long). But some of the countries such as Indonesia, Marshall Islands, Mongolia, Myanmar, Pakistan, the Philippines and Sri Lanka reported a very high open unemployment rate (either in double digit or close to that) among the females. The other striking pattern is that some of the countries experienced a decline in the female unemployment rate over time, but later in the recent past the unemployment rate again seems to have shot up. An increase in the female unemployment rate would mean shrinkage in the overall employment opportunities because recessionary tendencies are expected to have dampened the labour demand of which women are usually the victims in the first go.

As evident from Table A.8 in the Appendix, there are several countries that recorded a higher female unemployment rate than males. Though a sub-region generalization may not be appropriate, Southeast and partly South Asia are indicative of higher female unemployment rates. Since women have to engage themselves in the labour market while simultaneously pursuing the domestic work, their choice of jobs becomes highly limited. Besides, preoccupation in domestic work results in poor human capital formation not allowing them to enhance their capabilities and accept the available job opportunities. This results in a higher incidence of unemployment rate among the females. The rural–urban differences in the unemployment rates are also quite substantial. Though we do not have this information for very many countries, in general urban unemployment rates are higher than the rural rates because urban females are relatively more educated and skilled than their rural counterparts and they can afford a higher search cost.

In reality, it is difficult to compare the unemployment rates across countries due to the differences in the concepts, and therefore, information based on country-specific studies is used extensively. In Bangladesh, the unemployment rates among the population aged 15 and above rose over the period 1990–91 to 1999–2000 in each region and for both the sexes except for a slight decrease in the rate for urban females in 1995–96. This slight decrease was mainly due to growth in ready-made garments industries. On an average about 3.3% people of aged over 15 in Bangladesh were unemployed in 1999–2000. Taking unpaid family works into account according to the extended definition used by the labour force survey (LFS), it was 2.5% in 1995–96, which increased from 1.5% in 1990–91. Moreover, estimates show that there has been a significant rural–urban variation in the unemployment rate over the period with a concentration of unemployment in the urban areas. This is mainly because of the transfer of rural poverty to the urban areas through migration. On the other hand, unemployment among females is still higher than their male counterparts across regions, particularly in the urban areas. However, the incidence of underemployment remains very high as people struggle to survive by engaging themselves in many informal activities, though underemployment is not always well captured by the conventional employment-unemployment surveys. Rahaman (1998) pointed out that the demand for wage employment is not sufficient to absorb the entire supply; employment expansion could progress without causing an upturn in the wage trend.

In Bhutan, poverty exists in the rural areas among subsistence farmers relying largely on crops, large families with a higher proportion of children and elderly, households with limited livestock, off-farm income including remittances and limited schooling. In the urban areas, the poverty is more prevalent among migrants, households with higher dependency ratio, petty traders and casual labourers who do not have regular wage employment. Acharya (1998) brings out interlinks between the labour market situation in India, as well as Nepal since its economy is integrated with some of the provincial towns of India. A depressed Indian labour market is likely to depress the labour market in Nepal as well, and a blooming labour market in India would have a salutary effect on the labour market in Nepal. In India, the open unemployment rates are not high, but the relative size of unorganized or informal sector employment in both rural and urban areas is dominant (Mitra 1994). Ghayur (1998) points to the declining ability of the labour market in Pakistan to absorb work force productively. Unemployment rates are high among females, in general, children and senior citizens. Following the structural adjustment in Sri Lanka, a distinct bias is evident in the generation of employment outlets in favour of females (Rodrigo 1998).

In East Asia, the diffusion of primary education was possibly the single most important factor accounting for the reduction in poverty and income inequality. The East Asian countries in general allocated a much larger proportion of their public investment for agriculture and rural development than most other developing countries at comparable stages of their development. This together with universal primary education made growth broad based and labour intensive with skill intensity, resulting in higher growth and improved income distribution (Hashim 1998). Investment in physical and human capital with special emphasis on developing human resources and effective participation in international markets leading to expanding employment at higher productivity contributed to both the reduction in poverty and enhancement of growth.

Employment Structure and Employment Status

As the study by ILO (2000) pointed out, the share of women employment in agriculture is high in countries with low per capita income. The percentage of the female work force engaged in agriculture has been larger than its male counterpart in Bangladesh, Cambodia, the Republic of Korea, Malaysia, Pakistan, Sri Lanka and for some of the years in Thailand (Table A.9). It is possible that in these countries, as males look for better employment opportunities in activities other than agriculture, women engage in agriculture in an attempt to pursue the activity in the family farms. This reason seems to be a strong possibility, particularly in Bangladesh, Cambodia, Pakistan, Sri Lanka and Thailand where the proportion of female agricultural workers to total female workers has been sizeable Hong Kong, China (SAR), Macau, China (SAR), Maldives and Sri Lanka (two years) are countries where the female work force engaged in manufacturing has been larger than its male counterpart. In Hong Kong, China (SAR) and Macau, China (SAR), this may be explained in terms of rapid industrialization, which has generated demand for female labour. On the other hand, in several countries and for a number of years, the share of services in the female work force has been larger than that of males (see Table A.9 for positive differences between the female and male percentage of workers engaged in services; Fig. 3 gives the differences in all three activities for nine countries in 2005). This is possibly because of the fact that females have a strong preference to work in the services sector, and hence, the structural transformation away from agriculture to services in the case of females is much faster than in the case of males. With low human capital endowment, entry into the services sector is relatively easy compared to manufacturing as far as non-agricultural activities are concerned. Also, many of these countries are experiencing rapid tertiarization, and hence, absorption of female workers in services has possibly been more spontaneous. In Bangladesh, Indonesia, Lao People's Democratic Republic, Mongolia, Pakistan and the Philippines, where the pace of industrialization even in terms of male work force has been quite sluggish, it is understandable that the percentage of female workers engaged in manufacturing is also low. Though information on India has not been supplied by the KILM data of the ILO, we have noted from the NSS data that the discrepancy between the structural change in terms of value added and that in terms of work force is sizeable (Mitra 2008). This is usually explained in terms of technological reasons and factor price distortions leading to sluggish demand for labour in the industrial sector. Manufacturing activity is more skill intensive compared to agriculture and other tertiary sector activities such as community, social and personal services and retail trade. Women labour, as a result of possessing low human capital, is demanded usually after the available supplies of male labour are exhausted, and this would explain why the percentage of manufacturing in the female employment structure has been perceptibly low.

On the whole, limited spread of industry, technological reasons and factor price distortions leading to limited demand for labour in the industrial sector are some of the reasons for sluggish labour absorption in the manufacturing sector. On the other hand, many countries are experiencing rapid tertiarization, and hence, absorption of female workers in services has possibly been more spontaneous though the question whether this pattern of transition will be able to contribute to growth in a sustainable fashion is left unresolved.

Women's employment in the services sector has been vulnerable to and disadvantaged by the increased competition. With the rapid spread of the IT sector, both male and female job seekers seem to have benefited, but most of the benefits have reached only those who are in the higher echelons of the socio-economic ladder with higher levels of human capital endowments.

Employment status is given in terms of wage and salaried jobs and self-employment (Table A.10). Wage and salaried jobs include not only regular wage employment but also contractual and casual employment. The proportion of wage/salary employment among the male workers is higher than that among the females. Secondly, the proportion of wage/salary employment varies considerably across countries. Similarly, the relative size of self-employment also varies widely corresponding to both male and female workers. Usually, one expects the share of wage/salary employment to increase in the process of development, particularly in an inter-temporal sense. For many countries, inter-temporal data are not available, and hence, they could not be examined carefully. However, in the case of Maldives and Pakistan, a downward tendency is indicative. Sri Lanka also registered a slight decline, yet in Singapore where the relative size of wage employment has been on the high side, the decline is not taken seriously. Bangladesh, Cambodia, Lao People's Democratic Republic and Vietnam are some of the countries where the relative size of the wage/salaried employment has been quite small. The evidence on India (though not available from the same source) also points to the same direction if only the regular wage/salaried employment is considered, excluding the casual and contractual employment (Mitra 2008). On the whole, the low-income countries seem to be experiencing sluggish labour absorption in wage/salaried jobs, which may explain why South Asia is characterized by a relatively small proportion of its work force engaged in this category. In the face of sluggishly growing demand for hired labour, inadequate human capital endowment of female labour compels them to engage themselves as self-employed workers, which further accentuates gender inequality in the labour market. Also, as male workers look for better-paying opportunities in the job market, women workers in pursuance of their practical needs continue to work as home-based workers in order to augment family earnings.

In Table A.10, the relative size of the category of employment outside self-employment and wage/salaried employment is quite large in some of the countries. This category possibly includes 'employment not adequately defined'. However, in a country like Bangladesh, it is difficult to believe that around 80% of the female employment and 35% of the male employment was not 'adequately defined'. Possibly there is a mix-up of the categories. Usually in countries like India, national surveys report three categories of employment: regular wage/salaried employment, self-employment and casual employment. For these countries, if regular wage/salaried employment is compared with wage/salaried employment for countries, which define duality in terms of wage employment and self-employment, then naturally this kind of discrepancy is expected to occur.

Given these broad patterns relating to the labour market in the Asia-Pacific countries, we turn to the Indian situation in the next section.

3 Broad Patterns Relating to Participation in India

The male work participation rates pertaining to all age groups are relatively high and are nearly 50% both in the rural and in the urban areas if we consider the main or usual principal status workers (Table 1 for all-India and for states Figs. 1 and 2). Secondly, the interstate variations measured in terms of coefficient of variation are limited (17.5 and 15.5% in the rural and urban areas, respectively). On the other hand, the female participation rates are significantly lower than their male counterparts (Table 1 for all-India and for states Figs. 1 and 2), and more so in the urban areas, implying that the rural–urban differentials in the case of women are more pronounced than in the case of males (Table 1 and Figs. 3 and 4). Besides, the interstate variations are sizable in the case of females, reflecting the influence of economic, social and cultural factors (coefficient of variation being 53.2 and 36.0% in the rural and urban areas, respectively). The participation rates in the north-eastern and the southern regions, for example, are considerably higher than the northern states. A relatively lower magnitude of variation in the urban areas may be taken to signify the possibility of convergence (to a limited extent though), while the dominance of the social factors in the rural areas can be said to be more prominent. But the interpretation can be quite erroneous: the female work participation rates being by and large lower in the urban areas than in the rural areas indicate the limited impact of education on participation in the face of social factors. In fact, why the participation rate of Indian urban women is still so low, given that the per capita income and the educational attainment levels are higher than their rural counterparts, is an important research question. The plot of participation rates

Table 1 Work force participation rate (WFPR) and labour force participation rate (LFPR)

Category	WFPR (%) Population Census (2011)	LFPR (%) Labour Bureau (2011–12)
Rural male	41.6 (17.5)	79.4 (6.4)
Rural female	16.7 (53.2)	33.9 (48.0)
Urban male	48.7 (15.5)	73.7 (7.6)
Urban female	11.9 (36.0)	19.1 (46.9)
Persons rural	29.5	57.9
Persons urban	30.9	48.0
All males	43.8	77.9
All females	15.2	30.0
All persons all areas	29.9	55.4

Note (1) Though the Labour Bureau (LB) estimates refer to the year 2011–12—close to the population census year, 2011—they are not comparable with each other because the population census estimates are work participation rates for all age groups covering only the main (equivalent to the usual principal status) workers whereas the LB estimates are for age groups 15 and above and they cover all workers (usual principal and subsidiary status) and those who are unemployed. (2) Figures in parentheses are coefficient of variation based on the state-level data
Source Population Census, 2011 and Labour Bureau, 2011–12

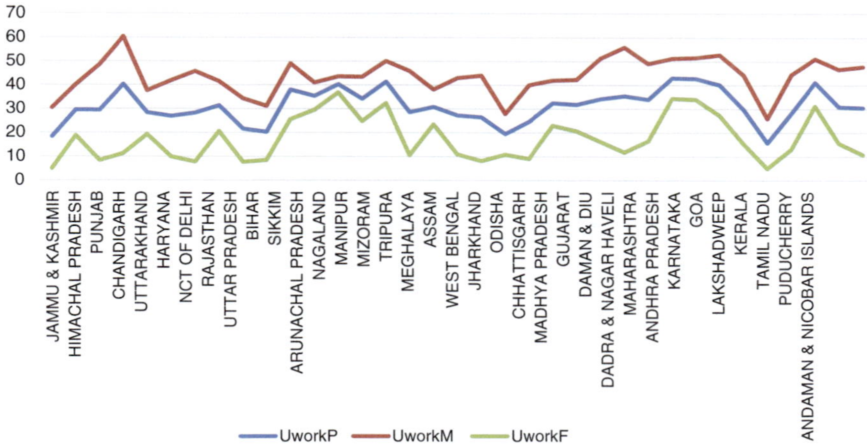

Fig. 1 Work force participation rate in rural areas of states and union territories: 2011. *Notes* (1) F for female, M for male and P for person. (2) Only main workers are being considered. *Source* Population Census, 2011

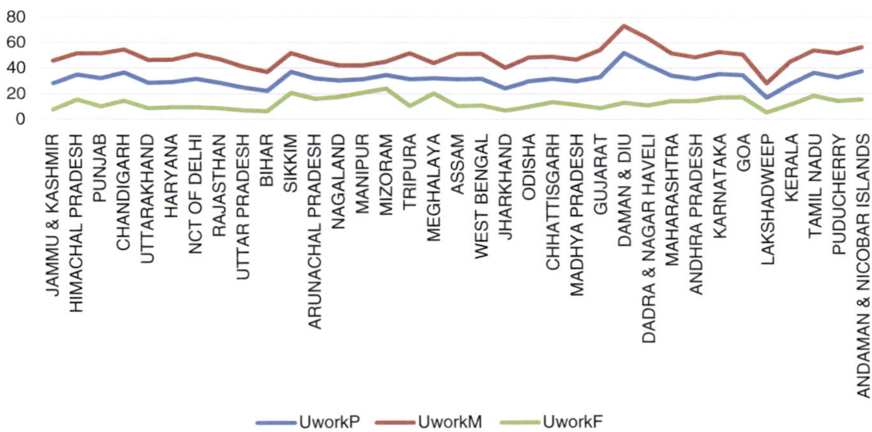

Fig. 2 Work force participation rate in urban areas of states and union territories: 2011. *Note* See notes to Fig. 1. *Source* Same as Fig. 1

against per capita income (Fig. 5) is not suggestive of any significant positive relationship in the case of females though among males such a pattern can be somewhat deciphered (Fig. 6). In relation to females, only a subset of the observations at the most may conform to this pattern.

Labour Bureau has been collecting information since 2009–10 on yearly basis (except 2010–11). Based on the estimates of labour force participation rate for the year 2011–12, corresponding to the age groups 15 and above, again similar

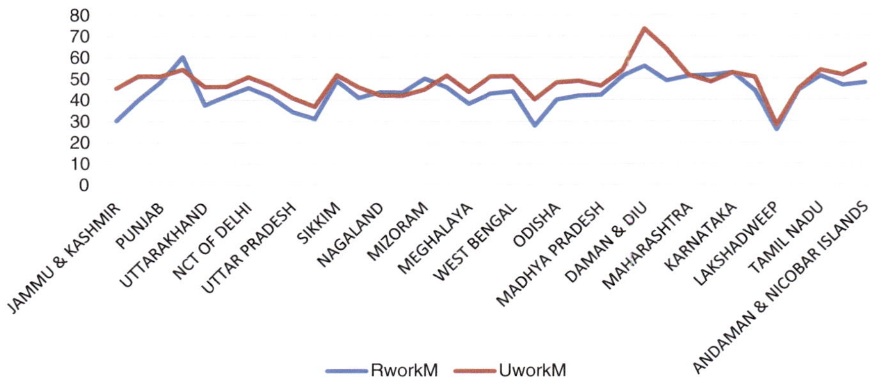

Fig. 3 Difference in rural and urban work participation rate of males: 2011. *Source* Same as Fig. 1

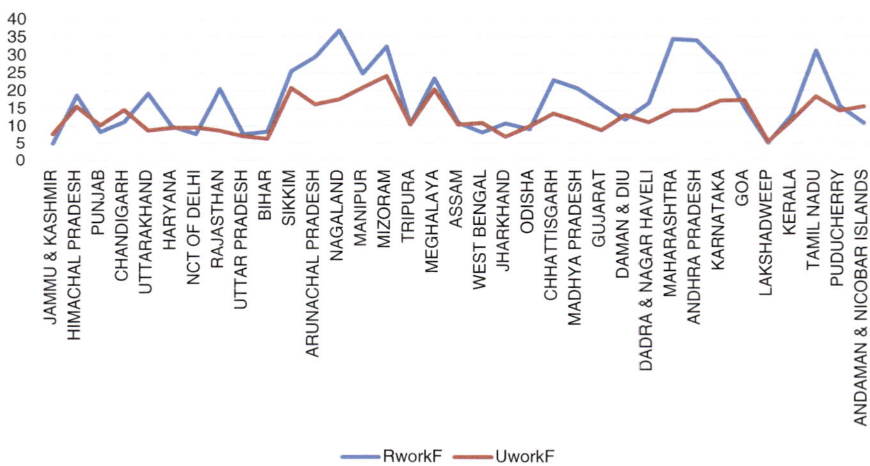

Fig. 4 Difference in rural and urban work participation rate of females: 2011. *Source* Same as Fig. 1

differences across gender are evident (Figs. 7 and 8). The coefficient of variation is much higher among the rural and urban females than among the males, indicating wide inter-spatial differences (Table 1).

Figures 9 and 10 provide Labour Bureau's estimates of gender-specific labour participation rate based on panel data, i.e. for each of the years since 2009–10 (except 2010–11) in the rural and the urban areas of the states and union territories. The estimates for a given category seem to have been consistent over time, and the gender differences in the estimates are pertinent for each of the years. The interstate variations in the rate of a given category and the rural–urban differences in the female rate particularly (Fig. 11) also seem to have remained stable over time, thus confirming the time invariance in the female participation rate which not only

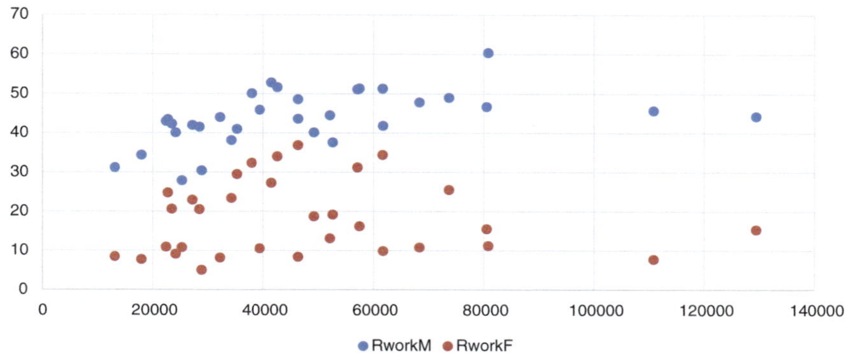

Fig. 5 Per capita income (2011–12) and rural work participation rate (2011). *Source* Data book for Planning Commission, Government of India and Population Census, 2011

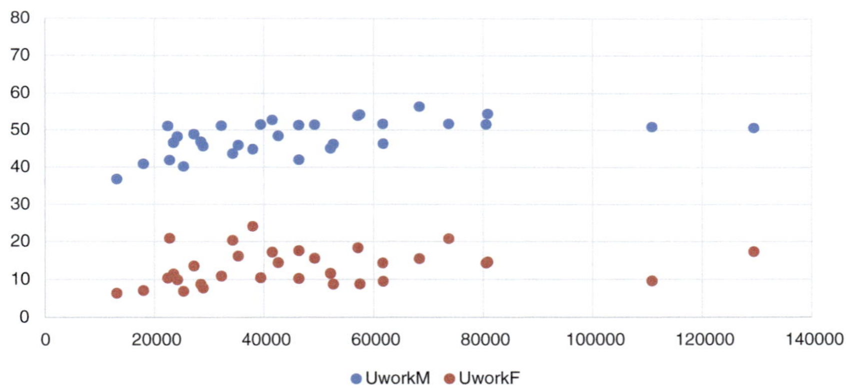

Fig. 6 Per capita income (2011–12) and Urban Work Participation rate (2011). *Source* Same as Fig. 5

hovers around a low magnitude but also varies widely across space. Though the time frame is too short to expect any significant change in the participation rate, the complete invariance in the female participation rate suggests that the gender concerns need to be addressed more seriously.

The Platform for Action adopted at the United Nations Fourth World Conference on Women (Beijing 1995) highlighted the concept of bringing gender issues into the mainstream of society. It is a necessity to ensure gender equality in all areas of social and economic development. Suggestions were made to make the concerns and experiences of women as well as of men an integral part of the design, implementation, monitoring and evaluation of policies and programmes in all

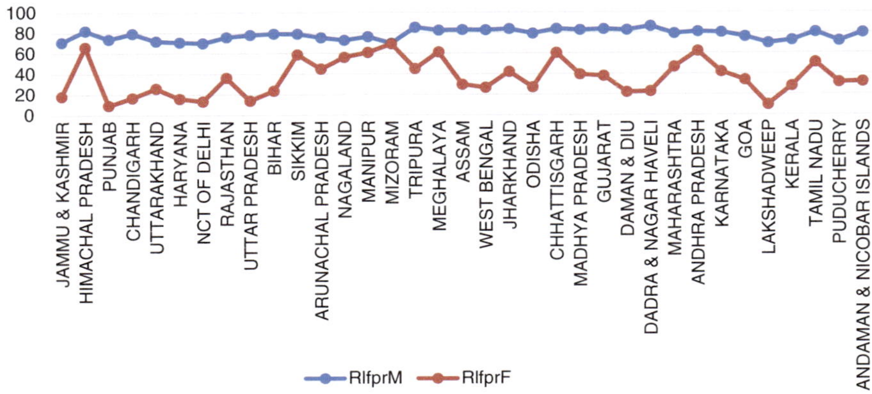

Fig. 7 Labour force participation rate in rural areas 2011. *Note* All workers based on usual principal-cum-subsidiary status. *Source* Labour Bureau, 2011–12, Ministry of Labour and Employment, Government of India

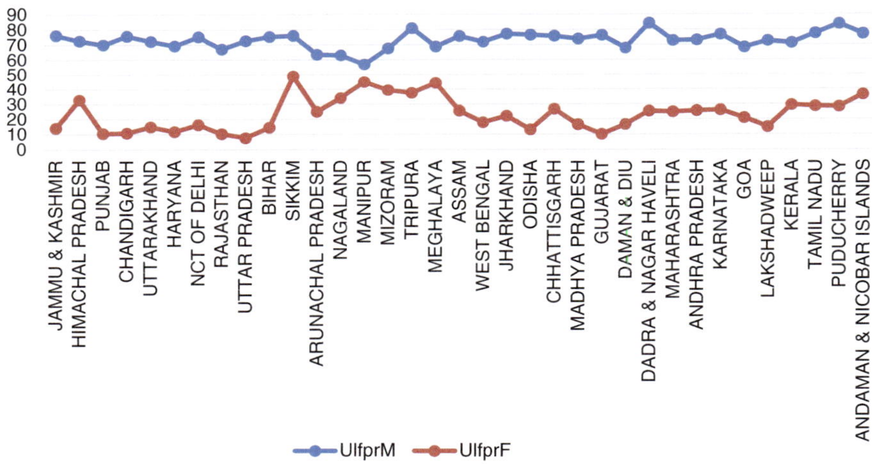

Fig. 8 Labour force participation rate in urban areas 2011–12. *Note and Source* Same as Fig. 7

political, economic and societal spheres, so that women and men benefit equally, and inequality is not perpetuated.[4]

One of the major suggestions in the gender studies literature is that women can be engaged directly in the development process and the benefits of growth can be

[4]International Labour Organization (ILO). Gender Equality Tool. Definition of Gender Mainstreaming. http://www.ilo.org/public/english/bureau/gender/newsite2002/about/defin.htm. Accessed Dec 2, 2016.

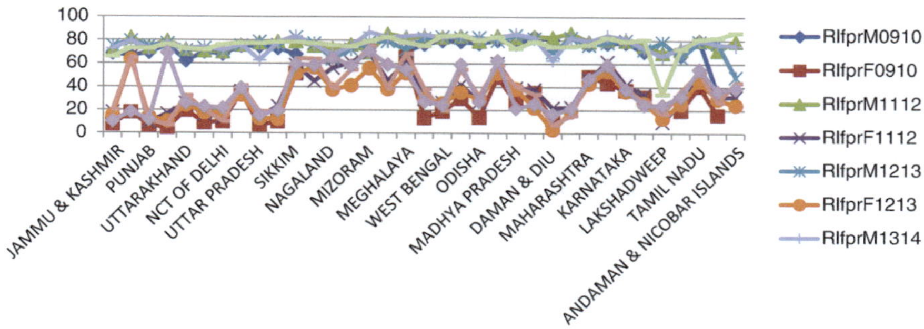

Fig. 9 Rural labour force participation rate: panel data. *Note and Source* Same as Fig. 7

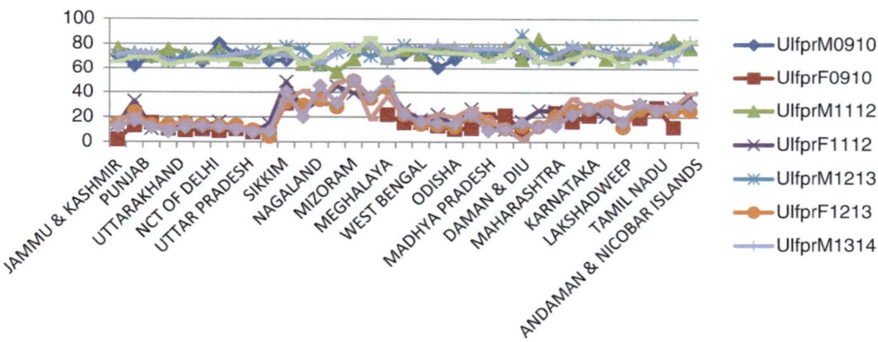

Fig. 10 Urban labour force participation rate: panel data. *Note and Source* Same as Fig. 7

distributed equitably by generating increasingly productive employment opportunities for women (Behrman and Zhang 1995). This can raise the degree of women's empowerment, as with increased resources they will be able to participate in the decision-making process, both within the household and outside the household. In other words, labour market participation would have positive spillover effects on various other aspects of well-being such as health, education and the overall attitude towards female sexuality. Employment aspect plays a pivotal role in relation to other capabilities of women such as health care and nutrition, self-respect and autonomy and full political functioning (Nussbaum and Glover 1995). Biases against girls/women lead to their inaccessibility to education and health which results in poor human capital formation and a low labour force participation rate. This in turn adversely affects the future human capital formation, female labour productivity, individual welfare, health and participation in the decision-making process and also the overall economic growth (United Nations 2007). However, other than skill differences between females and males, biases of employers against women employees also restrict their accessibility to high-income jobs. Patriarchy's

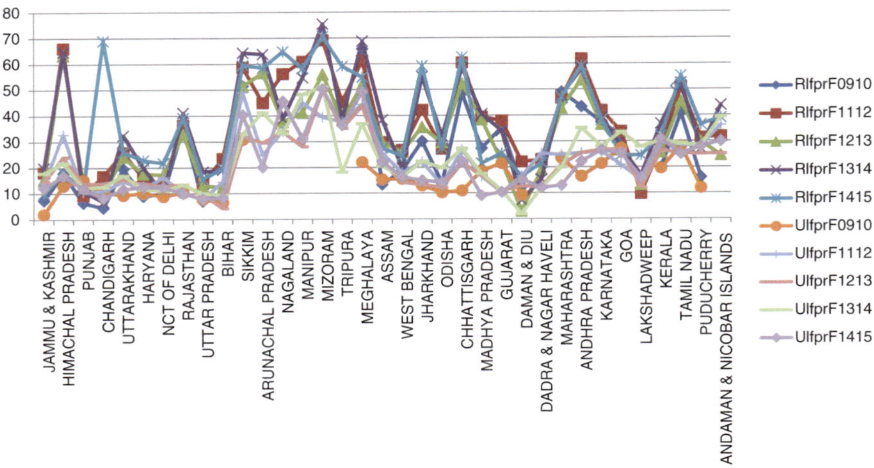

Fig. 11 Rural–urban differences in the female participation rate: panel data. *Note and Source* Same as Fig. 7

gendered division of labour often does not allow women to participate in the labour market on full-time basis, which in turn adversely affects their job market experience and bargaining power (Mitra 2005). As an outcome of a wide range of constraints impacting both from demand and supply sides on female labour market participation, the rates are indeed low and the gender differences are glaring irrespective of which source of data we use.

There are other alternative ways of empowering women instead of taking the labour market participation route. But the model of human capital formation and productive employment enhances the individual capabilities and, more importantly, empowers women to take part in the decision-making process. In the context of women employment, extensive citation has been made of the fact that arises in work accessibility of women improves the accessibility of children, particularly that of the girl children, to education and nutritious diet. Critics may find fault with the employment approach being a basic means of human development and generating pro-poor growth if women are largely employed in low-productivity activities in the informal sector. Therefore, while pursuing the labour market participation approach we explicitly highlight the concept of productive employment, which can contribute to human development and curb inequalities not only in economic terms but also in other respects. The participation rates which we are analysing are, however, too aggregative in nature and cannot throw much light on the quality of employment. Only as a rough measure of engagement in the growth process, these rates are examined in order to initiate the work.

4 Quantitative Analysis for India

Cross-sectional Results: Based on State-Level Data

In this section, we turn to the determinants of work and labour force participation (WFPR and LFPR) in the backdrop of the analytical frame presented in Sect. 1. The variables which are chosen are as follows: household size (HHSZ), literacy rate (LIT), child-to-woman ratio (CHILD), female-to-male ratio in the population (F/M), urbanization level (URBN), percentage of scheduled caste (SC) and scheduled tribe population (ST), per capita net state domestic product (PCNSDP), percentage of agriculture, industry and services in total gross state domestic product (AG, IND and SER), state-wise road length (in km) in relation to 100,000 population (ROAD), per capita consumption of electricity (ELEC), credit-to-deposit ratio of scheduled commercial banks (CRE-DEP), percentage of households with access to safe drinking water (WATER), infant mortality rate (IMR), fertility rate (FR) and gross enrolment rate in classes 1–8 (ENROL). As these variables have been gathered from various sources, they do not refer to one specific year. The appendix table gives the years for which the variables are available along with their sources. Secondly, while some of the variables are available for rural and urban areas and males and females separately, some other like infrastructure, growth and composition of growth and urbanization are aggregative in nature. IMR and enrolment are reported among girls and boys separately without any reference to area, while accessibility to safe drinking water is given for rural and urban areas.

Since the analysis is carried out at the state, district and city levels, we first discuss the results in detail with a view to highlighting the commonality at a later stage.

Some of these variables are self-explanatory. But some others need elaboration. For example, the female-to-male ratio is taken to represent visibility of women: with larger number of women in a region, the participation rate is likely to increase as solidarity and bargaining power of women may rise. A balanced sex ratio may mean less violence against women, which may motivate and provide a conductive environment to participate in the labour market. IMR is taken to represent the overall health condition of the population and so is the case with the access to safe drinking water. TFR or child-to-woman ratio (a broad indicator of fertility) covers the demographic pressure and the dependency on women. The overall household size is another indicator of dependency, keeping in view that in India the joint family system is still prevalent in many regions. ROAD and ELECT represent physical infrastructure, while CRE-DEP is an indicator of financial infrastructure.

The factor analysis has been carried out for males and females and for rural and urban areas separately. In relation to work participation rate among rural females (Table 2), four factors are seen to be statistically significant. Corresponding to the most important factor, i.e. Factor 1, women work participation rate does not have a significant factor loading. In Factor 2, however, it enters with a factor loading of 0.74. It has a strong positive relationship with the incidence of scheduled tribe women population, confirming the view that among the scheduled tribe population

Table 2 Factor analysis: rural female work participation rate

Variables	Factor 1	Factor 2	Factor 3	Factor 4
HHSZ(R)	0.2939	−0.0283	0.6949	0.0121
CHILD(R)	0.1180	0.1025	0.8878	0.1790
WPR(F,R)	0.0471	0.7419	−0.2058	0.1516
LIT(F,R)	−0.4945	0.1145	−0.5993	−0.4374
SC(F,R)	0.1186	−0.5926	−0.1541	−0.0253
ST(F,R)	0.0944	0.8396	0.2463	0.1134
F/M(R)	0.2869	0.1144	−0.5349	0.2783
URBAN	−0.8406	−0.0632	−0.0043	−0.2637
MPCE(R)	−0.5091	−0.0018	−0.1649	−0.7339
POV(R)	0.2633	0.2332	0.1563	0.7146
ELEC	−0.3281	−0.2369	−0.1902	−0.1206
ROAD	0.1431	0.7807	−0.1776	−0.0959
CR-DP	−0.2545	−0.2080	−0.0626	−0.0743
WATER(R)	−0.0572	−0.3597	−0.0518	−0.1071
IMR(F)	0.5907	−0.1382	0.4447	0.3198
% AGDP	0.7818	0.2717	0.2601	0.1715
Eigen value	5.39	3.04	1.62	1.12
% Explained	0.42	0.24	0.13	0.09

Note No. of observations (N) = 32, R within parenthesis represents rural and F female
Source Authors' calculation

women are earners in addition to their household responsibilities. On the other hand, the incidence of scheduled caste population reduces the women work participation rate. In the rural situation where caste system is more prevalent, it is possibly more difficult for scheduled caste women to find jobs. Poverty-induced participation is evident, and women being engaged largely in agriculture sector are also noticeable. What is most striking is the effect of physical infrastructure on women work participation. Other studies confirmed increased female enrolment in schools in response to improved infrastructure (Dreze and Gandhi-Kingdon 1999), and here, we notice the positive influence of road network on female work participation. Literacy is also seen to have a mild positive association with work participation, while infant mortality rate shows a negative one. The positive relationship between female-to-male ratio and participation is distinct, more so in Factor 3. Urbanization level is, however, not seen to raise women work participation rate in the rural areas. In other words, states with higher levels of urbanization though expected to have positive spillover effects in the rural areas are somehow not seen to have experienced so, at least in terms of women work participation rate. Large household size and child-to-women ratio affect women work participation adversely, as observed in Factor 3.

Instead of work if we consider the labour force participation rate, in Factor 1 itself some of these findings are discernible (Table 3). Scheduled caste incidence reduces the labour participation, while among the tribes, women join the labour

Table 3 Factor analysis: rural female labour participation rate

Variables	Factor 1	Factor 2	Factor 3
HHSZ(R)	−0.0174	0.2898	0.7006
CHILD(R)	0.1650	0.1133	0.8865
LFPR(F,R)	0.6955	0.1650	−0.2695
LIT(F,R)	0.1521	−0.4966	−0.6012
SC (F,R)	−0.6691	0.1162	−0.1428
ST(F,R)	0.9021	0.1001	0.2282
F/M(R)	0.1208	0.2895	−0.5208
URBAN	−0.1004	−0.8603	−0.0109
MPCE(R)	−0.0377	−0.5262	−0.1740
POV(R)	0.2463	0.2733	0.1571
ELEC	−0.2930	−0.3237	−0.1929
ROAD	0.7616	0.1448	−0.1999
CR-DP	−0.3097	−0.2702	−0.0690
WATER(R)	−0.4586	−0.0466	−0.0550
IMR(F)	−0.1171	0.5873	0.4615
% AGDP	0.2824	0.7781	0.2583
Eigen value	5.49	3.09	1.65
% Explained	0.43	0.25	0.13

Note No. of observations (N) = 32, and the rest same as Table 2
Source Authors' calculation

market extensively. Poverty-induced participation, requirement of female labour more in the agriculture sector, the positive effect of health and education, a strong impact of physical infrastructure on labour market participation and the lack of urbanization's spill effect on rural women labour participation are also evident. That the demographic pressure reduces labour market participation is brought out by Factor 3. The positive association between the increased presence of women, measured in terms of female–male population, and the labour market participation is also verifiable across all the three statistically significant factors (Table 3).

Turning to rural male work participation, it has the highest factor loading in Factor 4 compared to the other three (Table 4). The overall growth in the rural areas measured in terms of rural consumption expenditure per capita, the financial infrastructure (credit-to-deposit ratio) and the overall urbanization in the state are seen to raise the male participation. Rural diversification has a positive effect as the percentage of agriculture in gross state domestic product is negatively associated with participation. From Factor 2 in which the male work participation takes a moderate factor loading, the positive impact of literacy and the adverse effect of demographic variables are noticed evidently. Many of these findings are, however, not confirmed as we shift to labour force participation (Table 5). There is rather evidence on poverty-induced participation in agricultural activities, i.e. Factor 3. Besides, large household size tends to raise the male labour market participation which could be because of economic compulsions. Urbanization reduces the rural

Table 4 Factor analysis: rural male work participation rate

Variables	Factor 1	Factor 2	Factor 3	Factor 4
HHSZ(R)	0.0330	0.6608	−0.1955	−0.4429
CHILD(R)	0.1667	0.8944	−0.0210	−0.1266
WPR(M,R)	0.1223	−0.3631	0.2436	0.7715
LIT(M,R)	−0.0167	−0.7136	0.4474	0.0453
SC(M,R)	−0.7406	−0.1154	−0.1616	0.1574
ST(M,R)	0.8717	0.2447	−0.1139	−0.0359
URBAN	−0.0779	−0.0618	0.7492	0.4175
MPCE(R)	0.0157	−0.2332	0.3917	0.1548
POV(R)	0.2492	0.1958	−0.1864	−0.1303
ELEC	−0.3349	−0.2067	0.3194	0.1085
ROAD	0.8194	−0.1957	−0.2352	−0.0641
CR-DP	−0.4352	−0.0159	0.1661	0.7797
WATER(R)	−0.5049	−0.0691	0.0348	0.1278
IMR(M)	−0.1916	0.5284	−0.4633	−0.0723
% AGDP	0.2765	0.3100	−0.7619	−0.1629
Eigen value	5.86358	2.6534	1.14647	1.0349
% Explained	0.4983	0.2255	0.0974	0.0880

Note No. of Observations (N) = 32, R within parenthesis represents rural and M male
Source Authors' calculation

Table 5 Factor analysis: rural male labour participation rate

Variables	Factor 1	Factor 2	Factor 3
HHSZ(R)	−0.0090	0.6996	0.2745
CHILD(R)	−0.1940	0.8925	0.0336
LFPR(M,R)	0.0708	−0.0471	0.2205
LIT(M,R)	0.0343	−0.7322	−0.4432
SC(M,R)	0.7560	−0.1205	0.1340
ST(M,R)	−0.8766	0.2387	0.1291
URBAN	0.0793	−0.1316	−0.8239
MPCE(R)	−0.0136	−0.2923	−0.4591
POV(R)	−0.2530	0.2236	0.2695
ELEC	0.3627	−0.2141	−0.3339
ROAD	−0.7887	−0.2147	0.2669
CR-DP	0.4184	−0.0781	−0.3324
WATER(R)	0.5668	−0.0701	−0.0593
IMR(M)	0.1827	0.5730	0.4718
% AGDP	−0.2644	0.3210	0.8005
Eigen value	5.52720	2.62514	1.38563
% Explained	0.4885	0.2320	0.1225

Note No. of observations (N) = 32, R within parenthesis represents rural and M male
Source Authors' calculation

Table 6 Factor analysis: urban female work participation rate

Variables	Factor 1	Factor 2	Factor 3
HHSZ(U)	0.9053	−0.0611	−0.0909
CHILD(U)	0.9209	0.1570	−0.0126
WPR(F,U)	−0.4124	0.7570	0.0628
LIT(F,U)	−0.7754	0.3486	0.2176
SC(F,U)	−0.0728	−0.6424	0.0407
ST(F,U)	0.1053	0.9281	−0.0677
F/M(U)	−0.4064	0.2027	−0.0116
URBAN	−0.1199	0.0129	0.8717
ELEC	−0.1466	−0.2226	0.1497
ROAD	−0.2336	0.5771	−0.1607
CR-DP	−0.0858	−0.2531	0.4220
WATER(U)	−0.0058	−0.2040	0.0362
IMR(F)	0.4215	−0.0980	−0.4984
% SERDP	−0.0491	−0.0869	0.9008
Eigen value	3.71607	3.37977	1.50656
% Explained	0.3547	0.3226	0.1438

Note No. of observations (*N*) = 32, U within parenthesis represents urban and F female
Source Authors' calculation

male participation possibly because the economically active ones migrate out from the rural areas.

In the urban context, the female work participation with the highest factor loading in Factor 2 among all the three factors unravels the positive effect of literacy and road infrastructure (Table 6). The female-to-male ratio is also positively associated with participation. Again, the positive relationship with the incidence of scheduled tribe population and a negative one with scheduled caste population come out sharply. High demographic pressure and poor health reduce participation. Urbanization, industrialization and growth in services show positive effect on participation, very mildly though (Factors 1 and 4 in Table 7).

In relation to the labour force participation rate by and large, similar findings are obtained if we consider the most important factor and the one in which the female labour force participation takes the highest factor loading: Factor 1 and Factor 3, respectively (Table 8a, b). In Factor 1 (Table 8b) in fact, all the infrastructure variables are positively associated with urban female labour force participation. Financial infrastructure possibly allows women to set up small businesses which enable them to earn.

Among males in the urban areas, the demographic pressure is seen to reduce participation quite contrary to the belief that large family size or a large number of children forces men to participate in the labour market (Table 9). In low-income households, large family size and participation in petty activities coexist. But the male respondents often do not consider those activities as proper jobs, and hence,

Table 7 Factor analysis: urban female work participation rate with some different variables

Variables	Factor 1	Factor 2	Factor 3	Factor 4
HHSZ(U)	−0.9030	−0.0450	0.0396	−0.1403
CHILD(U)	−0.9166	0.1641	0.0786	−0.0510
WPR(F,U)	0.4143	0.7508	−0.0647	0.1126
LIT(F,U)	0.7927	0.3489	0.1367	0.1034
SC(F,U)	0.0701	−0.6593	0.0525	0.0218
ST(F,U)	−0.0992	0.9309	0.0122	−0.1092
F/M(U)	0.4107	0.2090	−0.0233	−0.0431
URBAN	0.1508	0.0068	0.4923	0.7884
ELEC	0.1349	−0.2506	−0.2774	0.6585
ROAD	0.2288	0.5634	−0.0108	−0.2043
CR-DP	0.0984	−0.2541	0.2756	0.3193
WATER(U)	0.0003	−0.2113	−0.0891	0.1901
IMR(F)	−0.4346	−0.0866	−0.2023	−0.5051
% SERDP	0.1070	−0.0676	0.9061	0.3427
% INDP	0.1464	−0.0255	−0.9301	0.1194
Eigen value	3.72865	3.42559	2.17373	1.07259
% Explained	0.3186	0.2927	0.1858	0.0917

Note No. of observations (N) = 32, U within parenthesis represents urban and F female
Source Authors' calculation

they claim to be outside the work force. Growth shows a positive impact on participation. At very high levels of income, participation is expected to decline, but India being one of the low-income countries, it is unrealistic to expect a negative association between them. Similarly, literacy and better health conditions tend to improve participation, irrespective of whether we use work or labour force participation rate (Table 10). Usually, literacy or enrolment is expected to cause withdrawal from the labour market, but our findings based on the cross-sectional data suggest that though in certain age groups it occurs in the short run, in the long run regions with better human capital formation reveal higher participation rates.

Cross-sectional Results: Based on District-Level Data

At the district level, a couple of new variables have been introduced such as sex ratio among children (CHILDSR), shares of agricultural labour (AGLAB), cultivators (CUL), household manufacturing (MFGHH) and other activities (OTHER) in total work force. The child sex ratio may represent the extent of gender discrimination at young age brackets. Districts with low levels of child sex ratio would mean high degree of gender discrimination. The employment composition is taken to assess how dynamic an area is.

The negative effect of fertility and household size on rural female work participation comes out sharply from Factor 1 (Table 11). Greater domestic burdens in large households do not allow women to participate in the work force. Literacy raises participation (Factor 1) though there are other districts forming a separate

Table 8 (a) Factor analysis: urban female labour participation rate. (b) Factor analysis: urban female labour participation rate with some different variables

Variables	Factor 1	Factor 2	Factor 3	Factor 4
(a)				
HHSZ(U)	0.2164	0.1944	−0.8739	−0.1184
CHILD(U)	−0.6172	0.2057	−0.5705	−0.1398
LFP(F,U)	0.2368	0.3743	0.5380	−0.0800
LIT(F,U)	0.2453	0.3402	0.7402	0.2769
SC(F,U)	0.1708	−0.6624	0.0005	−0.0894
ST(F,U)	0.0754	0.9108	−0.0294	0.0369
F/M(U)	0.8898	0.0960	0.1297	−0.0209
URBAN	−0.2073	0.0443	0.0732	0.8383
ELEC	−0.8908	−0.0374	0.1646	0.1847
ROAD	0.2092	0.4625	0.2989	−0.1619
CR-DP	0.1267	−0.4581	0.0349	0.2096
WATER(U)	−0.3161	−0.4819	0.0653	−0.0968
IMR(F)	−0.0475	−0.0135	−0.3521	−0.7285
Eigen value	3.32991	2.37299	2.15265	1.10843
% Explained	0.3544	0.2526	0.2291	0.1180
(b)				
HHSZ(U)	−0.9059	−0.0010	0.0139	−0.1253
CHILD(U)	−0.9050	0.0547	0.2164	−0.0524
LFPR(F,U)	0.5110	−0.1942	0.5526	−0.3422
LIT(F,U)	0.8061	0.1602	0.3405	0.0230
SC(F,U)	0.0511	0.0606	−0.6668	0.0751
ST(F,U)	−0.0565	−0.0116	0.9413	−0.1072
F/M(U)	0.4237	−0.0304	0.1849	−0.1366
URBAN	0.1462	0.6537	−0.0173	0.5601
ELEC	0.1214	−0.1157	−0.2612	0.8142
ROAD	0.2401	−0.0697	0.5684	−0.2188
CR-DP	0.0893	0.3629	−0.3486	0.2801
WATER(U)	−0.0079	−0.0430	−0.2161	0.2637
IMR(F)	−0.4234	−0.2888	−0.0458	−0.2299
% SERDP	0.0934	0.9616	−0.0833	0.1045
% INDP	0.1579	−0.8785	−0.0244	0.2866
Eigen value	3.83221	3.44993	2.18838	1.00253
% Explained	0.3238	0.2915	0.1849	0.0847

Note No. of observations (N) = 32, U within parenthesis represents urban and F female
Source Authors' calculation

Table 9 Factor analysis: urban male work participation rate

Variables	Factor 1	Factor 2	Factor 3	Factor 4
HHSZ(U)	−0.9019	−0.1639	0.0154	0.0408
CHILD(U)	−0.8910	−0.0729	−0.1879	0.0751
WPR(M,U)	0.7119	0.2945	0.2085	0.0227
LIT(M,U)	0.8691	0.2175	−0.2488	0.0201
SC(M,U)	0.0658	−0.0781	0.6973	0.0814
ST(M,U)	−0.0958	−0.0844	−0.8909	0.0174
URBAN	0.1422	0.7768	0.0559	0.4533
ELEC	0.1055	0.6646	0.3121	−0.3174
ROAD	0.2629	−0.1446	−0.6956	0.0019
CR-DP	0.1232	0.2019	0.3758	0.2758
WATER(U)	−0.0181	0.2178	0.2496	−0.0934
IMR(M)	−0.4138	−0.5361	0.0999	−0.1980
PCNSDP	0.3378	0.8770	0.0116	0.0968
% INDP	0.1434	0.0878	0.0641	−0.9468
% SERDP	0.0838	0.3889	0.1023	0.8801
Eigen value	4.70756	2.82700	2.29885	1.23276
% Explained	0.3892	0.2337	0.1900	0.1019

Note No. of observations (N) = 32, U within parenthesis represents urban and M male
Source Authors' calculation

Table 10 Factor analysis: urban male labour participation rate

Variables	Factor 1	Factor 2	Factor 3	Factor 4
HHSZ(U)	0.9059	−0.1819	−0.0097	0.0372
CHILD(U)	0.8851	−0.0891	−0.2157	0.0744
LFPR(M,U)	−0.2125	0.0616	0.5107	−0.0454
LIT(M,U)	−0.8651	0.2163	−0.2280	0.0211
SC(M,U)	−0.0456	−0.0695	0.6811	0.0827
ST(M,U)	0.0636	−0.0964	−0.8884	0.0163
URBAN	−0.1305	0.7738	0.0579	0.4674
ELEC	−0.0627	0.6900	0.3074	−0.3173
ROAD	−0.3030	−0.1534	−0.6958	−0.0015
CR-DP	−0.0825	0.2208	0.3746	0.2822
WATER(U)	0.0634	0.2759	0.2890	−0.1088
IMR(M)	0.4398	−0.5322	0.0889	−0.2089
PCNSDP	−0.3209	0.8867	0.0222	0.1019
% INDP	−0.1388	0.1007	0.0727	−0.9432
% SERDP	−0.0744	0.3851	0.0997	0.8840
Eigen value	4.18816	2.93519	2.31019	1.22377
% Explained	0.3653	0.2560	0.2015	0.1067

Note No. of observations (N) = 32, U within parenthesis represents urban and M male
Source Authors' calculation

Table 11 Factor analysis: rural female work participation rate at the district level

Variables	Factor 1	Factor 2	Factor 3	Factor 4
HHSZ(R)	−0.6820	−0.0478	0.2315	−0.1173
CHILD(R)	−0.8783	0.1008	0.0717	0.1659
WPR(F,R)	0.4626	0.5607	−0.0051	0.2973
LIT(F,R)	0.7067	−0.3227	0.1442	−0.0066
SC(F,R)	0.1048	−0.0205	−0.2099	−0.7008
ST(F,R)	−0.0695	0.2442	0.2478	0.7081
F/M(R)	0.4101	0.1304	−0.0642	0.1631
URBAN	0.3592	−0.2852	−0.0290	0.0236
AGLAB(F,R)	0.0185	0.2679	−0.9526	−0.1024
CUL(F,R)	−0.1301	0.6514	0.6790	0.1662
MFGHH(F,R)	−0.0726	−0.1470	0.0037	−0.0821
OTHER(F,R)	0.1467	−0.9531	0.2402	−0.0518
CHILDSR(R)	0.0967	0.1167	−0.1530	0.4789
Eigen value	2.91318	2.49798	1.78244	1.05884
% Explained	0.3283	0.2815	0.2009	0.1193

Note No. of observations (*N*) = 631, R within parenthesis represents rural and F female
Source Authors' calculation

group in which literacy reduces participation (Factor 2) possibly because enrolment of girls leads to labour market withdrawal. The positive association between tribal population and participation and the negative effect of low caste population on participation are evident.

The visibility of women and urbanization level seems to be enhancing women participation in the rural areas. With increased level of urbanization, the rural–urban dis-continuum tends to decline which brings in work opportunities even for rural women who do not migrate out. There is a cluster of districts which is indicative of women workers being engaged primarily as agricultural labour or cultivators (Factor 2) though there are some other districts which tend to show increased participation with improvement in activities other than agriculture and household manufacturing. The non-household manufacturing and the services sector offer possibilities of better earnings, encouraging women, particularly the literate ones, to join the work force. Also, some of the jobs in health sector, for example, are meant specifically for literate women. Unfortunately, rural diversification has been very sluggish in the Indian context with its limited impact on women work participation rate which can be seen from the low magnitude of the factor loading for the share of workers in non-household manufacturing and services in Factor 1. Gender discrimination at early ages is reflective of its continuation even in the later years: an improvement in the gender ratio among children improves the work participation to a very limited extent.

Among the rural males, the positive effect of urbanization on participation is evident (Table 12). Literacy raises the work participation rate, while demographic pressure reduces it. Large families with large number of children are not able to

Table 12 Factor analysis: rural male work participation rate at the district level

Variables	Factor 1	Factor 2	Factor 3
HHSZ(R)	−0.7141	−0.1482	0.1723
CHILD(R)	−0.8742	−0.2242	−0.0524
WPR(M,R)	0.6612	−0.0179	−0.0679
LIT(M,R)	0.5956	0.2986	0.2413
SC(M,R)	0.1588	−0.0013	−0.2127
ST(M,R)	−0.0818	−0.2575	0.1938
URBAN	0.2565	0.3895	0.1347
AGLAB(M,R)	0.0228	0.0286	−0.9928
CUL(M,R)	−0.1644	−0.9483	0.2152
MFGHH(M,R)	−0.0853	0.1331	−0.0280
OTHER(M,R)	0.1338	0.8054	0.5778
CHILDSR(R)	0.1189	−0.0092	−0.1499
Eigen value	3.19995	1.97325	1.73938
% Explained	0.3785	0.2334	0.2057

Note No. of observations (N) = 631, R within parenthesis represents rural and M male
Source Authors' calculation

generate better human capital formation which in turn reduces the possibility of being absorbed in high-productivity activities. Activities other than household manufacturing and agriculture have a positive effect on participation, suggesting the importance of rural diversification.

Among the urban females, the findings are again quite similar to those for rural females except in relation to gender ratio which does not have a positive effect on participation in the urban areas (Table 13). This is mainly because many educated women living in the urban areas remain confined to the domestic activities. Even when the gender ratio rises due to migration of women after marriage—the biggest reason of female migration in India (Mitra and Murayama 2009)—women do not necessarily participate in the labour market. Besides, women who accompany their husbands while migrating from the rural to the urban areas are not able to find employment in the urban labour market. At times, there is skill mismatch and at times the labour demand for women is limited and transient. For example, in the construction sector, demand for women labour is highly sporadic and, when there is a decline in labour demand, the women workers are the first ones to be retrenched. So the discrimination issue is much wide and deep-rooted, and it can exist even when at the time of birth it is not prevalent in the form of gender-selective feticide. As Table 13 shows, the child sex ratio has a positive association with work participation, but the overall gender ratio has a much stronger negative relationship with female work participation rate. With accessibility of women to job opportunities, female feticide seems to have declined, but rise in the women to men ratio has not resulted in enhanced participation due to cultural barriers.

Among the males, the findings are again not different from what we noted in the rural context. However, the association between the share of activities comprising

Table 13 Factor analysis: urban female work participation rate at the district level

Variables	Factor 1	Factor 2	Factor 3	Factor 4
HHSZ(U)	−0.7893	−0.0272	0.0657	0.0318
CHILD(U)	−0.8262	0.1174	0.2322	0.1146
WPR(F,U)	0.6137	0.1048	0.2320	0.4184
LIT(F,U)	0.7600	−0.2329	−0.0343	0.1495
SC(F,U)	0.1254	0.0876	−0.1199	−0.6222
ST(F,U)	0.0176	−0.0951	0.4184	0.7240
F/M(U)	−0.8262	0.1174	0.2322	0.1146
URBAN	0.3041	−0.1769	−0.1508	−0.0241
AGLAB(F,U)	−0.0445	0.9978	0.0138	−0.0404
CUL(F,U)	−0.0879	0.0914	0.9793	0.1661
MFGHH(F,U)	−0.1243	0.0239	−0.0724	−0.0562
OTHER(F,U)	0.1470	−0.6715	−0.4819	−0.0296
CHILDSR(U)	0.2846	0.1268	0.0424	0.5288
Eigen value	3.14689	2.37446	1.73720	1.01386
% Explained	0.3584	0.2705	0.1979	0.1155

Note No. of observations (*N*) = 637, U within parenthesis represents urban and F female
Source Authors' calculation

Table 14 Factor analysis: urban male work participation rate at the district level

Variables	Factor 1	Factor 2	Factor 3
HHSZ(U)	−0.7569	0.0513	0.1070
CHILD(U)	−0.8366	0.1671	0.2077
WPR(M,U)	0.6008	−0.1819	−0.2105
LIT(M,U)	0.7096	−0.3451	−0.0913
SC(M,U)	0.1605	0.0831	−0.0248
ST(M,U)	−0.0642	−0.1414	0.2994
URBAN	0.2488	−0.1746	−0.1904
AGLAB(M,U)	−0.1520	0.9731	0.1671
CUL(M,U)	−0.1462	0.1956	0.9631
MFGHH(M,U)	−0.1539	0.0851	0.0186
OTHER(M,U)	0.2178	−0.6645	−0.6270
CHILDSR(M,U)	0.2600	0.1206	0.0630
Eigen value	3.94216	1.67724	1.27130
% Explained	0.4961	0.2111	0.1600

Note No. of observations (*N*) = 637, U within parenthesis represents urban and M male
Source Authors' calculation

non-household manufacturing and services and the work participation rate is highly significant. Higher levels of urbanization are seen to raise the participation confirming the agglomeration effects. With greater concentration of infrastructure and activities, labour demand seems to have raised the participation rate (Table 14).

Cross-sectional Results: Based on City-Level Data

Since cities are considered to be the dynamic centres of growth compared to other medium-sized and small-sized towns, we have undertaken the analysis separately for the class 1 cities each with a population of 100,000 and above. As mentioned above, these cities comprise more than 60% of the urban population. The association between the overall gender ratio and the female work participation is positive and quite strong unlike at the level of all urban areas which means that women in relatively large cities are better off as far as the labour market outcome is concerned (Table 15). With their greater presence, women are able to participate in the labour market as the social restrictions are relatively less in large cities, whereas in smaller urban locations, the effect of larger presence gets neutralized by the cultural barriers. The demonstration effect of relatively advanced households on the rest is a strong possibility in large cities which comprise more heterogeneous households compared to the homogeneous habitation of the small towns. Also, large cities because of scale effects are able to conduct greater economic activities, generating larger demand for labour, while many of the activities in the services sector prefer women workers, specifically. Besides, women from low-income households in large cities are often forced to participate because of higher cost of living.

The findings for males in cities (Table 16) are not different from what was observed at the state or district level. The effect of city size on both male and female participation is noteworthy, suggesting that even within the set of large cities the participation of males and females both tend to improve as the city size increases. Very large cities naturally offer better prospects for employment; and the social restrictions which are more prevalent in the case of women tend to get dissipated.

Table 15 Factor analysis: urban female work participation rate at the city level

Variables	Factor 1	Factor 2
HHSZ(C)	−0.8032	0.1592
CHILD(C)	−0.8085	0.1752
WPR(F,C)	0.6377	0.3242
LIT(F,C)	0.6840	−0.3685
SC(F,C)	0.0849	0.0099
ST(F,C)	0.0781	−0.1276
F/M(C)	0.4687	0.1003
CTYSZ	0.1482	−0.1181
MFGHH(F,C)	−0.0507	0.8753
OTHER(F,C)	0.1828	−0.8652
CHILDSR(C)	0.3361	0.1900
Eigen value	3.24645	2.01018
% Explained	0.5628	0.3485

Note No. of observations (*N*) = 467, C within parenthesis represents city and F female
Source Authors' calculation

Table 16 Factor analysis: urban male work participation rate at the city level

Variables	Factor 1	Factor 2
HHSZ(C)	−0.8671	−0.2156
CHILD(C)	−0.6653	−0.1376
WPR(M,C)	0.7959	0.1823
LIT(M,C)	0.4724	0.3683
SC(M,C)	0.0222	0.0062
ST(M,C)	0.0438	0.1237
CTYSZ	0.1404	0.1180
MFGHH(M,C)	−0.1258	−0.8155
OTHER(M,C)	0.2558	0.8420
CHILDSR(M,C)	0.4167	−0.1573
Eigen value	3.28815	1.08844
% Explained	0.7008	0.2320

Note No. of observations (*N*) = 467, C within parenthesis represents city and M male
Source Authors' calculation

Panel Data Analysis

Since Labour Bureau has supplied data for five time points corresponding to each of the states and union territories, we have tried to carry out the panel data analysis as well. But in this exercise, only a limited number of variables such as per capita income, the sectoral shares in gross state domestic product and the infant mortality rate could be included.

The results from Table 17 indicate that the female participation rate in the rural areas is influenced by industrialization. The rural diversification possibly creates more opportunities in which women workers can step into. The services sector on the other hand reduces participation refuting some of the popular views which suggest about women's preference to work in this sector. The residual activities carried out in this sector with meagre earnings can discourage women from participating in the labour market ('discouraged dropouts'). However, the female health condition measured in terms of infant mortality rate is a strong determinant of their participation both in the rural and in the urban areas (Table 17).

For rural males, none of the variables turns out to be significant though in the fixed effect model (FE) the overall growth index is statistically significant (Table 18). The positive effect of industry and services is evident in the case of urban males, across all the three models (classical OLS, fixed effect and random effect).

Keeping in view the literature, suggesting the beneficial effect of women's access to income and its positive effect on nutrition, education and health of the children, we have turned the causality from participation to IMR after controlling for growth. Both female participation and economic growth are seen to reduce infant mortality rate among girls as well as boys. And this beneficial effect of female participation is evident across both rural and urban areas as can be seen from all the

Table 17 Regression results for labour force participation rate: panel data analysis (OLS results)

Variables	Dep var: LFPR(F,R) (OLS)	Dep var: LFPR(M,R) (OLS)	Dep var: LFPR(F,U) (OLS)	Dep var: LFPR(M,U) (OLS)	Dep var: LFPR(F,R) (OLS)	Dep var: LFPR(F,U) (OLS)
PCNSDP	−0.00002 (−0.28)	−0.0001 (−1.84)	0.0001 (2.22)*	−0.00005 (−1.70)	−0.0002 (−1.81)	−0.00002 (−0.39)
% INDP	0.5 (3.54)*	0.069 (1.29)	−0.29 (−1.39)	0.24 (2.62)*	0.69 (4.73)*	−0.22 (−1.09)
% SERDP			0.40 (−1.97)*	0.19 (2.17)*		−0.41 (−2.07)*
% AGDP	0.25 (0.80)	−0.073 (−0.61)			0.35 (1.08)	
IMR among girls					−0.43 (−3.61)*	−0.42 (−5.96)*
Constant	17.93 (1.69)	78.78 (19.56)	45.67 (3.13)*	56.81 (8.95)*	34.40 (2.70)*	68.25 (4.66)*
Adj. R2	0.09	0.02	0.19	0.04	0.23	0.24
N	154	154	154	154	122	122

* 5 per cent level

Note R within parenthesis represents rural, U urban, F female and M male

three models (classical OLS, FE and RE; Tables 19 and 20). However, the participation definitely has a beneficial effect on children's health, particularly that of a girl child: with an increase in female labour force participation, the infant mortality rate among girls both in the rural and the urban areas tends to decline.

5 Productivity and Female Participation

In this section, we assess whether female labour participation raises labour productivity as well. However, there are certain practical difficulties in doing this. A highly capital intensive technology which reduces the pace of labour absorption without reducing value added would mean higher labour productivity. Hence, there is difficulty in assessing the impact of labour force participation rate on labour productivity as lower employment levels would always mean higher labour productivity. So this needs to be interpreted very carefully. Secondly, labour productivity is defined as value added per labour. But no information is available on how much of value added is contributed by the male and the female workers separately. Hence, it becomes difficult to assess the association between female labour force participation and female labour productivity. Again, the information on rural and urban labour productivity is missing because value-added figures are given sector wise. So what is doable is as follows. We can only investigate whether there is a positive relationship between female labour force participation and overall labour productivity.

Table 18 Regression results for labour force participation rate: panel data analysis (fixed effect and random effect models)

Variables	Dep var: LFPR(F,R) (FE)	Dep var: LFPR(F,R) (RE)	Dep var: LFPR(M,R) (FE)	Dep var: LFPR(M,R) (RE)	Dep var: LFPR(F,U) (FE)	Dep var: LFPR(F, U)	Dep var: LFPR(M,U) (FE)	Dep var: LFPR(M,U) (RE)
PCNSDP	−0.0001 (−0.95)	−0.0002 (−1.7)	0.0002 (3.32)*	−0.00001 (−0.22)	0.0001 (0.80)	5.98e−06 (0.07)	−00006 (−1.04)	−0.00005 (−1.54)
% INDP	0.37 (1.28)	0.57 (2.83)*	−0.47 (−1.15)	0.06 (0.81)	0.25 (0.49)	−0.26 (−0.93)	1.26 (4.16)*	0.34 (2.63)*
% SERDP					0.49 (0.92)	−0.32 (−1.18)	1.11 (3.72)*	0.28 (2.23)*
% AGDP	−0.24 (−0.35)	0.34 (0.83)	−0.11 (−0.63)	0.03 (0.20)				
IMR among girls	−0.69 (−4.51)*	−0.67 (−5.43)*			−0.18 (−1.51)	−0.35 (−3.98)*		
Constant	61.35 (3.47)*	48.21 (3.39)*	74.69 (6.58)*	74.74 (13.86)*	−9.18 (−0.21)	60.56 (2.90)*	−22.80 (−0.96)	49.70 (5.48)*
R2	0.06	0.19	0.03	0.03	0.01	0.07	0.02	0.04
N	122	122	154	154	122	122	154	154

* 5 per cent level

Note R within parenthesis represents rural, U urban, F female and M male

Table 19 Impact of female LFPR in rural areas on IMR (panel data results)

	IMR(Girls) OLS	IMR(Girls) FE	IMR(Girls) RE	IMR(Boys) OLS	IMR(Boys) FE	IMR(Boys) RE
PCNSDP	−0.0004 (−9.36)*	−0.0005 (−5.18)*	−0.0004 (−7.16)*	−0.0004 (−9.55)*	−0.0004 (−4.43)*	−0.0004 (−6.62)*
LFPR (F,R)	−0.18 (−2.86)*	−0.31 (−4.81)*	−0.28 (−5.07)*	−0.18 (−2.87)*	−0.27 (−4.28)*	−0.25 (−4.50)*
Constant	64.37 (19.47)*	70.16 (17.31)*	68.5 (17.89)*	61.43 (18.36)*	61.96 (15.59)*	62.11 (16.23)*
Adj. R2	0.42	0.42	0.41	0.44	0.42	0.43
N	122	122	122	122	122	122

* 5 per cent level
Note R within parenthesis represents rural and F female

Table 20 Impact of female LFPR in urban areas on IMR (panel data results)

	IMR(Girls) OLS	IMR(Girls) FE	IMR(Girls) RE	IMR(Boys) OLS	IMR(Boys) FE	IMR(Boys) RE
PCNSDP	−0.0004 (−9.27)*	−0.0005 (−5.07)*	−0.0004 (−6.72)*	−0.0004 (−9.49)*	−0.0004 (−4.49)*	−0.0004 (−6.44)*
LFPR (F,U)	−0.514 (−5.64)*	−0.20 (−2.10)*	−0.30 (−3.54)	−0.53 (−5.70)*	−0.13 (−1.44)*	−0.24 (−2.88)*
Constant	67.60 (24.75)*	65.6 (15.24)*	64.03 (18.04)*	64.76 (23.47)*	57.48 (13.74)*	58.27 (16.39)*
Adj. R2	0.51	0.46	0.49	0.52	0.46	0.49
N	122	122	122	122	122	122

* 5 per cent level
Note U within parenthesis represents and F female

On a priori basis, the relationship between the variables can go in either direction—positive or negative. In ageing societies as labour supply shrinks, the shortages can be mitigated by raising the female labour force participation. Also, given the fact that female labour is docile and sincere, labour productivity can actually rise with increased participation of women in the labour market. Besides, female wages being lower than the male wages, the substitution of female labour for male labour can reduce the wage share (or labour cost) in value added. In other words, wage-to-labour productivity ratio can decline which means increased efficiency of the unit from the point of view of the employer. This can then contribute to overall growth.

However, from another angle, particularly in a typical neoclassical frame, female wages are lower because female productivity is believed to be lower than the male productivity: the rationalization is derived from the proposition that each of the factors of production gets paid according to its marginal productivity under perfect competition. This postulation has led to the concern that increased participation of females in the labour market can actually reduce labour productivity and growth.

Further, as we say low productivity means low wages which in turn raise labour demand, there is the possibility of a causal relationship running from productivity to participation as well. Or to put in plainly, lower productivity would mean more manpower to complete the job. So the bidirectionality issue is quite important. In addition, productivity cannot be measured as a function of participation only. Other relevant variables representing technology, skill, production structure, to cite a few, need to be controlled for. However, given the paucity of information and the lack of possibility of carrying out a rigorous quantitative exercise, we simply take overall labour productivity as a function of certain variables on which information is readily available. This is pursued basically to address the importance of certain policy options. For example, economic necessity may compel women to participate in the labour market, and without adequate education and skill, they may pursue petty activities. This sort of a situation will lead to increased participation but with low levels of productivity. On the other hand, with higher levels education and skill when women participate in the labour market, their productivity can be much higher. But with higher levels of education, women not necessarily can participate in the labour market as the social factors may pose major hindrances. Hence, based on the observed association between productivity and participation, certain broad inferences can only be drawn regarding the quality of jobs that women get absorbed into and, accordingly, suggestions can be made in favour of strategies which can help attain the twin objectives of productivity growth and increased participation.

When we take labour productivity as a function of participation rate, the endogeneity problem arises because participation itself is an endogenous outcome which is determined in terms of certain variables. We have, therefore, presented two sets of results below (Table 21). One set gives the OLS results, while the other set corrects for endogeneity by considering an appropriate instrument for participation. The instrument is generated by estimating the participation equation first and then considering the predicted value. The results tend to indicate that the female participation rate is statistically insignificant in most of the equations with labour productivity as the dependent variable. It has a negative sign, but it can be primarily because many women workers are engaged in petty activities in the informal sector, both in the rural and in the urban areas.

What is striking from Table 21 is that given participation, women's education (captured through enrolment), urbanization and infrastructure availability are some of the most important determinants of productivity. Also, the social infrastructure covering health- and education-specific variables, and physical and financial infrastructure impact on women participation in the labour market significantly. Poor health conditions measured in terms of higher infant mortality rate reduce the participation. The panel data analysis also confirms that poor health reduces women participation. These findings are important from policy point of view because different infrastructure variables are seen to improve both women participation and labour productivity. Infrastructure (social, physical and financial) can to certain extent help break the social and cultural barriers and help women participate in the labour market and make productive contribution. For voicing the women's need, overcoming the social constraints and enhancing their bargaining power, their

Table 21 Effect of female participation on labour productivity

Variables	Dep var: Lab Prod (OLS)	Dep var: Lab Prod (OLS)	Dep var: WORK (F,R) (OLS)	Dep var: WORK (F,U) (OLS)	Dep var: LFPR (F,R) (OLS)	Dep var: LFPR (F,U) (OSLS)	Dep var: Lab Prod (2SLS)	Dep var: Lab Prod (2SLS)
WORK (F.R)	−9474.98 (−0.21)						−26709.8 (−0.26)	
WORK (F,U)	−185178.5 (−1.84)						−385561.6 (−1.35)	
LFPR (F,R)		−185115.6 (−0.57)						−103884.6 (−2.0)
LFPR (F,U)		−0.36783.7 (−0.76)						−190538.2 (−1.84)
SERDP	75500.8 (1.82)	80466.8 (1.71)					68489.8 (1.54)	64334.9 (1.55)
URBAN	78042.7 (3.43)*	62162.9 (2.52)*					100857 (3.14)*	92146.9 (3.59)*
ROAD		150.1 (0.16)	0.013 (3.99)*	0.005 (2.96)*	0.017 (2.71)*	0.009 (2.05)	1817.1 (1.23)	3335.0 (2.05)*
CR-DP			0.180 (3.95)*	0.05 (2.26)*	0.19 (2.13)*	−0.02 (−0.35)		
ENROL of girls	44694.7 (2.57)*	40649.1 (2.07)*	0.136 (2.30)*	0.107 (3.61)*	0.389 (3.46)*	0.26 (3.52)*	59537 (2.31)*	109144.9 (3.21)*
IMR(F)				−0.12 (−2.62)*		0.28 (−2.47)*		
F/M			32.33 (1.78)		77.59 (2.24)*			
Constant	−8386365 (−2.89)*	−8751124 (−2.65)*	−43.35 (−2.42)*	0.51 (0.13)	96.22 (−2.81)*	2.58 (0.27)	−8347673 (−2.69)*	−1.10+e07 (−3.56)*
Adj. R2	0.64	0.66	0.55	0.48	0.47	0.50	0.59	0.64
N	32	32	35	35	35	35	32	32

* 5 per cent level

Note R within parenthesis represents rural, U urban and F female physical presence is essential as indicated by a positive association between female-to-male ratio and women participation, particularly in the rural areas where the social barriers are strong.

We also noted in the previous section the beneficial effect of female labour force participation rate (from the panel data analysis) on infant mortality of girls as well as boys after controlling for growth indicator which also has a very strong effect on infant mortality rate. Access of mothers to resources through labour market participation improves the health status of the children as their nutritional status also improves. Also, greater volume of resources is required for enhancing the provision of heathcare facilities which can be met through higher levels of growth.

Elsewhere, it has been shown based on data from a number of Asia-Pacific countries that decline in gender inequality in labour market through improvement in female labour force participation reduces inequality in many other spheres, and eventually, it leads to greater participation of women in the decision-making process both within the households and at the macrolevel (Mitra 2010). Particularly when it comes to fertility decisions, the working women are able to voice their preference better compared to the housewives. Similarly, the working women could vouch for gender budgeting and participate in the political process as well. Refuting the view that increased participation of females in the labour market would reduce growth, the study also casted evidence in favour of economic growth responding positively to a rise in female participation. The poor levels of skill resulting from gender discrimination, limited scope to undergo on the job training, information asymmetry aggravated by the inadequate access of women to job market information, inability to pursue job search on full-time basis due to domestic responsibilities, unavailability of productive jobs with flexi hours and weak bargaining power result in lower wages for women workers than their male counterparts. And this wage discrepancy has sent a wrong message about women being less productive.

An important way of showing the relevance of skill in the job market is to calculate the returns to skill and the differences in the returns across various levels of skills. One of the convenient ways of conceptualizing the returns is to estimate an earning function with dummies representing different educational levels. The weekly wage function estimated on the basis of the NSS unit-level data from the 66th round (2009–10) shows that the male wages are substantially higher than their female counterparts (Table 22). Education dummies (the general and technical both) tend to enhance earnings. Those who have general education receive higher earnings in comparison with the illiterates (the comparison group). In fact, most of the education dummies have positive coefficients and are significant except Gedu2 which represents literates without formal schooling. Similarly, technical education dummies are statistically significant. But those who have acquired vocational training are not better off in comparison with those who do not have it. Scheduled castes receive a lower wage compared to the general-cum-OBCs. Large households are also worse off in terms of earnings, suggesting lower productivity levels and poor quality of labour. Though age, taken to be a proxy for job market experience, is not significant, age square is, and it has a positive coefficient. All this tends to

Table 22 Dependent variable: regression equation for weekly wage (in Rs. per person)

Variables	Coefficient	*t* ratio
Age	−1.98	−0.58
Agesq	0.39	8.98*
hhhold_size	−10.28	−4.57*
Gedu2	18.63	0.24
Gedu3	201.06	13.44*
Gedu4	831.28	46.45*
Gedu5	2028.29	95.56*
Tedu2	2756.52	47.92*
Tedu3	690.78	20.12*
Tedu4	903.45	19.08*
vtrn1	−766.49	−24.02*
vtrn2	−124.35	−3.89*
vtrn3	−77.98	−3.59*
mst1	−8.88	−0.29
mst2	193.45	7.68*
gender1	371.49	27.14*
reldum1	−184.97	−10.26*
reldum2	−155.69	−6.42*
Socdum1	26.93	1.56
Socdum2	−101.55	−7.4*
occ1	−700.31	−16.03*
occ3	−412.47	−9.3*
occ4	−586.32	−13.42*
occ5	−750.70	−16.42*
occ6	−323.05	−7.09*
occ7	101.45	2.34*
Secdum1	−258.73	−22.27*

* 5 per cent level

Note Number of obs = 75518, F(27, 75490) = 1914.54, Adj. R-square = 0.41

Variables Age: age of the earner, Agesq: age square, hhhold_size: household size, Gedu2: literate without formal schooling, Gedu3: primary and middle level, Gedu4: secondary and higher secondary, Gedu5: graduation and postgraduation, Tedu2: technical degree in agriculture/ engineering/technology/medicine, etc., Tedu3: diploma or certificate (below graduate level) in: agriculture, engineering/technology, medicine, crafts, other subjects, Tedu4: diploma or certificate (graduate and above level) in: agriculture, engineering/technology, medicine, crafts, other subjects, vtrn1: receiving formal vocational training, vtrn2: received vocational training: formal, vtrn3: received non-formal: hereditary, self-learning, learning on the job and others, mst1: never married, mst2: currently married, gender1: gender dummy (1 for males and 0 for females), reldum1: Hindu, reldum2: Islam, Socdum1: schedule tribe, Socdum2: schedule caste, occ1: agriculture, hunting, forestry and fishing, occ3: manufacturing, electricity, gas and water supply, occ4: construction, occ5: wholesale and retail trade, hotel and restaurant, occ6: transport, storage and communication, occ7: other services including financing, secdum1: rural dummy (1 for rural and 0 for urban areas)

Source Based on NSS unit-level data (66th Round, 2009–10)

suggest that skill formation and experience do contribute to higher levels of earnings. The sector-specific dummies are mostly negative indicating lower earnings in most of the sectors in relation to the comparison group which is mining and quarrying. However, the occ7 which represents ‘other services’, including financing, has a positive coefficient, meaning higher earnings accruing to workers in this sector.

6 Conclusion and Policy Issues

This study on labour (and work) force participation rate has been pursued gender wise, at three spatial levels: state, district and city. Further, the state- and district-specific rates have been analysed at the rural and urban areas separately. Among the cities and towns, the relatively large ones, i.e. each with a population of 100,000 and above, have been considered in order to assess the effects of agglomeration economies and the cultural factors which are supposedly more advanced in the large cities.

Based on the population census data, the study noted that the female participation rates are significantly lower than those among the males. The interstate variations in the male-specific rates are rather limited. On the other hand, the rural–urban differentials are more pronounced and the interstate variations are sizable in the case of females, reflecting the influence of social, cultural and economic factors. Female rates in the urban areas are not necessarily higher than the rural rates despite higher levels of education and social advancement that urbanization is expected to usher in. Economic factors, particularly in the low-income households, dominate in the rural context, compelling more women to participate in the labour market. There does not seem to be any significant positive relationship between per capita income and participation rate in the case of females (except in a subset of sates) though among males such a pattern is somewhat distinguishable. This finding brings out the inadequacy of growth to usher in gender equality.

The Labour Bureau’s panel estimates of gender-specific labour participation rate have been consistent over time, and the gender differences in the estimates are again pertinent for each of the years. Though the time frame (2009–10 through 2014–15) is too short to expect any significant change in the participation rate, the rigidity in the female participation rate does raise concerns to be addressed in a larger ambit covering social, economic, political and cultural arena. On the whole, the female participation is considerably low. Even in the urban areas and in the relatively large cities, the social factors and the practice of gender-based division of labour are prevalent as a result of which the female labour market participation is lower than its rural counterpart.

Based on the inter-spatial variations, the study made an attempt to capture the important determinants. It clearly brings out the importance of infrastructure, education and health and urbanization on labour force participation of both the gender. This in turn points to three types of factors which are instrumental in resulting enhanced participation rate. The first set refers to creation of greater volume of jobs motivating participation, the second enhances the ability of the individuals to participate, and the third, the most important one, facilitates the accessibility of the capable ones to the locations where jobs are available. Hence, strategies for creating clusters with greater employment potentials (which in turn is cost-effective in making pro-poor growth happen), consecrated efforts for human capital formation and investments to remove barriers between jobs and their seekers need to be pursued aggressively.

The negative impact of fertility and household size on rural female work participation comes out sharply: greater domestic burdens in large households do not allow women to participate explicitly in the labour market. Though the urbanization level does not show a positive effect on rural women participation at the state level, the beneficial effects are evident at the district level for both the gender. On the other hand, in the urban context, the participation rates of both females and males vary positively with the level of urbanization. In other words, the urban areas in states and districts with higher levels of urbanization unravel higher levels of participation both for females and for males in comparison with the states or districts with lower levels of urbanization, revealing the agglomeration effects. With greater concentration of infrastructure and activities, labour demand tends to increase. Further evidence in this regard is brought out from the city-level data which confirm the positive effect of city size on both male and female participation. The urban-specific rates, particularly for females, may be lower than the rural rates, showing the persistence of cultural backwardness, but within the urban context, there is a positive impact of urban settlement; that is, the relatively large settlements are associated with better outcomes.

While industrialization and growth in services both show a positive effect on participation, though very mildly especially in the case of urban women, growth shows a rising impact only in the case of urban males. Also, there is evidence on poverty-induced participation in agricultural activities, suggesting clearly the importance of rural diversification for participation to pick up.

The positive relationship between the female-to-male ratio and the female participation is striking in both the rural and urban areas, at least at the state level. Greater presence of women in the society is a precondition to their participation in the labour market though there is evidence, particularly from the urban district-level data that it is not a sufficient condition. In fact, many educated women remain confined to domestic activities not being able to participate in the labour market. However, the association between the gender ratio and the female work participation rate is positive and quite strong in large cities compared to all urban areas which comprise medium-sized and small-sized towns. The social restrictions are likely to be less in large cities, enabling more women to participate in the labour market. The demonstration effect of relatively advanced households on the rest is also a possibility. Besides, large cities because of scale effects are able to conduct greater economic activities, generating larger demand for labour. Many of the activities in the services sector, especially, prefer to have women workers, motivating the potential entrants to join the job market. This, however, does not rule out the possibility of women from low-incomes households being residually absorbed in low-productivity services because of high living costs.

Women's participation does not reduce productivity. On the contrary, it improves child health significantly as noted from the beneficial effect of female labour force participation rate (from the panel data analysis) on infant mortality of girls as well as boys after controlling for growth, which too has a strong effect on infant mortality. Access of mothers to resources through labour market participation improves the health status of the children as their nutritional status and access to curative health care get better.

Regarding the negative effect of female labour force participation on labour productivity and economic growth, the study clears up the misgivings, suggesting that the negative sign is statistically not significant; and secondly, it arises because of women's residual absorption in petty activities in the informal sector, both in the rural and the urban areas. Further, the female–male wage differences are due to skill differences and not because males are more productive than females in relation to a given task. The results suggest that given participation, women's education (captured through enrolment), urbanization and infrastructure availability are some of the most important determinants of productivity. Further, as mentioned above, the social infrastructure (covering health- and education-specific variables) and physical and financial infrastructure impact on women participation as well.

On the whole, based on these results, it may be inferred that women participation in productive activities has a double effect: first, it raises the household income, and second, it contributes to well-being of the household as the health status of the children improves. A mere increase in participation without ensuring productive absorption may not be beneficial as it would only raise the burden on the women members. Also, institutional support to discourage the practice of gender-based discriminatory wages is instrumental to women's participation in the labour market and the beneficial effects which are expected to crop up subsequently.

These findings are important from policy point of view because different infrastructure variables are seen to improve both participation and labour productivity. With improved infrastructure, the quantum of investment is expected to shoot up and the accessibility to growth centres offering better livelihood opportunities can ameliorate. Infrastructure (social, physical and financial) can to certain extent break the social and cultural barriers and help women participate in the labour market and make productive contribution to the growth process. Though the level of urbanization raises the urban participation rate in an inter-spatial sense, a similar pattern is not evident in the context of rural females (at least at the state level). How urbanization can be made more generative with positive spillover effects in the rural neighbourhood is, therefore, an important policy question. Increased urbanization, ushering in greater concentration of non-farm activities, holds the potentiality to create employment prospects and result in productivity gains.

Higher fertility rate harms maternal health, reducing women's ability to work in the labour market. For voicing the women's need, overcoming the social constraints and enhancing their bargaining power, their physical presence is essential as indicated by a positive association between the female-to-male ratio and the women participation, particularly in the rural areas where the social barriers are strong. Ban on sex-selective termination of pregnancy requires greater enforceability. That despite higher levels of education women-specific participation rate in the urban areas is in general lower in comparison with the rural areas calls for introducing more effective strategies to make women more job-oriented. Rural women workers are mostly engaged in agriculture, and rural poverty forces many of them to pick up marginal activities outside agriculture. How productivity and earning of these workers can be enhanced is, therefore, another key policy concern.

The age structure shift in the Indian context, i.e. a relatively large percentage of population in working age brackets, can prove to be beneficial only when their accessibility to productive jobs develops. The improvement in the job market participation of both females and males and their absorption in productive activities would be possible when economic growth, human capital formation and social progress take place simultaneously. For all this to happen, strategic action is required. With enhanced equality between females and males in terms of work opportunities and labour market attributes, several positive outcomes in terms of economic, social, political, educational and health-related equality may take place in a significant way. All this would subsequently improve the overall social status of women and their participation in the decision-making process. Going a step ahead, one may argue that with specific interventions, enhanced labour market participation of women can result in higher productivity and growth as well, which will indeed be sustainable in the long run. Since women labour has remained unutilized in remunerative and economic activities to a large extent, higher participation of women, particularly in ageing societies, can mitigate the shortage of labour and contribute to pro-poor growth.

The government's effort to introduce the new manufacturing policy, urban policy with a thrust to create smart cities, 'skill India' programme to improve the employability of the labour force and 'make in India' programme to raise labour demand and production simultaneously are expected to have positive impact on both female and male labour force participation rates. Specifically for women, a series of measures which include maternity benefit, provision of childcare leave, equal remuneration for both male and female workers, prevention of domestic violence and workplace harassment are there which may encourage participation. A scheme on gender budgeting was introduced in 2007 to build capacity so that a gender perspective is retained at all levels of planning, budget formulation and implementation stages.[5] Shifting workers of both the gender from low- to

---

[5]Besides, there are literacy mission (Sakshar Bharat abhiyan), sanitation scheme, midday meal schemes in school and save the girl child (Beti Bachao, Beti Padhao: BBBP) programme. National rural Health Mission and National Urban Mission and High Level Expert Group on Universal Health Coverage aim at improving the access to health services for women, girls and other vulnerable genders, going beyond maternal and child health. The scheme relating to hostels for working women intends to promote mobility among women in the labour market by providing safe and cheap accommodation to those from the lower income households and living away from home. Provision and improvement of sanitation facilities in educational institutions is expected to

high-productivity activities has been a major challenge. On top of that if the participation rate has to improve, both demand- and supply-side factors, as our analysis highlights, will have to be considered.

References

Acharya, M. 1998. Structural Adjustment Policies and Labour Market Development in Nepal. In *Labour, Employment and Human Development in South Asia*, ed. A. Chandra, H. Mund, T. Sharan, and C.P. Thakur, 101–132. Delhi: B.R. Pub Corp.

Agarwal, B. 1988. Who Sows? Who Reaps? Women and Land Rights in India. *The Journal of Peasant Studies, London* 15 (4): 531–581.

Banerjee, B. 1984. "Information Flow, Expectations and Job Search: Rural to Urban Migration Process in India". *Journal of Development Economics*, 15 (2): 239–257.

Banerjee, N. 1997. How Real is the Bogy of Feminization? *The Indian Journal of Labour Economics* 40 (3): 427–438.

Behrman, Jere R., and Zheng Zhang. 1995. Gender Issues and Employment in Asia. *Asian Development Review* 13 (2): 1–49.

Besley, T., and R. Burgess. 2004. Can Labour Regulation Hinder Economic Performance? Evidence from India. *The Quarterly Journal of Economics* 119 (1): 91–134.

Bharadwaj, K. 1989. The Formation of Rural Labour Markets: An Analysis with Special Reference to Asia. World Employment Research Programme Working Paper (WEP 10-6/WP 98). Geneva: ILO.

Bhattacharjea, A. 2006. Labour Market Regulation and Industrial Performance in India: A Critical Review of the Empirical Evidence. *The Indian Journal of Labour Economics* 49 (2): 211–232.

Boserup, E. 1970. *Woman's Role in Economic Development*. London: Earthscan.

Cagatay, N., and S. Ozler. 1995. Feminisation of the Labour Force: The Effects of Long-Term Development and Structural Adjustment. *World Development* 23 (11): 1883–1894.

Cook, Cynthia, Tyrrell Duncan, Somchai Jitsuchon, Anil Sharma, and Wu Guobao. 2005. *Assessing the Impact of Transport and Energy Infrastructure on Poverty Reduction*. Manila: Asian Development Bank.

Currie, Janet and Brigitte C. Madrian. 1999. Health, Health Insurance and the Labour Market (Chapter 50). In *Handbook of Labor Economics*, ed. O. Ashenfelter, and D. Card, vol. 3, 3309–3415. Elsevier Science B.V.

Dreze, Jean, and Geeta Gandhi Kingdon. 1999. *School Participation in Rural India*. The Development Economics Discussion Paper Series, London School of Economics. Visited on 27 Dec 2016. http://workspace.unpan.org/sites/internet/Documents/UNPAN95932.pdf.

Dreze Jean, and Reetika Khera. 2009. The Battle for Employment Guarantee. *Frontline* 26 (1) (Jan 03–16).

Dreze, Jean, and Reetika Khera. 2015. *Child Development: How are Indian States Faring?* Posted On: 10 Dec 2015; Visited on 16 Nov 2016. http://ideasforindia.in/article.aspx?article_id=1544.

---

improve enrolment among girl children. There are other women development programmes too (Swyam Sidha programme, Swa-Shakti programme and Rashtriya Mahila Kosh programmes). The National Rural Employment Guarantee Programme (MNREGA), the Right to Free and Compulsory Education, National Rural Health Mission, National Rural Livelihood Mission and National Skill Development Mission aim at improving the ability to access better livelihood opportunities.

Forsythe, N.R., P. Korzeniewicz, and V. Durrant. 2000. Gender Inequalities and Economic Growth: A Longitudinal Evaluation. *Economic Development and Cultural Change* 48 (3): 573–617.

Ghayur, S. 1998. Labour Market in Pakistan: Existing Situation, Issues and Emerging Pressures. *Labour, Employment and Human Development in South Asia*, ed. A. Chandra, H. Mund, T. Sharan, and C. P. Thakur, 133–157. Delhi: B.R. Pub Corp.

Goldin, C. 1994. *The U-shaped Female Labour Force Function in Economic Development and Economic History*. NBER Working Paper No. 4707, National Bureau of Economic Research, Cambridge.

Grossman, Michael. 1975. The Correlation Between Health and Schooling. In *Household Production and Consumption*, ed. Nestor E. Terleckyj, 147–211. New York: Columbia University Press.

Harris, John R., and Michael P. Todaro. 1970. "Migration, Unemployment and Development: A Two-Sector Analysis". *The American Economic Review* 60 (1): 126–142

Hashim, S.R. 1998. Foreword to the Book. In *Labour, Employment and Human Development in South Asia*, ed. A. Chandra, H. Mund, T. Sharan, and C. P. Thakur. Delhi: B.R. Pub Corp.

Hayase, Y. 2005. Gender Perspectives in Family Planning in Postwar Japan and Policy Implications from the Japanese Experience. In *Gender and Development: The Japanese Experience in Comparative Perspective*, ed. M. Murayama. Palgrave-Macmillan: IDE-JETRO.

Hirway, I. 2010. Time-Use Surveys in Developing Countries: An Assessment. In *Unpaid Work and the Economy: Gender, Time Use and Poverty in Developing Countries*, ed. R. Antonopoulos, and I. Hirway. London, UK: Palgrave Macmillan.

ICDF Report. 2002. *The Importance of Microcredit Programs in Sustainable Development*. Visited on 16 Nov. https://www.icdf.org.tw/web_pub/20030429170522PP171-174%20C3-3.pdf.

ILO (International Labour Organisation). 2000. *Towards Full Employment*. Section 2.4 "Gender Inequalities", Regional Office for the Asia and the Pacific, Bangkok. http://www.ilo.org/public/english/region/asro/bangkok/feature/f-emp24.htm.

Jalan, J. 2000. Does Economic Progress Close the Gender Gap in Human Resource Development. *Journal of Quantitative Economics* 18 (1): 19–32.

Mathur, O.P. 1994. Women, Urban Poverty and Economic Development. In *Gender, Economic Growth and Poverty: Market Growth and State Planning in Asia and Pacific*, ed. Nolen Heyzer, and Gita Sen, 173–205. New Delhi: Asia and Pacific Development Centre and Kali for Women.

Mitra, Arup. 1994. *Urbanisation, Slums, Informal Sector Employment and Poverty: An Exploratory Study*. Delhi: B. R. Publishing Corporation.

Mitra, Arup. 2005. Women in the Urban Informal Sector: Perpetuation of Meagre Earnings. *Development and Change* 36 (2): 291–316.

Mitra, Arup. 2008. *The Indian Labour Market: An Overview. ILO-Asia Pacific Working Paper Series*. New Delhi: International Labour Organisation.

Mitra, Arup. 2010. *Women's Employment in Asia-Pacific*. Asia-Pacific Human Development, Report Background Papers Series, 2010/07, UNDP.

Mitra, Arup. 2013a. *Can Industry be the Key to Pro-Poor Growth?* An Exploratory Analysis for India. ILO Asia-Pacific Working Paper Series, December.

Mitra, Arup. 2013b. *Insights into Inclusive Growth, Employment and Wellbeing in India*. Springer.

Mitra, A., and M. Murayama. 2009. Rural to Urban Migration: A District-Level Analysis for India. *International Journal of Migration, Health and Social Care* 5 (2): 35–52.

Mohanty, Bidyut. 2008. Status of Women in an Agrarian Economy: Deconstruction of Oriya LaksmiVrat-Katha. In *The Constant and Changing Faces of the Goddess: Goddess Traditions of Asia*, ed. Deepak Shimkhada, and Phyllis K. Herman. Cambridge Scholars Publishing, New Castle.

Murayama, M. (Ed.). 2005. *Gender and Development: The Japanese Experience in Comparative Perspective*. Palgrave-Macmillan, IDE-JETRO.

Nord, S. 1989. The Relationship among Labour Force Participation and Service Sector Employment and Underemployment. *Journal of Regional Science* 29 (3): 407–421.

Nussbaum, Martha C., and Jonathan Glover. 1995. *Women, Culture and Development: A Study of Human Capabilities*. New Delhi: Oxford University Press.

Okada, Aya. 2004. Skill Development and Inter-Firm Learning Linkages Under Globalisation: Lessons from the Indian Automobile Industry. *World Development* 32 (7): 1265–1288.

Okada, Aya. 2012. Skills Development for Youth in India: Challenges and Opportunities, CICE Hiroshima University. *Journal of International Cooperation in Education* 15 (2): 169–193.

Oppenheimer, V. 1970. *The Female Labour Force in the United States*. Berkeley, CA: Institute for International Studies.

Patrick, Martin. 2001. Unorganised Women in an Urban Setting: Opportunities and Challenges. In *Informal Sector in India: Perspectives and Policies*, ed. A. Kundu, and A.N. Sharma, 349–360. New Delhi: Institute for Human Development-Institute for Applied Manpower Research.

Pradhan, B.K., S. Singh, and A. Mitra. 2015. Female Labour Supply in a Developing Economy: A Tale from a Primary Survey. *Journal of International Development* 27 (1): 99–111.

Rahaman, R.I. 1998. Structure of the Labour Market, Unemployment and Poverty in Bangladesh. In *Labour, Employment and Human Development in South Asia*, ed. A. Chandra et al., 47–67. Delhi: B.R. Pub Corp.

Rodrigo, C. 1998. Structural Reforms and Labour Market in Sri Lanka. In *Labour, Employment and Human Development in South Asia*, ed. A. Chandra, H. Mund, T. Sharan, and C. P. Thakur, 159–200. Delhi: B.R. Pub Corp.

Schultz, T.P. 1990. Women's Changing Participation in the Labour Force: A World Perspective. *Economic Development and Cultural Change* 38: 457–488.

Sen, A. 1981. Market Failure and Control of Labour Power: Towards an Explanation of Structure and Change in Indian Agriculture, Part 2. *Cambridge Journal of Economics* 5 (4): 327–350.

UN (United Nations). 2001. *World Population Monitoring 2000: Population, Gender and Development*. New York: United Nations.

United Nations. 2007. *Economic and Social Survey of Asia and the Pacific, 2007, Surging Ahead in Uncertain Times*. Delhi: Economic and Social Commission for Asia and the Pacific, Academic Foundation.

Wadsworth, M.E. 1986. Serious Illness in Childhood and Its Association With Later-Life Achievement. In *Class and Health: Research and Longitudinal Data*, ed. R. Wilkinson, 50–74. London: Tavistock.

Appendix

See Tables A.1 and A.2.

A. Mitra and A. Okada, *Labour Market Participation in India*, SpringerBriefs in Economics, https://doi.org/10.1007/978-981-10-7143-0

Table A.1 Labour force participation rate for females (age 15+)

Country	Region	LFPR 1980	LFPR 1985	LFPR 1990	LFPR 1995	LFPR 2000	LFPR 2005	LFPR 2006	Change: 1980–90	Change: 1990–06
Cambodia	Northeast	79	78.5	77.9	77.2	75.4	74.7	74.7	−1.1	−3.2
China	Northeast	71.1	71.8	73.2	72.8	71.3	68.9	68.5	2.1	−4.7
Hong Kong, China (SAR)	Northeast	45.5	48.8	47.2	47.4	49.6	53.2	53.8	1.7	6.6
Korea, Democratic People's Republic of	Northeast	52.9	52.7	52.2	50.1	49.2	48.3	48.2	−0.7	−4.0
Korea, Republic of	Northeast	43.6	42.8	47.1	48.5	48.6	50.2	50.3	3.5	3.2
Lao People's Democratic Republic	Northeast	51.5	54.5	53.3	54.2	53.8	54	54.1	1.8	0.8
Macao, China (SAR)	Northeast	39.4	41	44.8	48.7	55.2	60.7	61.8	5.4	17.0
Mongolia	Northeast	53.1	53.3	55.5	54.6	54.3	53.9	53.9	2.4	−1.6
Vietnam	Northeast	73.3	73.9	73.8	73.5	72.9	72.1	72	0.5	−1.8
Fiji	Pacific	54.7	52.6	48.8	48.9	49.9	51.3	51.6	−5.9	2.8
Papua New Guinea	Pacific	70.6	71	71.6	70.7	71.3	71.7	71.7	1.0	0.1
Samoa	Pacific	38.6	39.8	39.4	40.6	40.5	39.4	39.3	0.8	−0.1
Solomon Islands	Pacific	52.3	54.2	55.6	55.1	54.7	54.1	54.1	3.3	−1.5
Tonga	Pacific	38	36.4	36.8	45.7	44.7	44.9	44.9	−1.2	8.1
Vanuatu	Pacific	78.3	78.5	79.6	78.4	78.7	79.4	79.5	1.3	−0.1
Brunei Darussalam	Southeast	32.4	36.2	44.9	46.1	46.1	44	43.7	12.5	−1.2
Timor-Leste	Southeast	56.8	54.1	49.5	48.1	50.6	55.1	55.8	−7.3	6.3
Indonesia	Southeast	44	43.4	50.3	49.4	50.7	51	51.2	6.3	0.9
Malaysia	Southeast	42.2	42.1	44.1	43.8	45.5	46.5	46.9	1.9	2.8
Myanmar	Southeast	69.7	69.5	68.8	68.3	68.2	68.2	68.3	−0.9	−0.5
The Philippines	Southeast	50.2	48	47.4	49.1	48.5	54.7	55.7	−2.8	8.3
Singapore	Southeast	44.9	44.9	50.3	49.8	52.3	50.6	50.4	5.4	0.1

(continued)

Table A.1 (continued)

Country	Region	LFPR 1980	LFPR 1985	LFPR 1990	LFPR 1995	LFPR 2000	LFPR 2005	LFPR 2006	Change: 1980–90	Change: 1990–06
Thailand	Southeast	75.6	75.1	74.5	66.1	65.4	65.8	66	−1.1	−8.5
Afghanistan	South and west	37.5	37.4	37.4	37.1	37.5	38.9	39.5	−0.1	2.1
Bangladesh	South and west	64.8	65.9	63.4	56.6	54.8	52.6	52.4	−1.4	−11.0
Bhutan	South and west	36.6	36.1	35	33.1	37.3	46.9	49.4	−1.6	14.4
India	South and west	36.1	36.5	36.5	35.5	34.1	34	34	0.4	−2.5
Maldives	South and west	24.2	23.7	20.1	28	37.4	48	49.8	−4.1	29.7
Nepal	South and west	45.3	46.4	48.1	48.3	49.4	49.9	50.1	2.8	2.0
Pakistan	South and west	27	27.2	27.9	28.7	29.4	32.6	33.3	0.9	5.4
Sri Lanka	South and west	39.6	37.5	45.1	36.4	37.1	35.2	35	5.5	−10.1
French Polynesia	NA	45	45.6	48.5	49.1	47.8	46.9	46.9	3.5	−1.6
Guam	NA	45.8	50.4	52.1	52.5	52.1	51.8	51.9	6.3	−0.2
New Caledonia	NA	43.1	45.5	45.6	45.1	44.5	43.5	43.3	2.5	−2.3
Average		50.61	50.77	51.62	51.32	52.08	53.25	53.55		
Standard deviation		15.42	15.39	14.98	13.74	12.81	12.08	12.00		
Coefficient of variation		30.47	30.30	29.02	26.77	24.60	22.69	22.41		

Note (1) French Polynesia, Guam and New Caledonia are not included in the TOR. However, they fall into the Asia-Pacific region as given in the KILM data set. Hence, they have been included in the analysis. However, the figures on average, standard deviation and the coefficient of variation do not include these countries. (2) All these countries in this table are termed as developing countries in ESCAP region; see ESCAP Report, 2007. The developed countries in the ESCAP region include Australia, Japan and New Zealand, which are not included in the analysis as the focus is primarily on the developing countries
Source KILM Data, Fifth Edition, ILO

Table A.2 Labour force participation rate for males (age 15+)

Country	Region	LFPR 1980	LFPR 1985	LFPR 1990	LFPR 1995	LFPR 2000	LFPR 2005	LFPR 2006
Cambodia	Northeast	86	85.6	85.2	85	81	80.2	80.2
China	Northeast	87.5	86	85.1	85.2	84.1	82.2	81.9
Hong Kong, China (SAR)	Northeast	81.5	80.6	79.5	76.3	73.4	70.8	70.2
Korea, Democratic People's Republic of	Northeast	81.7	81.5	82	81.5	79	78.5	78.2
Korea, Republic of	Northeast	75.2	72.3	73.4	75.2	73.1	73.9	73.7
Lao People's Democratic Republic	Northeast	79.1	79.4	79.5	80.1	80.4	80.3	80.3
Macao, China (SAR)	Northeast	71.4	72.4	72.3	72.8	75.4	75.3	75.2
Mongolia	Northeast	80.9	81	81.5	81.8	81.8	81.4	81.6
Vietnam	Northeast	81.7	81.9	81.1	80.2	79	78	77.9
Fiji	Pacific	81.8	81.5	79.7	79.6	80	80.3	80.3
Papua New Guinea	Pacific	73.9	74.3	75.1	72.9	73.7	74.8	74.9
Samoa	Pacific	81.4	82	76.9	78.7	78.8	77.4	77.1
Solomon Islands	Pacific	79.3	80.2	80.8	81.9	81.9	82.1	82.2
Tonga	Pacific	78.7	75.8	77.6	75.4	73.6	73.2	73
Vanuatu	Pacific	87.3	87.5	88.9	87.3	87.5	88.2	88.3
Brunei Darussalam	Southeast	83.1	82.9	82.6	81.6	80.8	79.2	78.8
Timor-Leste	Southeast	84.1	83.3	79.2	78.3	78.1	82.5	83.1
Indonesia	Southeast	82.9	80.7	81.4	82.2	84.8	85	85.1
Malaysia	Southeast	78.4	78.2	81.2	81.9	81.6	81.4	81.3
Myanmar	Southeast	89.2	88.7	87.5	86.6	86.4	86.2	86.2
The Philippines	Southeast	80.4	81.1	82.6	83.2	81.5	83.1	83
Singapore	Southeast	81.5	80.6	79.9	78.9	78.7	76.2	75.5

(continued)

Table A.2 (continued)

Country	Region	LFPR 1980	LFPR 1985	LFPR 1990	LFPR 1995	LFPR 2000	LFPR 2005	LFPR 2006
Thailand	Southeast	87.4	88	87.9	84.4	82.1	81.1	80.8
Afghanistan	South and west	87.2	87.3	87.6	87.9	87.9	87.8	87.8
Bangladesh	South and west	89.3	89.4	88.8	88.6	86.8	86.2	86.1
Bhutan	South and west	86.4	86	85.3	85.3	83	81.3	80.9
India	South and west	86.3	85.6	84.7	83.8	82.9	81.8	81.6
Maldives	South and west	74.5	78.5	77.6	74.2	72.4	71.7	71.8
Nepal	South and west	87	84.3	80.4	79.5	78.7	78.3	78.2
Pakistan	South and west	86.9	88.1	86.1	83.8	84.1	83.2	83.1
Sri Lanka	South and west	81.4	81.2	78.8	74.7	76.4	76.5	76.4
French Polynesia	Na	78.3	76.3	74.3	75.1	73.9	72.4	72.3
Guam	Na	73.3	77.2	80.4	80.4	80.3	79.7	79.4
New Caledonia	Na	67.5	70.8	72.8	72.6	71.9	70.5	70.3
Average		82.37	82.13	81.62	80.93	80.29	79.94	79.83
Standard deviation		4.58	4.49	4.28	4.37	4.29	4.42	4.51
Coefficient of variation		5.56	5.47	5.24	5.41	5.34	5.53	5.65

Notes The figures on average, standard deviation and the coefficient of variation do not include French Polynesia, Guam and New Caledonia

For other Notes and Source, see Table A.1.

See Table A.3.

Table A.3 Ratio of female-to-male LFPR

Country	F/M 1980	F/M 1985	F/M 1990	F/M 1995	F/M 2000	F/M 2005	F/M 2006
Afghanistan	0.43	0.43	0.43	0.42	0.43	0.44	0.45
Bangladesh	0.73	0.74	0.71	0.64	0.63	0.61	0.61
Bhutan	0.42	0.42	0.41	0.39	0.45	0.58	0.61
Brunei Darussalam	0.39	0.44	0.54	0.56	0.57	0.56	0.55
Cambodia	0.92	0.92	0.91	0.91	0.93	0.93	0.93
China	0.81	0.83	0.86	0.85	0.85	0.84	0.84
Timor-Leste	0.68	0.65	0.63	0.61	0.65	0.67	0.67
Fiji	0.67	0.65	0.61	0.61	0.62	0.64	0.64
French Polynesia	0.57	0.60	0.65	0.65	0.65	0.65	0.65
Guam	0.62	0.65	0.65	0.65	0.65	0.65	0.65
Hong Kong, China (SAR)	0.56	0.61	0.59	0.62	0.68	0.75	0.77
India	0.42	0.43	0.43	0.42	0.41	0.42	0.42
Indonesia	0.53	0.54	0.62	0.60	0.60	0.60	0.60
Korea, Democratic People's Republic of	0.65	0.65	0.64	0.61	0.62	0.62	0.62
Korea, Republic of	0.58	0.59	0.64	0.64	0.66	0.68	0.68
Lao People's Democratic Republic	0.65	0.69	0.67	0.68	0.67	0.67	0.67
Macao, China (SAR)	0.55	0.57	0.62	0.67	0.73	0.81	0.82
Malaysia	0.54	0.54	0.54	0.53	0.56	0.57	0.58
Maldives	0.32	0.30	0.26	0.38	0.52	0.67	0.69
Mongolia	0.66	0.66	0.68	0.67	0.66	0.66	0.66
Myanmar	0.78	0.78	0.79	0.79	0.79	0.79	0.79
Nepal	0.52	0.55	0.60	0.61	0.63	0.64	0.64
New Caledonia	0.64	0.64	0.63	0.62	0.62	0.62	0.62
Pakistan	0.31	0.31	0.32	0.34	0.35	0.39	0.40
Papua New Guinea	0.96	0.96	0.95	0.97	0.97	0.96	0.96
The Philippines	0.62	0.59	0.57	0.59	0.60	0.66	0.67
Samoa	0.47	0.49	0.51	0.52	0.51	0.51	0.51
Singapore	0.55	0.56	0.63	0.63	0.66	0.66	0.67
Solomon Islands	0.66	0.68	0.69	0.67	0.67	0.66	0.66
Sri Lanka	0.49	0.46	0.57	0.49	0.49	0.46	0.46
Thailand	0.86	0.85	0.85	0.78	0.80	0.81	0.82
Tonga	0.48	0.48	0.47	0.61	0.61	0.61	0.62
Vanuatu	0.90	0.90	0.90	0.90	0.90	0.90	0.90
Vietnam	0.90	0.90	0.91	0.92	0.92	0.92	0.92
Average	0.61	0.62	0.63	0.63	0.65	0.67	0.67
Standard deviation	0.18	0.18	0.17	0.16	0.16	0.15	0.15
Coefficient of variation	29.13	28.67	27.48	25.76	23.99	22.33	22.09

Notes The figures on average, standard deviation and the coefficient of variation do not include French Polynesia, Guam and New Caledonia

For other Notes and Source, see Table A.1.

See Tables A.4, A.5, A.6, A.7, A.8, A.9 and A.10.

Table A.4 (a) Worker-to-population ratio of females and males aged 15 and above, (b) change in the worker-to-population ratio of females and males

(a)

Country	Female			Male		
	1995	2000	2006	1995	2000	2006
Afghanistan	30	30.2	33.8	79.9	79.9	81.1
Bangladesh	55.2	53	50	85.9	83.9	82.6
Bhutan	27.8	31.5	43.4	78.9	76.7	75.4
Brunei Darussalam	43.8	43.8	41.6	78.1	77.2	75.5
Cambodia	74.2	73.3	73.2	82.1	79.2	78.8
China	71	69.4	66.8	81.8	80.6	78.9
Timor-Leste	46.3	48.7	53.4	75.6	75.4	79.7
Fiji	46.2	46.8	48.8	75.4	75.2	76
Hong Kong, China (SAR)	46	47.5	51.4	73.7	69.3	66.1
India	33.7	32.7	32.2	79.8	79.3	77.7
Indonesia	46.7	47.1	44.3	78.5	80.1	77.5
Korea, Democratic People's Republic of	49	47.2	46.2	79	74.6	73.8
Korea, Republic of	47.7	46.9	48.8	73.4	69.4	70.8
Lao People's Democratic Republic	53.1	52.9	53.5	77.8	78.6	79
Macao, China (SAR)	47.1	52.8	59.5	69.9	69.1	72
Malaysia	42.4	44.1	45.2	79.4	79.2	78.4
Maldives	27.6	36.4	48.6	73.7	71.2	70.6
Mongolia	46.4	45.2	46.9	69.8	67.1	71.3
Myanmar	65.7	66	66	83.4	83.5	83.2
Nepal	42.8	43.9	43.7	74.8	73.8	72.8
Pakistan	25.5	25.2	30.2	81.3	80	79
Papua New Guinea	68.2	69.3	69.8	70.4	71.6	72.9
The Philippines	44.4	43.6	51.6	76.8	73.3	76.9
Singapore	48.4	49.9	48	76.8	75	72.7
Solomon Islands	52.7	51.8	51.9	78.7	77.8	79
Sri Lanka	29.2	32.9	31.6	68.2	72.2	72.7
Taiwan, Province of China	43	43.3	46.5	70.2	65.5	62.3
Thailand	65.3	63.9	65.2	83.6	80.1	79.7
Vietnam	71.9	71.2	70.3	78.4	77.2	76.6
Average	47.97586	48.63793	50.42759	77.08	75.72	75.62
Standard deviation	13.69308	12.75381	11.63876	4.56	4.80	4.73
Coefficient of variation	28.5416	26.22193	23.08014	5.92	6.34	6.26

(b)

Country	Female		Male	
	Between 1995 and 2000	Between 2000 and 2006	Between 1995 and 2000	Between 2000 and 2006
Afghanistan	0.20	3.60	0	1.20
Bangladesh	−2.20	−3.00	−2	−1.3
Bhutan	3.70	11.90	−2.2	−1.3
Brunei Darussalam	0.00	−2.20	−0.9	−1.7
Cambodia	−0.90	−0.10	−2.9	−0.40
China	−1.60	−2.60	−1.2	−1.7
Timor-Leste	2.40	4.70	−0.2	4.30
Fiji	0.60	2.00	−0.2	0.80
Hong Kong, China (SAR)	1.50	3.90	−4.40	−3.2
India	−1.00	−0.50	−0.5	−1.60
Indonesia	0.40	−2.80	1.60	−2.6
Korea, Democratic People's Republic of	−1.80	−1.00	−4.4	−0.8
Korea, Republic of	−0.80	1.90	−4	1.40
Lao People's Democratic Republic	−0.20	0.60	0.80	0.40
Macao, China (SAR)	5.70	6.70	−0.8	2.90
Malaysia	1.70	1.10	−0.2	−0.8
Maldives	8.80	12.20	−2.5	−0.6
Mongolia	−1.20	1.70	−2.7	4.20
Myanmar	0.30	0.00	0.10	−0.3
Nepal	1.10	−0.20	−1	−1
Pakistan	−0.30	5.00	−1.3	−1
Papua New Guinea	1.10	0.50	1.20	1.30
The Philippines	−0.80	8.00	−3.5	3.60
Singapore	1.50	−1.90	−1.8	−2.3
Solomon Islands	−0.90	0.10	−0.90	1.20
Sri Lanka	3.70	−1.30	4	0.5
Taiwan, Province of China	0.30	3.20	−4.7	−3.2
Thailand	−1.40	1.30	−3.5	−0.4
Vietnam	−0.70	−0.90	−1.2	−0.6

Source See Table A.1

Table A.5 Illiteracy rate

Country	Year	Female		Male	
		Youth illiteracy rate (%)	Adult illiteracy rate (%)	Youth illiteracy rate (%)	Adult illiteracy rate (%)
Afghanistan	2000	81.6	87.4	49.2	56.9
China	1990	8.5	31.9	3	13
China	2000	1.5	13.5	0.8	4.9
Indonesia	1990	4.9	24.7	2.6	12
Lao People's Democratic Republic	1995	35.9	52.1	21.2	26.5
Malaysia	2000	2.7	14.6	2.8	8
Maldives	1985	3.8	7.6	5.1	7.9
Maldives	1990	1.7	3.9	1.9	4.1
Maldives	1995	1.7	3.6	2	3.8
Maldives	2000	1.7	3.6	2	3.8
Mongolia	2000	1.6	2.5	3	2
Myanmar	2000	6.6	13.6	4.3	6.1
Pakistan	2005	46.9	64.6	23.3	35.9
Papua New Guinea	2000	35.9	49.1	30.9	36.6
The Philippines	1990	3.1	6.8	3.7	6
The Philippines	2000	4.3	7.3	5.5	7.5
Singapore	1990	0.9	17	1.1	4.9
Thailand	2000	2.2	9.5	1.9	5.1

Table A.6 Enrolment and expenditure on education

Country	Year	Expenditure per student: primary (% of GDP per capita)	Expenditure per student: secondary (% of GDP per capita)	Expenditure per student: tertiary (% of GDP per capita)	Pupil-to-teacher ratio (primary, %)	School enrolment: primary (% gross)	School enrolment: secondary (% gross)	School enrolment: tertiary (% gross)
Afghanistan	2000				64	19.2		
Afghanistan	2005				83.4	86.5	16.2	
Bangladesh	2000	8.2	11.4	43.5	57.1	108.9	50.3	5.8
Bangladesh	2005	7.7	14.7	49.7				6.5
Bhutan	2000	14.4	103.2	574	41.1			
Bhutan	2005				31.1			
Brunei Darussalam	2000				13.5	109.7	85.5	12.6
Brunei Darussalam	2005				10.1	107.5	95.6	15
Cambodia	2000	5.9			50.1	106.3	17	2.2
Cambodia	2005				53.2	134.1		3.3
China	2000						62.9	7.6
China	2005				18.6	112.8	74.3	20.3
Cook Islands	2000	0.9	1		17.8	87.9	66.1	
Timor-Leste	2005				34.2	151.1	51.8	
Fiji	2000				28.1	109.1	80.8	
Fiji	2005				28.2	106	87.8	15.3
Hong Kong, China (SAR)	2000				21.3	106.2		

(continued)

Table A.6 (continued)

Country	Year	Expenditure per student: primary (% of GDP per capita)	Expenditure per student: secondary (% of GDP per capita)	Expenditure per student: tertiary (% of GDP per capita)	Pupil-to-teacher ratio (primary, %)	School enrolment: primary (% gross)	School enrolment: secondary (% gross)	School enrolment: tertiary (% gross)
Hong Kong, China (SAR)	2005	14.9	19.9	60.6	18.3	104.7	87.2	31.4
India	2000	14.5	24.3	90.5	40	98.8	47.9	10.2
India	2005					119.2	56.6	11.4
Indonesia	2000	3.7	7.3	21.3	22.4	110.9	54.9	
Indonesia	2005				20.4	117.3	63.1	17.1
Kiribati	2000	37.3			31.7	109.5	98.7	
Kiribati	2005				24.7	112.2	87.1	
Korea, Republic of	2000				32.2	98	97.6	72.6
Korea, Republic of	2005				29	104.8	92.9	89.9
Korea, Republic of	2006				27.9	104.5	95.7	91
Lao People's Democratic Republic	2000	3.9	5.6	69	30.1	115.3	35.6	2.8
Lao People's Democratic Republic	2005	9.7	4.9	26.8	31.5	115.8	46.7	7.9

(continued)

Table A.6 (continued)

Country	Year	Expenditure per student: primary (% of GDP per capita)	Expenditure per student: secondary (% of GDP per capita)	Expenditure per student: tertiary (% of GDP per capita)	Pupil-to-teacher ratio (primary, %)	School enrolment: primary (% gross)	School enrolment: secondary (% gross)	School enrolment: tertiary (% gross)
Macao, China (SAR)	2000	8.4	11.3	61	30	102.9	78.9	26.4
Macao, China (SAR)	2005				23.2	106.3	97.3	61.4
Malaysia	2000	12.8	22.3	83.3	19.6	97.1	69.3	26.3
Maldives	2000				22.7	127.3	55.6	
Maldives	2005	22			20.1	93.7		
Marshall Islands	2000					100.6		
Marshall Islands	2005					102.7	76.5	
Mongolia	2000				32.6	100	62.6	28.8
Mongolia	2005				34.2	93.3	91.8	43.2
Myanmar	2000				32.8	89.4	37.6	11.3
Myanmar	2005				30.9	99.6	40.3	
Nauru	2000				21.5	75.6	45.4	
Nepal	2000	10.3	11.6	141.7	42.6	116.5	35.3	4.1
Nepal	2005				39.7	113.3	45.7	
Nepal	2006				39.7	126	43.1	
Niue	2000				14.7	93.3	95.9	

(continued)

Table A.6 (continued)

Country	Year	Expenditure per student: primary (% of GDP per capita)	Expenditure per student: secondary (% of GDP per capita)	Expenditure per student: tertiary (% of GDP per capita)	Pupil-to-teacher ratio (primary, %)	School enrolment: primary (% gross)	School enrolment: secondary (% gross)	School enrolment: tertiary (% gross)
Niue	2005				11.9	86.4	99	
Pakistan	2000				33	71.2		
Pakistan	2005				38.3	87.3	26.9	4.6
Papua New Guinea	2000				35.9	78.9	22.8	
The Philippines	2000	12.5	10.7	15				
The Philippines	2005				35.1	112.5	85.2	28.1
Samoa	2000	8.2	9.6	137.5	24	99.2	77.9	7.4
Samoa	2005					99.8	80.3	
Solomon Islands	2000					85.6	19.2	
Solomon Islands	2005					96.5	29.5	
Thailand	2000	17.6		35.5	20.8	94.7		34.2
Thailand	2005			24.9		97.1	70.3	43
Thailand	2006				18.7	95.7	70.6	42.7
Tokelau	2000				9.9	101.2	94.7	
Tonga	2000				22.1	110.6	101.1	4.7
Tonga	2005				20.3	114.7		
Tuvalu	2000				19.7	108.7		

(continued)

Table A.6 (continued)

Country	Year	Expenditure per student: primary (% of GDP per capita)	Expenditure per student: secondary (% of GDP per capita)	Expenditure per student: tertiary (% of GDP per capita)	Pupil-to-teacher ratio (primary, %)	School enrolment: primary (% gross)	School enrolment: secondary (% gross)	School enrolment: tertiary (% gross)
Vanuatu	2000	15.3	70.6	167.9	22.5	112.9	33.8	4
Vanuatu	2005				20	118		
Vietnam	2000				29.5	106.6	64.6	9.5
Vietnam	2005				21.6	94.5	75.8	16

Note In some of the countries, expenditure as a percentage of GDP per capita exceeds 100% precisely because the per capita income is too low
Source See Table A.1

Table A.7 Female employment elasticity

Country	Region	Female employment elasticity			Female employment growth			Difference between female and male employment elasticity		
		93-97 F elasticity	97-01 F elasticity	01-05 F elasticity	93-97 Fempgr	97-01 Fempgr	01-05 Fempgr	93-97 elasf-m	97-01 elasf-m	01-05 elasf-m
Cambodia	Northeast	0.36	0.43	0.31	2.41	3.61	2.95	−0.08	0	−0.04
China	Northeast	0.09	0.12	0.1	0.97	0.97	0.98	0	−0.02	−0.03
Hong Kong, China (SAR)	Northeast	0.86	0.71	0.53	4.04	1.56	2.76	0.76	0.64	0.37
Korea, Republic of	Northeast	0.43	0.4	0.34	3.14	1.40	1.60	0.16	0.19	0.02
Lao People's Democratic Republic	Northeast	0.37	0.45	0.5	2.70	2.61	3.15	0.01	−0.02	0.04
Mongolia	Northeast	0.34	0.71	0.46	2.89	1.56	2.99	−0.04	0.12	−0.03
Vietnam	Northeast	0.31	0.38	0.35	2.76	2.32	2.66	0.05	−0.06	0.01
Fiji	Pacific	0.63	0.48	0.78	1.64	1.20	1.87	0.08	0.07	0.33
Papua New Guinea	Pacific	0.87	0.95	1.3	1.22	0.57	2.47	0.19	0.13	0.04
Solomon Islands	Pacific	0.73	−0.35	0.58	2.63	2.03	2.55	−0.06	0.02	−0.04
Brunei Darussalam	Southeast	1.41	0.93	0.86	3.38	1.02	1.89	0.32	0.04	−0.03
Indonesia	Southeast	0.3	−0.16	0.2	2.13	0.21	1.00	−0.09	−0.08	−0.1
Malaysia	Southeast	0.34	0.93	0.56	3.09	1.67	3.02	−0.05	0.37	0.14
The Philippines	Southeast	0.81	0.97	0.85	4.05	2.52	4.34	0.17	0.4	0.28
Singapore	Southeast	0.37	0.5	0.31	3.29	1.65	1.67	0.06	0.06	0.09
Thailand	Southeast	0.35	0.35	0.35	1.92	0.00	2.06	0.17	0.08	0.21
Bangladesh	South and west	0.17	0.44	0.21	0.80	2.33	1.15	−0.38	0.04	−0.2
Bhutan	South and west	0.26	1.05	1.28	1.43	7.03	9.47	0.4	0.39	0.49
India	South and west	0.24	0.33	0.25	1.63	1.82	1.85	−0.06	−0.03	0

(continued)

Table A.7 (continued)

Country	Region	Female employment elasticity			Female employment growth			Difference between female and male employment elasticity		
		93-97 F elasticity	97-01 F elasticity	01-05 F elasticity	93-97 Fempgr	97-01 Fempgr	01-05 Fempgr	93-97 elasf-m	97-01 elasf-m	01-05 elasf-m
Maldives	South and west	1.23	1.37	1.46	10.21	8.49	6.86	0.88	0.93	0.92
Nepal	South and west	0.82	0.39	0.99	4.59	1.87	2.28	0.27	0.03	−0.03
Pakistan	South and west	0.48	1.15	1.08	1.73	3.56	6.05	−0.17	0.26	0.55
Sri Lanka	South and west	0.11	0.7	0.11	0.57	2.38	0.57	−0.25	0.28	−0.09

Source See Table A.1

Table A.8 Unemployment rate

Country	Year	Female unemployment rate (%)	Male unemployment rate (%)	Female–male diff.
Afghanistan	2005	9.5	7.6	1.9
Bangladesh	1985	5.6	1.4	4.2
Bangladesh	2000	3.3	3.2	0.1
Cambodia	2000	2.8	2.2	0.6
Guam	1980	12.1	8.4	3.7
Guam	1985	8.8	5.6	3.2
Hong Kong, China (SAR)	1980	4	4.5	−0.5
Hong Kong, China (SAR)	1985	2.6	3.5	−0.9
Hong Kong, China (SAR)	1990	1.3	1.3	0
Hong Kong, China (SAR)	1995	2.9	3.4	−0.5
Hong Kong, China (SAR)	2000	4	5.6	−1.6
Hong Kong, China (SAR)	2005	4.4	6.5	−2.1
India	2000	4.1	4.4	−0.3
Indonesia	1985	2.1	2.2	−0.1
Indonesia	2005	13.6	8.3	5.3
Korea, Republic of	1980	3.5	6.2	−2.7
Korea, Republic of	1985	2.4	5	−2.6
Korea, Republic of	1990	1.8	2.9	−1.1
Korea, Republic of	1995	1.7	2.3	−0.6
Korea, Republic of	2000	3.6	5	−1.4
Korea, Republic of	2005	3.4	4	−0.6
Lao People's Democratic Republic	1995	2.6	2.6	0
Lao People's Democratic Republic	2005	1.4	1.3	0.1
Macao, China (SAR)	1990	4	2.5	1.5
Macao, China (SAR)	1995	3	4.1	−1.1
Macao, China (SAR)	2000	4.4	8.6	−4.2
Macao, China (SAR)	2005	3.8	4.4	−0.6
Malaysia	1995	3.8	2.8	1
Malaysia	2000	3.1	2.9	0.2
Maldives	1995	1.3	0.6	0.7
Maldives	2000	2.7	1.6	1.1
Marshall Islands	1980	11.3	9	2.3
Marshall Islands	2005	24.3	26.4	−2.1
Mongolia	2000	16.6	18.2	−1.6
Myanmar	1990	8.8	4.7	4.1

(continued)

Table A.8 (continued)

Country	Year	Female unemployment rate (%)	Male unemployment rate (%)	Female–male diff.
Pakistan	1980	14	2.9	11.1
Pakistan	1985	1.4	3.8	−2.4
Pakistan	1990	0.7	2.8	−2.1
Pakistan	1995	14	3.7	10.3
Pakistan	2000	15.8	5.5	10.3
Pakistan	2005	12.8	6.6	6.2
Papua New Guinea	1990	5.9	9	−3.1
Papua New Guinea	2000	1.3	4.3	−3
The Philippines	1980	7.5	3.2	4.3
The Philippines	1985	8.2	4.8	3.4
The Philippines	1990	9.8	7.1	2.7
The Philippines	1995	9.4	7.7	1.7
The Philippines	2000	9.9	10.3	−0.4
The Philippines	2005	7.3	7.4	−0.1
Singapore	1980	3.4	2.9	0.5
Singapore	1985	4.4	4.5	−0.1
Singapore	1990	1.4	1.9	−0.5
Singapore	1995	2.8	2.6	0.2
Singapore	2005	5	3.7	1.3
Sri Lanka	1985	20.3	9.8	10.5
Sri Lanka	1990	23.5	9.1	14.4
Sri Lanka	1995	19.9	8.7	11.2
Sri Lanka	2000	11.1	5.4	5.7
Sri Lanka	2005	11.9	5.5	6.4
Taiwan, Province of China	1980	1.5	1.1	0.4
Taiwan, Province of China	1985	2.9	2.9	0
Taiwan, Province of China	1990	1.7	1.7	0
Taiwan, Province of China	1995	1.8	1.8	0
Taiwan, Province of China	2000	2.4	3.4	−1
Thailand	1980	0.8	1	−0.2
Thailand	1985	4.4	3.2	1.2
Thailand	1990	2.4	2	0.4
Thailand	1995	1.4	0.9	0.5
Thailand	2000	2.3	2.4	−0.1
Thailand	2005	1.2	1.5	−0.3
Vietnam	2000	2.1	2.4	−0.3

Source See Table A.1

Table A.9 Employment structure

Country	Year	Female			Male			Female–male difference		
		Agriculture (%)	Industry (%)	Services (%)	Agri (%)	Industry (%)	Services (%)	Ag.	Ind.	Ser.
Bangladesh	1990	84.9	8.8	2.1	54.4	15.7	25.3	30.5	−6.9	−23.2
Bangladesh	2000	76.9	9	12.1	53.3	11	30.3	23.6	−2	−18.2
Cambodia	2000	74.9	9.6	15.4	72.4	7.1	20.2	2.5	2.5	−4.8
Hong Kong, China (SAR)	1980	1.2	56.2	42.6	1.5	46.9	51.5	−0.3	9.30	−8.9
Hong Kong, China (SAR)	1985	1.5	47	51.4	1.7	42.8	55.5	−0.2	4.20	−4.1
Hong Kong, China (SAR)	1990	0.7	33	66.2	1	38.9	60.2	−0.3	−5.9	6.00
Hong Kong, China (SAR)	1995	0.4	18.7	80.9	0.7	32.2	67.1	−0.3	−13.5	13.8
Hong Kong, China (SAR)	2000	0.2	10.4	89.3	0.3	27.6	72.1	−0.1	−17.2	17.2
Hong Kong, China (SAR)	2005	0.2	6.6	93.2	0.4	22.3	77.3	−0.2	−15.7	15.90
Indonesia	1980	54.2	13.1	32.7	57.5	13.1	29.4	−3.3	0	3.30
Indonesia	1985	53.6	12.2	34	55.3	14.1	30.6	−1.7	−1.9	3.4
Indonesia	1990	56.3	12.4	31.1	55.6	14.6	29.7	0.70	−2.2	1.4
Indonesia	1995	43.8	16	40.1	44.1	19.7	36.2	−0.3	−3.7	3.90
Indonesia	2000	46.6	14.9	38.5	44.2	19.1	36.6	2.40	−4.2	1.90
Indonesia	2005	45.2	14.7	40.1	43.4	19.8	36.8	1.80	−5.1	3.30
Korea, Republic of	1980	39	23.8	37.2	31	32.2	36.9	8	−8.4	0.30
Korea, Republic of	1985	27.8	24.4	47.8	23.1	34.9	42	4.70	−10.5	5.80
Korea, Republic of	1990	20.3	30.2	49.6	16.3	39	44.7	4	−8.8	4.90
Korea, Republic of	1995	14.6	23.7	61.6	10.9	39.8	49.2	3.70	−16.1	12.4
Korea, Republic of	2000	12.2	19.2	68.6	9.5	34.5	55.9	2.7	−15.3	12.7
Korea, Republic of	2005	8.9	16.6	74.4	7.2	34.1	58.5	1.7	−17.5	15.9

(continued)

Table A.9 (continued)

Country	Year	Female			Male			Female–male difference		
		Agriculture (%)	Industry (%)	Services (%)	Agri (%)	Industry (%)	Services (%)	Ag.	Ind.	Ser.
Lao People's Democratic Republic	1995	89.3	2.7	7.9	81.2	4.4	14.4	8.10	−1.7	−6.5
Macao, China (SAR)	1990	0.1	50.4	49	0.2	36.7	62.8	−0.1	13.7	−13.8
Macao, China (SAR)	1995	0.1	34.4	65.1	0.3	30.1	69.5	−0.2	4.30	−4.4
Macao, China (SAR)	2000	0.1	30.2	69.6	0.2	26.5	73.3	−0.1	3.70	−3.7
Macao, China (SAR)	2005	0.2	23.1	76.6	0.2	27.1	72.7	0	−4	3.90
Malaysia	1980	43.8	20	36.3	33.9	25.6	39.9	9.90	−5.6	−3.6
Malaysia	1985	33.8	20.5	45.7	28.6	25.6	45.9	5.20	−5.1	−0.2
Malaysia	1990	25.3	28	46.8	26.4	27.3	46.3	−1.1	0.70	0.5
Malaysia	1995	16.9	31.4	51.8	21.6	32.8	45.6	−4.7	−1.4	6.20
Malaysia	2000	14	28.9	57	20.7	33.9	45.4	−6.7	−5	11.6
Maldives	1995	9	42.9	44.2	27	16.9	52.7	−18	26	−8.5
Maldives	2000	5.4	24.1	39	17.9	16.4	55.8	−12.5	7.70	−16.8
Mongolia	1995	45	16.1	38.9	47.1	19.6	33.3	−2.1	−3.5	5.60
Mongolia	2000	46.5	11.3	42.2	50.6	16.8	32.6	−4.1	−5.5	9.60
Mongolia	2005	36.8	14.8	48.4	43	18.9	38.1	−6.2	−4.1	10.3
Pakistan	1985	75.1	11.8	13.1	47.9	21	30.4	27.2	−9.2	−17.3
Pakistan	1990	72.2	14.1	13.5	48.4	20.6	30.9	23.8	−6.5	−17.4
Pakistan	1995	67.4	10.7	21.9	43.9	19.6	36.4	23.5	−8.9	−14.5
Pakistan	2000	72.9	9	18.1	44.4	19.5	36.1	28.5	−10.5	−18
Pakistan	2005	67.3	15	17.6	38.1	21.4	40.5	29.2	−6.4	−22.9
The Philippines	1980	37.3	14.9	47.8	59.8	15.6	24.6	−22.5	−0.7	23.2

(continued)

Table A.9 (continued)

Country	Year	Female			Male			Female–male difference		
		Agriculture (%)	Industry (%)	Services (%)	Agri (%)	Industry (%)	Services (%)	Ag.	Ind.	Ser.
The Philippines	1985	35	12.8	52.2	58.3	14.5	27.3	−23.3	−1.7	24.9
The Philippines	1990	31.3	12.8	55.8	53.1	16.3	30.5	−21.8	−3.5	25.3
The Philippines	1995	31.1	13.2	55.6	51.7	17	31.2	−20.6	−3.8	24.4
The Philippines	2000	24.5	13.2	62.3	45.3	17.7	37	−20.8	−4.5	25.3
The Philippines	2005	24.8	11.7	63.5	44.7	16.9	38.5	−19.9	−5.2	25
Singapore	1980	0.9	40.3	58.8	1.5	33.3	64.6	−0.6	7	−5.8
Singapore	1985	0.4	33.4	66	0.8	36.3	62.4	−0.4	−2.9	3.60
Singapore	1995	0.1	25	74.5	0.3	34.7	63.8	−0.2	−9.7	10.7
Singapore	2000	0	20.9	78.8	0	42.2	56.9	0	−21.3	21.9
Singapore	2005	0	20.5	79.1	0	36	62.9	0	−15.5	16.2
Sri Lanka	1985	54.2	19.9	24.4	47.2	18.3	29.4	7	1.6	−5
Sri Lanka	1995	41.5	28.7	27.6	35.5	21	36.3	6	7.70	−8.7
Thailand	1980	74.1	7.8	18.1	67.8	12.6	19.6	6.30	−4.8	−1.5
Thailand	1985	64.1	10.7	25.2	67.2	12.6	20.2	−3.1	−1.9	5
Thailand	1990	65	12.3	22.7	63.1	15.5	21.3	1.90	−3.2	1.40
Thailand	1995	53.4	17.1	29.4	50.8	22	27.3	2.60	−4.9	2.1
Thailand	2000	47.5	17.3	35.2	49.8	20.4	29.7	−2.3	−3.1	5.5
Thailand	2005	40.7	18.7	40.5	44.2	21.6	34.1	−3.5	−2.9	6.40
Vietnam	2000	66.3	10.1	23.6	64.2	14.7	21	2.10	−4.6	2.6

Source See Table A.1

Table A.10 Status of employment

Country	Year	Female: wage and salaried workers (employees) (%)	Female: total self-employed workers (%)	Female: the rest	Male: wage and salaried workers (employees) (%)	Male: total self-employed workers (%)	Male: the rest
Bangladesh	2000	8.3	11	80.7	15.2	49.8	35
Cambodia	2000	12.1	28.9	59	18.6	54.6	26.8
Hong Kong, China (SAR)	1995	94.8	3.8	1.40	85.7	14.2	0.10
Hong Kong, China (SAR)	2000	95	3.8	1.2	85.5	14.4	0.1
Hong Kong, China (SAR)	2006	93.5	5.3	1.2	83	16.9	0.1
Indonesia	2006	33.8	29.2	37	40.1	51.7	8.20
Korea, Republic of	1980	39.2	23.3	37.5	52.2	40.6	7.20
Korea, Republic of	1985	48.2	21.3	30.5	58	37.6	4.40
Korea, Republic of	1990	56.8	18.7	24.5	63.1	34.4	2.5
Korea, Republic of	1995	59.1	19.6	21.3	64.9	33.5	1.60
Korea, Republic of	2000	61.5	19.2	19.3	64.3	33.8	1.90
Korea, Republic of	2006	67.7	18.8	13.5	66.8	32	1.20
Lao People's Democratic Republic	1995	5.4	57.1	37.5	14.3	56.6	29.1
Macao, China (SAR)	2000	92	5.1	2.9	84.8	14.9	0.30

(continued)

Table A.10 (continued)

Country	Year	Female: wage and salaried workers (employees) (%)	Female: total self-employed workers (%)	Female: the rest	Male: wage and salaried workers (employees) (%)	Male: total self-employed workers (%)	Male: the rest
Macao, China (SAR)	2006	93.8	4.5	1.70	88.1	11.7	0.20
Malaysia	1995	72.9	13.9	13.2	72.5	24.2	3.30
Malaysia	2000	77.9	12.7	9.40	71.7	23.8	4.50
Maldives	1995	43.9	38.6	17.5	33.9	57.5	8.60
Maldives	2000	28.8	37.4	33.8	21.3	69.4	9.30
Mongolia	2000	43.6	17.6	38.8	39.3	46.1	14.6
Pakistan	1995	24.8	13.5	61.7	35.4	47.4	17.2
Pakistan	2000	33.1	16.8	50.1	36	47.3	16.7
Pakistan	2006	25.7	15.1	59.2	40	40.8	19.2
The Philippines	2006	49.7	31.1	19.2	51	39.8	9.20
Singapore	1995	93.5	4.7	1.8	85.3	14	0.70
Singapore	2000	94.2	5.1	0.70	86.5	13.3	0.2
Singapore	2006	89.9	9	1.10	81.3	18.4	0.30
Sri Lanka	2000	55.5	18	26.5	56.6	36.9	6.5
Sri Lanka	2006	54.5	23.9	21.6	56	39.6	4.40
Thailand	1990	25.6	18.3	56.1	31	42	27
Thailand	1995	32.4	21	46.6	38.3	43.2	18.5
Thailand	2000	38.8	21.4	39.8	40.2	43.3	16.5
Thailand	2006	42.9	26.6	30.5	44.3	41.8	13.9
Vietnam	2000	15.1	30.3	54.6	21.7	56	22.3

Source See Table A.1

Data for India: Variables, Year of Availability and Source:

WPR: Work force participation rate among females and males in rural and urban areas: Population Census, 2011
LFPR: Labour force participation rate among females and males in rural and urban areas, 2011–12 in cross-sectional study and from 2009–10 through 2014–15 except 2010–11 in the panel data analysis, Labour Bureau, Ministry of Labour and Employment, Government of India
AGDP: Share of agriculture in gross state domestic product, 2011–12
INDP: Share of industry in gross state domestic product, 2011–12
SERDP: Share of services in total gross state domestic product, 2011–12
URBAN: % of population residing in urban areas, 2011
ROAD: State-wise road length in relation to population, 2011, Ministry of Road Transport and Highways
ELEC: State-wise annual per capita consumption of electricity in kWh, 2012–13, Ministry of Power
CR-DP: Credit-to-deposit ratio, 2010, Data Book for Planning Commission, 2014
ENROL: Gross enrolment in classes I–VIII, 2010–11; Data Book for Planning Commission, 2014
LIT: Literacy rate among females and males in rural and urban areas, Population Census, 2011
IMR: Infant mortality rate, boys and girls: for cross-sectional study 2011 and for panel 2006, 2010, 2011 and 2012 Sample Registration System 46, 47 and 48, Office of Registrar General, Ministry of Home Affairs
WATER: % of households with access to safe drinking water, rural and urban, 2011; Data Book for Planning Commission, 2014
F/M: Female per thousand male, Population Census, 2011
PCNSDP: Per capita net state domestic product in Rs. 2011–12; for panel data analysis, 2008–09, 2009–10, 2010–11, 2011–12 and 2012–13 are taken in 2004–05 prices, Data Book for Planning Commission, 2014
AGDP: Share of agriculture in gross state domestic product, 2011–12; for panel data analysis, 2008–09, 2009–10, 2010–11, 2011–12 and 2012–13 are taken in 2004–05 prices, Data Book for Planning Commission, 2014
INDP: Share of industry in gross state domestic product, 2011–12; for panel data analysis, 2008–09, 2009–10, 2010–11, 2011–12 and 2012–13 are taken in 2004–05 prices; Data Book for Planning Commission, 2014
SERDP: Share of services in total gross state domestic product, 2011–12; for panel data analysis, 2008–09, 2009–10, 2010–11, 2011–12 and 2012–13 are taken in 2004–05 prices; Data Book for Planning Commission, 2014
Lab Prod: Labour productivity in Rs. 2011–12 calculated by the author from state domestic product and workers reported by population census
SC: Percentage of scheduled castes among females and males in rural and urban areas, Population Census, 2011
ST: Percentage of scheduled tribes among females and males in rural and urban areas, Population Census, 2011
CTYSZ: City size in log terms, Population Census, 2011
AGLAB: Share of agriculture labour in total work force, male and female, Population Census, 2011

(continued)

(continued)

CUL: Share of cultivators in total work force, male and female, Population Census, 2011
MFGHH: Share of household manufacturing in total work force, females and males in rural and urban areas, Population Census, 2011
OTHER: Share of non-household manufacturing and services in total work force, female and male and rural and urban areas, Population Census, 2011
CHILDSR: Child sex ratio (age bracket: up to 4 years): Population Census, 2011
CHILD: Children (up to 4 years) to women ratio, Population Census, 2011
HHSZ: Average household size, Population Census, 2011
TFR: Total fertility rate for 2009 (since 2010 figures are not available for a number of states); Data Book for Planning Commission, 2014
MPCE: Monthly mean per capita consumption expenditure in Rs, in rural and urban areas, 2011–12, Data Book for Planning Commission, 2014
POV: Incidence of poverty in rural and urban areas, 2011–12, Data Book for Planning Commission, 2014

MIX
Papier aus verantwortungsvollen Quellen
Paper from responsible sources
FSC® C105338

If you have any concerns about our products,
you can contact us on
ProductSafety@springernature.com

In case Publisher is established outside the EU,
the EU authorized representative is:
Springer Nature Customer Service Center GmbH
Europaplatz 3, 69115 Heidelberg, Germany

Printed by Libri Plureos GmbH
in Hamburg, Germany

Coastal Research Library

Volume 10

Series Editor

Charles W. Finkl
Department of Geosciences
Florida Atlantic University
Boca Raton, FL 33431, USA

The aim of this book series is to disseminate information to the coastal research community. The Series covers all aspects of coastal research including but not limited to relevant aspects of geological sciences, biology (incl. ecology and coastal marine ecosystems), geomorphology (physical geography), climate, littoral oceanography, coastal hydraulics, environmental (resource) management, engineering, and remote sensing. Policy, coastal law, and relevant issues such as conflict resolution and risk management would also be covered by the Series. The scope of the Series is broad and with a unique crossdisciplinary nature. The Series would tend to focus on topics that are of current interest and which carry some import as opposed to traditional titles that are esoteric and non-controversial. Monographs as well as contributed volumes are welcomed.

More information about this series at http://www.springer.com/series/8795

Mohamed Maanan • Marc Robin
Editors

Sediment Fluxes in Coastal Areas

Springer

Editors
Mohamed Maanan
Institut de Géographie et
d'Aménagement Régional
de l'Université de Nantes
Géolittomer, LETG UMR 6554-CNRS
Nantes Cedex 3, France

Marc Robin
Institut de Géographie et
d'Aménagement Régional
de l'Université de Nantes
Géolittomer, LETG UMR 6554-CNRS
Nantes Cedex 3, France

ISSN 2211-0577 ISSN 2211-0585 (electronic)
ISBN 978-94-024-0587-3 ISBN 978-94-017-9260-8 (eBook)
DOI 10.1007/978-94-017-9260-8
Springer Dordrecht Heidelberg New York London

Printed on acid-free paper

Springer is part of Springer Science+Business Media (www.springer.com)

Preface

Sediment Fluxes: Natural and Anthropogenic Changes in Coastal Areas at Various Spatial and Temporal Scales

The world's coastal area is a long narrowed feature of mainland, island and adjacent seas denoting a zone of transition between land and ocean. If we consider a world coastal band 20 km wide, we can compute that this area represents nearly 4 % of total Earth surface. Nearly 30 % of people in the world live in this relatively small but highly valued and highly dynamic area. Humans have lived in the coastal area for millennia utilising its many and rich resources for their survival and socio-economic benefit.

Sedimentary processes occurring along coastal areas are a very complex issue and result from the interaction between deep processes (tectonics with subsidence/uplift) and superficial processes (climate, sea level change and hydrodynamic) (Cloetingh 2007). The pattern and distribution of sedimentary facies in depositional basins are under sediment fluxes control (Jones and Frostick 2002).

Coastal processes and natural ecosystems are subject to changes that vary greatly in geographic scales, timing and duration, combining to create dynamic and biologically productive coastal systems vulnerable to additional pressures resulting from human activities (Dean 2004). In turn, the sustainability of human economic and social hazards can be seen as a result of our poor understanding of the dynamics of land-ocean interactions, coastal processes and influence of poorly planned and managed human interventions (Crossland et al. 2007). Indeed a major problem for coastal studies is the constant changing coastal systems, from both natural and human causes (Maanan & Robin 2010). Changing wave and current regimes, climate, morphological processes and fluxes of materials from land, atmosphere and oceans are causes of high natural variabilities, which are still imperfectly understood. Moreover, major questions remain unanswered such as sedimentary fluxes quantification and precise models of both solid matter transport from source-to-sink areas and their consequences on building sedimentary architecture of continental shelf at various spatial scales (Milliman and Farnsworth 2011).

Conditions of erosion, timing and processes of sedimentary deposition and preservation as a function of environmental, climatic conditions and with human interplay are still a challenge in science (Anthony 2009).

Land-ocean sediment fluxes are one of the most important components in the sediment cycle of the Earth system and are also a major influencing factor in the processes of land-ocean interactions in coastal zones (Einsele 1992). The fluxes of continental water and sediment to a continental shelf largely depend on a region's climate and local drainage-basin characteristics, which together affect the hydrology of contributing rivers (Jones and Frostick 2002; Burt and Allison 2010). There are certainly other local factors that impact sediment delivery, including the anthropic influence.

Sediment is an integral part of coastal system. The term "sediment" refers mainly to sand, silt, clay, gravel, and bioclastic material that are transported by waves and currents along or near the coast but also by wind, along desert or arid coastline or between beach and dune.

The sources of beach material are the landmasses bordering the sea and the rivers, supplying the coastal area with cohesive and non-cohesive materials. In order to fully understand the coastal morphology in a specific area, it is necessary to have some knowledge of the geology of the area and of the sediment supply from the rivers. Other more special factors may influence the characteristics of the coastal area, such as the local flora and fauna as in the cases of coral coastlines and mangrove coastal areas. However, coasts defined by biological systems will receive little attention here.

Figure 1 gathers the main elements of the sediment cycle seen on a short time scale on coastal areas. It is inspired by a concept of sediment budget which is an

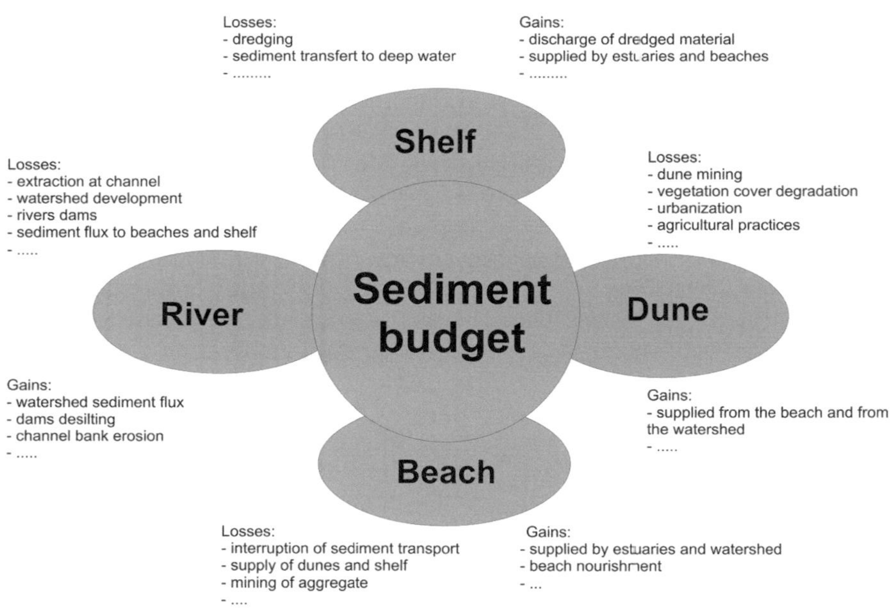

Fig. 1 Sediment budget principle on a coastal zone

accounting of the sources and disposition of sediment as it travels from its point of origin to its eventual outlet from a defined landscape unit like a drainage basin (Reid and Dunne 1996). We are concerned by sediment budget from land to see through four main coastal compartments which are trapping sediments over a given period or are providing sediments at other coastal compartments (shore, coastal dunes and cliffs, costal hinterland watersheds and rivers, nearshore zone and beyond offshore zone forming a sink on a short period beyond the depth of closure – nevertheless the sediments of offshore compartments can be mobilized in case of severe climatic changes involving the decrease of sea level).

Sediment fluxes are driven by different factors, such as proximal (climate/glaciation, land cover, topography), distal (base level) and local controls (human activity). The principal influences on sediment flux during the Holocene are driven primarily by geography (temperature, runoff, biogeography and pedology), geomorphology (basin area and relief), geology (tectonic, lithology) and climate change (sea level change, flooding, storms, length of the season and El Niño events or Asian monsoon) (Jones and Frostick 2002).

Sediment fluxes to the ocean during the period from the late Jurassic to the Pliocene ranged between 2.7 and 5.2 $Gt \cdot year^{-1}$, but increased up to 9.6–15.5 $Gt \cdot year^{-1}$ in Pliocene-Holocene (Panin 2004). The contemporary sediment flux is 2, higher due to human disturbance of the coast and the land (Milliman and Syvitsky 1992). Over the Anthropocene which spreads over the last three centuries, however, large-scale human activities like dam, jetty and seawall construction challenge natural processes like changing sea level and major storms have influences on the shoreline position (Pilkey and Dixon 1996). Quick land cover changes over wide areas into watershed also impact water and sediment fluxes. From a quantitative point of view, the impact of watershed management by humans has first led to an increase in natural sediment supply to the ocean due to soil erosion (+2.3 +/−0.6 billion tonnes/year) and now leads to a decrease (1.4 +/−0.3) due to sediment trapping in dams (about 30 % of the sediment flux coming from inland) (Syvitski et al. 2005; Vorosmarty et al. 2003). At this decrease overlap subsidence processes in the majority of large muddy deltas (Syvistki et al. 2009) because of a large pumping water, oil and gas in coastal sedimentary layers. Finally, on an annual-decadal time scale, human activities, such as dredging, spoil disposals and beach replenishment, along with storm-generated waves, are probably the most important factors in shaping the coast (Hill et al. 2004). Quantitative assessment of the relative importance of these processes and prediction of future beach behaviour remain important problems for coastal geologists and engineers (Thieler et al. 2000).

Today, the coastal erosion which is felt in a generalized way is thus the result of a well-known convergence of the following factors: (a) climatic changes: increase of the marine level, modification of the modes weather-sailors (winds, swell); (b) reduction in the sedimentary contributions of the rivers because of the extractions of sands and gravels or the stopping, and the progressive unpacking, of the basins slopes; (c) reduction in sand stocks available on the spot because of urbanization; and (d) disturbances of the sedimentary transit by harbour works or protections which can defer the problem on the close sectors (Fig. 2). Hence coastal and marine sediments are limited in quantity and should be managed sustainably.

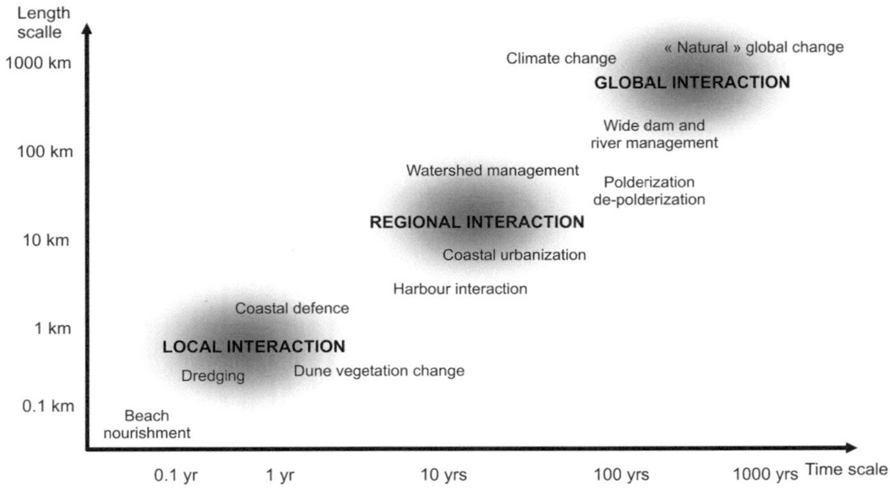

Fig. 2 Examples of human interaction with sediment fluxes in coastal area at various spatial and temporal scales

Moreover large amounts of sediment have been consumed on Earth for beach nourishment, land reclamation and construction.

Several studies gathering a wide and synthesized knowledge have been published concerning sedimentary fluxes at different spatial and temporal levels and different scientific issues. Jones and Frostick (2002) present a current perspective on controls and constraints on sediment supply, a model and empirically based driven understanding of sediment fluxes and the interaction of geomorphology, landscape evolution and sedimentary geology to provide a more complete picture of the Earth system. Crossland et al. (2007) addressed key elements of material flux between land, sea and atmosphere through the coastal zone and indications of: (i) change in land use, climate, sea level and human activities alter the fluxes in the coastal zone, and affect coastal quality and morphodynamic; and (ii) change in coastal systems, including responses to varying terrestrial and oceanic inputs, will affect the global carbon cycle and the trace gas composition of the atmosphere with an assessment of the influence of human society, before looking at future needs for targeted research and management actions in the coastal zone. More recently Burt and Allison (2010) published a volume entitled *Sediment Cascades: An Integrated Approach*. The aim of the book is to deal with sediment transport through the fluvial landscape with implications for catchment management, and consideration of larger-scale landform evolution. No single text integrates the landscape components we decided to include in the present book, covering the transfer of sediments from watershed environments, through transport pathways to the coastal zone under natural control (climatic and tectonic) at different time scales from the Holocene to the Anthropocene.

The book is a collection of many case studies carried out by researchers from several countries. These studies are provided by a large international spectrum of researchers and presented in a uniform structure, focussing particularly on sediment fluxes in different coastal regions and at various spatial and temporal scales.

The aim of the first part is to show the impact of the climatic change on sediment fluxes over a long period (Holocene) through the study of three cases. The first case concerns drastic Holocene environmental change on the north-east Atlantic coast (Baltzer et al.), the second case concerns impact of deglaciation during Holocene upon sediment flux in a polar coastal zone (Strzelecki et al.). The last one is a case-study along the coast of Rhone Delta over a shorter period during the little ice age which ends at the beginning of Anthropocene period (Provansal et al.).

The aim of the second part is to focus on processes and resulting landforms over the Antropocene period which is ongoing since the development of the industrial time. Three studies have been chosen in three different climatic areas: the first takes place in the tropical area of the French Guiana coast and is related to mud sediments (Anthony et al.). The second case studies a semi-arid country along the northwest coast of Morocco (El Mrini et al.). The last case takes place along the Channel Coast of France in Normandy characterized by high chalk cliffs, in a temperate climate (Costa et al.).

The third part of the book points out the use of modelling approaches of sediment fluxes at a higher spatial and temporal scale. In order to discuss the use of such modelling approach, we have chosen three cases: the first case addresses sediment exchange through the inlets of the Venice Lagoon in Italia (Umgiesser et al.). The second case highlights tidal inlet dynamics and relocation in response to artificial breaching on the west coast of Morocco (Zourarah et al.). The third case is focusing upon sediment transport formulae for coastal morphodynamic simulation, comparing calculated sediment flux against in situ data (Larroudé et al.).

We propose a fourth party concerning extreme events such as tsunamis and associated sediment fluxes (Regnauld and Mastronuzzi). Tsunamis are not linked to climate changes nor to climate but must be taken into account because of their major and instantaneous impacts on sediment fluxes and sediment cells.

This book is an essential reading for academics, students and professionals belonging to a wide range of disciplines like geography, biology, modelling, environmental sciences, land planning and marine policy.

Nantes, France

Mohamed Maanan
Marc Robin

References

Anthony EJ (2009) Shore processes and their palaeoenvironmental applications. Elsevier, Amsterdam/Boston, 519 p

Burt T, Allison R (2010) Sediment cascades: an integrated approach. Wiley-Blackwell, Chichester, West Sussex/Hoboken, 482 pp

Cloetingh S et al (2007) Topo-europe: the geoscience of coupled deep earth-surface processes. Glob Planet Change 58(1–4):1–118

Crossland CJ, Kremer HH, Lindeboom HJ, Marshall Crossland JI, Le Tissier MDA (2007) Coastal fluxes in the anthropocene. Springer, Berlin, 231 p

Dean RG, Dalrymple RA (2004) Coastal processes with engineering applications. Cambridge University Press, Cambridge/New York, 488 p

Einsele G (1992) Sedimentary basins. Evolution, facies, and sediment budget. Springer, Berlin/New York, 628 p

Hill HH, Kelley JT, Belknap DF, Dickson SM (2004) The effects of storms and storm-generated currents on the sand beaches in southern Maine. Mar Geol 210:149–168

Jones SJ, Frostick LE (eds) (2002) Sediment flux to basins: causes, controls and consequences. Geological Society, London, Special Publications, vol 191, 284 pages

Maanan M, Robin M (2010) Geomatic solution for coastal environments. Nova Science Publishers, New York, 371 pages

Milliman JD, Farnsworth KL (2011) River discharge to the coastal ocean: a global synthesis. Cambridge University Press, Cambridge/New York, 392 p

Milliman JD, Syvitsky JPM (1992) Geomorphic/tectonic control of sediment discharge to the ocean: the importance of small mountainous rivers. J Geol 100:525–544

Panin A (2004) Land-ocean sediment transfer in palaetimes, and implications for present-day natural fluvial fluxes. Sediment Transfer through the Fluvial System, pp 115–124

Pilkey OP, Dixon K (1996) The shore and the corps. Island Press, Washington, DC, 272 pp

Reid, Leslie M, Thomas Dunne (1996) Rapid evaluation of sediment budgets. Catena Verlag (GeoEcology paperback), Reiskirchen, 164 p

Schwab WC, Thieler ER, Allen JR, Foster DS, Swift BA, Denny JF (2000) Influence of inner continental shelf framework on the evolution and behavior of the barrier island system between Fire Island Inlet and Shinnecock Inlet, Long Island, New York. J Coast Res 16:396–407

Syvitski JPM, Vorosmarty CJ, Kettner AJ, Green P (2005) Impact of humans on the flux of terrestrial sediment to the global coastal ocean. Science 308:376–380

Syvitski JPM, Kettner AJ, Overeem I, Hutton EWH, Hannon MT, Brakendridge HGR, Day J, Vorosmarty CJ, Saito Y, Giosan L, Nicholls RJ (2009) Sinking deltas due to human activities. Nat Geosci 2:681

Thieler ER, Pilkey Jr. OH, Young RS, Bush DM, Chai F (2000) The use of mathematical models to predict beach behaviour for U.S. coastal engineering: a critical review. J Coast Res 16:48–70

Vörösmarty JV, Meybeck M, Fekete B, Sharma K, Green P, Syvitski JPM (2003) Anthropogenic sediment retention: major global impact from registered river impoundments. Glob Planet Change, n° 39(1–2):169–190

Contents

Contributors

Carl L. Amos School of Ocean and Earth Science, National Oceanography Centre, Southampton, Hampshire, UK

César Andrade Centro e Departamento de Geologia, Faculdade de Ciências, Universidade de Lisboa, Lisboa, Portugal

Giorgio Anfuso Dpto. de Ciencias de la Tierra, Facultad de Ciencias del Mar y Ambientales, Universidad de Cádiz, Cádiz, Spain

Edward J. Anthony Aix Marseille Université, Institut Universitaire de France, CEREGE, UM 34, Europôle Méditerranéen de l'Arbois, Aix en Provence Cedex, France

Agnès Baltzer CNRS – UMR 6554, Laboratoire Géolittomer/IGARUN, Université de Nantes – Campus du Tertre, Nantes Cédex 3, France

Jean-François Bourillet IFREMER Brest, REM, Plouzané, France

Guillaume Brunier CEREGE, Université Aix Marseille, UMR 34, Europôle Méditerranéen de l'Arbois, Aix en Provence Cedex, France

Adrien Cartier Laboratoire D'Océanologie et des Géosciences, UMR 8187 LOG, Université du Littoral Côte d'Opale, Wimeureux, France

Stéphane Costa Lab. Géophen., UMR CNRS-LETG Caen Géophen 6554, University of Caen Basse-Normandie, Caen, Cedex, France

Giuseppe Cultrone Departamento de Mineralogía y Petrología, Universidad de Granada, Granada, Spain

Mehdi Daou UMR 5519, LEGI, Université de Grenoble, Saint-Martin-d'Hères, France

Franck Dolique Univ. Antilles-Guyane, Martinique, Schoelcher, France

Abdelmounim El Mrini Département de Géologie, Faculté des Sciences, Université Abdelmalek Essaâdi, Tétouan, Morocco

Christian Ferrarin Institute of Marine Sciences, ISMAR-CNR, Venezia, Italy

Jérôme Fournier Muséum National d'Histoire Naturelle, Station Marine, Dinard, France

CNRS – UMR 7208 BOREA, Muséum National d'Histoire Naturelle, Paris cedex 05, France

Maria da Conceição Freitas Centro e Departamento de Geologia, Faculdade de Ciências, Universidade de Lisboa, Lisboa, Portugal

Antoine Gardel Université du Littoral Côte d'Opale, Laboratoire d'Océanologie et de Géosciences, CNRS UMR 8187 LOG, Wimereux, France

CNRS Guyane, USR3456, Immeuble Le Relais, Cayenne, France

Evelyne Goubert Geoarchitecture EA2219, Geosciences marines & Géomorphologie littorale, Université de Bretagne Sud, Vannes, France

Rachel Helsby School of Ocean and Earth Science, National Oceanography Centre, Southampton, Hampshire, UK

Arnaud Hequette Laboratoire D'Océanologie et des Géosciences, UMR 8187 LOG, Université du Littoral Côte d'Opale, Wimeureux, France

Nathalie Labourdette UPMC Univ Paris 06, CNRS, UMR 7193, ISTeP, Paris cedex 05, France

Benoit Laignel Department of Geology, UMR 6143 CNRS M2C, University of Rouen, Mont-Saint-Aignan, France

Philippe Larroudé UMR 5519, LEGI, Université de Grenoble, Saint-Martin-d'Hères, France

Franck Lartaud UPMC Univ Paris 06, CNRS, Laboratoire d'Écogéochimie des Environnements Benthiques (LECOB) UMR 8222, Observatoire Océanologique de Banyuls, Banyuls-sur-mer, France

UPMC Univ Paris 06, CNRS, UMR 7193, ISTeP, Paris cedex 05, France

Pauline Letortu Lab. Géophen., UMR CNRS-LETG Caen Géophen 6554, University of Caen Basse-Normandie, Caen, Cedex, France

Mohamed Maanan Institut de Géographie et d'Aménagement Régional de l'Université de Nantes, Géolittomer, LETG UMR 6554-CNRS, Nantes Cedex 3, France

Jakub Małecki Cryosphere Research Department, Adam Mickiewicz University, Poznań, Poland

Elena Marrocchino Department of Physics and Earth Sciences, University of Ferrara, Ferrara, Italy

Giuseppe Mastronuzzi Dipartimento di Scienze della Terra e Geoambientali, Università degli Studi "Aldo Moro", Bari, Italy

Khalid Mehdi Environment – Integrated Coastal Zone Management, Department of Geology, Faculty of Sciences, UFR: ST/18/05, El Jadida, Morocco

Faculté des Sciences, Laboratoire des Geosciences Marines et Sciences du Sol (Unité associée CNRST-URAC 45), El Jadida, Morocco

Asmae Mhamdi Alaoui Environment – Integrated Coastal Zone Management, Department of Geology, Faculty of Sciences, UFR: ST/18/05, El Jadida, Morocco

Faculté des Sciences, Laboratoire des Geosciences Marines et Sciences du Sol (Unité associée CNRST-URAC 45), El Jadida, Morocco

Zohra Mokeddem IFREMER Brest, LGG, Plouzané, France

Driss Nachite Faculté Polydisciplinaire, Larache, Morocco

Christina Péron Université du Littoral Côte d'Opale, Laboratoire d'Océanologie et de Géosciences, CNRS UMR 8187 LOG, Wimereux, France

CNRS Guyane, USR3456, Immeuble Le Relais, Cayenne, France

Georges Pichard Département d'Histoire, Université Aix-Marseille, Aix-en-Provence, France

Mireille Provansal Europôle de l'Arbois, CNRS, UM CEREGE, Aix-en-Provence, France

UMR 6635 CEREGE, Europôle Méditerranéen de l'Arbois, Université Aix Marseille, Aix-en-Provence, France

Hervé Regnauld Laboratoire Costel UMR 6554 LETG et IFR Caren, Université de Rennes 2, Rennes, France

UMR CNRS 6554 LETG, Université de Rennes 2, Rennes, France

Marc Robin Institut de Géographie et d'Aménagement Régional de l'Université de Nantes, Géolittomer, LETG UMR 6554-CNRS, Nantes Cedex 3, France

Mateusz Czesław Strzelecki Department of Geomorphology, University of Wrocław, Wrocław, Poland

Rui Taborda LATTEX/IDL, Departamento de Geologia, Faculdade de Ciências, Universidade de Lisboa, Lisboa, Portugal

Georg Umgiesser Institute of Marine Sciences, ISMAR-CNR, Venezia, Italy

Carmela Vaccaro Department of Physics and Earth Sciences, University of Ferrara, Ferrara, Italy

Piotr Zagórski Department of Geomorphology, Maria Curie-Skłodowska University, Lublin, Poland

Bendahhou Zourarah Environment – Integrated Coastal Zone Management, Department of Geology, Faculty of Sciences, UFR: ST/18/05, El Jadida, Morocco

Faculté des Sciences, Laboratoire des Geosciences Marines et Sciences du Sol (Unité associée CNRST-URAC 45), El Jadida, Morocco

About the Editors

Mohamed Maanan is an Associate Professor at University of Nantes (France). His research is concerned with the interaction between coastal environment processes, earth surface materials and impact of human activities. In particular, attention is focussed on sediment delivery processes – the temporal and spatial dynamics of sediment production and transfer (continent-ocean).

Marc Robin is Professor of the University of Nantes (France). He is specialised in watershed and coastal dynamics, policy making and management of coastal areas, risks and hazards issues along coastline, remote sensing of coastal resources and management of coastal data into geographical information systems.

Part I
Sediment Fluxes Changes Link to Climatic Change During Holocene

Chapter 1
The "*Turritella* Layer": A Potential Proxy of a Drastic Holocene Environmental Change on the North–East Atlantic Coast

Agnès Baltzer, Zohra Mokeddem, Evelyne Goubert, Franck Lartaud, Nathalie Labourdette, Jérôme Fournier, and Jean-François Bourillet

Abstract A collection of data including sub-bottom VHR seismic (Seistec boomer), bathymetry and cores, was conducted in three sea lochs of the north west coast of Scotland, as part of an investigation of the sedimentological and climatic change records since the Last Glacial Maximum. Five acoustic facies have been correlated to the sediment of the core MD04-3204 and interpreted in terms of glacial activity, ice retreat and subsequent Holocene sedimentation. Grain size, pollen, foraminifera, geochemical analyses together with ^{14}C dating, indicate a

---

A. Baltzer (✉)
CNRS – UMR 6554, Laboratoire Géolittomer/IGARUN, Université de Nantes – Campus du Tertre, BP 81227, 44 312 Nantes Cédex 3, France
e-mail: agnes.baltzer1@univ-nantes.fr

Z. Mokeddem
IFREMER Brest, LGG, BP 70, 29280 Plouzané, France

E. Goubert
Geoarchitecture EA2219, Geosciences marines & Géomorphologie littorale, Université de Bretagne Sud, 56 017 cédex Vannes, France

F. Lartaud
UPMC Univ Paris 06, CNRS, Laboratoire d'Écogéochimie des Environnements Benthiques (LECOB) UMR 8222. Observatoire Océanologique de Banyuls, 66650 Banyuls-sur-mer, France

UPMC Univ Paris 06, CNRS, UMR 7193, ISTeP, 75252 cedex 05 Paris, France

N. Labourdette
UPMC Univ Paris 06, CNRS, UMR 7193, ISTeP, 75252 cedex 05 Paris, France

J. Fournier
Muséum National d'Histoire Naturelle, Station Marine, 38 rue du Port Blanc, 35801 Dinard, France

CNRS – UMR 7208 BOREA, Muséum National d'Histoire Naturelle, 43 rue Cuvier, CP 26, 75231 Paris cedex 05, France

J.-F. Bourillet
IFREMER Brest, REM, BP 70, 29280 Plouzané, France

M. Maanan, M. Robin (eds.), *Sediment Fluxes in Coastal Areas*, Coastal Research Library 10, DOI 10.1007/978-94-017-9260-8_1

complex series of palaeoclimate changes in the loch since the Last Glacial Maximum including "Rapid Climate Changes" described in literature.

A characteristic acoustic reflector, identified into the holocene sedimentary deposit, occurring into the different studied lochs, corresponds to a unique *Turritella* layer. A similar reflector has been identified on the continental shelf of South Brittany and is correlated to a *Turritella* layer. This *Turritella* layer seems to be related, in both case, to a drastic environmental change beginning around the 8,200 year BP cold event and finishing abruptly at 7,500 year BP in the North Atlantic.

1.1 Introduction

As the western Scottish sea lochs (Fig. 1.1) are located at an important junction between the North Atlantic Ocean and the European waters of the North Sea, these sites are adapted for observations on climatic variations at high latitudes, and in particular variations in sedimentation that have resulted from climatic changes since the Last Glacial Maximum (LGM) at high latitudes 56°N. Previous studies

Fig. 1.1 Location of the two studies areas in the north west coast of Scotland and in south Brittany. The *white square* in Scotland, north of Oban, shows the location of two sea-lochs: Loch Sunart and Loch Creran. A first géophysic survey (SUCRE, 2002), allowed to acquire seismic profiles in both lochs and short cores in Creran. An oceanographic cruise with the Marion Dufresne (ORSANE 2004) permit to acquire 2 long cores. The *black square* on the south coast of Brittany shows the location of the "Grande vasière", a huge muddy sand patch occurring on the shelf, up to 100 m of water depth

(Mokeddem et al. 2010; Baltzer et al. 2010) established the chronostratigraphy of sedimentary deposits in the Loch Sunart, based on the correlation between a long core (12 m) and seismic acoustic facies constrained by ^{14}C ages together with sediment analysis. An unusual reflector frequently occurs in the Holocene thick transparent sedimentary unit of Loch Sunart and Loch Creran which corresponds to a 15 cm thick layer of *Turritella communis* (Graham 1938, 1988) dated from base to top at 8,260–7,460 cal year BP.

On the southern part of Brittany, the core VK03-58bis retrieved in the Bay of Biscay gives an integrated image of the climate evolution at mid latitudes (45°N) through pollen and Dinocysts analyses (Naughton et al. 2007) from 8,850 year BP to present days. This core was acquired in "la Grande vasière" (Fig. 1.1) in a homogeneous silt sequence marked by a specific level rich in *T. communis* (Folliot 2004) dated at 8,482–7,520 year BP. In both cases the sudden disparition of *T. communis* seems to correspond to a drastic change of environmental conditions.

This paper presents hypothesis for the establishment and extinction of this *Turritella* layer, and its potential signification.

1.2 General Settings: Scottish Sea Lochs and South Brittany Shelf

1.2.1 Scottish Sea Lochs

The two Lochs presented in this paper, are localised on the West coast of Scotland. Loch Creran is located in the north of Argyll and Bute council whereas Loch Sunart is located near the Ardnamurchan peninsula (Fig. 1.1). These lochs are bordered by mountains whose altitude does not exceed 1,000 m. Vegetation cover is variable, including spaces of forests and grassland.

These lochs present a characteristic morphology of "fjord style lochs" with a steep sided narrow cross section and flat loch floor (Syvitski et al. 1987). This typical morphology provides protection from swell and wave action and could preserve long sedimentation records (Howe et al. 2002). Loch Sunart (Fig. 1.2) is the second longest Scottish loch with 31 km length (Bates et al. 2004), an average of 1.5 km width and has a maximum depth of 124 m. The length and the narrowness of this loch make it possible to meet a spectrum of hydrodynamic conditions, from well exposed conditions at the mouth, to extremely calm conditions at the head of the loch.

The Loch Creran (Fig. 1.3) is smaller than Loch Sunart, with 12.8 km length and a maximum depth of 49 m. Located at 8 km north of Loch Etive, its ocean connection is restricted by the Island of Eriska which protects the inner basin from the energy of the swell. The Loch Creran includes four basins and Glen Creran constitutes the principal supply of fresh water. The water of the Loch Creran is extremely well mixed (Edwards and Sharples 1986; Austin and Inall 2002).

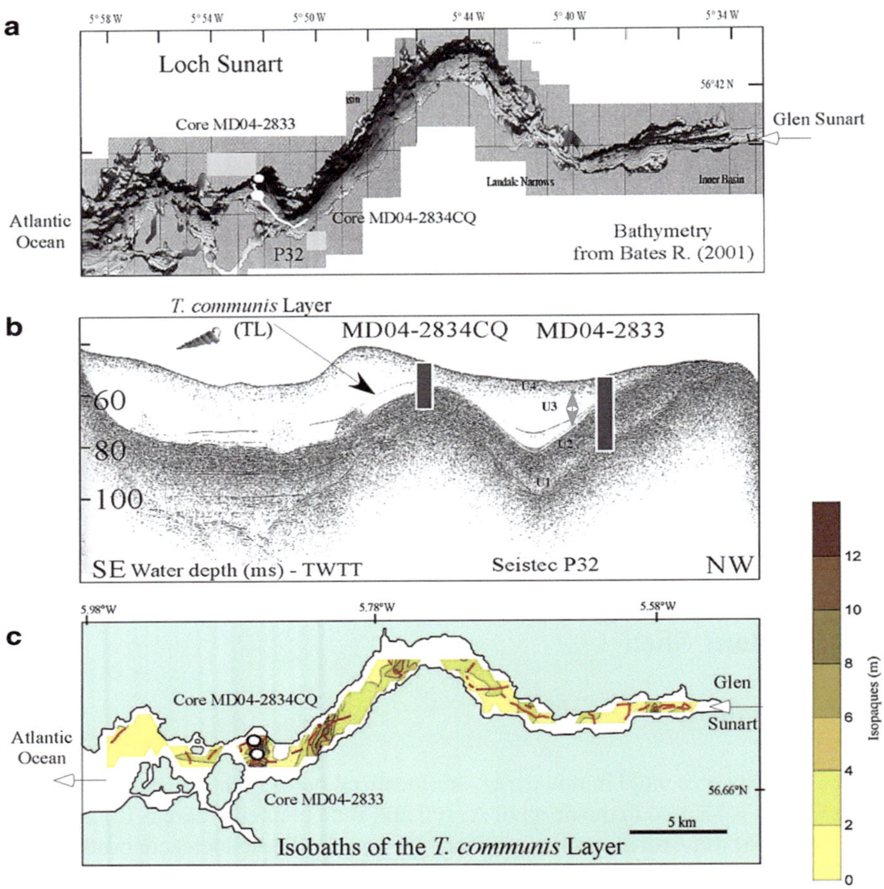

Fig. 1.2 Loch Sunart. (**a**) Bathymetric map of Loch sunart realized by Bates (Bates and Byham 2001). Location of the 2 long cores MD04-2833 and core MD04-234CQ acquired with the Marion Dufresne and the situation of the boomer seismic profile P32. (**b**) Seistec profile P32: characteristic profile with the different seismic units. The Turitella communis Layer is indicated by an *arrow* in the transparent unit (U3). The position of the long CALYPSO core MD04-2833 and the CASQ core MD04-2834CQ are indicated, showing the variation of Turritella Layer (noticed T.L. further on) depth. (**c**) Map of the T.L. isobaths. The seismic reflector related to the TL has been mapped. The resulting isobaths are shown on the figure and reveal the paleo-bathymetry at 7,500 cal year BP (age of the top of the TL.)

1.2.2 South Brittany Shelf

The Bay of Biscay presents a 300 km wide continental shelf in it's north-westernmost area and becomes narrow with a steep slope further south (30 km wide) (Fig. 1.1). This shelf is composed of two small and one large open-shelf mud patches: the West and South Gironde shelf mud fields and the "Grande Vasière"

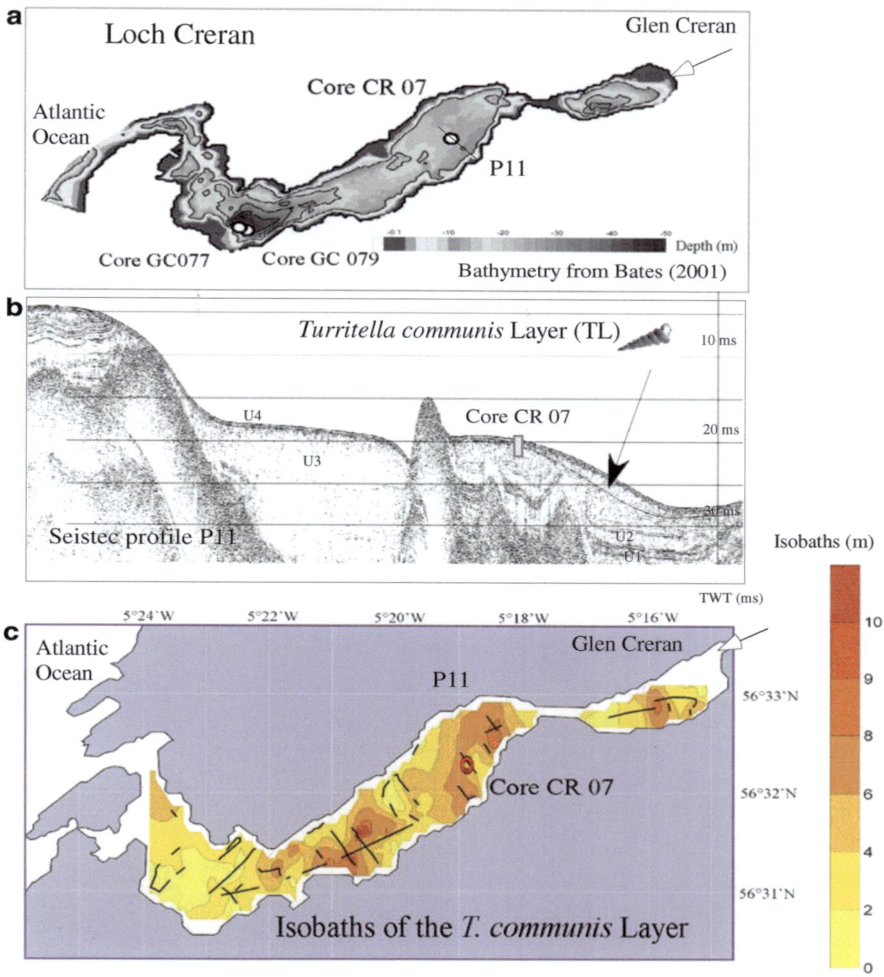

Fig. 1.3 Loch Creran. (**a**) Bathymetric map of Loch Creran realized by Bates (Bates and Byham 2001). Location of the short core CR07 acquired by divers during the SUCRE mission, and the situation of the boomer seismic profile P11. (**b**) Seistec profile P11: characteristic profile with the different seismic units. The Turitella communis Layer is indicated by an *arrow* in the transparent unit (U3). The position of the short core CR 07 is indicated, showing the variation of TL depth. (**c**) Map of the TL isobaths. The seismic reflector related to the TL has been mapped. The resulting isobaths are shown on the figure and reveal the paleo-bathymetry at 7,500 cal year BP (age of the top of the T.L.)

(Fig. 1.4) (Allen and Castaing 1977). According to McCave's classification the "Grande Vasière" is a mid-shelf mud belt (McCave 1972). The "Grande Vasière" is large (more than 225 km length and 40 km wide), located between 80 and 110 m water depth and presents an annual mean sedimentary rate of 0.1–0.2 cm year^{-1} (Lesueur et al. 2001) (Fig. 1.1). Shelf upkeep depends essentially on: (a) continental supply by nepheloid layers (Jouanneau et al. 1999; Lesueur et al. 2001); (b) wave

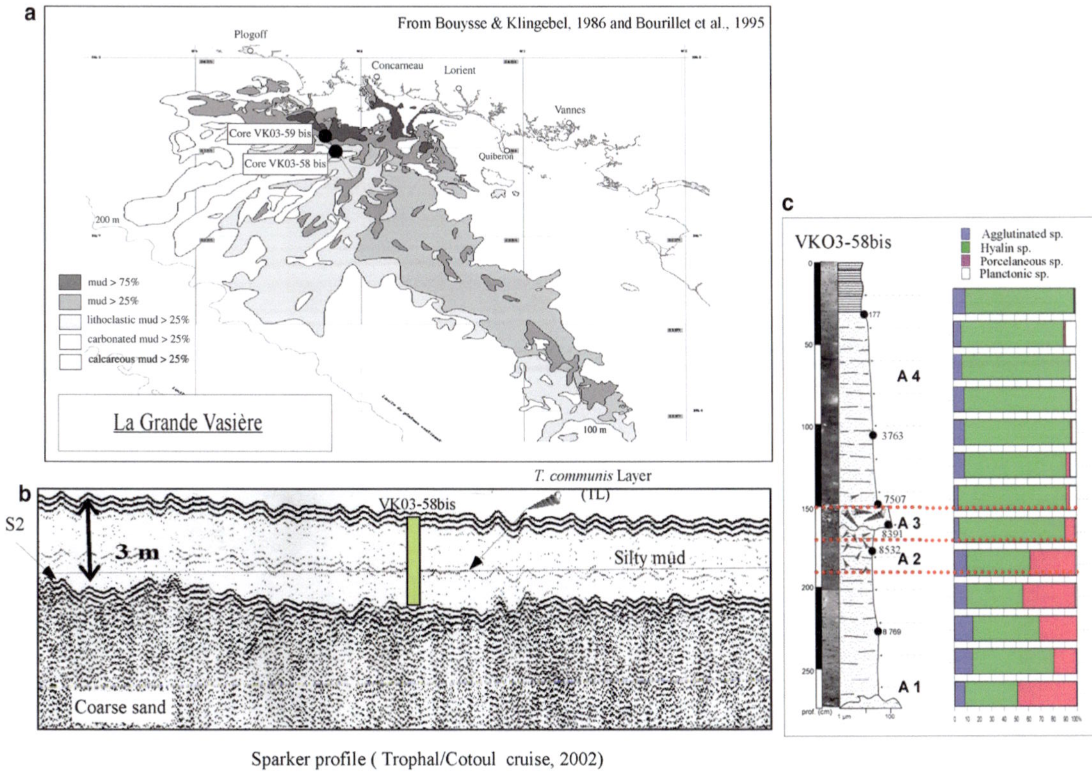

Fig. 1.4 The Grande Vasière. (**a**) Bathymetric map of the south Brittany shelf showing the surface of 8,000 km^2 covered by the "Grande Vasière", a mid-shelf mud belt, centered around 100 m of water depths. The repartition of the different mud facies is linked to the source of the sediments. Sands and gravels come from remobilization of the shelf sediments and the clays are supplied by the different rivers, especially the Gironde. (**b**) The Sparker profile shows the acoustic facies units: basal facies is constituted by coarse sands eroded by an erosional surface S2, which has a regional extension. The above unit is essentially composed of silty mud of varying thickness (from 3à cm to a maximum of 3 m). Within this unit, a dark continuous reflector reveals the presence of the Turritella Layer, sampled by the core VK03-58bis. (**c**) The log of the core VK03-58bis is presented here with the percentages of different foramonifera assemblages: Agglutinated species, Hyalin species, Porcelaneous species and Planctonic species

action (Pinot 1974) and hydrology, and (c) sea level changes (Lesueur and Klingebiel 1976). The "Grande Vasière" rests over two sandy units and consists of a thin (few decimetres) Holocene feature of muddy autochthon sand (Bourillet et al. 2002, 2005).

1.3 Material and Methods

In this paragraph, we only present materiel and methods deployed for our studies in Scottish lochs. The comparison with the work done by Naughton et al. (2007) on the cores acquired on the Brittany shelf will be tackled in the discussion part.

1.3.1 Geophysical Surveys

A complete set of data was acquired in the Loch Sunart: two geophysical surveys (bathymetric sidescan and a Seistec Boomer) where completed by the acquisition of a Calypso long core of 12 m. A Seistec Boomer System (IKB Ltd) was used to record sub-bottom profiles. It has a frequency range from 1 to 10 kHz, a pulse duration ranging from 75 to 250 ms at a power of 150 J, allowing a spatial resolution of 25 cm, with a penetration up to 100 m in soft sediments and 200 m in deep water soft sediments (Simpkin and Davis 1993). Thirty four profiles, recovering 60 km, were acquired in the loch with an average penetration of 50 m except in some areas where gas occurrence prevented any signal penetration. The Seistec sub-bottom profile 32 (Fig. 1.2b) shows a representative section of all five seismic facies that are present in the inner basin.

1.3.2 Sediment Cores

The long core MD04-2833 (Fig. 1.2b) was acquired by the giant Calypso core system on board the RV Marion Dufresne. This piston corer is similar to a gravity corer but a piston is used to reduce internal friction in the barrel, enabling the corer to recover complete and less disturbed sediment sequences than an open barrel gravity corer. The MD04-2833 core was 12 m long and was acquired in the middle loch to the west of Isle of Carna at a water depth of 38 m (Fig. 1.2). MD04-2834CQ is a casq long core (11.80 m) acquired close to the MD04-2833. The combined pollen, foraminifera and sedimentological analysis help us to interpret many of the features observed in seismic sections. The correlation of the seismic facies with the sediments units (Mokeddem et al. 2007, 2010; Baltzer et al. 2010) allowed to follow the evolution of the sediment fluxes linked to environmental changes. In these both cores, a specific layer of 15 cm thick, composed at 98 % of *Turritella communis* shells, occurs within the upper seismic section. Another short core CRE07, acquired in the Loch Creran, reveals a similar *Turritella* layer. Geochemical analyses have been realised on this *Turritella* layer (noticed TL) to complete this study.

1.3.3 ^{14}C Ages

Core MD04-2833 was analysed for sedimentation and microfauna with seven ^{14}C ages acquired on different shell samples, all in life positions (see Table 1.1) and one ^{14}C ages for the core MD08-2334CQ. A standard reservoir correction R(t) of 400 years was used as the regional average value for western Britain (Harkness 1983) and calibrated calendar ages were obtained from the calibration tables in Stuiver and Reimer (1993), Stuiver et al. (1998) by means of the CALIB 5.1.0b software.

1.3.4 Foraminifera Analysis

A preliminary analysis of foraminiferal assemblages, based on dominant species of 87 samples taken from the core has been conducted. Approximately 20 g of sediment samples were washed through 2 mm and 500 μm, 125 μm and 45 μm sieves. Residues were oven dried (40 °C) and dry sample weights recorded. The 125 μm and 45 μm fractions were observed under a binocular at 80× magnification

Table 1.1 ^{14}C ages acquired from core MD04-2833 *(italic)* and MD04-2834CQ (normal)

Material	Depth (cm)	Laboratory code	Radiocarbone age (year BP)	Corrected[b] (calibrated) age (cal year BP)	± 2[c] (cal year BP)
Turritella communis	81	[a]Poz-23471	1,405 ± 30	994	777–1,211
Wood fragment	198	[a]Poz-23648	4,885 ± 35	5,623	5,584–5,663
Turritella communis	265	[a]Poz-1054	6,910 ± 40	7,414	7,325–7,503
Turritella communis	270	[a]Poz-23648	6,920 ± 35	7,459	7,411–7,507
Turritella communis	271	[a]Poz-23472	6,950 ± 40	7,468	7,389–7,548
Pecten species	385	[a]Poz-13368	8,710 ± 50	9,374	9,262–9,447
Pecten maximus	776	[a]UL-2853	14,020 ± 210	16,760	16,067–17,454
Turritella communis	178	[a]Poz-23473	6,750 ± 40	7,320	7,212–7,407

[a]Poznan Radiocarbon Laboratory, °Laval University Laboratory
[b]Marine reservoir correction: 405 ± 40 year (Harkness 1983)
[c]Standard deviation (Stuiver et al. 1998)

to determine the dominant species. A total of 300 specimens were counted. The generic and specific identifications were based on taxonomic sources (Murray 1971; Loeblich and Tappan 1988; Murray 2000, 2003; Fontanier et al. 2002). The paleoenvironmental reconstitution is based on ecological and morphological groups of benthic foraminifers (Goubert et al. 2001; Mokeddem et al. 2010). The ecological significances of the species come from Murray (2006), Scourse (2002) and Mokeddem et al. (2010).

1.3.5 Geochemical Analyses (Oxygen and Carbon Isotope Composition) on Core MD2833

Mollusk gastropods are considered to precipitate their shells in isotopic equilibrium with seawater (Grossman and Ku 1986; Latal et al. 2004). Particularly, turritelid shells are considered to be a reliable archive of paleoenvironmental and paleoclimatic conditions (Andreasson and Schmitz 1996; Huyghe et al. 2012).

Two aragonitic *Turritella communis* shells were used for oxygen and carbon isotope composition. The first one was taken at 265 cm depth in the core MD04-2833 (shell ID: 265), corresponding to the center of the Loch Sunart and the other one was taken at 178 cm in the core MD04-2834CQ (shell ID: 178), corresponding to the edge of the same *Turritella* layer. The two samples were dated at 7,414 cal year. BP.

Sampling for $\delta^{18}O$ and $\delta\ ^{13}C$ analyses was achieved each millimeter along the transect of growth from the uppermost layer, by using a 0.5 mm drill bit. The powdered $CaCO_3$ samples were analysed according to standard techniques (Jones and Quitmyer 1996) which involved an initial reaction in vacuo with 100 % orthophosphoric acid at 90 °C for 15 min. An on-line automated carbonate-preparation system facilitated the production and purification of evolved CO_2 gas. The isotopic differences between the derived CO_2 gas and the VPDB standard were determined with a VG Instruments Isoprime mass spectrometer. Isotopic data were reported in conventional delta (δ) notation relative to the Vienna Pee Dee Belemnite (VPDB). The standard used for the analyses was an internal standard calibrated on the NBS-19. Standard deviation for $\delta\ ^{18}O$ and $\delta^{13}C$ is ± 0.05‰.

1.4 Results

1.4.1 Seismic Data: Mapping of the "Turritella's *Reflector*"

Sedimentary processes in this loch have been grouped into four units (Mokeddem et al. 2007, 2010; Baltzer et al. 2010) from the Last Glacial Maximum (Fig. 1.5).

Unit 1 corresponds to a basal till sequence (numerous dropstones and gravels in a clayey silty mud matrix). Effective deglaciation processes appear only after

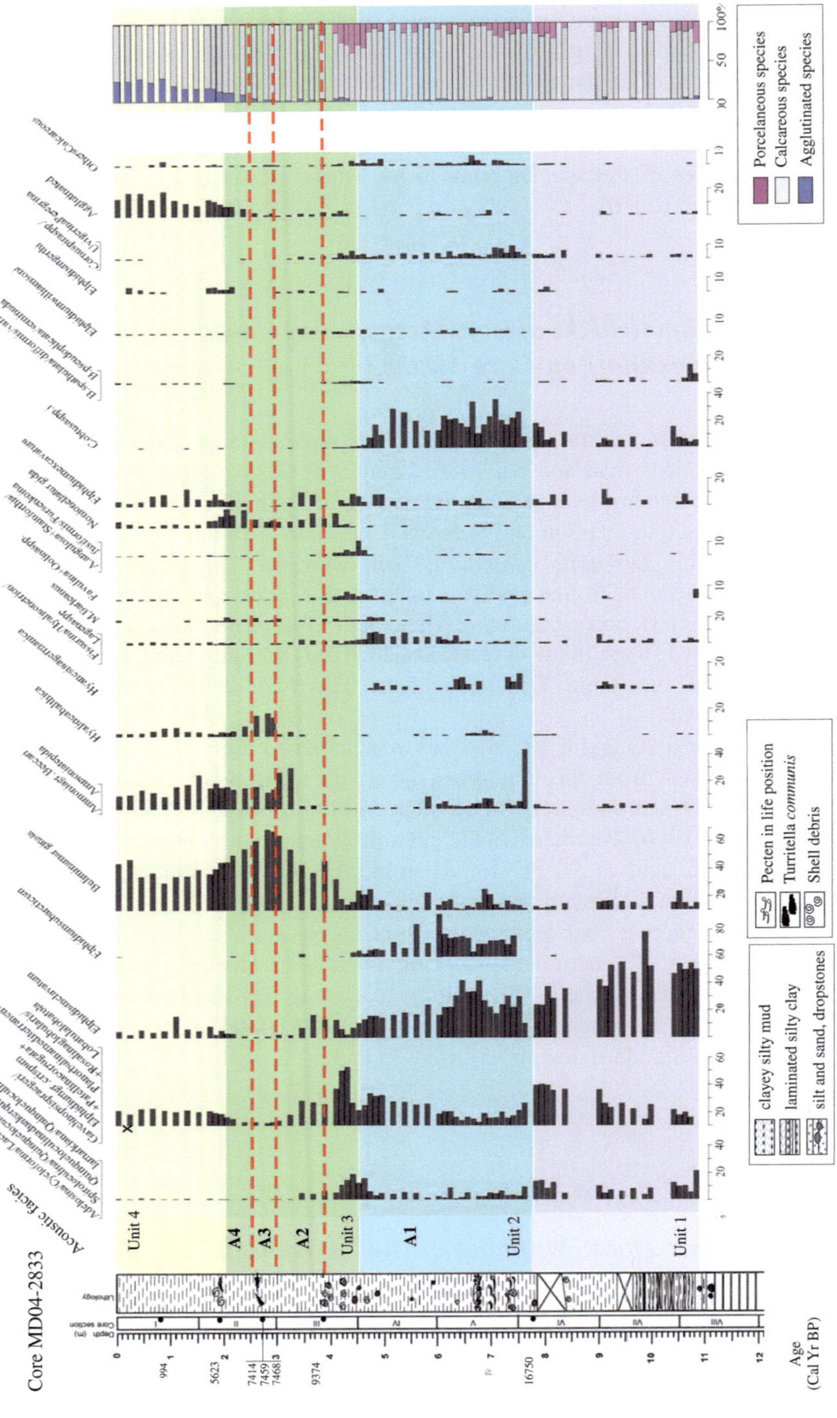

Fig. 1.5 Stratigraphic distribution of benthic foraminifera assemblages (percentages of total benthic faunas) in core MD04-2833. Four domains are delimited by global species changes and correspond to the four seismic unit facies (Unit 1, Unit 2, Unit 3, Unit 4). Three main species of foraminifera have been grouped: the Porcelaneous species, the Calcareous species and the Agglutinated species

16,750 cal year BP. The more temperate Bölling period (15,730 cal year BP), occurs at the end of this unit. Unit 2 presents fine acoustic layering of glaciomarine origin which corresponds to a period including the Younger Dryas sedimentation, when the ice cap re-advanced, stopped and retreat. A major unconformity surface cuts across the top of this unit with up to 40 cm of vertical erosion, probably related to the lowest position of the relative sea level (around 4 m) at these times. Unit 3 is interpreted as a time of rapid and large volume sediment supply where significant reworking was taking place, even under weak currents. The transparent facies of this unit suggests an unconsolidated state of the sediments associated with rapid sedimentation. A continuous and high amplitude reflector frequently occurs into this transparent facies (Figs. 1.2b and 1.3b) which corresponds to a 15 cm thick layer of *Turritella* shells dated from 7,468 to 7,414 cal year BP in the core MD04-2833. This TL was sampled in the "sister core" MD04-2834CQ acquired on the edge of the basin. The Unit 4, characterised by thin laminated beds of silty clay reveals a low sediment supply in a quiet environment and corresponds to recent sedimentation patterns with decreasing sediment supply.

The high amplitude of the "Turritella reflector" related to the TL, reveals a very high impedance which is in accordance with a shelly layer included in a soft deposit. The spatial extension of this reflector (Figs. 1.2 and 1.3) appears to follow paleo-bathymetry in loch Sunart and Creran. *Turritella communis* (Risso 1826) occurs locally and abundantly in gravelly muddy, more or less buried, in shallow water sediments up to 200 m (Graham 1988). *T. communis*, who have a highly specialized mud-burrowing habit, maintains contact with the water, from which the gill filters suspended particles (Yonge 1946) but without disturbing the surrounding mud. The actual distribution ranges from northern Norway (Lofoten Isles) to North Africa, including the Mediterranean Sea (Graham 1938).

These observations mean that the TL exactly underlines the paleo-bottom floor of the lochs.

1.4.2 Foraminifera Analyses

The Fig. 1.5 shows that the TL corresponds to abrupt variations of the different foraminifera curves.

The cold species abundance, *Hyalinea balthica* and the extinction of *Hyanesina germanica*, show a cooling event which began at 380 cm (8,200 cal year BP) and finished at 240 cm (7,400 cal year BP). This event is short in time and underlines an abrupt change of temperature. A net increase of *Bulimina marginata* and *Becarii* abundance traduces a complete environmental change with occurrence of confinement conditions. Simultaneous extinction of *Clavatum* species confirms a very low oxygen content. At 4,000 cal year BP climatic conditions improve with a net increase of the temperature, illustrated by the development of the porcelaneous species around the "climatic optimum".

The benthic foraminiferal assemblages show that the trophic equilibrium of the environments is disrupted according to the large dominance of opportunistic and infaunal species like *Bulimina marginata* and *Ammonia* spp.

1.4.3 Oxygen and Carbon Isotopic Composition of T. communis Shells

The two shells exhibit equivalent mean oxygen isotope composition ($\delta^{18}O_{265} = 2.28 \pm 0.25‰$ and mean $\delta^{18}O_{178} = 2.27 \pm 0.25‰$). The maximum range is closely similar: 1.10‰ for the shell 265 and 1.03‰ for the shell 178. Oxygen isotope values were converted into seawater temperatures using the paleotemperature equation of Grossman and Ku (1986), for the temperature-dependent fractionation of aragonite in mollusks relative to seawater: T (°C) = 21.8 − 4.69 [shell $\delta^{18}O_{VPDB}$ − (seawater $\delta^{18}O_{SMOW}$ − 0.2‰)]. The measured oxygen isotope composition of North-West Scottish coastal waters and sea lochs is 0.18‰ SMOW (Austin and Inall 2002). The mean estimated temperature is 11 ± 1.2 °C for shell 265 and 11.1 ± 1.2 °C for shell 178. The two profiles show clear seasonal cycles, with a winter average of 8.8 ± 0.7 °C (shell 265) and 9.5 ± 0.7 °C (shell 178), and a summer average of 12.4 ± 0.7 °C and 12.8 ± 0.4 °C (for shell 265 and 178 respectively) (Fig. 1.6).

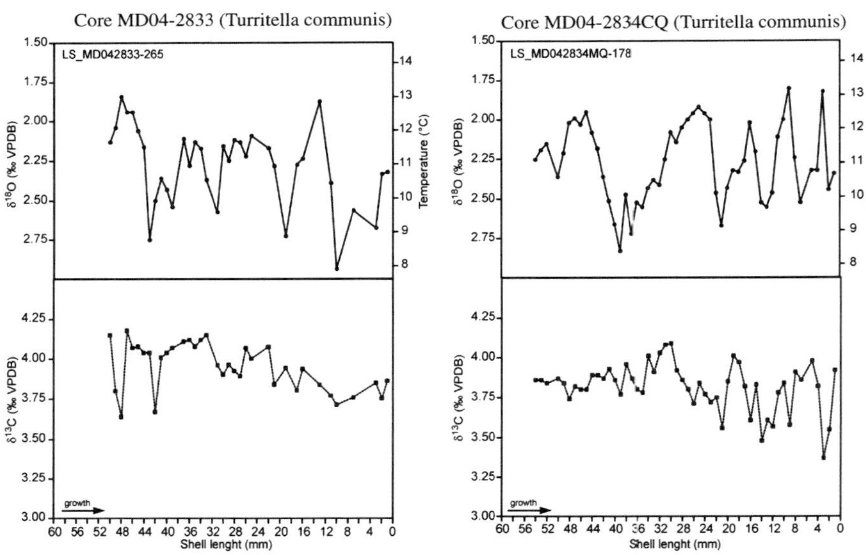

Fig. 1.6 High-resolution oxygen and carbon stable isotope profiles from *Turritella communis* shells, and $\delta^{18}O$-converted temperatures. On the left diagram, the shell was issued from the long core MD04-2833, sampled in the T.L. and aged of 7,414 cal year BP. The diagram on the right shows a shell sampled in the casq core MD04-2834CQ and aged of 7,320 cal year BP

The mean carbon isotope values of the two shells are close similar ($\delta^{13}C_{265} = 3.95 \pm 0.15‰$ and $\delta^{13}C_{178} = 3.82 \pm 0.13‰$). The shell $\delta^{13}C$ profiles are less variable than $\delta^{18}O$, with a range of 0.54‰ for shell 265 and 0.72‰ for shell 178. These $\delta^{13}C$ positive values are consistent with stable normal marine conditions for the two shell locations, without significant freshwater or organic inputs (Gillikin et al. 2006; Lartaud et al. 2010).

Calculated seawater paleotemperatures by the 7,414 cal year BP turritellid shells show data close to present day North-West Scottish seas (Austin et al. 2006). The estimated seasonal gradient is very low (3.5 °C). This may be related to seasonal thermal stratification of the water column, which conducts to significantly less intra-annual bottom water temperature variation than mixed regions (Austin et al. 2006). Scourse (2002) evaluated the timing of the onset of seasonal stratification in the Central Celtic Sea at 8,720 cal year BP.

1.5 Comparison and Discussion

1.5.1 Comparison with the Turritella *Layer of the "Grande Vasières" in South Brittany*

The chirp profile (Fig. 1.4) acquired during the Cotoul cruise (2001) shows an acoustic reflector similar to the *Turritella* reflector within a thick transparent acoustic facies. Three cores have been collected in the South-west of the Glénan sector of the "La Grande Vasière", retrieved at 96.8 m of water depth (Bourrillet et al. 2005), in south Brittany. This mud patch (47°36′ N and 4°08′ W) has been sampled using a vibrocorer during the "Vibarmor" oceanographic cruise (integrated in the "Défi Golfe de Gascogne", an Ifremer program). The Glénan sector is one of the end members of the "Grande Vasière" and is composed of 3 m of sediments with high percentages of fine material (greater than 80 %). Core description and sedimentological analyses including micro-granulometry, calcimetry, x-ray (SCOPIX image-processing; Migeon et al. 1999) and benthic gastropod *Turritella communis* counts were performed by Folliot (2004). Pollen and dynocists analyses have been realised and complete this approach (Naughton et al. 2007).

Five accelerator mass spectrometer (AMS) ^{14}C dates on *T. communis* were obtained on the core VK03-58Bis, indicating that this core sedimentary sequence covers the last 8850 years (Table 1.2). All AMS ^{14}C dated levels were calibrated using CALIB Rev 5.0 program and the global marine calibration dataset (marine 04.14c) (Stuiver and Reimer 1993; Hughen et al. 2004; Stuiver et al. 2005). This dataset uses the global marine age reservoir correction (R) of 400 years. *T. communis* dated levels from twin cores, "VK03-58" (47°36′ N, 4°08′ W; 97.3 m water depth) and "VK03-59Bis" (47°38′ N, 4°09′ W; 94.6 m water depth), were correlated with core "VK03-58Bis" for the age model construction

Table 1.2 ^{14}C ages acquired from core VK03-58bis

Lab code	Core-depth (cm)	Material	Conventional AMS ^{14}C age BP	Conv. AMS ^{14}C age BP (−400 year)	error	Weighted Mean Δr Arcachon France	95.4 % (2σ) Cal BP age ranges	Cal BP age median probability
POZ-10166	VK03 58Bis 106	*T. communis*	3,820	3,420	30	3	3,667 BP:3,865 BP	3,763
POZ-10167	VK03 58Bis 149	*T. communis*	7,020	6,620	30	3	7,427 BP:7,576 BP	7,507
POZ-10168	VK03 58Bis 160	*T. communis*	8,030	7,630	30	3	8,391 BP:8,576 BP	8,479
POZ-10170	VK03 58Bis 177	*T. communis*	8,170	7,770	30	3	8,532 BP:8,808 BP	8,652
POZ-10171	VK03 58Bis 226	*T. communis*	8,240	7,840	30	3	8,613 BP:8,938 BP	8,764

(Fig. 1.4c). As the ages have been obtained in the same laboratory (Poznan laboratory), it should be relevant to compare the ages from these different cores.

The core "VK03-58Bis" is characterised by an homogenous silt sequence marked between 210 and 150 cm by a level containing *T. communis* (Fig. 1.4). Between 210 and 160 cm this *T. communis* community presents all the characteristics of a biocenose: the shells are deposited in life position; both young and adult specimens are present within the same level; they do not present any evidence of shelf destruction by transport. Between 160 and 150 cm, there is an increase in *T. communis* abundance, and in contrast with the underlying level they are not in life position. This indicates a drastic change in the environmental conditions which probably resulted in their mortality. This single drastic episode has also been observed in the twin cores. Considering the shortness of this drastic *T. communis* mortality episode Naughton et al. (2007) can assume that this event has been synchronous in the three cores. *T. communis* death and the decrease of the *Lingulodinium machaerophorum* dinocyst, between 8,480 and 8,390 cal year BP, was most probably triggered by the opening of the English Channel.

1.5.2 Discussion

The stationary life is typical of ciliary feeders and *T. communis* is known to remain stationary for very long periods and possibly indefinitely under natural conditions (Riso 1826; Graham 1988), unless disturbed by external stresses. But they are able to survive in environments with fluctuations of salinity and temperatures. Thus, the establishment of *T. communis* populations indicates a very low sediment supply because of their life mode.

The decrease of temperature combined to the lower salinity are parameters characterizing the 8,200 cold event. The variations of these parameters could explain the absence of other fauna species and they will permit the *T. communis* development. Thus the occurrence of the T.L. corresponds to a change in environmental conditions (T° and S%) together with a stop or at least a slowing down of sediment fluxes which will avoid the burial of shells.

On a second phase, the brutal disparition of the *T. communis* could be explained by the lack of oxygen, as variations of the temperature and salinity are supported by this species.

To explain a decrease of the oxygen, we could propose three scenarii:

- The arrival of a cold water mass coming from the Agassiz and Ojibway lakes (supposed to initiate the 8,200 cold event) which implies stratification of the waters and thus diminution of oxygen conditions.
- The opening of the Channel Pas de Calais, which would drastically change the hydrodynamic and sedimentation conditions of the north west coast of France
- The increase of the sediment supply related to the rapid amelioration of the climatic conditions

The cold water temperatures could not only explain the disappearing of the *T. communis* as they are not especially sensitive to temperature either salinity variations. Another point is that chemical analyses do not show any variations of the salinity or temperature within the months before they died as demonstrated by the carbon and oxygen isotopic composition (Fig. 1.6).

The potential opening of the Channel proposed by Naughton et al. (2007), whereas the actual scientific papers are not confident with an opening of the Pas de Calais strait after 12,500 year BP (Cohen 2007), would probably change the environmental conditions and the sediment fluxes in the south of Brittany but would not reach the north western part of Scotland.

The rapid amelioration of the climate conditions after 7,800 cal year BP correspond to the beginning of the temperate humid Atlantic period. Thus, the erosion power of the fluvial systems is increased and allowed important sedimentation ratios. The seismic profiles show in both cases a transparent facies usually related to unconsolidated sediments linked to rapid sediment deposits. At this point, it is difficult to distinguish the part of the sediment supply increase and the part of the rapid rising sea level on the reduction of the oxygen content which cold explain the abrupt mortality of the *T. communis*. Further studies will be needed to better understand the role of the sediment fluxes on the TL existence.

The "Turritellids event" marks a great variation in biological, hydrological and sedimentological conditions of proximal environments such as Lochs or continental shelf of the Glenan islands.

1.6 Conclusions

This study establishes for the first time the relative importance of a *Turritella* layer signification. This work shows that a specific *T. communis* Layer, dated from 8,300–7,400 cal year BP in sea lochs on the northwestern coast of Scotland and on the south Brittany coast, marks an important change in environmental conditions, confirmed by the foraminifera species assemblages. On a first step, the establishment of this layer, exclusively composed of *Turritella* shells, illustrates rapid deteriorations of T° and S% probably due to the 8,200 cold event. On a second step, the brutal death of these *T. communis* populations at 7,500 cal year BP could be related to a drastic lack of oxygen. These anoxic or semi-anoxic conditions would be linked either to the stratification of water masses due to the rapid increase of sea level rise or/and to the abrupt increase of sediment supply which would burry the shells. Nevertheless, this layer materializes a global and rapid change in environmental parameters like sediment fluxes and/or sea level variations, depending on climate fluctuations. The global mapping of this *Turritella* Layer in other north Atlantic coastal areas would help us to understand the complete signification of this layer.

Acknowledgements The writers are especially grateful to the Marion Dufresne Captain: Jean-Marc Lefèvre and the Chief operator Yvon Balut for the tenacity they show to obtain these incredible cores. The authors would like to thanks the team, P. Bretel, Dr J. Fournier, F. Lelong, E. Poizot and Dr J.M. Rousset, J. & J-C Rousset and Dr A. Stépanian, for their participation during data acquisition.

References

Allen GP, Castaing P (1977) Carte de répartition des sédiments superficiels sur le plateau continental du Golfe de Gascogne. *Bulletin de l'Institut de Géologie du Bassin d'Aquitaine*. Talence, France, pp 255–260

Andreasson FP, Schmitz B (1996) Winter and summer temperatures of the early middle Eocene of France from *Turritella* $\delta^{18}O$ profiles. Geology 24(12):1067–1070

Austin WEN, Inall ME (2002) Deep water renewal in a Scottish fjord: temperature, salinity and oxygen isotopes. Polar Res 21(2):251–258

Austin WEN, Cage AG, Scourse JD (2006) Mid-latitude shelf seas: a NW European perspective on the seasonal dynamics of temperature, salinity and oxygen isotopes. Holocene 16:937–947

Baltzer A, Bates R, Clet-Pellerin M, Mokeddem Z, Bonnot-Courtois C, Walter-Simonnet A-V (2010) Combined pollen and acoustic seismic facies analyses: evaluating climatically-driven changes in a Scottish sea loch (fjord) over the last 20,000 years. In: Howe JA, Austin WEN, Forwick M, Paetzel M (eds) Fjord systems and archives, vol 344, Special Publications. Geological Society, London, pp 357–371

Bates CR, Byham P (2001) Swath-sounding techniques for near shore surveying. Hydrogr J 100:13–18

Bates CR, Moore CG, Harries DB, Austin W, Lyndon AR (2004) Broad scale mapping of sublittoral habitats in Loch Sunart, Scotland. Scottish Natural Heritage Commissioned Report No. 006 (ROAME No. F01AA401C), Scotland

Bourrillet J-F, Loubrieu B, Levron L, Apprioual R, Weber O (2002) Reconnaissance sédimentologique du nord de la Grande Vasière: résultats préliminaires de la mission Trophal 1. In Ifremer Ed Colloque du Défi Golfe de Gascogne. Ifremer, Brest, 11–13 December 2002

Bourrillet J-F, Dubrulle C, Goubert E, Jouanneau J-M, Cortijo E, Weber O, Lesueur P, Vicaire O (2005) La Grande Vasière: architecture, mise en place et estimation des facteurs de son évolution. In: Ifremer Ed Colloque Défi Golfe de Gascogne. Ifremer, Brest, 22–24 March 2005

Cohen K (2007) A pervasive millennial cycle in North Atlantic. Assemblée des Sédimentologistes de France 2007, CAEN

Edwards E, Sharples F (1986) Scottish Sea Lochs – a catalogue. Scottish Marine Biological Association/Nature Conservancy council, Oban, 110 pp

Folliot B (2004) "La grande Vasière": étude sédimentologique de deux secteurs septentrionaux. DEA Lille-Caen-Rouen, 38 p

Fontanier C, Jorissen FJ, Licari L (2002) Live benthic 519 foraminifera faunas from the Bay of Biscay: faunal density, composition, and microhabitats. Deep-Sea Res I 49(4):751–785

Gillikin DP, Lorrain A, Bouillon S, Willenz P, Dehairs F (2006) Stable carbon isotopic composition of *Mytilus edulis* shells: relation to metabolism, salinity, δ13C DIC and phytoplankton. Org Geochem 37:1371–1382

Goubert E, Neraudeau D, Rouchy JM, Lacour D (2001) Foraminiferal record of environmental changes: Messinian of the Los Yesos area (Sorbas Basin, SE Spain). Palaeogeogr Palaeoclimatol Palaeoecol 175:61–78

Graham A (1938) On a ciliary process of food-collecting in the gastropod Turritella Communis Risso. Proc Zool Soc Lond A(108):456–463

Graham A (1988) Molluscs: Prosobranch and Pyramidellid Gastropods, Keys and notes for the identification of the species. Synopses of the British Fauna (New Series) (eds) Kermack DM, Barnes RSK, n°2, 2nd edn. Published for the Linnean Society of London & The Estuarine and Brackish-Water Sciences Association by E.J. Brill and W. Backhuys, Leiden, New-York, Kobenhaven, Koln, 662p

Grossman EL, Ku TL (1986) Oxygen and carbon isotope fractionation in biogenic aragonite: temperature effects. Chem Geol 59:59–74

Harkness D (1983) The extent of the natural ^{14}C deficiency in the coastal environment of the United Kingdom. J Eur Stud Group Phys Chem Math Tech Appl Archaeol PACT 8(IV.9):351–364

Howe JA, Shimmield T, Austin WEN, Longva O (2002) Post-glacial depositional environments in a mid latitude glacially-overdeepened sea loch, inner Loch Etive, western Scotland. Mar Geol 185:417–433

Hughen K, Lehman SJ, Southon JR, Overpeck JT (2004) Cariaco Basin 50KYr Radiocarbon Calibration and Reconstruction. Map of data site Science 9, 303(5655):202–207

Huyghe D, Merle D, Lartaud F, Cheype E, Emmanuel L (2012) Middle Lutetian climate in the Paris Basin: implications for a marine hotspot of paleobiodiversity. Facies 58:587–604

Jones DS, Quitmyer IR (1996) Marking time with bivalve shells: oxygen isotopes and season of annual increment formation. Palaios 11:340–346

Jouanneau JM, Weber O, Cremer M, Castaing P (1999) Fine-grained sediment budget on the continental margin of the Bay of Biscay. Deep-Sea Res II 46:2205–2220

Lartaud F, Emmanuel L, de Rafelis M, Pouvreau S, Renard M (2010) Influence of food supply on the $\delta^{13}C$ signature of mollusc shells: implications for palaeoenvironmental reconstitutions. Geo-Mar Lett 30:23–34

Latal C, Piller WE, Harzhauser M (2004) Palaeoenvironmental reconstructions by stable isotopes of Middle Miocene gastropods of the Central Paratethys. Palaeogeogr Palaeoclimatol Palaeoecol 211:157–169

Lesueur P, Klingebiel A (1976) Carte des sédiments superficiels du plateau continental du Golfe de Gascogne (échelle 1/500,000). BRGM-IFREMER *Ed Carte Géologique de la marge continentale française*, 23 pp

Lesueur P, Jouanneau J-M, Boust D, Tastet J-P, Weber O (2001) Sedimentation rates and fluxes in the continental shelf mud fields in the Bay of Biscay (France). Cont Shelf Res 21:1383–1401

Loeblich AR, Tappan H (1988) Foraminiferal genera and their classification (2 vols). Van Nostrant Reinhold/Chapman & Hall, New York/London. ISBN 0 442 25937 9, xi + 970pp; ix + 213 pp + 847 plates

McCave IN (1972) Transport and escape of fine-grained sediment from shelf areas. In: Swift DJP, Duane DB, Pilkey OH (eds) Shelf sediment transport process and pattern. Dowden, Hutchinson and Ross, Inc., Stroudsburg, pp 225–248

Migeon S, Weber O, Faugères J-C, Saint-Paul J (1999) SCOPIX: a new X-ray imaging system fore core analysis. Geo-Mar Lett 18:251–255

Mokeddem Z, Baltzer A, Clet-Pellerin M, Walter-Simonnet A-V, Bates R, Balut Y, Bonnot-Courtois C (2007) Fluctuations climatiques enregistrées depuis 20,000 ans dans le remplissage sédimentaire du loch Sunart (Nord-Ouest de l'Écosse), Climatic fluctuations recorded in the sediment fillings of Loch Sunart (northwestern Scotland) since 20,000 BP. Comptes Rendus à l'Académie des Sciences 339(2):150–160

Mokeddem Z, Baltzer A, Goubert E, Clet-Pellerin M, Walter-Simonnet A-V (2010) Multiproxy reconstruction of palaeoenvironmental evolution since the Last Glacial maximum in a fjord environment: Loch Sunart (NW Scotland). In: Howe JA, Austin WEN, Forwick M, Paetzel M (eds) Fjord systems and archives, vol 344, Special Publications. Geological Society, London, pp 343–355

Murray JW (1971) An atlas of British recent foraminiferids. Heinemann, London, pp 623–656

Murray JW (2000) Revised taxonomy, atlas of British Recent foraminiferids. J Micropalaeontol 19:44

Murray JW (2003) An illustrated guide to the benthic foraminifera of the Hebridean Shelf, West of Scotland, with notes on their mode of life. Palaeontol Electron 5(2), 31p

Murray JW (2006) Ecology and applications of benthic foraminifera. Cambridge University Press, Cambridge, 426 p

Naughton F, Bourrillet J-F, Sanchez Goñi MF, Turon J-L, Jouanneau J-M (2007) Long-term and millennial-scale climate variability in north-western France during the last 8 850 years. Holocene 7:939–953

Pinot J-P (1974) Le précontinent Breton entre Penmarch, Belle Î}\^{I}{le et l'escarpement continental. Etude géomorphologique. PhD Thesis, Brest University, France, 256 pp

Risso A (1826) Histoire naturelle des principales productions de l'Europe méridionale et particulièrement de celles des environs de Nice et des Alpes Maritimes. Tome quatrième.[1–7], 1–439, pl. 1–1. Paris. (Levrault)

Scourse J (2002) Editorial. J Quat Sci 17:1. doi:10.1002/jqs.668

Simpkin PG, Davis A (1993) For seismic profiling in very shallow water, a novel receiver. In Sea Technology, p 9

Stuiver M, Reimer PJ (1993) Extended ^{14}C data base and revised CALIB3.0 ^{14}C age calibration program. Radiocarbon 35(1):215–230

Stuiver M, Reimer PJ, Bard E, Beck JW, Burr GS, Hughen KA, Kromer B, McCormac G, van der Plicht J, Spurk M (1998) INTCAL98 Radiocarbon Age Calibration, 24000–0 cal BP. Radiocarbon 40(3):1041–1083

Stuiver M, Reimer PJ, Reimer RW (2005) CALIB 5.0. [program and documentation]. http://calib.qub.ac.uk/calib/

Syvitski JPM, Burrel DC, Skei JM (1987) Fjords processes and products. Springer, New York, p 681, 379 p

Yonge CM (1946) On the habits of Turritella communis Risso. J Mar Biol Assoc UK 26:377–380

Chapter 2
The Influence of Recent Deglaciation and Associated Sediment Flux on the Functioning of Polar Coastal Zone – Northern Petuniabukta, Svalbard

Mateusz Czesław Strzelecki, Jakub Małecki, and Piotr Zagórski

Abstract The pristine coasts of Spitsbergen, major island of Svalbard Archipelago provide a superb opportunity to quantify how High Arctic coasts are responding to glacier retreat and associated intensified sediment flux to the fjord and shelf zones. This study focuses on the mechanisms controlling the recent coastal evolution (1990–2009) in Northern Petuniabukta, one of the most sheltered bays of central Spitsbergen, characterised by a semi-arid subpolar climate, limited wave action and rapid retreat rate of all surrounding glaciers. The formation of the coastal landforms here was to a large degree dependent of the rate of sediment excavation from alluvial fans and outwash plains that developed across a wide coast plain between the glacier valleys and the fjord. During last two decades most of the sediments transported from proglacial zones has been accumulated on outwash plains and after reworking supplied a prograding tidal flat system. Despite sheltered location and drier climate the rates of coastal evolution in Petuniabukta are comparable to those seen along the W and S coasts of Spitsbergen.

M.C. Strzelecki (✉)
Department of Geomorphology, University of Wrocław,
pl. Uniwersytecki 1, 50-137 Wrocław, Poland
e-mail: mat.strzelecki@gmail.com

J. Małecki
Cryosphere Research Department, Adam Mickiewicz University,
ul. Dzięgielowa 27, 61-680 Poznań, Poland

P. Zagórski
Department of Geomorphology, Maria Curie-Skłodowska University,
al. Kraśnicka 2cd, 20718 Lublin, Poland

M. Maanan, M. Robin (eds.), *Sediment Fluxes in Coastal Areas*,
Coastal Research Library 10, DOI 10.1007/978-94-017-9260-8_2

2.1 Introduction

In contrast to mid- and low- latitude coasts, relatively little is known regarding the potential impacts of climate and sea-level change on the high latitude coastal margins (Overduin et al. 2014). Indeed, many of the existing intellectual paradigms regarding the functioning of polar coastal zone are now out-dated, based on descriptive geomorphology and a limited process-based understanding. Not only is the number of academic papers on high latitude coastal environments lower than from temperate and tropical regions, but also their qualitative nature seems to be insufficient to allow numerical modelling and more sophisticated data analyses (Byrne and Dionne 2002). Lantuit et al. (2010) indicated that only 1 % of Arctic coastlines have been investigated in sufficient detail to allow quantitative description of processes operating on them.

The most recent advances in high latitude coastal geomorphology is marked by significant discrepancy (Fig. 2.1a). Last decades have seen major development in Arctic coastal research due to projects of the Arctic Coastal Dynamics (ACD) Group (e.g. Rachold et al. 2005; Forbes 2011; Lantuit et al. 2012) and the reopening of Russian works to the wider scientific community, especially in the field of thermoabrasion (e.g. Aré 1988; Aré et al. 2008; Lukyanova et al. 2008; Streletskaya et al. 2009).

However, the major focus in these initiatives has been on understanding of the evolution of the ice-rich permafrost coastlines, particularly in N Alaska, NW

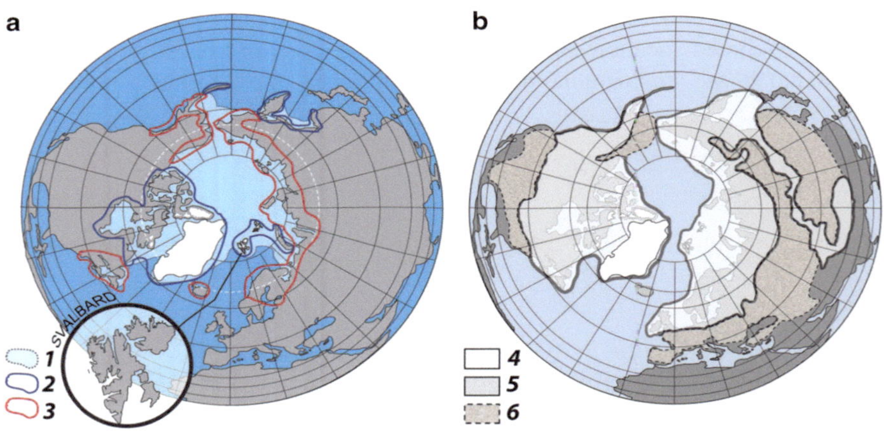

Fig. 2.1 (**a**) Simplified map of cold region coasts in the northern hemisphere (Modified after Byrne and Dionne 2002). *1* – Extent of winter sea ice cover; *2* – Zone of still relatively poorly studied cold region coasts where the mechanisms controlling coastal evolution remain unknown, *3* – Zone of relatively well-studied cold region coasts with running coastal erosion monitoring programmes, and number of high quality papers published in a last decade; (**b**) Map of palaeo – and modern paraglacial and paraperiglacial landsystems and landscapes in the northern hemisphere (Modified after Mercier 2008). *4* – Potential future paraglacial environments currently occupied by Greenland Ice Sheet and glaciers which duo to the climate warming may be exposed from ice in coming decades; *5* – Paraglacial environments during Holocene deglaciation; *6* – Paraglacial and periglacial environments during Holocene warming

Canada, and along the Siberian seas – regions characterised by some of the most rapid erosion rates in the world (Lantuit et al. 2012). In contrast, much less work has been done on the coastal environments of High Arctic archipelagos such as Svalbard, Franz Joseph Land, Canadian Arctic Archipelago or Greenland.

One of the characteristic features distinguishing High Arctic coastal environments from those along Siberian, Chuckchi and Beaufort Seas is the influence of former and recent glacial systems on the coastal morphology, sediment supply and long-term evolution.

This strong effect of glacial legacy in the form of relatively high relief (steep-walled fjords), abundance of coarse glacigenic sediments in the coastal zone delivered from erosion of relict and modern glacial landforms, rapid sea-level changes driven by glacio-isostatic rebound inscribes vast sections of High Arctic coasts into the paraglacial coastal environments (Fig. 2.1b).

2.1.1 Paraglacial Coastal Environments

According to Forbes and Syvitski (1994) paraglacial coastal environments are *'those on or adjacent to formerly ice-covered terrain, where glacially excavated landforms or glacigenic sediments have a recognizable influence on the character and evolution of the coast and nearshore deposits'*. It is noteworthy that the major developments in our understanding of paraglacial coastal system were achieved along coasts of Ireland, NE United States and Atlantic Canada (Forbes and Taylor 1987; Carter et al. 1989; Orford et al. 1991; Shaw et al. 1990; Forbes et al. 1995; Orford et al. 2002). These are coasts that develop by the reworking of inherited sources of glacigenic sediments, thus transforming relict glacial landforms into active coastal landforms until their full destruction. The mid-latitude paraglacial coasts have already adjusted to non-glacial conditions and their evolution is controlled mainly by trend in relative sea-level change and the energy of the surrounding body of water. In the High Arctic coastal zone development is much strongly linked with climate-driven processes including ongoing deglaciation and sediment fluxes from still actively accumulated glacial and periglacial landforms e.g. moraine belts, outwash plains, talus slopes, alluvial fans (e.g. Lønne and Nemec 2004).

Mid-latitude paraglacial coasts which were often formed by submergence of lowlands are commonly characterised by gentle slopes and shallow nearshore zone, whereas the High Arctic coasts are dominated by high relief fjord topography. This is an important factor controlling the wave climate and the accommodation space for sediments delivered to the coastal zone. For instance the barriers formed by ocean waves that approach gentle slopes tend to be wider and thinner than along the coasts with steep slopes where their thickness and height increases (St-Hilaire-Gravel et al. 2010).

The climate amelioration that followed the last major glaciation ended also the operation of periglacial processes on glacigenic sediments in mid-latitudes and led to the complete melt out of permafrost, which is still an important *'sediment binder'* in the high latitudes. The Arctic beach morphology is also strongly influenced by sea ice processes, which are very limited if not absent along present-day mid-latitude paraglacial coasts.

Another significant factor controlling the sediment availability along paraglacial coasts is the presence of vegetation cover. The majority of glacial landforms in mid-latitudes are covered by vegetation, whereas freshly exposed moraines, drumlins, or eskers as well as Arctic coastal landforms (deltas, spits, barrier islands) are barren and more vulnerable to washout, wind action or mass wasting.

In fact, vast sections of mid-latitude paraglacial coasts are already in the 'post-paraglacial period' and their evolution is no longer controlled by glacial history (i.e. Hein et al. 2012).

Despite several differences between the functioning of paraglacial coastal zone in the mid-latitudes and polar regions the latter did not received much attention. Until recently the major advances in understanding of the mechanisms controlling High Arctic paraglacial coastal systems has been made in Svalbard Archipelago (e.g. Mercier and Laffly 2005; Zagórski et al. 2013).

2.1.2 Svalbard Paraglacial Coasts

During the twentieth century large areas of Svalbard have experienced significant shift from glacial-dominated into the non-glacial dominated environments (Mercier 2000). This process is associated with the rapid retreat of glaciers since the termination of the Little Ice Age (LIA), which on Svalbard occurred around AD 1900 (Szczuciński et al. 2009).

The post-LIA glacier retreat exposed vast proglacial and valley systems filled with unstable glacigenic sediments prone to paraglacial transformation (e.g. Lukas et al. 2005; Lønne and Lyså 2005; Etienne et al. 2008; Rachlewicz 2009; Irvine-Fynn et al. 2011; Evans et al. 2012). In addition, the warming of climate and occurrence of extreme precipitation events observed in the last century, destabilised and reactivated sediment delivery to the coast from numerous periglacial landforms including debris flows, slush avalanche lobes and solifluction tongues (Jahn 1967; Åkerman 1984; André 1990; Mercier et al. 2009). Those processes have influenced the evolution of Svalbard coastal zone by providing huge amounts of unconsolidated sediments, which have been used to accumulate new coastal landforms such as spits, tombolos, lagoons, barriers, deltas and tidal flats (e.g. Moign and Guilcher 1967; Klemsdal 1986; Héquette and Ruz 1990; Kowalska and Sroka 2008). For instance on Brøggerhalvøya Mercier and Laffly (2005) have documented *ca.* 90 m of coastal progradation between 1966 and 1995 and linked it with a period of accelerated glaciofluvial sediment delivery from extending proglacial zone of Midre and Austre Lovénbreen. The strong link between glaciofluvial sediment input and coastal evolution has been also observed in Calypsostranda by Zagórski (2011). His study suggests that during 1936–2007 the shift in direction of sediment delivery from the retreating Renardbreen resulted in the cessation of sandur seaward progradation and, in consequence of expanded open water conditions, over

100 m coastal erosion. In Recherchefjorden post-LIA deglaciation led to the transformation of Renardbreen from a marine-terminated into a land-terminated glacier type and resulted the formation of entirely new coastlines composed of unstable glacigenic sediments prone to abrupt modification by marine processes (e.g. Zagórski et al. 2012b). In southern Spitsbergen (Sørkappland) Ziaja et al. (2009) found an evidence of even more dramatic coastal change in the form of ca. 200–460 m shoreline retreat between 1936 and 2005 which led to the destruction of Davislaguna lake.

It is important to notice that the most of previous studies describing the adjustment of coastal zone to deglaciation were located in western and southern parts of Spitsbergen, directly influenced by West Spitsbergen Current (Fig. 2.2) and

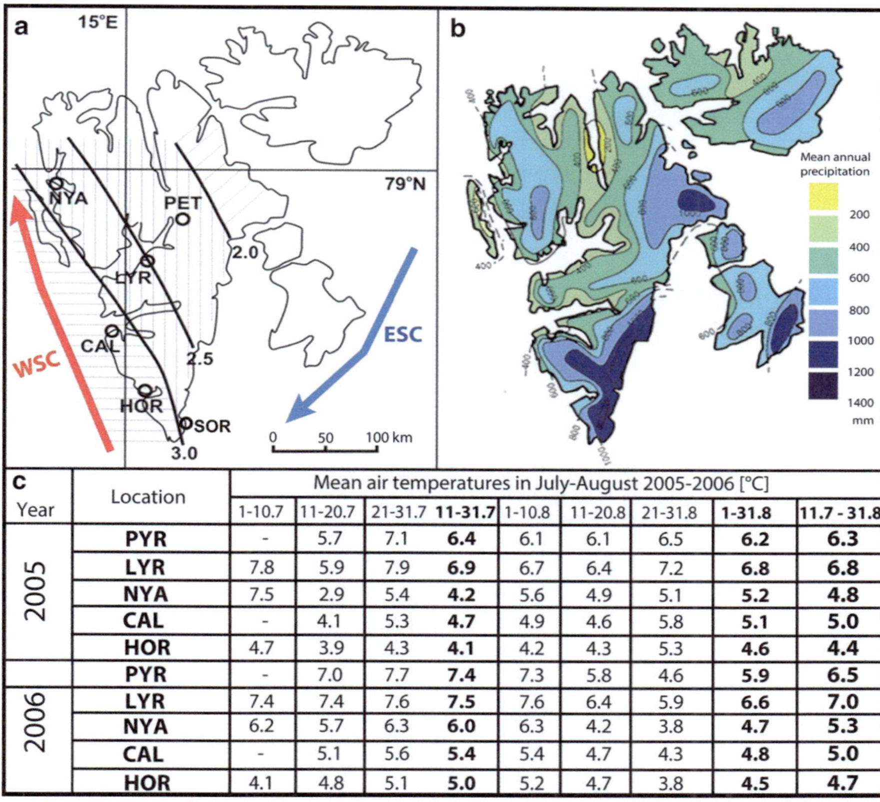

c

Year	Location	Mean air temperatures in July-August 2005-2006 [°C]								
		1-10.7	11-20.7	21-31.7	**11-31.7**	1-10.8	11-20.8	21-31.8	**1-31.8**	**11.7 - 31.8**
2005	**PYR**	-	5.7	7.1	**6.4**	6.1	6.1	6.5	**6.2**	**6.3**
	LYR	7.8	5.9	7.9	**6.9**	6.7	6.4	7.2	**6.8**	**6.8**
	NYA	7.5	2.9	5.4	**4.2**	5.6	4.9	5.1	**5.2**	**4.8**
	CAL	-	4.1	5.3	**4.7**	4.9	4.6	5.8	**5.1**	**5.0**
	HOR	4.7	3.9	4.3	**4.1**	4.2	4.3	5.3	**4.6**	**4.4**
2006	**PYR**	-	7.0	7.7	**7.4**	7.3	5.8	4.6	**5.9**	**6.5**
	LYR	7.4	7.4	7.6	**7.5**	7.6	6.4	5.9	**6.6**	**7.0**
	NYA	6.2	5.7	6.3	**6.0**	6.3	4.2	3.8	**4.7**	**5.3**
	CAL	-	5.1	5.6	**5.4**	5.4	4.7	4.3	**4.8**	**5.0**
	HOR	4.1	4.8	5.1	**5.0**	5.2	4.7	3.8	**4.5**	**4.7**

Fig. 2.2 (**a**) Variability of climatic conditions on Spitsbergen after Rachlewicz (2009) based on Marsz (1995) oceanity index distribution: *horizontal lines – oceanic conditions, vertical lines – sub-oceanic conditions, oblique lines – continental conditions. WSC* warm West Spitsbergen Current, *ESC* cold East Spitsbergen Current. *Circles* indicates the location of former coastal studies on Spitsbergen discussed in this study: *PET* Petuniabukta, Billefjorden (this study), *LYR* Longyearbyen, Adventfjorden, *NYA* Ny Ålesund, Kongsfjorden, *CAL* Calypsostranda, Bellsund, *HOR* Hornsund, *SOR* Sørkappland, open coast of Barents Sea; (**b**) Mean annual precipitation [mm] on Svalbard based on Hagen et al. 1993; (**c**) 10-day mean air temperatures between July–August 2005–2006 in PET, LYR, NYA, and CAL sites

exposed to storm waves developed on Greenland and Barents Seas (e.g. Moign and Héquette 1985; Héquette and Ruz 1986; Héquette 1992; Marsz 1996; Mercier and Laffly 2005; Ziaja et al. 2009; Ziaja 2012; Zagórski et al. 2012a, b). On the contrary, the coastal behaviour in inner fjord environments of Spitsbergen, characterised by sheltered location, prolonged sea-ice conditions, low tidal range and ephemeral pulses of sediment delivery from landforms developing in semi-arid, polar desert climate is largely unexplored. Only recently, Lønne and Nemec (2004) have provided a new insight into the nature of High Arctic coastal sedimentation by studying Holocene evolution of a fan delta in Adventfjorden, Sessford (2013) has reported on the rates of coastal erosion in southern Sassenfjorden and Strzelecki (2011) has characterised the degree of surface weathering of rocky coasts using Schmidt hammer rock tests in northern Billefjorden.

Present study aims to address this deficiency in understanding of High Arctic coastal systems by describing coastal evolution in central Spitsbergen focusing on the last two decades of intensified climate warming and associated increased rate of deglaciation. The geographical focus is Petuniabukta (Fig. 2.2), one of the most protected bays of Spitsbergen constituting the exact opposite of storm wave coastal environments of W and S Spitsbergen.

2.2 Regional Setting

Petuniabukta (78°42′ N; 16°36′ E) is a small, sheltered, microtidal bay located in the northern Billefjorden (Fig. 2.3). The mosaic of Precambrian, Devonian and Carboniferous-Permian outcrops disturbed in Billefjorden Fault Zone (BFZ) makes the geology of study area one of the most diverse in Svalbard (Dallmann et al. 2004). This region lies in the zone of semi-arid polar climate, with a mean annual air temperature of −6.5 °C, annual precipitation usually lower than 200 mm and prolonged sea-ice conditions limiting operation of waves to summer months (June–September) (Rachlewicz 2009).

The seasonal thawing of active layer ranges in study area between 0.5 and 2.5 m (Gibas et al. 2005). The present spring tidal range in Petuniabukta is *ca.* 1.5 m, with the active storm ridge located *ca.* 0.25–0.75 m above mean tide level. The longest wave fetch potential is from the south, showing strong relation with the prevailing winds entering central Spitsbergen from the S-SSE (along the axis of Billefjorden). The local wave conditions are influenced also by N and NE katabatic winds descending from major glacier valleys of Hørbyebreen, Ragnarbreen, Ebbabreen and Nordenskiöldbreen (Fig. 2.3).

The coastal landscape in Petuniabukta region is rich in cold region littoral landforms created by the interplay of glacial heritage (source of coarse clastic sediments), glacioisostasy (control of access to sediment sources and formation

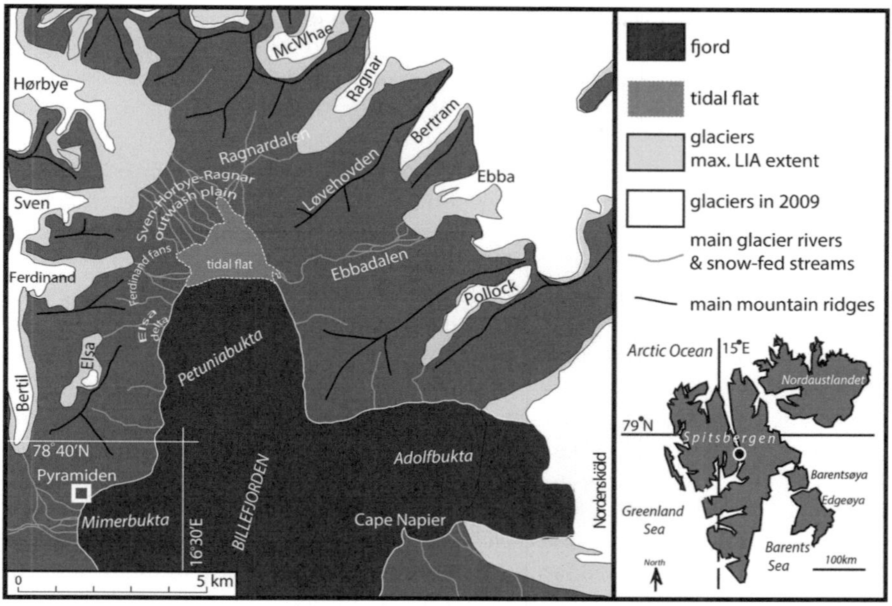

Fig. 2.3 Location of study area, Petuniabukta, Billefjorden. The present-day and LIA extent of glaciers modified after Rachlewicz et al. (2007) and Małecki (2013)

of uplifted/submerged forms) and climate-driven processes (including sea-ice, nival, permafrost and periglacial action).

Due to the common presence of sharp break in beach slope separating sand from gravel parts the modern barrier can be describe as composite gravel beach type *sensu* Jennings and Schulmeister (2002). Active layer thickness in the upper part of the barrier exceeds 1.5 m what allows highest tides to seepage through barrier and flood lagoons and depressions in the back of barrier. In the last decade a gravel-dominated barrier has blocked majority of small snow-fed stream outlets in the surroundings of Petuniabukta what led to the characteristic accumulations of fine sediments (muddy and sandy) in the back of the barrier. Occasional breaching of barriers during summer high discharges related to intensified snow-melting and rainfalls leads to delivery of fine material to the coast and progradation of micro-deltas. We have also noticed the importance of seaweed and driftwood accumulations for reinforcement of barrier structure making them abnormally resilient even for the highest waves in the summer season.

Observations of barrier microrelief over the last decade indicated that regardless the prolonged sea-ice conditions the effects of sea-ice erosion, deposition and melting on the beach are ephemeral and destroyed in the first few days of open water conditions each year. The characteristic for Arctic beaches pitted morphology including kettle-like hollows, kaimoo and ice-push ridges were found in the upper parts of gravel-dominated barriers only in two sites along eastern and western coast, suggesting the decaying role of sea-ice in shaping the shoreface that occurred in recent decades.

Currently, the sculpting of the surrounding landscape is dominated by the reworking of glacial and periglacial landforms left after the last Pleistocene glaciation and LIA glacier advances by paraglacial slope, aeolian, fluvial and coastal processes (Rachlewicz 2010; Szpikowski et al. 2014). Previous studies on the ice-masses in the surroundings of Petuniabukta emphasised the huge variety in terms of size, elevation, thermal state, the geomorphology of marginal zones and retreat rates of local glaciers (Rachlewicz et al. 2007; Rachlewicz 2009; Małecki 2013). According to Rachlewicz et al. (2007) since the termination of LIA all glaciers in the northern Billefjorden experienced rapid retreat exposing ca. 25 km^2 of new areas (Fig. 2.3). Their study indicated that the glacier recession for LIA-2002 period reached up to 5–15 m $year^{-1}$ for land-terminating glaciers and 35 m $year^{-1}$ for the marine-terminating Nordenskiöldbreen. They have also stated that such retreat rates are within typical range for retreat rates in the other parts of Spitsbergen, excluding large fast flowing glaciers, not present in the study area. In general the post-Little Ice Age recession of local glaciers is controlled by the air temperature warming, although several factors modify the rate of change including: the occurrence of glacier surge (faster retreat than non-surging), the elevation of glacier accumulation zone, the aspect of glacier, the shape of glacier margin and the bedrock relief which have the reducing effect on the ice flow speed (Małecki 2013; Małecki et al. 2013).

According to Long et al. (2012) the RSL in study area was about 40–45 m asl ca. 10,000 cal. year BP and fell to within a meter of present sea-level by c. 3,100 cal. year BP. Later the RSL probably fell below present and rose again in the last few millennia. The effect of land uplift related to the post-Little Ice Age deglaciation on RSL fluctuations is not yet determined although continuing accretion of barrier-platform in the mouth of Ebba River or uninterrupted development of beach-ridges on Cape Napier in the neighbouring Adolfbukta observed throughout the twentieth century suggest the counterbalancing of sea transgression by land rebound.

The twentieth century glacier retreat has exposed valley systems filled with fresh, unstable glacigenic sediments which are easily reworked by proglacial meltwater streams and modified by paraglacial slope processes (slumping, gullying and debris flows). This paraglacial sediment cascade is additionally reinforced by melting of ice-cores in glacial landforms (controlled ridges, eskers, lateral moraines) that maintain high rates of sediment flux to the tidal flat and fjord system. A recent study of sediment accumulation rates in Billefjorden (Szczuciński et al. 2009) suggests that the post-LIA transfer of sediment released from decaying glaciers to the bay is almost four times higher than during the LIA and the rest of Holocene.

Fig. 2.4 Main features of the glacial and coastal landscape in N Petuniabukta investigated in this case study. *1* – alluvial fans fed by Ferdinandelva; *2* – Svenbreen outwash plain; *3* – Hørbyebreen outwash plain; *4* – Ragnarbreen outwash plain

Taking into the consideration the post-LIA rates of ice-mass loss, the geomorphology of exposed forelands and the diversity of coastal landforms – one of the most intriguing zones for investigations of the *'glacier retreat – coastal zone response'* is a system of prograding tidal flat merging with an extensive outwash plain accumulated by rivers of Svenbreen, Hørbyebreen and Ragnarbreen in N Petuniabukta (Fig. 2.4).

This paper will now explore the main patterns of proglacial and coastal landscape changes that occurred in N Petuniabukta the last two decades (1990–2009) – the warmest period on Svalbard since the termination of the Little Ice Age (Nordli et al. 2014).

2.3 Methods

In order to describe and quantify recent coastal zone changes in N Petuniabukta we applied geomorphological field observations, differential GPS (DGPS) surveying, aerial photogrammetric analysis and digital elevation modelling (DEM) in geographic information systems (GIS).

In years 2008–2010 geomorphological mapping was carried out during each summer season. This was combined with field sketches and interpretation from aerial photos and old maps (ground truthed in the field) to produce the final geomorphological maps. For the purpose of this study we collected and analysed the following maps of the central Spitsbergen region:

- Karczewski et al. (1990) geomorphological map of Petuniabukta region, 1: 40,000;
- Dallmann et al. 2004 Geological map of Billefjorden, 1: 50,000;

Field verification of images was accompanied with DGPS surveying. In 2008 and 2009 Leica A500 system was used to carry out barrier profiling and coastal landform mapping which was replaced by Leica 1200 system in summer 2010. DGPS receivers provided horizontal and vertical accuracy of 0.02 m. All surveys were tied back to a benchmark established during the 2008 expedition, so their elevation indicates height above mean tide level in meters.

DGPS was used to precisely measure the altitude of stable surfaces on bedrock or large boulders for orthorectification of images and DTM (Digital Terrain Model) production. Over 50 points from stable surfaces were complemented by DGPS measurements of several reference markers (2×3 m white geofiber rectangles) placed in advance of the Norwegian Polar Institute aerial photography flights carried out in summer 2009 as part of this research project. Rectangles were placed on stable natural points for ground control such as rocky outcrops and boulders to improve the precision of the constructed orthophotos and DTMs.

A selection of sites in N Petuniabukta including tidal flat, coastal barriers, alluvial fans and proglacial landforms was investigated for patterns of multidecadal change using information from aerial imaginary spanning the period 1990–2009 taken by Norwegian Polar Institute and old maps.

The following aerial images have been used in the study:

- fifteen 1990 NPI aerial images lines: S90 1706-1711; S90 1760-61; S90 1796-1807
- twenty-eight digital 2009 NPI aerial lines: s2009_13822_00001-00008; 00027-00034; s2009_13833_00477-00485;00491-493

The 2009 aerial photographs were also used to produce a set of DTMs which serve as a basis for morphometric analysis of landscape changes in the N Petuniabukta. A ground-truthing was carried out on the majority of sites using DGPS surveys, ground (oblique) photography and surface sediment sampling of selected landforms.

Delimitation of shorelines position was estimated using the middle of the first, fully emerged storm ridge visible on the image to minimise the error stemming from different phases of tidal cycle captured on individual photographs. In general, shoreline changes smaller than 2.5 m were not considered in interpretation of results. This is because it was impossible to distinguish if the emerging forms comprised ephemeral gravel berms or storm ridges.

The error cited was also based on the observations of the present-day shoreface where the distance between these shoreline elements is ca. 2 m.

DTMs based on 2009 images were automatically produced in ERDAS Leica Photogrammetry Suite 2010 (LPS). Software employs the bundle block adjustment, using least squares estimation, to establish the relationship between the positions of a set of photographs and a ground coordinate system, based on the interior and exterior parameters input into the software and the location of ground control points. As aerial images from summer 2009 (27 July and 11 August) were taken by NPI with an UltraCam Xp Large Format Digital Aerial Camera manufactured by Vexcel the interior parameters were already inserted in image files so only exterior parameters had to be manually entered into the software. Each set of photographs was then processed as for a digital camera. The projection used was UTM, with the spheroid WGS 84 for zone 33 N. The selection of strategy parameters was based on a visual inspection of DTMs and orthophotos output using different strategy parameters.

For each 2009 image used for DTM creation at least five ground control points were collected using DGPS. Set of DTMs were generated from the 2009 images with ground resolutions ranging from 1 to 20 m. DTM of 20 m resolution covered the whole study area and was suitable for comparison with the DTM produced by NPI from the set of 1990 images obtained for this project.

Differencing of the 2009 and 1990 DTMs was done for the N part of Petuniabukta. The difference was calculated by subtracting two DTMs in ArcGIS software. Estimation of surface elevation changes is an extremely useful method for landscape evolution studies and allows identification of zones of surface erosion and surface aggradation. In high latitudes this technique has been commonly applied to measure surface elevation changes of glaciers (e.g. Wangensteen et al. 2006; Muskett et al. 2009; Barrand et al. 2010) and proglacial landforms (e.g. Schomacker and Kjær 2008; Irvine-Fynn et al. 2011; Bennett and Evans 2012). In this study the subtracting of DTMs was carried out to investigate surface elevation change in the proglacial zone of Ferdinandbreen, Svenbreen and Hørbyebreen and to estimate the amount of sediment removed by paraglacial processes (fluvial, slope, aeolian activity) towards the coastal zone.

2.4 Results

Previous studies on recent Svalbard coastal zone changes have focused on the rate of shoreline progradation and erosion (Mercier and Laffly 2005; Ziaja et al. 2011; Zagórski 2011; Zagórski et al. 2012a, b). In this study we sought to estimate the vertical relief changes associated with sediment erosion and deposition over last two decades. To do this we used the 20 m resolution DTM of 2009 and 20 m resolution DTM of 1990 from the Norwegian Polar Institute to calculate the vertical surface change by subtracting the 1990 model from the 2009 model in ArcGIS software (Fig. 2.5).

To calculate data on surface elevation changes between the proglacial and the coastal zone of N Petuniabukta the following steps were made in the analysis:

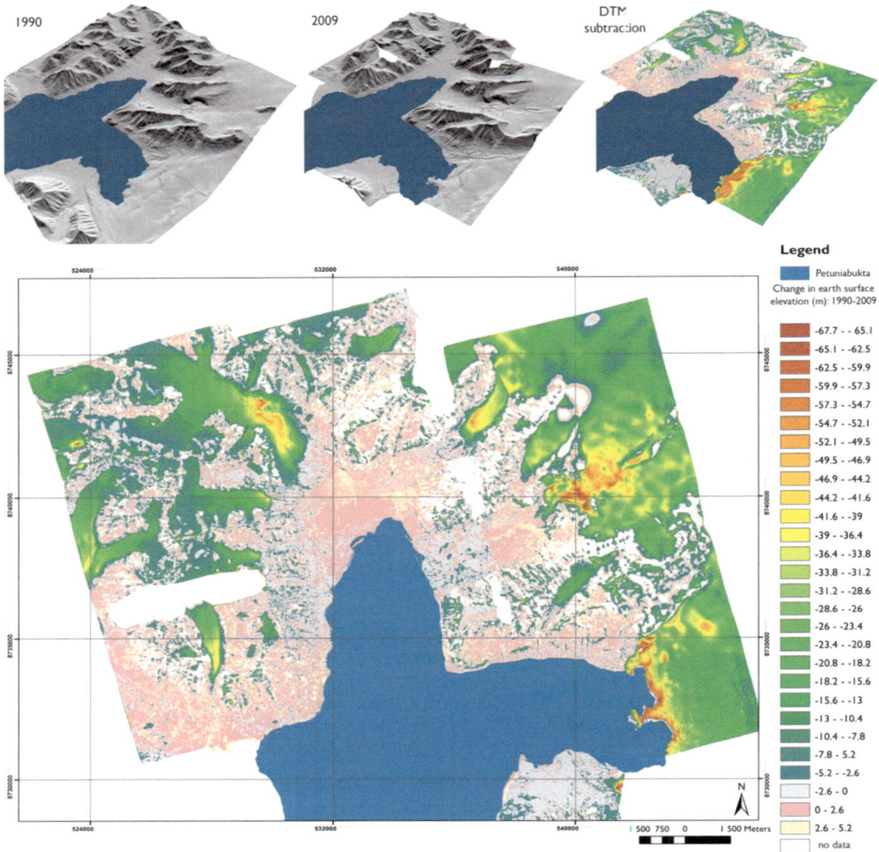

Fig. 2.5 DTM differencing of 1990 and 2009 models. The map summarises surface elevation changes (m) that occurred between 1990 and 2009 in Petuniabukta region

(a) Having two DTMs from 1990 to 2009 it was possible to study surface elevation changes only for a short phase of post-LIA period (19 years). This period was characterised by a rapid increase in retreat rates of all Petuniabukta glaciers apart from Ferdinandbreen and Svenbreen (Rachlewicz et al. 2007; Małecki 2009). We hypothesised that such conditions significantly increased sediment availability and the efficiency of sediment release and transport processes from deglacierised areas towards the coastal zone.

(b) Between 1990 and 2009, recession of Petuniabukta glaciers exposed *ca.* 5 km^2 of area covered by fresh and unconsolidated material which was easy to transport and further modify by paraglacial processes dominated by fluvial, mass-wasting and wind action.

(c) Amongst the glaciers supplying sediments to the N coast of Petuniabukta the largest area was exposed in front of Hørbyebreen (*ca.* 2.5 km^2). Small valley glaciers along western coast exposed in total *ca.* 0.66 km^2: Elsabreen (*ca.* 0.28 km^2), Svenbreen (*ca.* 0.22 km^2) and Ferdinandbreen (*ca.* 0.16 km^2). Ragnarbreen supplies sediments to the tidal flat via an outwash plain that is linked with the Hørbyebreen outwash plain, exposed *ca.* 0.6 km^2 of new area. The role of Ragnarbreen in sediment delivery to the coast is limited by a proglacial lake that acts as a sediment trap for sediments released from the glacier and ice-marginal zone (Ewertowski et al. 2012; Ewertowski 2014).

(d) The retreat of small glaciers (Elsabreen, Ferdinandbreen, and Svenbreen) led to the elongation of their rivers (815 m, 105 m, 95 m respectively). Since 1990, these glaciers were already hidden deep in their valleys (Elsabreen, Ferdinandbreen) and behind a bedrock sill (Svenbreen) that significantly focused sediment transfer from freshly exposed proglacial areas towards the coast.

(e) To check the vertical accuracy of surface elevation change, a vertical elevation error resulting from a potential mismatch of models during the overlying process was estimated. To do so 54,000 points lying along the contour lines on the 1990 DTM were selected from stable surfaces i.e. rocky outcrops, edges of rockwalls, coastal lowlands with bedrock outcrops avoiding unstable glacial and glaciofluvial landforms. Points were then re-measured on the 2009 DTM and the resulting elevation difference was plotted with height above sea-level and slope inclination ascribed to each point. Error analysis showed that the DTMs were matched closely and that the calculated surface elevation differences were not related to slope inclination or height a.s.l with both values close to 0 m. To estimate the vertical error range between models the root mean squared error (RMSE) was calculated. As the RMSE increases exponentially with the slope inclination it was assumed that detailed calculations of sediment volume change should be limited only to low-inclined areas distant from steep-sided mountain slopes.

(f) The largest surface lowering, excluding that resulting from ice thickness changes of retreating glaciers fronts (over 60 m $\pm$ 1.6 m), occurs in the ice-marginal zones of glaciers: up to 50 m $\pm$ 8 m (Hørbyebreen); up to 39 m $\pm$ 10.2 m (Svenbreen); up to 35 m $\pm$ 4.7 m (Ferdinandbreen), up to 24 m $\pm$ 2.8 m (Elsabreen) and up to 55 m $\pm$ 3.9 m (Ragnarbreen). Such large decreases of surface elevation cannot be associated solely with sediment erosion and redistribution and likely records decay of dead-ice in ice-cored landforms. Dead-ice melting is a characteristic process controlling surface lowering over ice-cored landforms (moraines, eskers, kames) in ice-marginal and proglacial areas (Schomacker 2008). It was assumed that the mean annual downwasting rate of ice-cored areas is *ca.* 0.9 m following the measurements made by Schomacker and Kjær (2008), across the ice-marginal zone of Holmströmbreen which is a glacier located in central Spitsbergen that supplies an extensive outwash plain that merges into the muddy tidal flat of Ekmanfjorden. We treated surface elevation change values observed in these areas as a sum of dead-ice melting and sediment removal. Using Schomacker and Kjær (2008) calculations, the estimated surface lowering related to decay of dead-ice is *ca.* 17 m over the 19 years of analysis. In support of this assumption are slower lowering rates observed over the Hørbyebreen frontal moraine, which according to a DC resistivity survey by Gibas et al. (2005) is devoid of ice, compared with faster lowering of the frontal moraine of Ebbabreen, which is ice-cored. Thus, the maximum surface lowering of moraines in front of Ebbabreen was *ca.* 28 m $\pm$ 5.4 m, whereas remnants of Hørbyebreen frontal moraine lowered up to 13 m $\pm$ 3.9 m.

(g) Finally, it was assumed that the ice-marginal and proglacial zones acts as the largest sediment supplier to the N coast of Petuniabukta, and the sediment removal from these environments is recorded in accumulation of material on alluvial fans, outwash plains and tidal flat system.

Taking into consideration the input assumptions described above, an attempt was made to calculate the volume of sediments accumulated and eroded in 19 years over the outwash plains and fans formed by Hørbyebreen, Ragnarbreen, Svenbreen, Ferdinandbreen and Elsabreen (Table 2.1). This shows that the alluvial fans and outwash plains of N Petuniabukta act as an effective trap for sediment released from decaying ice-marginal and proglacial landforms. During the analysed 19 years the majority of landforms gained more sediment than they lost due to erosion.

Erosion dominated the sediment budgets of only two landforms – the outwash plain of Svenbreen and the fan formed by Elsaelva. In the case of the former, this may be related to the presence of dead-ice in remnants of the frontal moraine and eskers eroded by Svenelva. Melting of dead-ice may have caused the loss of up to 603,309 m^3 of landform volume that would significantly reduce the amount of eroded sediments (to *ca.* 544,777 m^3). Regarding the latter, this relates mainly to the remnants of old features (relict fans, uplifted beaches) that form islands dividing braided streams of the glacier river. It is important to note that the area of Elsaelva fan and river channel has been commonly washed out and incised by snow-melt

Table 2.1 Volumes of sediments stored and eroded from selected landforms in N Petuniabukta between 1990 and 2009

Landform	Area [m^2]	Accumulation [m^3]	Erosion [m^3]	Net change [m^3]
Hørbyebreen outwash plain	3,824,847	6,133,192	−87,109	6,046,083
Ragnarbreen outwash plain	1,308,222	2,391,380	−352,242	2,039,138
Svenbreen outwash plain	917,943	423,800	−1,148,086	−724,286
Ferdinandbreen relict and modern fans	1,286,584	1,195,849	−517,270	678,579
Elsabreen fan and delta	132,464	21,450	−196,253	−174,803
Tidal flat	1,839,156	2,396,362	−112,061	2,284,301
Total:	9,309,216	12,562,033	−2,413,021	10,149,012

streams with reduced glaciofluvial sediment supply from the decaying Elsabreen (*ca.* 46 m year^{-1} of glacier front retreat over 1990–2009 period) and this explains the process of sediment loss quite well. It was also observed in years 2005–2010 that fragments of uplifted beaches located in the Elsaelva fan delta area were subject to wave erosion.

Between 1990 and 2009 the modern and relict alluvial fans supplied from Ferdinandbreen were the biggest sediment storage systems along the western coast of Petuniabukta. Interestingly, sediment accumulation dominated the areas abandoned by Ferdinandelva channels (Ferdinand fans) suggesting a significant role of sediment influx from snow-melt streams, slope movements (solifluction) or aeolian deposition. Conversely, in those parts of fans where the modern Ferdinandelva was active, erosion was dominant. According to the DTMs subtraction a relatively strong surface lowering occurred over small snow-fed fans that accumulated between the relict lagoon and the prograding alluvial fan. The erosion of the barrier and opening of outlets linking the lagoon with Petuniabukta that occurred between 1990 and 2009 may have led to increased erosion from fan aprons and the back of the barrier, but it is also probable that the results are biased by the presence of a steep rockwall that may have distorted the elevation change calculations processed in ArcGIS.

Certainly the largest sediment storage system in the analysed area was the outwash plain of Hørbyebreen in which over 60 % of sediments accumulated in the studied landforms between 1990 and 2009. Sediment loss was observed only along the sandur margins which border on remnants of the ice-cored western lateral moraine of Hørbyebreen and a retreating cliff formed in uplifted marine sediments (NW margin), the eroding slopes of the Hørbyebreen LIA frontal moraine (N margin) and the eroding slopes of old rock glacierised moraine of Late Weichselian age (NE margin).

The second largest sediment storage was found in the Ragnarelva outwash plain and alluvial fans formed on southern slopes of Ragnardalen that supplies sediments to outwash plain and directly to tidal flat during snow-melt flood events.

Since the formation of a proglacial lake in the late 1980s, the sediment supply from Ragnarbeen ice-marginal had been significantly reduced. The surface analysis changes suggest that the major source of sediments accumulated in outwash plain comes from three sources: erosion and redistribution of sediments accumulated in the Ragnarbeen LIA frontal moraine, lateral erosion of river banks in the central sector of Ragnardalen and incision of river channel close to the proximal sector of Ragnar outwash plain (Ewertowski 2014).

One of the largest surface changes in the entire area occurred over fans that accumulated on slopes of Løvehovden in Ragnardalen. During the 19 years these gained *ca.* 2,400,000 m^3 of sediments derived mainly from ephemeral snow-fed streams, debris flows, slush avalanches and solifluction.

The final feature selected for sediment volume change analysis was the tidal flat system. The lower part of tidal flat was fully flooded in 1990 and it was partly flooded in 2009, so it was assumed that the elevation difference over this area was unsuitable for further calculations. Therefore, only that sector of the tidal flat adjacent to the Hørbyebreen outwash plain to the north, and limited to the southern extent of main tidal islands to the south, was considered in calculations.

Interestingly, the amount of sediments stored in the upper part of tidal flat (2,396,362 m^3) was about the same as the total amount of sediments eroded from the rest of analysed landforms (2,413,021 m^3). This shows that the tidal flat is a very effective sediment trap for sediments eroded from outwash plains and fans. The further progradation of the tidal flat is expected to facilitate the development of the barrier coast in N Petuniabukta by providing the stable submarine platform for future spits and barriers supplied by proglacial rivers and snow-fed streams.

2.5 Discussion

The post-LIA retreat of glaciers has arguably triggered the most dramatic change of Svalbard landscape since deglaciation at the start of the Holocene. Retreating glaciers have exposed vast areas of fresh glacigenic sediments that were easily released, eroded, transported and redistributed by an array of processes: dead-ice melting (e.g. Schomacker and Kjær 2008), meltwater streams (e.g. Etzelmüller et al. 2000), jökulhlaups (e.g. Etienne et al. 2008), slope processes (e.g. Mercier et al. 2009), wind action (e.g. Rachlewicz 2010) and finally coastal processes (e.g. Mercier and Laffly 2005). Intensified operation of those processes was strengthened by warming of the climate that thawed permafrost and destabilised unlithified river banks or fjord shores because of thinner ice cover and/or weaker thermal insulation of slopes and rockwalls by reduced snow cover. The response of the Svalbard coastal zone to the post-LIA paraglaciation, which in theory constitutes 'the ultimate sink' (Ballantyne 2002) for paraglacially eroded, reworked and transported sediments before they are moved further offshore, has been observed in several sites along W and S Spitsbergen. Previous studies have linked coastal progradation and rapid development of depositional landforms with uninterrupted periods of sediment supply from glacial rivers (Héquette 1992; Mercier and Laffly 2005), episodes of dramatic coastal erosion in areas no longer covered or protected by glacier ice (Ziaja et al. 2009), and coastal reworking of glacigenic landforms (mainly frontal moraines, margins of outwash plains and smaller proglacial features) exposed after the retreat of glaciers (Zagórski et al. 2012a, b).

It is important to note that despite the enhanced post-LIA sediment supply to the coastal zone in all previously investigated sites (Sørkappland – Ziaja et al. 2009, 2011; Hornsund – Zagórski et al. 2012b; Bellsund – Zagórski 2011), except for the section of Kongsfjorden coast described by Mercier and Laffly (2005), the observed rates of coastal erosion exceeded the rates of coastal progradation. These observations contradict the picture of Svalbard coastal zone as classified on the most recent map of Arctic coast erosion rates as being a 'stable' or 'aggrading' coastline (Lantuit et al. 2012).

The dominance of erosion along those mostly open-type coasts in W and S Spitsbergen can be explained by: the prolongation of exposure of coasts to the operation of waves and more frequent storms caused by the earlier disappearance and later formation of sea-ice and ice-foot; the increased influx of warmer Atlantic waters that weaken sea-ice cover and disturb the thermal state of coastal permafrost; the thickening of the active layer in coastal areas that leads to the destabilization of coastal sediments and increases their permeability by both groundwater and seepage of seawater, and; the rutting of the coastal sediments by heavy machines in the vicinity of research stations (e.g. the Polish Polar Station in Hornsund or bases in Ny-Ålesund).

The general image of the post-LIA paraglacial coasts in Svalbard that can be determined from previous studies suggests very responsive and unstable systems that rapidly react to changes in sediment supply delivered from retreating glaciers and climate-driven forcings of coastal erosion (retreat of tide-water glaciers, prolongation of open water conditions and influx of warmer waters).

The results of the research presented in this paper confirm an increase in the post-LIA sediment delivery to the coastal zone, but have also shown that the link between coastal evolution and glacier retreat and sediment supply change seen along the W and S coasts of Spitsbergen has been less dramatic in the protected, inner-fjord environment of Petuniabukta.

Geomorphological evidence and information derived from aerial imagery indicate that the recent development of the coasts of N Petuniabukta is strongly influenced by local factors that include local climate, basement topography and inherited landscape, wave climate and surface circulation pattern, and to some extent the pattern of relative sea-level change.

Since summer periods in Petuniabukta are warmer and drier than along W and S coasts of Spitsbergen (see climate conditons on Fig. 2.2), retreat of glaciers drives them high into their valleys. This, in turn, increases the distance between glacier snouts and the coastal zone. On average glacier rivers draining to the N Petuniabukta have to overcome almost twice the distance to the coast compared with rivers transporting sediments from comparable proglacial zones of W and S Spitsbergen (e.g. Bayelva, Scottelva, Werenskioldelva). This decreases the stream power, reduces sediment transport and increases the sediment load loss in intermediate sinks such as river banks, river bars, floodplains or proglacial lakes. Therefore, even though glacier retreat rates in Petuniabukta are similar with those observed in the other parts of Spitsbergen (Rachlewicz et al. 2007; Małecki 2013) coastal responses are less dramatic than in W and S Spitsbergen.

In W and S Spitsbergen it is common to observe erosional and depositional shorelines that are distributed in time and space according to sediment supply and delivery rates or the appearance of protective sea-ice before the arrival of storms (e.g. Calypsostranda responding to pulses of sediment supply from Scottbreen and Renardbreen as described by Zagórski (2011)).

In N Petuniabukta, coastal erosion in the last two decades was limited to a short (300–350 m) section of coastline located between the Elsaelva delta and the

Ferdinand fans (Fig. 2.3). This occurred despite continuous sediment delivery to the coast by the Elsaelva and Ferdinandelva and continued severe sea-ice conditions throughout the last century. It is difficult to explain this section of erosion coast, although it is possible that the coastline orientation with reference to the prevailing winds and surface water circulation directions in the fjord has been influential.

Sea ice is another important factor in controlling coastal change. The western and southern coasts of Spitsbergen are generally ice-free for longer periods and exposed to storms originating far away in the Barents and Greenland Seas that define local wind directions and shape coastal geomorphology. In contrast to Petuniabukta, coastal development at a site like Hornsund (SW Spitsbergen) is strongly influenced by the rapid decay of tide-water glaciers and an associated influx of warm Atlantic waters delivered by West Spitsbergen Current. Due to the post-LIA retreat of glaciers the fjord areas here have increased by over 172 km^2 (Błaszczyk et al. 2013). The post-LIA ice decay not only lengthened Hornsund shorelines, but also increased the exchange of waters between the fjord and open sea, leading to the acceleration of tidal currents velocity that might have intensified the coastal erosion (Piotr Głowacki pers. comm.).

Another important difference between N Petuniabukta coast and coasts from W and S Spitsbergen is the lack of a direct connection between the coastal zone and glacial landforms (moraines, eskers, kames, crevasse fills etc.). The erosion of landforms left by retreating glaciers by waves and longshore currents constitutes an important source of coarse-clastic sediment delivery to Kongsfjorden, Bellsund, Hornsund and to the bays around Sørkappland. This mode of glacigenic sediment delivery make them similar to mid-latitude paraglacial coasts supplied with sediment from erosion of drumlins and other landforms left along the coast by last ice sheets (e.g. the paraglacial coasts of Ireland and Nova Scotia (Taylor et al. 1986; Shaw et al. 1990; Orford et al. 1991)). Evolution of this type of paraglacial coastal systems is characterised by episodes of rapid reorganization associated with gaining access to and reworking of glacigenic landforms. According to Forbes et al. (1995) the lifespan of paraglacial coast is dependent on the volume and endurance of the (glacial) sediment source, so that often the phase of intensified growth and migration of paraglacial barriers is abruptly terminated by the exhaustion of sediments supply that occurs when a glacigenic landform is fully eroded.

The relatively dry and warm climate of the study area (compared with the W Spitsbergen coast) limits the growth of local glaciers to high elevations. This meant that the post-LIA sediment supply to the N Petuniabukta coast was more distant to that in W Spitsbergen. Therefore it can be assumed that the shorelines here experienced the decaying phase of paraglacial sedimentation associated with reworking of former glacigenic sediments already transported and modified by non-glacial fluvial, slope and aeolian processes.

This situation resembles the fourth stage of fjord evolution model proposed by Syvitski and Shaw (1995) who determined the following steps of fjord infilling: Stage One – the complete coverage of fjord by glacier ice; Stage Two – the ice-contact sedimentation associated with retreating tide-water glacier; Stage Three – distal proglacial sedimentation after transformation of the glacier into a land-based type; Stage Four – paraglacial sedimentation associated with the reworking of glacigenic deposits left by a retreating and later a fully disappearing glacier; and Stage Five – complete infilling of the fjord basin. As noted by Ballantyne (2002) such a sequence of events can be disturbed, stopped or reversed by a shift of climate conditions, and can be either slowed down or accelerated by sea-level change.

2.6 Conclusions

This paper provides a new insight into the functioning of High Arctic paraglacial coastal environments developing in sheltered fjord settings and supplied by sediments derived from glacial (glacierised catchments) and non-glacial (snow-fed streams and talus slopes) sources. In such low energy environments one might expect the limited modification of coastal landforms. However, information from aerial photogrammetric analyses and geomorphological mapping shows that Petuniabukta coastal zone quickly adjusts to climatic and geomorphic changes.

The formation of new coast landforms here is to a large degree dependent of the rate of sediment excavation from relict sediment storage systems, such as alluvial fans and outwash plains that developed across a wide coast plain between the glacier valleys and the fjord. Majority of the sediments eroded between 1990 and 2009 from outwash plains and alluvial fans has been stored in a prograding tidal flat system. Progradation of tidal flat over the study period provided the depositional platform on which new coastal features have developed.

Rates of coastal evolution, over the analysed period, in these contexts are comparable to those seen along the W and S coasts of Spitsbergen.

Our work highlights the need for a greater understanding of the controls on High Arctic coastal sediment budgets, especially given the potential for accelerated warming and sea-level rise in the coming decades and centuries.

Acknowledgements This paper is a contribution to the National Science Centre project '*Model of the interaction of paraglacial and periglacial processes in the coastal zone and their influence on the development of Arctic littoral relief*' (award no. 2013/08/S/ST10/00585).

David Milledge from the Durham University helped in photogrammetric analysis of aerial images provided by Harald Aas from the Norwegian Polar Institute.

Matt Strzelecki is supported by the National Science Centre Postdoctoral Fellowship, Research Council of Norway Yggdrasil fellowship and Foundation for Polish Science HOMING PLUS grant no. 2013-8/12.

Review by Denis Mercier and his valuable comments on this manuscript are highly appreciated.

References

Åkerman J (1984) Notes on talus morphology and processes in Spitsbergen. Geogr Ann 66A:267–284
André M-F (1990) Frequency of debris flows and slush avalanches in Spitsbergen: a tentative evaluation from lichenometry. Pol Polar Res 11:345–363
Aré FE (1988) Thermal abrasion of sea coasts. Polar Geogr Geol 12:1–157
Aré FE, Reimnitz E, Grigoriev M, Hubberten H-W, Rachold V (2008) The influence of cryogenic processes on the erosional Arctic shoreface. J Coast Res 24:110–121
Ballantyne C (2002) Paraglacial geomorphology. Quat Sci Rev 21:1935–2017
Barrand NE, James TD, Murray T (2010) Spatio-temporal variability in elevation changes of two high-Arctic valley glaciers. J Glaciol 56:771–780
Bennett G, Evans DJA (2012) Glacier retreat and landform production on an overdeepened glacier foreland: the debris-charged glacial landsystem at Kvíárjökull Iceland. Earth Surf Process Landf 37:1584–1602
Błaszczyk M, Jania J, Kolondra L (2013) Fluctuations of tidewater glaciers in Hornsund Fjord (Southern Svalbard) since the beginning of the 20th century. Pol Polar Res 34:327–352
Byrne M-L, Dionne J-C (2002) Typical aspects of cold regions shorelines. In: Hewitt K, Byrne M-L, English M, Young G (eds) Landscapes in transition landform assembladges and transformations in cold regions. Kluwer Academic Publishers, Dordrecht, pp 141–158
Carter RWG, Forbes DL, Jennings SC, Orford JD, Shaw J, Taylor RB (1989) Barrier and lagoon coast evolution under differing sea-level regimes: examples from Ireland and Nova Scotia. Mar Geol 88:221–242
Dallmann WK, Pipejohn K, Blomeier D (2004) Geological map of Billefjorden Central Spitsbergen Svalbard with geological excursion guide 1:50 000. Norsk Polarinstitutt Tematkart No 36
Etienne S, Mercier D, Voldoire O (2008) Temporal scales and deglaciation rhythms in a polar glacier margin Baronbreen Svalbard. Nor J Geogr 62:102–114
Etzelmüller B, Ødegård RS, Vatne G, Mysterud RS, Tonning T, Sollid JL (2000) Glacier characteristics and sediment transfer system of Longyearbreen and Larsbreen western Spitsbergen. Nor J Geogr 54:157–168
Evans DJA, Strzelecki M, Milledge DG, Orton C (2012) Hørbyebreen polythermal glacial landsystem Svalbard. J Maps 8:1–11
Ewertowski M (2014) Recent transformations in the high-Arctic glacier landsystem, Ragnarbreen, Svalbard. Geogr Ann: Ser A Phys Geogr. doi:10.1111/geoa.12049
Ewertowski M, Kasprzak L, Szuman I, Tomczyk A (2012) Controlled ice-cored moraines: sediments and geomorphology an example from Ragnarbreen Svalbard. Zeitschrift für Geomorphologie 51:53–74
Forbes DL (ed) (2011) State of the Arctic Coast 2010 – Scientific Review and Outlook. International Arctic Science Committee Land-Ocean Interactions in the Coastal Zone Arctic Monitoring and Assessment Programme International Permafrost Association Helmholtz-Zentrum Geesthacht Germany, 178 pp. http://arcticcoasts.org
Forbes DL, Syvitski JPM (1994) Paraglacial coasts. In: Carter RWG, Woodroffe C (eds) Coastal evolution Late Quaternary shoreline morphodynamics. Cambridge University Press, Cambridge, pp 373–424
Forbes DL, Taylor RB (1987) Coarse-grained beach sedimentation under paraglacial conditions Canadian Atlantic Coast. In: Fitzgerald D, Rosen P (eds) Glaciated coasts. Academic, New York, pp 51–86
Forbes DL, Orford JD, Carter RWG, Shaw J, Jennings SC (1995) Morphodynamic evolution self-organisation and instability of coarse-clastic barriers on paraglacial coasts. Mar Geol 126:63–85

Gibas J, Rachlewicz G, Szczuciński W (2005) Application of DC resistivity soundings and geomorphological surveys in studies of modern Arctic glacier marginal zones Petuniabukta Spitsbergen. Pol Polar Res 26:239–258

Hagen JO, Liestøl O, Roland E, Jørgensen T (1993) Glacier Atlas of Svalbard and Jan Mayen, Meddelelser 129. Norsk Polarinstitutt, Oslo, 141 pp

Hein CJ, FitzGerald DM, Carruthers EA, Stone BD, Barnhardt WA, Gontz AM (2012) Refining the model of barrier island formation along a paraglacial coast in the Gulf of Maine. Mar Geol 307–310:40–57

Héquette A (1992) Morphosedimentological dynamics and coastal evolution in the Kongsfjorden area Spitsbergen. Polar Geogr Geol 16:321–329

Héquette A, Ruz M-H (1986) Migration of offshore bars by a process of overtopping by storms within the framework of a marine transgression (Kvadehuk Brøggerhalvøya Spitsbergen). Géographie physique et Quaternaire 40:197–206

Héquette A, Ruz M-H (1990) Coastal sedimentation along glacial outwash plain shorelines in northwest Spitsbergen. Géographie physique et Quaternaire 44:77–88

Irvine-Fynn TDL, Barrand NE, Porter PR, Hodson AJ, Murray T (2011) Recent High-Arctic proglacial sediment redistribution: a process perspective using airborne lidar. Geomorphology 125:27–39

Jahn A (1967) Some features of mass movement on Spitsbergen slopes. Geogr Ann 49A:213–225

Jennings R, Schulmeister J (2002) A field based classification scheme for gravel beaches. Mar Geol 186:211–228

Karczewski A, Borówka M, Gonera P, Kasprzak L, Kłysz P, Kostrzewski A, Lindner L, Marks L, Rygielski W, Stankowski W, Wojciechowski A, Wysokiński L (1990) Geomorphology – Petuniabukta Billefjorden Spitsbergen 1: 40 000. Adam Mickiewicz University Press, Poznań

Klemsdal T (1986) Lagoons along the coast of the Svalbard archipelago and the island of Jan Mayen. Nor J Geogr 40:37–44

Kowalska A, Sroka W (2008) Sedimentary environment of the Nottinghambukta delta SW Spitsbergen. Pol Polar Res 29:245–259

Lantuit H, Overduin P, Solomon S, Mercier D (2010) Coastline dynamics in polar systems using remote sensing. In: Maanan M, Robin M (eds) Geomatic solutions for coastal environments. Nova Science Publishers, New York, 163–174 pp

Lantuit H, Overduin PP, Couture N, Wetterich S, Are F, Atkinson D, Brown J, Cherkashov G, Drozdov D, Forbes D, Graves-Gaylord A, Grigoriev M, Hubberten HW, Jordan J, Jorgenson T, Ødegård RS, Ogorodov S, Pollard W, Rachold V, Sedenko S, Solomon S, Steenhuisen F, Streletskaya I, Vasiliev A (2012) The Arctic Coastal Dynamics database: a new classification scheme and statistics on Arctic permafrost coastlines. Estuar Coasts 35:383–400

Long AJ, Strzelecki MC, Lloyd JM, Bryant C (2012) Dating High Arctic Holocene relative sea level changes using juvenile articulated marine shells in raised beaches. Quat Sci Rev 48:61–66

Lønne I, Lyså A (2005) Deglaciation dynamics following the Little Ice Age on Svalbard: implications for shaping of landscapes at high latitudes. Geomorphology 72:300–319

Lønne I, Nemec W (2004) High-Arctic fan delta recording deglaciation and environment disequilibrium. Sedimentology 51:553–589

Lukas S, Nicholson LI, Ross FH, Humlum O (2005) Formation meltout processes and landscape alteration of high-Arctic ice-cored moraines—examples from Nordenskiold Land Central Spitsbergen. Polar Geogr 29:157–187

Lukyanova SA, Safyanov GA, Soloveva GD, Shipilova LM (2008) Types of Arctic coasts of Russia. Oceanology 48:268–274

Małecki J (2009) Changes in the extent and geometry of glaciers in Petuniabutka region (Dicksonland Spitsbergen) in 20th and 21st century. Unpublished M.Sc. thesis (in Polish), Faculty of Geographical and Geological Sciences Adam Mickiewicz University, Poznań, 149 pp

Małecki J (2013) Elevation and volume changes of seven Dickson Land glaciers Svalbard 1960–1990–2009. Polar Res 32:18400. http://dxdoi.org/103402/polarv32i018400

Małecki J, Faucherre S, Strzelecki MC (2013) Post-surge geometry evolution and thermal structure of Hørbyebreen central Spitsbergen Svalbard Archipelago. Pol Polar Res 34:305–321
Marsz A (1995) Wskaźnik oceanizmu jako miara klimatycznego współdziałania w systemie ocean-atmosfera-kontynenty. WSM Gdynia, 110 p
Marsz A (1996) Processes controlling shore morphology in recently developing fjords (based on examples from Hornsund and Admirality Bay). In: Proceedings of the department of Navigation Naval Academy in Gdynia, vol 3, pp 85–141
Mercier D (2000) Du glaciaire au paraglaciaire: la métamorphose des paysages polaires au Svalbard. Annales de Géographie 616:580–596
Mercier D (2008) Paraglacial and paraperiglacial landsystems: concepts, temporal scales and spatial distribution. Géomorphologie Relief Processus Environ 4:223–233
Mercier D, Laffly D (2005) Actual paraglacial progradation of the coastal zone in the Kongsfjorden area western Spitsbergen (Svalbard). In: Harris C, Murton JB (eds) Cryospheric systems: glaciers and permafrost. Geological Society London Special Publication 242, London, pp 111–117
Mercier D, Étienne S, Sellier D, André M-F (2009) Paraglacial gullying of sediment-mantled slopes: a case study of Colletthøgda Kongsfjorden area West Spitsbergen (Svalbard). Earth Surf Process Landf 34:1772–1789
Moign A, Guilcher A (1967) A coastal spit in periglacial arctic environment: Sarstangen Spitsbergen. Norois 14:5–17
Moign A, Héquette A (1985) Summertime evolution of an arctic coast Broggerhalvoya Spitsbergen. Norois 32:5–17
Muskett RR, Lingle CS, Sauber JM, Post AS, Tangborn WV, Rabus BT, Echelmeyer KA (2009) Airborne and spaceborne DEM- and laser altimetry-derived surface elevation and volume changes of the Bering Glacier system Alaska USA and Yukon Canada 1972–2006. J Glaciol 55:16–26
Nordli Ø, Przybylak R, Ogilvie AEJ, Isaksen K (2014) Long-term temperature trends and variability on Spitsbergen: the extended Svalbard Airport temperature series 1898–2012. Polar Res 33:21349. http://dxdoi.org/103402/polarv3321349
Orford JD, Carter RWG, Jennings SC (1991) Coarse clastic barrier environments: evolution and implications for quaternary sea-level interpretation. Quat Int 9:87–104
Orford JD, Forbes DL, Jennings SC (2002) Organisational controls typologies and time scales of paraglacial gravel-dominated coastal systems. Geomorphology 48:51–85
Overduin PP, Strzelecki MC, Grigoriev MN, Couture N, Lantuit H, St-Hilaire-Gravel D, Günther F, Wetterich S (2014) Coastal changes in the Arctic. In: Martini IP, Wanless HR (eds) Sedimentary coastal zones from high to low latitudes: similarities and differences. Geological Society London Special Publications 388. http://dxdoi.org/101144/SP38813
Rachlewicz G (2009) Contemporary sediment fluxes and relief changes in high Arctic glacierised valley systems (Billefjorden Central Spitsbergen). Wydawnictwo Naukowe UAM, Poznań, 203 pp
Rachlewicz G (2010) Paraglacial modifications of glacial sediments over millennial to decadal time-scales in the high Arctic (Billefjorden central Spitsbergen Svalbard). Quaestiones Geographicae 29:59–67
Rachlewicz G, Szczuciński W, Ewertowski M (2007) Post-"Little Ice Age" retreat rates of glaciers around Billefjorden in central Spitsbergen Svalbard. Pol Polar Res 28:159–186
Rachold V, Are F, Atkinson D, Cherkashov G, Solomon S (2005) Arctic Coastal Dynamics (ACD): an introduction. Geo-Mar Lett 25:63–68
Schomacker A (2008) What controls dead-ice melting under different climate conditions? A discussion. Earth Sci Rev 90:103–113
Schomacker A, Kjær KH (2008) Quantification of dead-ice melting in ice-cored moraines at the high-Arctic glacier Holmströmbreen Svalbard. Boreas 37:211–225

Sessford EG (2013) Spatial and temporal analysis of Holocene coastal development: applications to erosion assessment and cultural heritage mitigation in Svalbard. M.Sc. thesis, The University of Oslo, Oslo

Shaw J, Taylor RB, Forbes DL (1990) Coarse clastic barriers in eastern Canada: patterns of glaciogenic sediment dispersal with rising sea levels. J Coast Res Spec Issue 9:160–200

St-Hilaire-Gravel D, Bell TJ, Forbes DL (2010) Raised gravel beaches as proxy indicators of past sea-ice and wave conditions Lowther Island Canadian Arctic Archipelago. Arctic 63:213–226

Streletskaya ID, Vasiliev AA, Vanstein BG (2009) Erosion of sediment and organic carbon from the Kara Sea coast. Arct Antarct Alp Res 41:79–87

Strzelecki MC (2011) Schmidt hammer tests across a recently deglaciarized rocky coastal zone in Spitsbergen – is there a "coastal amplification" of rock weathering in polar climates? Pol Polar Res 32:239–252

Syvitski J, Shaw J (1995) Sedimentology and geomorphology of fjords. In: Perillo GME (ed) Geomorphology and sedimentology of estuaries. Elsevier, Amsterdam, 113–178 pp

Szczuciński W, Zajączkowski M, Scholten J (2009) Sediment accumulation rates in subpolar fjords – impact of post-Little Ice Age glaciers retreat Billefjorden Svalbard. Estuar Coast Shelf Sci 85:345–356

Szpikowski J, Szpikowska G, Zwoliński Z, Rachlewicz G, Kostrzewski A, Marciniak M, Dragon K (2014) Character and rate of denudation in a High Arctic glacierized catchment (Ebbaelva Central Spitsbergen). Geomorphology. http://dxdoi.org/101016/jgeomorph201401012

Taylor RB, Forbes DL, Carter RWG, Orford JD (1986) Beach sedimentation in Ireland: similarities and contrasts with Atlantic Canada. Geol Surv Can Pap 86-1B:55–64

Wangensteen B, Gudmunsson A, Eiken T, Kääb A, Farbot H, Etzelmüller B (2006) Surface displacements and surface age estimates for creeping slope landforms in Northern and Eastern Iceland using digital photogrammetry. Geomorphology 80:59–79

Zagórski P (2011) Shoreline dynamics of Calypsostranda (NW Wedel Jarlsberg Land Svalbard) during the last century. Pol Polar Res 32:67–99

Zagórski P, Gajek G, Demczuk P (2012a) The influence of glacier systems of polar catchments on functioning of the coastal zone (Recherchefjorden Svalbard). Zeitschrift für Geomorfologie 56 (Suppl 1):101–122

Zagórski P, Malczewski A, Łęczyński L (2012b) Shoreline changes of Isbjørnhamna (Hornsund Svalbard) in years 1960–2011. Field report UMCS University, 34 pp

Zagórski P, Rodzik J, Strzelecki MC (2013) Coastal geomorphology. In: Zagórski P, Harasimuik M, Rodzik J (eds) The geographical environment of NW part of Wedel Jarslberg Land (Spitsbergen Svalbard). University Marie Curie-Sklodowska Press, Lublin, 212–247 pp

Ziaja W (2012) Current changes in the south Spitsbergen landscape: a comparison of the Sørkappland eastern and western coasts. In: Churski P (ed) Contemporary issues in Polish geography. Bogucki Wydawnictwo Naukowe, Poznań, 83–93 pp

Ziaja W, Maciejowski P, Ostafin K (2009) Coastal landscape dynamics in NE Sørkapp Land (SE Spitsbergen) 1900–2005. Ambio 38:201–208

Ziaja W, Lisowska M, Olech M, Osyczka P, Węgrzyn M, Dudek J, Ostafin K (2011) Transformation of the natural environment in Western Sørkapp Land (Spitsbergen) since the 1980s. Jagiellonian University Press, Kraków, 92 pp

Chapter 3
Geomorphic Changes in the Rhône Delta During the LIA: Input from the Analysis of Ancient Maps

Mireille Provansal, Georges Pichard, and Edward J. Anthony

Abstract The morphogenesis of the mouths and shores of the Rhône river delta has been strongly influenced by changes in hydrology associated with climatic deterioration during the Little Ice Age (LIA). The present shape of the delta is related to two avulsions. The progradation of delta-mouth lobes, their morphology (digitated or lobate), and their reworking by marine processes are described here from ancient maps, the interpretation of which has been comforted jointly by the critical viewpoint of the historian and input from previous geomorphic studies. The impacts of climatic oscillations proper to the LIA are analysed and confronted with other factors implied in deltaic morphogenesis such as sediment transfers, accommodation space, marine processes and human interventions, notably from an engineering perspective. The successive metamorphoses of the Rhône delta are, thus, seen to be related to the conjunction of some or all of these factors, depending on the time frame under consideration.

M. Provansal (✉)
Europôle de l'Arbois, CNRS, UM CEREGE, 13545 Aix-en-Provence, France

UMR 6635 CEREGE, Europôle Méditerranéen de l'Arbois, Université Aix Marseille, Aix-en-Provence, France
e-mail: provansal@cerege.fr

G. Pichard
Département d'Histoire, Université Aix-Marseille, 13100 Aix-en-Provence, France
e-mail: georgpichard@yahoo.fr

E.J. Anthony
Aix Marseille Université, Institut Universitaire de France, CEREGE, UM 34, Europôle Méditerranéen de l'Arbois, B.P. 80, 13545 Aix en Provence Cedex, France
e-mail: anthony@cerege.fr

M. Maanan, M. Robin (eds.), *Sediment Fluxes in Coastal Areas*, Coastal Research Library 10, DOI 10.1007/978-94-017-9260-8_3

3.1 Introduction

The last five centuries in Western Europe were punctuated by a cold and humid climatic crisis that affected hydro-fluvial systems, resulting in abundant liquid and solid discharge and in a high frequency of strong river floods. Starting from the seventeenth century, this crisis coincided with a strong increase in human occupation of mountain catchments, favouring slope erosion and increased solid fluvial discharge. This climatic crisis ended at the turn of the nineteenth to the twentieth centuries, at a time when rural exodus and reforestation had already been contributing to slope stabilisation for nearly 50 years. At about the same time, between the end of the eighteenth and the first half of the twentieth centuries, fluvial engineering was progressively engaged in the stabilization of riverbanks and river mouths and contributing to reduced solid discharge. The study period, between the fourteenth and the end of the nineteenth century, corresponds, therefore, to the conjunction and succession of two remarkable forcing factors, anthropogenic and natural, that impacted fluvial dynamics and river-mouth mobility. At the same time, progress in cartography, under the impetus of monarchies in Europe and of technological advances, was generating a corpus of ancient maps of remarkable spatial and chronological precision. Subject to the filter of historical scrutiny and analysis, these maps enable a fine-scale analysis of shoreline and river-mouth changes in the Rhône delta. The geomorphic interpretation of this multi-secular environmental history is supported by a remarkable hydro-climatic data bank that has been recently revised and expanded to give exhaustive datasets (HistRhône 2013), and by numerous geomorphic/sedimentological and GIS studies conducted over the last two decades on the Rhône river delta. The historical documentation and the ensuing analysis and conclusions have been reported Pichard et al. (2014).

3.2 The Rhône River Delta

The Rhône delta forms the terminus of a fairly large catchment covering an area of 98,000 km^2 (Fig. 3.1), and corresponding to several climatic zones ranging from Alpine mountains to the warmer shores of the Mediterranean. The relatively large liquid discharge (1,750 m^3·s at Beaucaire station, Fig. 3.1) and the river regime reflect this diversity (Pardé 1925). 100-year floods exceed 11,000 m$^3 \cdot$ s, the most reputed historical flood peak being that of May 1856 (11,800 m$^3 \cdot$ s). Models of liquid discharge and suspended sediment concentrations (SSC) highlight the overwhelming role of floods in the overall sediment budget of the river, with about 80 % of SSC being transported during floods, especially from the Mediterranean tributaries formed by the Ardèche and the Durance (Arnaud-Fassetta 2000; Antonelli 2002; Pont et al. 2002).

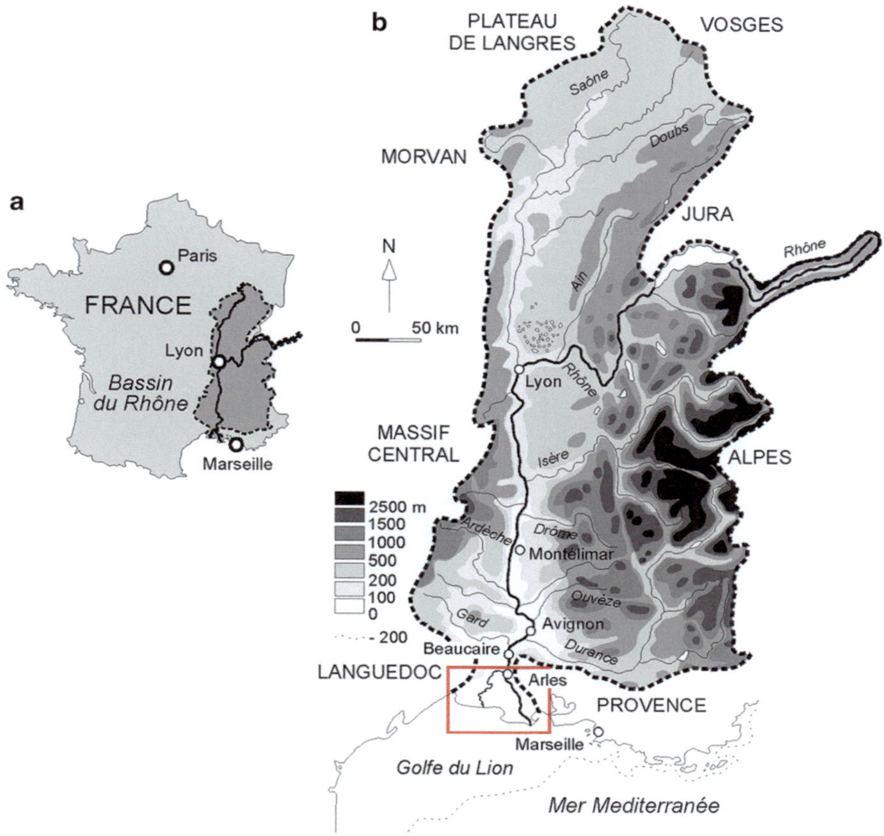

Fig. 3.1 The Rhône river catchment and delta: (**a**) catchment location in France; (**b**) catchment topography and the river delta

In the delta, the Holocene and historical mobility of the distributaries, the mouths and the shoreline have been described by L'Homer et al. (1981), Arnaud-Fassetta (2000) and Maillet (2005). Traces of ancient distributaries dating back to the Upper Middle Ages (Ulmet and St. Ferréol branches), and beyond, are still visible on the first edited modern maps as well as on the recent geological maps.

Since the end of the Middle Ages, variations in water levels have been measured at Arles and Beaucaire (Fig. 3.1), and they attest to a complex hydro-climatic history characterised by marked fluctuations in discharge (Pichard 1995). The hydrological, sedimentary and geomorphic impacts of the LIA (fourteenth to nineteenth centuries) on the Rhône fluvial system have been abundantly documented for the upper and middle reaches (Salvador 1991; Landon 1999; Bravard 2010) and for the lower reaches and the delta (Arnaud-Fassetta and Provansal 1999; Provansal et al. 2003; Antonelli et al. 2004; Provansal and Bravard 2009). At the end of the Middle Ages, when the long LIA commenced, the main fluvial branch, the Grand Passon, was

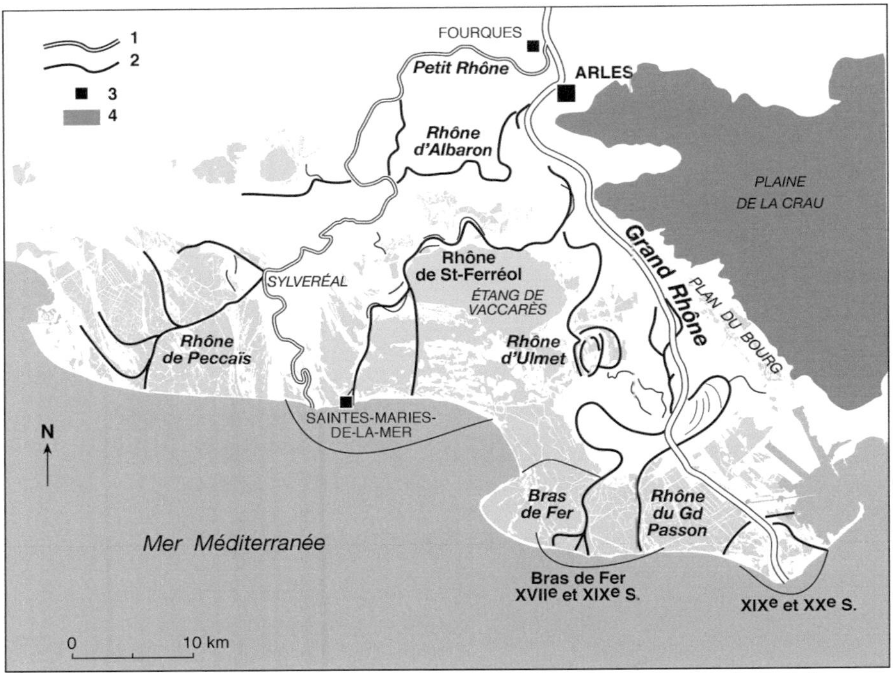

Fig. 3.2 Distribution of branches inherited from the Holocene and the historic period of the Rhône delta. *1*. Currently active branches, *2*. Traces of inherited branches, *3*. Main places cited in the text, *4*. Crau Plateau

situated in the eastern confines of the delta, near Crau, whereas the western part of the delta was characterised by secondary branches, among which the present Petit Rhône is a heritage (Fig. 3.2). This study focuses on the western part of the delta, where the present main branch, the Grand Rhône, is now located.

The present article focuses on old cartographic archives of the Rhône delta and shoreline dating to between the end of the sixteenth and the middle of the nineteenth centuries. Since the eighteenth century, historians have established a tradition of studies of the delta and its mouths and have attempted to appreciate their morphological changes. Among the more recent historical approaches are those Rossiaud (1993, 2007) for the Middle Ages, and Pichard (2005) and Pichard et al. (2014) for the sixteenth to nineteenth centuries. The historical data generated by these studies are interpreted in the light of knowledge on fluvial and delta dynamics acquired by geomorphologists over the last two decades.

The aim of the present study is to describe the evolution of the deltaic system and to propose a geomorphic interpretation that addresses the following questions. What has been the response of the delta mouths and shoreline to hydro-climatic forcing factors? How do these factors interact with the coastal dynamics? What are the response times of the deltaic system?

3.3 Ancient Maps of the Rhône Delta: Their Utility and Limits

The evolution of the Rhône delta river mouths and the delta shoreline has been described by numerous texts and illustrated documents. Maps constitute the essential basis for comprehending events in a spatial frame. The utilisation of ancient maps to document geomorphic fluvial changes has been practised for several river systems (Bravard and Bethemont 1989; Miramont et al. 1998; Gurnell and Peiry 2005; Bravard 2011; Forget 2013). In the Rhône delta, critical studies are now quite antiquated and often obsolete (Desjardins 1866; Guérard 1895). The studies conducted by engineers (Surrell 1847) are generally erroneous as far as dates and the historical context are concerned. Collaboration with historians is, nevertheless, indispensable from a methodological point of view. Historians have elaborated a critical system of analysis indispensable in using ancient maps and the numerous interpretations derived from these maps. A map cannot be read directly without prior investigations on the conditions relating to its production (Pichard et al. 2014). Research in this area is typically faced with two main problems.

The first is the date of the documents, which are commonly copied from an original, sometimes several times over, with or without modifications, often without the original being clearly cited. There is a need, therefore, to be aware of misleading directions in interpreting morphological changes. However, topographic descriptions and the cartography were often of very good precision, and the chronology of buildings and other infrastructure sometimes enables identification of the exact date of the document. It would, therefore, be unfortunate to neglect ancient maps as a source of geomorphic information (Pichard 2005; Pichard et al. 2014).

The second concerns the precision of mapping and the system of geographic references of mapped objects. In first available maps, between the end of the sixteenth century and the first half of the eighteenth century, mapping techniques were not sufficiently advanced as to enable precise geometric restitution of field objects. The interpretation of these earlier maps thus remains necessarily qualitative. Starting from the second half of the eighteenth century, the systematic use of triangulation in order to establish the first general maps of France (the Cassini Maps) permitted the creation of a geographic 'referential' that enabled better comparisons with present maps and more accurate measurements. Finally, starting from the mid-nineteenth century, several general levelling networks were created to cover the French territory, establishing a 3-D referential that enabled the integration of documents within Geographic Information Systems, and therefore the precise measurement of geomorphic changes.

Finally, historians have at their disposal an important corpus of texts that provide data on depths, that describe sedimentary processes and deposits, and that specify the dates and nature of human interventions, thus enabling confirmation or discussion of the cartographic data. This article therefore proposes utilising documents that antedate 'modern' cartography, of which only the Plan of the Rhône Mouth, drawn in 1852, will finally be presented. These documents will then be interpreted from a geomorphic standpoint.

3.4 Results

The evolution of the mouths of the Rhône since the end of the sixteenth century is represented by two major morphological yardsticks: abandonment, by avulsion, of the medieval Passon branch to the benefit of the formation of the Bras de Fer branch in 1587, and then the avulsion of the latter to the benefit of a new mouth in 1711 oriented towards the southeast.

3.4.1 Avulsion of the Medieval Passon Branch and Appearance of the Bras de Fer Branch at the End of the Sixteenth Century

Up to the end of the Middle Ages, the only documents describing the Rhône delta were Portulans and a set of dispersed texts (Rossiaud 1993). The first available maps date from the end of the sixteenth century. Two of them enable a description of the abandonment of the Passon branch and the avulsion resulting in a new mouth.

3.4.1.1 The Bompar/Solier Map (Before 1587): The State Prior to Avulsion in 1587

The first map of Provence (Fig. 3.3), called the 'Bompar map', dates from 1591. In reality, it appears to be anterior to the 1857 avulsion of the medieval Passon branch by 10 years, and drawn by Solier sometime between 1530 and 1594 (Pichard 1993; Pichard et al. 2014). The main branch of the river in its deltaic reach flowed along the vast Crau gravel fan of Pleistocene age. This course, inherited from ancient times, has been identified from aerial photographs and cores (L'Homer et al. 1981; Vella et al. 2005). The map exaggerates the width of the fluvial branches, but underlines the importance of solid discharge that may correspond to sediment plumes or mud banks called "tignes". At the mouth, numerous islets separate the flow into narrow "graus" or passages (Passon, Enfer, Grant, and Paulet graus).

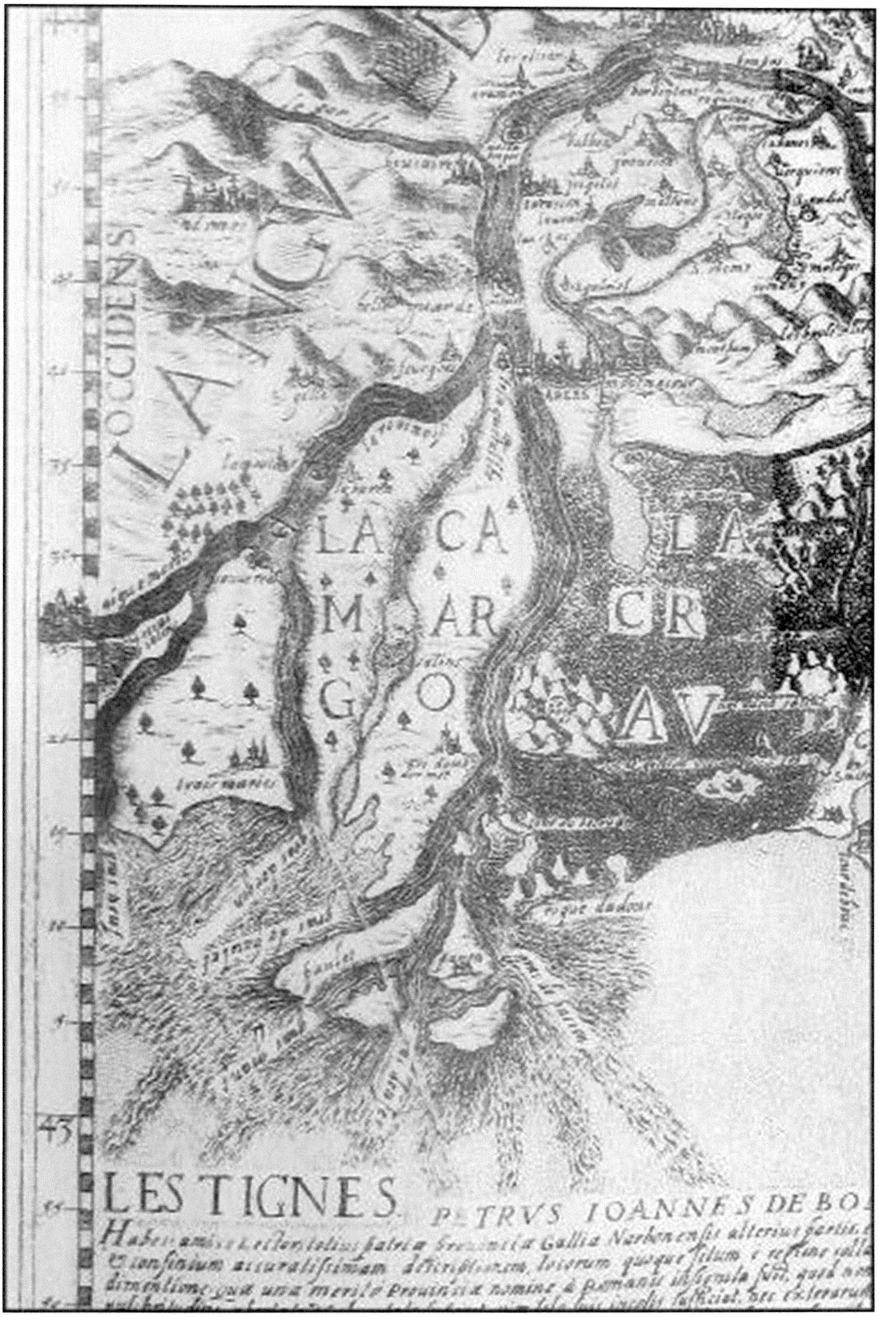

Fig. 3.3 Bompar's map dating from 1591 (*Accuratissima Patriae Provinciae Descriptio*). Details of the mouths of the Rhône (Photo *Terra Incognita*, Quimper)

3.4.1.2 The Camargo (1591–1592): Appearance of a New Branch, the "Bras de Fer"

Drawn by military engineers from the Italian Piemont, the Camargo map is certainly close to the field reality. Unfortunately, the shoreline was cut out in the vicinity of the mouth of the Rhône, even though beginnings of offshore prolongation of the mouth deposits are seen (Fig. 3.4).

This map describes a new branch, called Bras de Fer, characterised by anastomosing, with a sinuous course and numerous channels separated by wooded islets. The river vegetation on the banks and constructions near the river could reflect a rather quiescent hydrological regime. To the west, the Orgon (present Petit Rhône) and Peccais branches are also seen to be active. The first of these branches surrounds what was then the hamlet of Saintes-Maries de la mer, still far from the sea at the time. The pine forests colonising old beach ridges (Arnaud-Fassetta 2000) are well represented in the centre and in the west of the delta. The environment appears very "humid", however, with numerous swamps on the right bank of the Petit Rhône, in the centre of the "island" of Camargue, and in the Plan du Bourg on the left bank of the main branch.

3.4.2 *The Bras de Fer from 1630 to 1711: From Accelerated Progradation to a New Avulsion*

Three precisely dated maps are used to describe the later evolution of the Bras de Fer branch.

Fig. 3.4 Map of the Italian Piemont engineers dating from 1591 to 1592 (*The Camargo and the two branches of the Rhône in 1591–1592*), *Archivio di Stato di Torino* (Photo G. Pichard)

3.4.2.1 Maps Drawn by Flour (1633–1638) and Vortcamp (1656)

The original map drawn by Flour in 1633 no longer exists, but was redrawn by the Dutchman Vortcamp in 1656 (Fig. 3.5a), who dated it at 1638. An annotated extract, also available (Fig. 3.5b), shows the extreme complexity of the mouths during the 1630s.

The map shows three coexisting systems. In the east, the medieval Passon branch has regressed to become a minor channel that no longer empties into the sea. To the west, the two secondary branches, Gras d'Orgon (the future Petit Rhône) and Gras Nou, emptied into the sea after crossing the great pine forest. In the centre, the Bras de Fer, the most important branch, ends in a broad and very well drawn meander. Compared to the previous map (cf. the location of the large wooded island), the shoreline has strongly prograded up to the new mouth of the "Gras du Midy". The Tampan tower, constructed on the coast in 1610, had already fallen into disuse by 1633–1638 as a result of this shoreline advance. The main channel is bordered to the west by numerous banks or islets separated from firm land by the "Rageyrol" channel, These banks (or *illons*) often formed around shipwrecks, as attested by the local toponymy: Polacre, Vessel and Quarantaine illons. They attest to the difficulties of navigation in the Rhône during the seventeenth century (Illouze 1997). To the west of the mouth, the smooth concave plan shape of the shoreline corresponds to one or several large beach ridges comprising swales and cut by numerous "graus". The succession of these beach ridges highlights the phases of progressive coastal progradation. The Rascaillan spit running parallel to the coast confirms longshore drift to the west and prefigures the present Beauduc spit. The first half of the seventeenth century was thus characterised by important sediment inputs, which modified the shape of the new mouth. They testify to the importance of fluvial processes in determining the shape of the deltaic shoreline.

3.4.2.2 The Arnoul Map (1678)

Two maps, drawn by Arnoul in 1678 and 1688, show the persistent progradation of the mouth (Fig. 3.6 depicts the 1678 map). The rate of shoreline advance was of the order of 100 m/year between 1635 (map of Flour) and 1788, and 90 m/year between 1678 and 1688 (Caritey 1995; Pichard et al. 2014). The islets on the right bank are now attached to firm land and the Ragueyrol channel is infilled. New islets also appear (Ste Anne, Raymond, Janatan) between which embankments are constructed in order to channel outflow and favour navigation. The depth points clearly confirm a large sediment supply and reduction of available sediment accommodation space.

Two new phenomena appear, however. In the first place, the river channel becomes deformed. The increase in radius of the meander curve through point-bar development and the appearance of median and lateral banks indicate difficulties in downstream transport of the sediment load. Arnaud-Fassetta and Provansal (1999) and Arnaud-Fassetta (2000) have in fact shown that channel infill had begun as early as the second half of the seventeenth century, the thickness of this infill

Fig. 3.5 (**a**) Vortcamp's map from 1656, based on that of Flour (dated 1638 in the title), National Library (BNF), Paris. Note that the south is at the top. (Photo G. Pichard). (**b**) Details of the map of Flour (between 1635 and 1638, the original having disappeared), National Library (BNF), Cartes et Plans Service hydrographique (Photo G. Pichard)

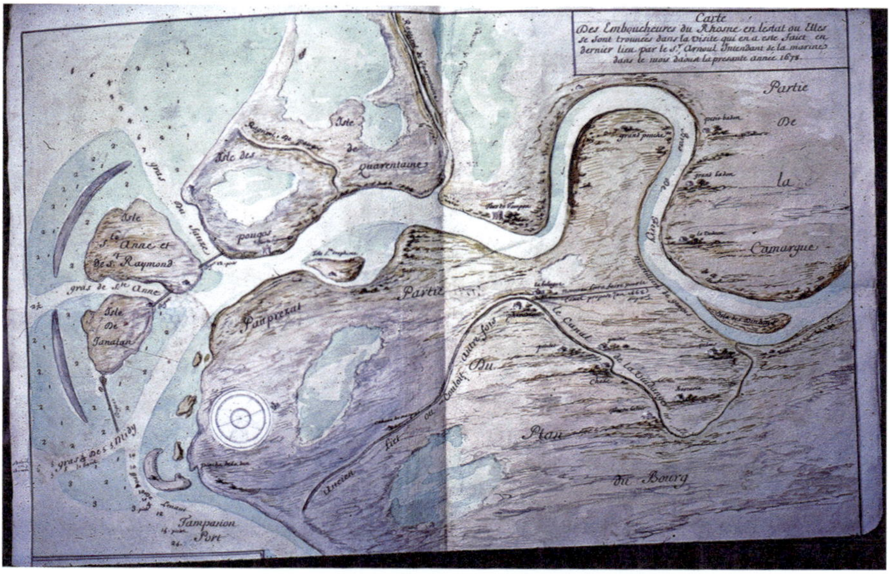

Fig. 3.6 Map of Arnoul, 1678, SHD Vincennes, Inspection du Génie, Art (Photo G. Pichard)

attaining 10 m between 1587 and 1711. Secondly, the elongation of sediments deposited on the delta front lobe into convex transverse bars denotes the importance of coastal processes.

3.4.2.3 The French Naval Engineers' Map (1709–1711)

Between the Arnoul map (1678) and the map of the naval engineers (Fig. 3.7), the channel has been modified. A new channel that had appeared a few years earlier now cuts through the meander, which is thus no longer capable of evacuating all the liquid and solid discharge during floods. The shoreline prograded 2.6 km between 1668 and 1711, i.e., 60 m/year, and locally, the distance between the Tampan tower and the Pointe de la Dent (or *Ponche de la Den*), had grown by 4 km, indicating an average progradation rate of 118 m/year (Pichard et al. 2014). At the mouth of the main left bank branch, the curved islet on the previous map is now welded to the shoreline. The embankments linking the islets have disappeared (destroyed by floods?), as well as the convex bars situated in front of these islets. Finally, on the right bank, the lagoons of Pougas islet had become infilled with sediment. The map also shows a rectilinear artificial canal, initially constructed to divert the river's freshwater into the coastal lagoons in order to hinder the illicit production of salt. This canal was finally exploited by the river avulsion of 1711–1712, leading to the abandonment of the Bras de Fer. Increasingly starved of sediment, this branch finally ended up as a simple drain.

Fig. 3.7 Map of the French naval engineers, Archives Nationales, Paris (Photo G. Pichard.)

3.4.3 Evolution of the New Mouth in the Eighteenth Century: The Cassini (1778) and Isnard (1783) Maps

Starting from the new mouth that formed in 1711, the progress of cartography and the unpublished reports of engineers in the nineteenth century had led to more reliable measurements. After 1711, floods and river mouths entered a relatively quiet phase for about 30 years, apart from the major 1725 flood (Pichard et al. 2014).

On the Cassini map of 1778, (Fig. 3.8a), the Faraman coast adjacent to the ancient Bras de Fer mouth had retreated by 2.5 km since 1711, i.e., 37–38 m/year. The eroded sediments source the formation of Beauduc spit. This feature, the precursor of which had been sketched in the map of Flour (1633–1638) as the recurved island of Rascaillan, thus reappears here in a similar position. Its highly recurved distal tip reflects the importance of longshore processes in this sector now cut off from fluvial influence. At its western extremity appears Beauduc bay, limited by a sandy barrier the concave plan form of which may reflect a decreasing sediment supply. In the western part, the Petit Rhône still feeds a prograding mouth that protects the village of Saintes-Maries de la Mer. The new mouth of the Grand Rhône (Fig. 3.8b) becomes divided into three branches, separated by two islets or *teys* (the Béricle and Bicle *teys*), giving an overall bird's foot morphology. In the course of its construction in 1740 in order to assure surveillance of the new mouth, the St Louis tower was situated 3 km from the sea. By the end of the eighteenth

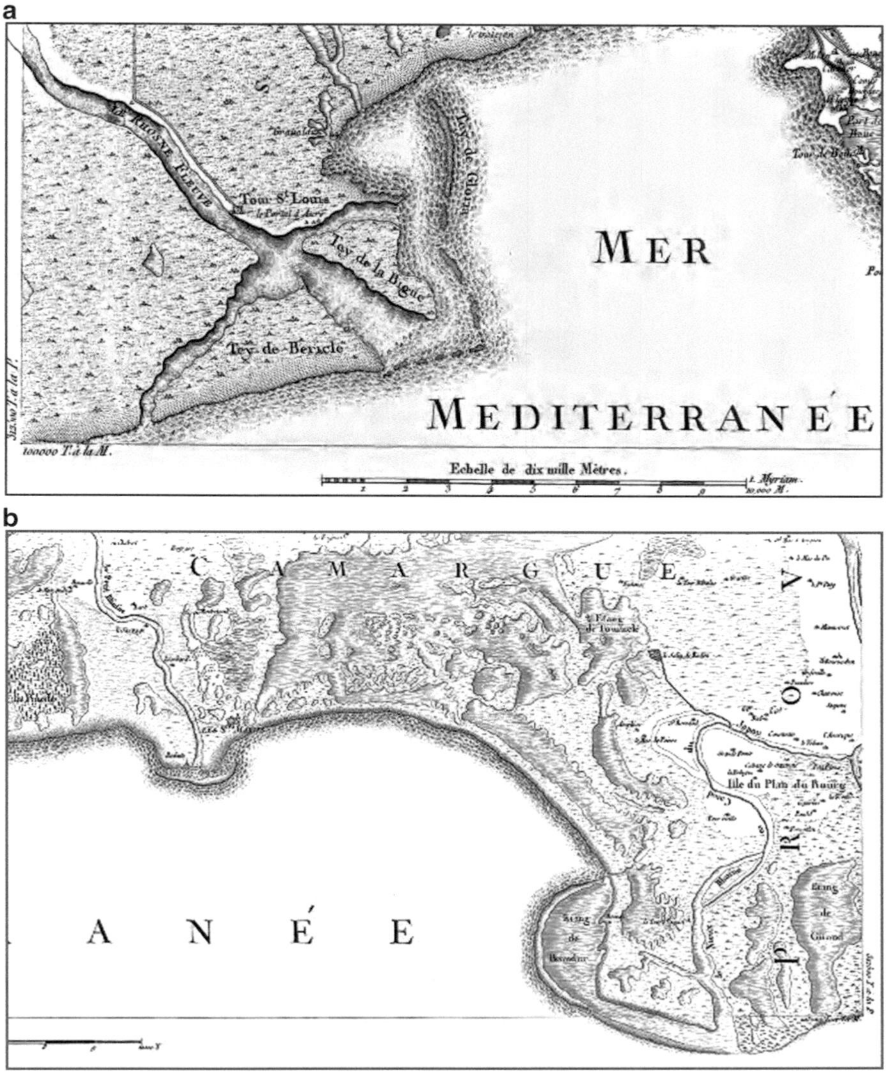

Fig. 3.8 (**a**) Extract of the map of Cassini (Photo G. Pichard.). (**b**) Map of Cassini showing details of the mouth of the Grand Rhône (Photo G. Pichard.)

century, it was already 6.2 km inland, giving a shoreline progradation rate of 65 m/year. According to the calculations of Surrell (1847), the delta gained an area of 30 ha/year from 1725 to 1778 (Pichard et al. 2014).

This configuration is confirmed by the Isnard map (Fig. 3.9) of 1783. The two islets of the former mouth are still very clearly visible, fronted by the large bank called the "Sabion de St Véran", which, judging by a tower built on it, is apparently

Fig. 3.9 Map of Isnard, 1783 (Photo AC Arles)

stabilised. This bank is associated towards the west with a relatively complex set of two successive sand spits and a subaerial longshore bar extending continuously to the mouth of the Petit Rhône and beyond. The longshore sediment cell presently at the core of the Rhône delta shoreline was thus already operational at this time. Erosion of the sediment mass formed by the former Bras de Fer mouth sources Beauduc spit and bay. The two maps (Figs. 3.8b and 3.9) show that these deposits are reworked by an efficient longshore dtift system, which constructed the Gloria *tey* towards the east, heralding the future Gracieuse spit, which presently bars the Gulf of Fos.

3.4.4 A Progressively Engineered Delta Mouth in the Nineteenth Century: The Sketches of Guérard

The nineteenth century, especially after 1840, saw successive embanking of the mouth of the Grand Rhône, notably for purposes of increasing navigation, and these engineering operations interfered with the natural dynamics. Surrell (1847), Desjardins (1866) and several other engineers carried out numerous precise depth measurements in the branches and at sea. They analysed both ancient and modern maps and conducted historical studies.

The sketch made in 1852 by A. Guérard (Fig. 3.10) depicts a complex mouth. The Béricle *tey* has grown in size and new *teys* formed around shipwrecks, such as the Roustan, which foundered in 1780, the Tartane and the Annibal in 1822, and the Eugène, in 1828, a manifestation of the difficulties of navigation due to rapid sedimentation. These deposits separate four branches: Piémançon in the west, which was to be rapidly shut off by a transverse dike, Eugène and Roustan in the centre, and Est or Pégoulier in the east. The left bank of this last branch is lined with

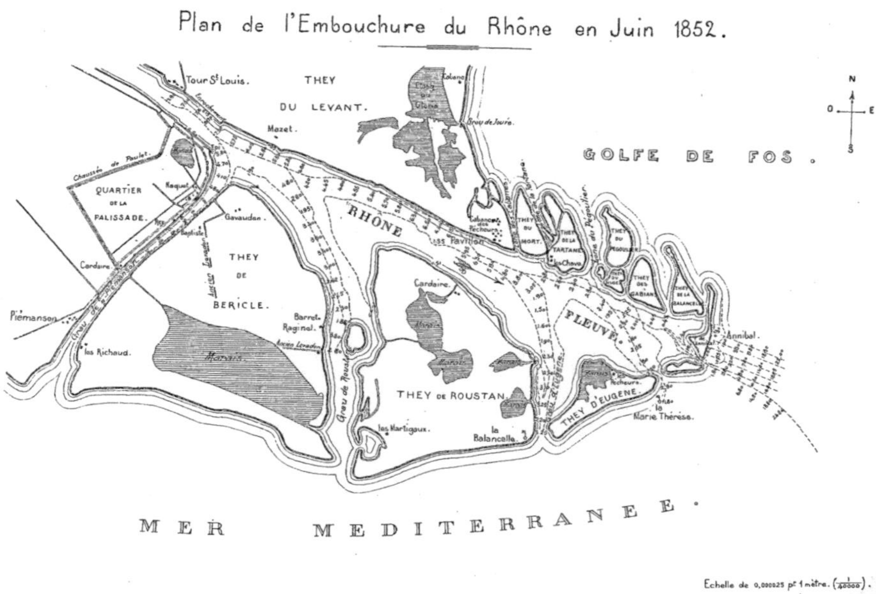

Fig. 3.10 Sketch by A. Guérard of the main mouth of the Rhône in 1852, Ref. AD13 6 S 1054 (Photo G. Pichard.)

numerous oblique islets indicating successive past positions of the river-mouth bar. It became embanked in 1852 in order to maintain sufficient energy to evacuate sediments. Its outlet became obstructed however by an important new mouth bar. Progradation of this branch turned out to be extremely rapid: 43.4 m/year from 1778 to 1855 on its right bank, and 31.2 m/year on its left bank.

By 1886 only the Pégoulier branch is still in activity (Fig. 3.11). The *theys* are aligned in the axis of river flow, which had constructed a lobe with a radius of about 2 km corresponding to the top of a large prodelta. Longshore drift is active on either side, resulting in northward elongation of ancient abandoned left bank *theys* and smoothing out of the former protruberance corresponding to the Roustan branch. The persistent difficulties in navigation ended up in abandonment of the Pégoulier branch, now completely infilled with sediment, and in the reopening of the Roustan branch in 1885. The latter has persisted and currently forms the mouth of the Grand Rhône, now stable, and perhaps even in retreat (Sabatier et al. 2006).

Bathymetric measurements show the advance of the sediment prism of the prodelta in front of the Roustan mouth, where the -10 m isobath extended seaward by 900 m (Pichard et al. 2014). A comparison of bathymetric charts between the shoreline and the 20 m-depth, confirms this growth, but it especially shows a diminution of the amount of sediment accumulating at the mouths of the Grand Rhône, which drops from +12 Mm^3/year between 1842 and 1872 to about +8 Mm^3/year between 1872 and 1895, and along the delta shoreline since the middle of the nineteenth century (Sabatier et al. 2006; Maillet et al. 2006a, b).

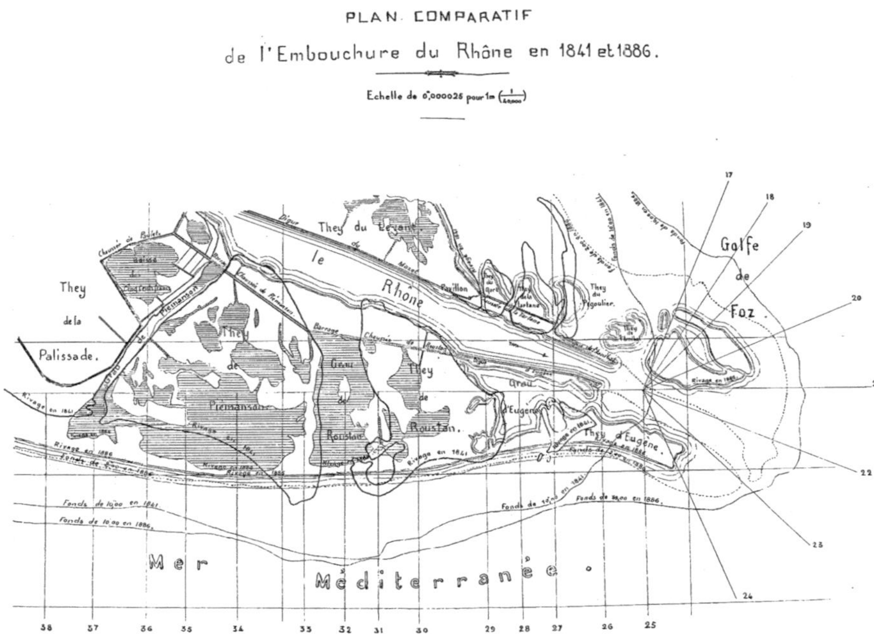

Fig. 3.11 Comparative sketches of the mouth of the Rhône in 1841 and 1886 by A. Guérard

The shoreline mobility was quite precisely measured. The delta gained 23 ha/year from 1778 to 1841 (Surrell 1847), corresponding to a rate of advance that was slightly weaker than in the previous decades. At the same time, shoreline retreat was affecting the entire central and western parts of the delta, with the exception of Beauduc spit, sourced by erosion of the mouth of the abandoned Bras de Fer branch. The rhythms and spatial distribution of these changes have been described by Provansal et al. (2003) and Maillet et al. (2006a, b).

3.4.5 Historical Mobility of the Rhône Delta Shoreline

Shoreline progradation needs to be considered separately, first from maps describing the period of the Bras de Fer (1635–1712), and for which the error margin is not precisely known but presumably important, and then from maps corresponding to the Grand Rhône era, and for which measurements are more reliable.

In the former case, the rates of advance following the initial avulsion in 1587 up to the 1650s are not measurable. There are a large number of maps that have not been presented in this study, but which have already been analysed from a historical point of view. Progradation rates go through two very strong peaks (>about 100 m/year), between 1650 and 1680, and between 1706 and 1712, separated by a period of slower advance (<about 90 m/year) in the course of the last 20 years of the seventeenth century (Pichard et al. 2014). Starting from the last decades of the eighteenth century, the measurements show inexorable retreat of the central and eastern parts of the delta (from −30 to −15 m/year), with the exception of Beauduc spit, which grew from the products of this erosion. Displacement of the main mouth to the east has definitively deprived these sectors of sediment supply. In the west, the disappearance of the secondary mouths and the progressive reduction of the discharge of the Petit Rhône have deprived this part of the delta shoreline of sediments. This evolution very seriously threatens the village of Saintes-Maries de la Mer. At the mouth of the Grand Rhône, the Piémanson branch became extinct in the course of the first half of the nineteenth century, whereas the Roustan and Pégoulier branches exhibited rapid advance, but nevertheless not as pronounced as the two peaks experienced by the Bras de Fer.

3.5 Interpretation and Discussion

The mobility of the mouths and shoreline of the Rhône delta are related to the interaction of fluvial and marine processes. Starting from the beginning of the eighteenth century, progressive intervention of the corps of engineers becomes an important factor. These data are therefore a first key in interpreting the geomorphic variations that have affected the mouths and shoreline of the Rhône delta.

3.5.1 Forcing Variables in the Morphogenesis of the Mouth and the Shoreline

The history of marine processes affecting the Rhône delta is still poorly known. The role of the sea (longshore drift, storms) has no doubt been fundamental, and still needs to be properly established, such as for instance the great storms of the end of the seventeenth century, described in archives, and threats to the village that had grown into the small town of Saintes-Maries de la Mer. It is nevertheless likely that climatic conditions responsible for the present coastal morphogenesis were already active. Sabatier (2001), Sabatier and Suanez (2003), and Brunel (2010) have shown that the geomorphic evolution of the Rhône delta was under the predominant influence of longshore currents generated by waves from the south and southeast These waves were diffracted by the inherited prodelta lobes, resulting in bi-directional drift cells oriented, respectively, east in the central part of the delta, and west in the western part. The orientation of the sand spits of Beauduc and Gracieuse on historical maps clearly highlights these two opposed drift directions. The central part of the delta corresponding to the ancient and powerful lobe of the Bras de Fer branch has thus served, and still does, as a central sediment source.

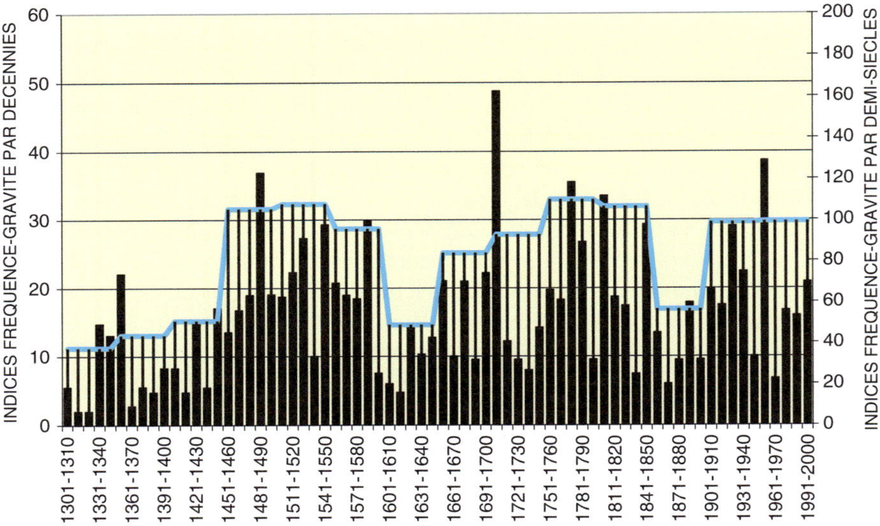

Fig. 3.12 Decadal frequency-gravity indices summed up for each half-century for floods in the lower Rhône from the fourteenth to the twentieth centuries (Modified after Pichard and Roucaute (2014))

Sabatier et al. (2006) have suggested the existence of a "time shift" between the input of river sediment to the sea and the build up of the shoreline. In an initial stage, the sediments are trapped in the prodelta lobe, and later, when the mouth location has shifted, they are reworked to build spits.

The impact of fluvial forcing on deltaic morphogenesis depends on the importance of the river's liquid and solid discharge and on the channel transport capacity. These three variables are presented here.

Hydrological variations are well known as they form the Histrhône hydroclimatic data base (http://histrhone.cerege.fr) generated by the historical work of Pichard and Roucaute (2014). On the basis of an index of decadal frequency-gravity, smoothed by half a century, these authors highlight two long periods of abundand floods between 1460 and 1610, and between 1660 and 1850 (Fig. 3.12). Within these two periods, there are several oscillations characterised by major identified floods. The estimation of past discharge from limnigraphic scales remains, however, hypothetical in part. Changes in channel morphology in the course of the twentieth century do not allow for a simple deduction of flow regimes for periods earlier than the mid-nineteenth century simply on the basis of the twentieth century discharge/height curves.

The solid discharge comes from erosion of the Rhône catchment, especially mountain areas. The main purveyors of suspended sediment to the lower Rhône are the Isère river, and the Mediterranean tributaries, the Drôme, Ardèche and Durance rivers. The last of these streams drains the fragile lithological environments of the southern Alps and has played a determining role in the sediment supply to the Rhône delta. Starting from the second half of the sixteenth century, wood-cutting, deforestation, and excessive grazing generated soil erosion in the Durance catchment and a highly torrential river regime (Sclafert 1959; Jorda 1985). The first bills of law of the Parliament of Aix, regarding control of deforestation, date back to 1555 and 1606. Notwithstanding, generalised deforestation became even more common in the following decades for demographic and social reasons (Pichard 1999, 2001). Contrary to a generally held belief, the inception of soil erosion occurred early, and became more intense at the end of the sixteenth century. It is therefore quite possible that solid discharge in the course of the seventeenth and eighteenth centuries was just as important, if not more so, than in the mid-nineteenth century. Since the middle of the nineteenth century, changes in the Rhône River catchment have led to a significant reduction in sediment flux into the river. These changes were often attributed to a decline in mountain agriculture, reforestation and regularisation of mountain torrents, and also to the natural decrease in frequency of the major floods on the tributaries and the main river at the end of the LIA (Pichard 1995; Landon 1999; Miramont and Guilbert 1997). Total Suspended Sediment transport (TSS), measured in the SORA Arles gauging station, has been reduced by about 60 % over the last 150 years, from about 18 Mm^3·year at the end of the nineteenth century (Pardé 1925), to 6.7 Mm^3·year at present (Pont et al. 2002; Maillet et al. 2007; Antonelli et al. 2008).

The sediment transport capacity in the channel down to the river mouth is constrained by several factors. In the first instance, the longitudinal bed profile and water surface slope decrease from 0.07 m km^{-1} at the upstream of Avignon to 0.06 m km^{-1} at Beaucaire and then drastically in the delta (0.003 m km^{-1}), contributing to a drop in specific stream power (equal or $<50\ N \cdot m^2$) and increasing sedimentation along the fluvial margins (Bravard 2010). On the Grand-Rhône River, the gravel bed load disappears about 8 km downstream from Arles, replaced by a sandy load (Arnaud-Fassetta et al. 2010). Delta-mouth and shoreline progradation therefore depend not only on the suspended load, composed for about 85–90 % of silt, but also on sand, which makes up 10–15 % of the total load. The transfer of this load only becomes effective at flood discharge levels of 3,000 $m^3 \cdot s$. Antonelli (2002) have also demonstrated that bedload and near-bed transport is only effective beyond a discharge level of 3,800 $m^3 \cdot s$. Furthermore, the highly changing thalweg profile of the Grand Rhône induces strong spatial variations in specific stream power (Antonelli et al. 2004). The present longitudinal profile is uneven, characterised by riffles and pools (4–20 m deep), which modify the transport of solid fluxes to the mouth.

Transfer of the solid load near the bed thus occurs in a relayed fashion involving storage and differed resuspension during floods (Maillet 2005). It is very likely that this pattern also prevailed during preceding phases. However, Arnaud-Fassetta (2003) has suggested that sediment transport has been facilitated by engineering of the Rhône channel, during the twentieth century.

It is therefore necessary to take all these factors into account when attempting to explain the geomorphic changes that affected the Rhône delta in the course of, and following the LIA. Interpretation is, however, faced with a major obstacle: the insufficiencies in data on marine processes as well as on solid discharge variations, the latter which, from a preliminary analysis, appear important starting from the sixteenth century, but without any further details. The only available information concerns hydro-climatic data and variations in the state of the channel.

3.5.2 *Attempts at Interpretation of the Variations of the Delta Mouths and Shoreline*

We will briefly highlight the succession of delta morphogenetic phases over the last five centuries.

3.5.2.1 Two Phases of Rapid Progradation Corresponding to a River-Dominated Delta in the Terminology of Galloway (1975)

These two phases coincide with two hydrological "crises" in a context of rural population increase. The first phase, at the end of the sixteenth century, is illustrated by the Bompar/Solier maps (around 1580), and then by the maps of the Piemont engineers (1591–1592). It corresponds to the end of the first part of the late sixteenth century crisis (Pfister 1988; Leroy-Ladurie 1983) and to the exceptional floods of 1548, 1570, 1573 and 1580. The flood frequency-gravity index attained 95.6 from 1451 to 1600 (Pichard and Roucaute 2014).

On the Bompar/Solier map, the bird's foot morphology of the mouth of the Passon branch attests to massive sediment inputs that exceeded the capacity of alongshore distribution by waves. The orientation of the islets in the axis of fluvial flow confirms the importance of the latter in shaping the delta mouth. The significant accumulation off the mouth and at the top of the delta lobe reduced sediment accommodation space, resulting in rapid progradation. This massive accumulation finally favoured avulsion and branch shifting towards a more westward location. Persistence of high liquid and solid discharges explains the rapid seaward advance of the new Bras de Fer mouth on the 1591–1592 and 1636 maps. However, the appearance of wooded islets characteristics of a tendency towards fluvial anastomosis attests to a fluvial energy decrease as early as the end of the nineteenth century.

The second crisis, during the last decades of the seventeenth century and the beginning of the eighteenth century, is illustrated by the maps of Arnoul (1678 and 1688) and of the naval corps of engineers in 1709–1711. This phase coincided with floods that became important once again after 1656, and especially during the first decade of the eighteenth century (Pichard et al. 2014). The flood frequency-gravity index attained 83.8 between 1651 and 1700, and even went up to 132.6, when the decade 1701–1710 is considered (Pichard and Roucaute 2014). The 1678 Arnoul map describes a situation of transition, still characterised by wave influence on river-mouth deposits. However, river processes once again take command, confirmed by the 1709–1711 maps, and explaining the new switch of the morphology of the mouth into a more bird's foot shape. Arnaud-Fassetta (2000) demonstrated, on the basis of a study of heavy minerals, that much of the sediment supplied at this time came from energetic floods originating in the Cevennes Mountains, which form the southern flanks of the Massif Central (Fig. 3.1). These rapid and violent floods probably enabled fluvial reworking and downstream transport of sediment that had accumulated in the course of the previous phase. Confronted with the infill of the mouth of the Grand Rhône, which affected through-flow to the sea, the increase in Rhône discharge resulted in strong offshore sediment transport and in the displacement of the mouth in 1711. It is worth noting that this river-mouth shift was guided and facilitated by the Launes canal, which, created in 1706 in the fight against illicit salt makers, provided a short cut towards the southeast. Its rectilinear course was designed by engineers, who had to counter the hazards of navigation in the lower part of the river mouth.

3.5.2.2 Two "Pauses" Corresponding to Slower Progradation and Evolution to a Lobate Delta (Terminology of Galloway 1975)

The first of these two "pauses", in the first half of the seventeenth century, is illustrated by the Flour and Vortcamp maps. It corresponds to a period of relatively calm hydrological conditions between 1601 and 1646 during which the river flood frequency-gravity index was only 48.6, notwithstanding a number of floods of secondary importance (Pichard and Roucaute 2014). The reduction in the frequency of floods weakened the capacity of downstream river transport. During this period, massive channel sediment loading occurred on other parts of the coast of Provence (Pichard 1999) and on the lower Rhône (Longchambon 1996). The ensuing upstream sediment storage thus reduced or slowed down sediment supply to the Rhône delta mouth. Several morphological indicators point to a decrease in fluvial influence matched by stronger marine processes. The meandering of the Bras de Fer and of the Petit Rhône very near to the coast, the numerous islets organised into a fan-shaped plan morphology at the mouth, and the shallow depths around these islets, and even to significant distances offshore, highlight clogging by sediment that the river mouth is incapable of evacuating. The formation of the Rascaillan spit shows that longshore drift becomes very efficient in redistributing sediments alongshore, associated with increasing wave domination.

The second, illustrated by the maps of Cassini and Isnard at the end of the eighteenth century, highlights the succession of fluvial- and marine-dominated processes in the course of the second half of the eighteenth century. The marked progradation of the Grand Rhône branch owes much to the return of large floods after 1740 (Pichard et al. 2014). These floods were strongly linked to an upsurge in liquid and solid discharge by the Durance, the floods of which appeared to have been strongly favoured by the important degradation of the vegetation and soil cover of the catchment of this tributary at the time. At the end of the century, marine processes seem to have taken command once again, as attested by the significant development of spits, which reflect a decrease in the Rhône sediment input compared to the preceding period. The Rhône delta assumed, for the first time, a multilobate morphology. The maps of Cassini and numerous studies by geomorphologists (Miramont and Guilbert 1997; Landon 1999; Salvador 1991; Bravard 2010; Provansal and Bravard 2009) show that during this period the entire Rhône channel was characterised by a braided pattern, implying important channel sediment storage and significant latency in sediment transfer downstream. The state of the channel therefore had a significant influence on the evolution of the mouth.

3.5.2.3 The Determinant Human Impact on Evolution of the Mouth and Delta in the Nineteenth Century

Starting from the mid-nineteenth century, the mouth adopts once again a bird's foot shape as shown by the sketches of Guérard in 1841, 1852 and 1886 in the Roustan and East branch sectors. It is likely that the strong floods of the 1840s, and then that of 1856 had significant effects on shoreline advance. The suspended sediment supply by the Rhône has been estimated by the naval corps of engineers at 24 Mm^3/year (Maillet et al. 2007). The bathymetric measurements describe the accretion of the prodelta, giving a measure of the important sediment inputs of the floods.

However, delta lobe advance is slowed down and the river-mouth deposits assumed a much more complex morphology at this time. These changes can be explained by many factors. In the first place, the channel maintains a braided style likely to be associated with upstream sediment storage, up to the start of the twentieth century, thus underlining quite clearly the latency necessary for the transition towards another fluvial style (Provansal et al. 2010). In the second place, the suspended load had no doubt started diminishing under the influence of stabilization of land-use patterns in the mountains upstream. Finally, progradation became faced with a large sediment accommodation space (Maillet 2005) that necessitated prior infill (Fanget et al. 2013), thus slowing down the surface expression of the mouth deposits. The modern prodelta started growing at this time. It is presently more than 100 m thick. It is also likely that embanking of the mouths favoured their seaward growth for some time and has, perhaps, been the major agent in shaping the mouths.

During the same period, shoreline retreat increased at the mouths of the Bras de Fer (also named the Old Rhône) and Petit Rhône, while the tip of Beauduc spit grew progressively, starting from the end of the seventeenth century.

3.6 Conclusion

The most characteristic feature of the mouths of the Rhône between the end of the sixteenth and middle of the nineteenth centuries is, without doubt, their remarkable seaward advance, associated with lateral mobility through two avulsions. These avulsions are responsible for the present shape of the delta, having resulted in marked shoreline advance in the central and eastern parts compared to the other earlier shoreline sectors inherited from the Roman period and the Middle Ages. The large amounts of sediment supplied to the mouths still contribute to shoreline stability, and have sourced the formation of the two major sand spits of Beauduc and La Gracieuse.

This evolution owes much to the hydrological regime generated by the cold and wet climatic conditions that accompanied the LIA and its numerous internal oscillations. The data analysed from ancients maps, and corroborated by geomorphic interpretation, highlight two main phases of river-mouth progradation that coincided with the two most drastic "crises" that occurred, respectively, at the end of the sixteenth century, and start of the eighteenth century. The latter coincided in fact with the so-called "Maunder" phase (1650–1715). Periods corresponding to a reduction in river energy are marked by a clear command of marine processes on river-mouth and shoreline dynamics, associated notably with the construction of the afore-mentioned spits. However, hydrological forcing was only efficient when coupled with abundant sediment fluxes generated following agricultural stripping of mountains and development of agrarian territories generated by strong demographic growth after the crisis of the fourteenth to fifteenth centuries. The waxing and waning of sediment supply combined with river discharge fluctuations hinged on LIA oscillations thus resulted in changes in delta shape from bird's foot to lobate. The present period has been characterised by a reduction in solid discharge due to upstream sediment retention in reforested catchments, and also by a lower frequency of strong floods, as well as by engineered river regularisation, all of which have contributed to the stabilization of the mouths of the Rhône.

Even when declined into several more or less severe "phases", this general overarching context of coupled high liquid and solid discharge has not, however, been the only driver of the geomorphic evolution of the Rhône delta and its shoreline. We have shown in this study that several other factors intervened, modulating the influence of the dominant hydrological and sediment supply factors. Among these, marine processes have certainly played an important role. It is hard to envisage a temporally uniform marine process context over five centuries. Unfortunately, there is a lack of data on this component of delta evolution.

The conditions of sediment transfer through the river channel down to the mouth, and even along the coast, also very likely involved periods of latency between catchment stripping and the net morphological resultant downstream. The specific power necessary for downstream transport varies depending on the fluvial style (anastomosed, braided or meandering). Depending on each case, sediment storage or active downstream transfer prevails in the channel. The braided front, which started in the Alpine catchments, and which involved significant sediment storage, progressively migrated downstream, a few km per century, and did not seem to have attained the lower Rhône before the eighteenth century (Provansal and Bravard 2009). However, the unique and deep channel existing today is still capable of locally storing sediment, with lags in downstream transfers that occur during each flood.

Sediment abundance can also have a local feedback effect on hydrology. In an infilled channel, such abundance raises the water levels attained by floods (and thus introduces bias in limnigraphic levels reached by floods). It can also result in changes in channel bed, and even in avulsion in the course of discharge levels that do not necessarily need to be excessive. This theme of interactivity between hydrology and sediments clearly transpires in the interpretation of some of the maps analysed here, and needs to be better studied. Sediment accomodation space at the mouth of the delta is also a very important element. It directly conditions the possibilities of progradation of the delta lobe and its shape.

A final important aspect in the course of the LIA was the will to master, from an engineering point of view, the delta mouths. An immediate but inefficient attempt was made, for instance, in 1587, following the first avulsion, to get the Rhône back into its pre-avulsion channel. Engineering efforts were more efficient in 1711 in maintaining and reinforcing flow in a new channel. These interventions were even stronger after 1852 in order to limit the mouth to a single channel, and have been the main forcing agent in the dynamics of the Grand Rhône mouth. The channelling of river flow in the unique Pégoulier branch in 1852 explains the rapid rogradation of this branch, and paradoxically, its equally rapid infill, resulting in flow diversion into the present branch in 1895.

References

Antonelli C (2002) Flux sédimentaires et morphogenèse récente dans le chenal du Rhône aval. Thesis, Aix-Marseille Université

Antonelli C, Provansal M, Vella C (2004) Recent morphological channel changes in a deltaïc environment. The case of the Rhône River, France. Geomorphology 57:385–402

Antonelli C, Eyrolle F, Rolland B, Provansal M, Sabatier F (2008) Suspended sediment and ^{137}Cs fluxes during the exceptional December 2003 flood in the Rhône River, southeast France. Geomorphology 95:350–360

Arnaud-Fassetta G (2000) Quatre mille ans d'histoire hydrologique du Rhône de l'âge du bronze au siècle du nucléaire. Graphigéo, Prodig, Paris

Arnaud-Fassetta G (2003) River channel changes in the Rhône Delta (France) since the end of the Little Ice Age: geomorphological adjustment to hydroclimatic change and natural resource management. Catena 51:141–172

Arnaud-Fassetta G, Provansal M (1999) High frequency variation of water flux and sediment discharge during the Little Ice Age (1586–1725 AD) in the Rhône delta (Mediterranean France). Hydrobiologia 410:241–250

Arnaud-Fassetta G, Carcaud N, Castanet C, Salvador PG (2010) Fluviatile palaeoenvironments in archaeological context: geographical position, methodological approach and global change – hydrological risk issues. Quat Int 216:93–117

Bravard JP (2010) Discontinuities in braided patterns: Rhône river from Geneva to the Camargue delta before river training. Geomorphology 117:217–233
Bravard JP (2011) La valorisation de la cartographie historique des rivières d'Europe, de la recherche sur la dynamique des paysages à la gestion des eaux. In: Federzoni L, Masotti L (eds) Il paesaggio dei technici. Attualità delle cartographie historica per ilgoverno delle acque. Coll. Bologna, Cremona 2008, ed. Marsilio, Venezia
Bravard JP, Bethemont J (1989) Cartography of rivers in France. In: Petts G (ed) Historical changes of large alluvial rivers. Wiley, London
Brunel C (2010) Evolution séculaire de l'avant-côte de la Méditerranée française, impact de l'élévation du niveau de la mer et des tempêtes. Thesis, Aix-Marseille Université
Caritey C (1995) L'évolution de l'embouchure du Rhône du milieu du XVIIe à la fin du XIXe siècle. Relation avec le régime du fleuve. Mémoire Université Aix-Marseille 1
Desjardins E (1866) Aperçu historique sur les embouchures du Rhône. Travaux anciens et modernes. Mémoires de la Société de Géographie Paris
Fanget AS, Bassetta MA, Arnaud M et al (2013) Historical évolution and extrême climate évents during the last 400 years on the Rhône prodelta (NW Mediterranean). Mar Geol 346:375–391
Forget M (2013) Le rôle des sources historiques dans la compréhension des dynamiques fluviales d'un grand fleuve de plaine. Le cas du Parana argentin. Géomorphologie Relief Processus Environnement 4:445–462
Galloway WE (1975) Process framework for describing the morphologic and stratigraphic evolution of deltaic depositional systems. In: Broussard ML (ed) Deltas: Models for Exploration. Texas Geological Society, Houston, pp 87–98
Guérard A (1895) Etude sur l'amélioration des embouchures des fleuves dans les mers sans marée, note 1. Mémoire de l'Institut des Ingénieurs civils de Londres, vol LXXXII session 1884–85 Part IV
Gurnell A, Peiry JL (2005) Using historical data in fluvial geomorphology. In: Kondolf M, Piegay H (eds) Tools in fluvial geomorphology. Wiley, Chichester
HistRhône (2013) Base de données hydro-climatiques sur le Bas Rhône. http://histrhone.cerege.fr/
Illouze A (1997) Epaves de Camargue d'Aigues-Mortes à Fos-sur-Mer, du XVe au XIXe siècle, Contribution à l'histoire des naufrages. Editions, Camarigo, Nîmes
Jorda M (1985) La torrentialité holocène des Alpes françaises du sud. Facteurs anthropiques et paramètres naturels de son évolution. Symposium International: les modifications de l'environnement dans lebassin méditerranéen occidental à la fin du Pléistocène et pendant l'Holocène. Toulouse, Cahiers Ligures de la Préhistoire, H.S., n°2, pp 49–70
L'Homer A, Bazile A, Thommeret J, Thommeret Y (1981) Principales étapes de l'édification du delta du Rhône de 7000BP à nos jours. Variations du niveau marin. Oceanis 7(4):389–408
Landon N (1999) L'évolution contemporaine du profil en long des affluents du Rhône moyen. Constat régional et analyse d'un hydrosystème complexe, la Drôme. Thesis Université Paris-Sorbonne, 2 vol
Leroy-Ladurie E (1983) Histoire du climat depuis l'An Mil, 2 vols. Flammarion, Paris
Longchambon C (1996) La déviation du lit de la Durance au XVe siècle. Histoire d'une conquête provençale en terre avignonnaise. Annuaire de la société des Amis du Palais des Papes:23–33
Maillet GM (2005) Relations sédimentaires récentes et actuelles entre un fleuve et son delta en milieu microtidal: exemple de l'embouchure du Rhône. Thesis Aix-Marseille Université
Maillet GM, Vella C, Sabatier F, Rousseau D, Provansal M, Fleury J (2006a) Connexions entre le Rhône et son delta (partie 1): évolution du trait de côte du delta du Rhône depuis le milieu du XIXe siècle. Géomorphologie Relief Processus Environnement 2:111–124
Maillet GM, Vella C, Sabatier F, Rousseau D, Provansal M, Fleury J (2006b) Connexions entre le Rhône et son delta (partie 2): Evolution de l'embouchure du Rhône depuis le début du XVIIIème siècle. Géomorphologie Relief Processus Environnement 2:125–140
Maillet GM, Raccasi G, Provansal M, Sabatier F, Antonelli C, Fleury J (2007) Transferts sédimentaires dans le bas Rhône depuis le milieu du 19ème siècle. Revue de géographie physique et quaternaire 61(1):39–54

Miramont C, Guilbert X (1997) Variations historiques de la fréquence des crues et évolution de la morphogenèse fluviale en moyenne Durance (France du sud-est). Géomorphologie Relief, Processus, Environnement 3:325–337
Miramont C, Jorda M, Pichard G (1998) Evolution historique de la morphogenèse et de la dynamique fluviale d'une rivière méditerranéenne: l'exemple de la moyenne Durance (France du SE). Géographie Physique et Quaternaire 52:381–392
Pardé M (1925) Le régime du Rhône, étude hydrologique, Etude et travaux de l'Institut de Géographie Alpine de l'Université de Grenoble. Thesis Université de Grenoble, 2 vol
Pfister C (1988) Une rétrospective météorologique de l'Europe. Un système de reconstitution de l'évolution du temps et du climat en Europe depuis le Moyen-Age central. Histoire et mesure II:313–358
Pichard G (1993) La première carte de Provence – 1591 – P.-J. BOMPAR. Fac-simile et étude l'accompagnant. Terra Cognita, Leuhan
Pichard G (1995) Les crues sur le bas Rhône de 1500 à nos jours. Pour une histoire hydro-climatique. Méditerranée 82(3–4):105–116
Pichard G (1999) Espaces et Nature en Provence. L'environnement rural 1540–1789, 4 vols. Thesis Aix-Marseille Université
Pichard G (2001) L'Espace absorbé par l'économique? Endettement communautaire et pression sur l'environnement en Provence (1640–1730). Histoire & Sociétés Rurales 16:81–115
Pichard G (2005) La découverte géologique de la Camargue, du xvie au début du xixe siècle, Travaux du Comité Français d'Histoire de la Géologie, série3, t. XIX
Pichard G, Roucaute E (2014) Pluies et crues en bas Rhône et caractérisation du Petit Age Glaciaire (PAG), Méditerranée, in press
Pichard G, Provansal M, Sabatier F (2014) Les embouchures du Rhône, l'apport de la cartographie à l'étude de leur évolution géomorphologique au cours du Petit Age Glaciaire, Méditerranée, in press
Pont D, Simonnet JP, Walter A (2002) Medium-term changes in suspended sediment delivery to the ocean: consequences of catchment heterogeneity and river management (Rhône river, France). Estuarine Coastal et Shelf Science 54:1–18
Provansal M, Bravard JP (2009) Le croisement d'approches naturalistes et historiques dans l'étude de l'histoire des fleuves: le cas du Rhône français. Cahiers de Vallesia 21, Archives Etat du Valais ed
Provansal M, Vella C, Aranaud-Fassetta G, Sabatier F, Maillet G (2003) Role of the fluvial sediment input in the mobility of the Rhône delta coast, (France). Géomorphologie Relief Environnement 4:271–282
Provansal M, Villiet J, Eyrolle F, Racassi G, Gurriaran R, Antonelli C (2010) High resolution evolution of recent bank accretion rate of the managed Rhone: a case study bu multi-proxy approach. Geomorphology 117:289–297
Rossiaud J (1993) Réalités et Imaginaire d'un fleuve. Recherches sur le Rhône médiéval. Thesis Grenoble Université
Rossiaud J (2007) Le Rhône au Moyen-Âge. Aubier, collection Historique, Paris
Sabatier F (2001) Fonctionnement et dynamiques morphosédimentaires du littoral du delta du Rhône. Thesis, Aix-Marseille Université
Sabatier F, Suanez S (2003) Evolution of the Rhône delta coast since the end of the 19th century. Géomorphologie Relief Processus Environnement 4:283–300
Sabatier F, Maillet G, Fleury J, Provansal M, Antonelli C, Suanez S, Vella C (2006) Sediment budget of the Rhône delta shoreface since the middle of the 19th century. Mar Geol 234(1–4):143–158
Salvador PG (1991) Le thème de la métamorphose fluviale dans les plaines alluviales du Rhône et de l'Isère; bassin de Malville et ombilic de Moirans, Bas-Dauphiné. Thesis Université Lyon 3
Sclafert T (1959) Cultures en Haute Provence. Déboisements et pâturages au Moyen-Age. S.E.V. P.E.N, Paris
Surrell A (1847) Mémoire sur l'amélioration des embouchures du Rhône, Imprimerie Ballivet & Fabre, Nîmes
Vella C, Fleury TJ, Raccasi G, Provansal M, Sabatier F, Bourcier M (2005) Evolution of the Rhône delta plain in the Holocene. Mar Geol 222–223:235–265

Part II
Studies Case About Sediment Fluxes in Three Different Climatic Zones (Wet Tropical, Semi-Arid, Temperate) During Anthropocene

Chapter 4
Mud Banks, Sand Flux and Beach Morphodynamics: Montjoly Lagoon Beach, French Guiana

Edward J. Anthony, Antoine Gardel, Franck Dolique, Guillaume Brunier, and Christina Péron

Abstract Sandy beaches affected by mud in an open-coast, wave-dominated setting are rare. Such beaches can also show rapid response patterns where large mud banks affect the nearshore wave regime, as on the Amazon-influenced coast of French Guiana. The sand flux patterns and morphodynamic changes affecting Montjoly beach, in Cayenne, have been analysed from interpretation of beach plan-view patterns deduced from four satellite images (1986, 1996, 2003, 2011) and from topographic monitoring at a shorter timescale. The data show the prevalence of beach rotation induced by the gradual approach and alongshore migration of mud banks. An irregular rotation pattern is highlighted, commanded in part by regional-scale and global climatic and hydrodynamic influences on mud bank dynamics. This irregularity denotes the difficulties of elaborating a predictive temporal scheme of beach change.

E.J. Anthony (✉)
Aix Marseille Université, Institut Universitaire de France, CEREGE, UM 34, Europôle Méditerranéen de l'Arbois, B.P. 80, 13545 Aix en Provence Cedex, France
e-mail: anthony@cerege.fr

A. Gardel • C. Péron
Université du Littoral Côte d'Opale, Laboratoire d'Océanologie et de Géosciences, CNRS UMR 8187 LOG, 32, Avenue Foch, 62930 Wimereux, France

CNRS Guyane, USR3456, 2, Avenue Gustave Charlery, Immeuble Le Relais, 97300 Cayenne, France

F. Dolique
Univ. Antilles-Guyane, Martinique, 97275 Schoelcher, France

G. Brunier
CEREGE, Université Aix Marseille, UMR 34, Europôle Méditerranéen de l'Arbois, B.P. 80, 13545 Aix en Provence Cedex, France

M. Maanan, M. Robin (eds.), *Sediment Fluxes in Coastal Areas*, Coastal Research Library 10, DOI 10.1007/978-94-017-9260-8_4

4.1 Introduction

Intertidal beaches affected periodically or permanently by mud on wave-dominated coasts are extremely rare, because of hydrodynamically controlled non-deposition of mud, and the common lack of substantial nearby mud supplies. Generally, sandy beaches evolve alongshore into muddy tidal flats as a function of wave energy (Masselink and Short 1993). Where mud supplies are important, this longshore energy segregation may also occur across shore with low-tide mud fronting a high-tide sandy beach. Such mud-affected sandy beaches are generally found associated with high fine-grained discharge deltas such as the Mekong (Tamura et al. 2010) or in settings subject to spates of more or less important mud mobilization from nearby sources such as offshore mud shoals, as on the Kerala coast in India (Tatavarti and Narayana 2006), or lagoonal mud as in the case of the Cassino beach and lagoon system in Brazil (Calliari et al. 2009). Such beaches are fine examples of the importance of sediment heterogeneity in coastal systems (Holland and Elmore 2008). The influence of mud on sandy beaches has, however, elicited little interest in the literature, no doubt because of the rarity evoked above. Where abundant mud supplies occur, their effect on sandy beaches is generally invested in varying degrees of dissipation of wave energy. This dissipation can range from partial to total. In the former case, this can induce longshore and cross-shore variations in sand flux and the ensuing beach morphodynamics, and in the latter case, in no sand flux.

Fine examples of mud-affected sandy beaches in an open-coast, wave-dominated setting occur in French Guiana, which lies on the world's longest muddy coast between the mouths of the Amazon and the Orinoco Rivers (Fig. 4.1). These beaches fall into three categories: (1) highly embayed short pocket beaches (0.1–1 km-long), locally referred to as *anses* (literally small bays), (2) longer (>2 < 5 km-long) more open beaches between bedrock headlands, and (3) open, non-embayed chenier beaches. Types 1 and 2 beaches are essentially limited to the bedrock promontory of Cayenne (Fig. 4.1), the hard-rock headlands of which consist of migmatites and granulites. The embayments between these headlands are bound by narrow (<500 m) sandy fringing beaches that generally abut older, probably Pleistocene, deposits that form a stiff, widespread reddish clay deposit. Locally, pronounced beach erosion may lead to exposure of these deposits in the backshore area. Cheniers are generally formed in the vicinity of river mouths.

The aim of this paper is to show the effects of mud from the Amazon on sand flux and, hence, the morphodynamics of a sector of beach in Cayenne (Fig. 4.1). Montjoly beach is the longest of the embayed beaches of Cayenne. The studied sector concerns the northwestern sector of Montjoly beach, and includes the inlet of a small lagoon, Montjoly Lagoon (ML sector) that is seasonally closed from the sea. The presence of mud alters the behavioural patterns of this beach, which is normally under the command of seasonal changes in wave energy due to trade-wind activity. Using aerial photographs covering the period 1958–2000 and aerial videographs obtained in 1998–1999, Anthony et al. (2002) showed that this beach undergoes rotation induced by migrating mud banks from the Amazon. This rotation pattern was further confirmed by high-resolution topographic surveys (Anthony and Dolique 2004). These authors further defined the beach morphological changes in

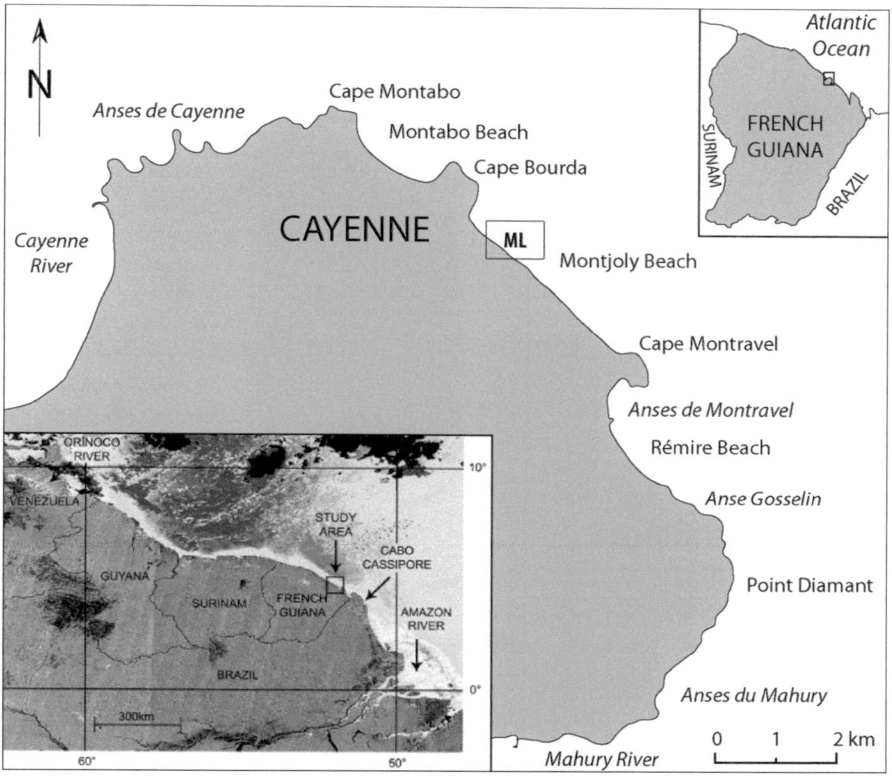

Fig. 4.1 The muddy coast of South America between the Amazon and the Orinoco river mouths and the bedrock-headland-bound sandy beaches of Cayenne, French Guiana. *Box* shows the monitored Montjoly Lagoon sector of Montjoly beach

terms of a simple, four-stage conceptual model (Anthony and Dolique 2006) comprising ‘bank’, ‘interbank’ (see Sect. 4.2) and transitional phases (Fig. 4.2).

In this paper, we analyse the sand flux patterns and beach morphodynamic changes involved in this rotation, based on the interpretation of beach plan-view patterns deduced from four satellite images (1986, 1996, 2003, 2011) and from topographic monitoring at a shorter timescale. An irregular rotation pattern is highlighted, commanded in part by regional-scale and global climatic and hydrodynamic influences on mud bank dynamics. This irregularity denotes the difficulties of elaborating a predictive temporal scheme of beach change.

4.2 The Regional Beach Setting

The sedimentary geology and morphodynamics of the northwestern coast of South America between the mouths of the Amazon and the Orinoco (Fig. 4.1) are dominated by the massive fine-grained discharge of the Amazon. The influence

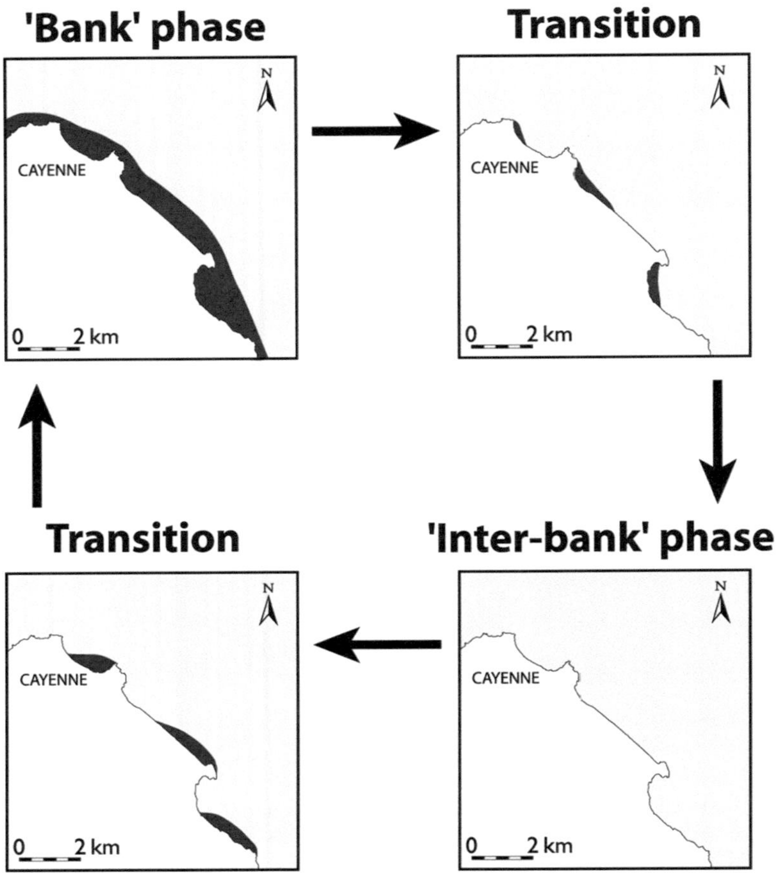

Fig. 4.2 A mud bank on the French Guiana coast showing incipient colonization by mangroves. This mud bank is one of several (up to 15 or more) banks migrating at any time from the mouth of the Amazon river in Brazil to that of the Orinoco river in Venezuela

of the Amazon is essentially imprinted on this coast via a unique system of successive mud banks that circulate alongshore. Each mud bank (Fig. 4.3) can be up to 60 km-long and 30 km-wide, and can contain several times the annual mud supply of the Amazon (Anthony et al. 2010), estimated at ca. 750–1,000 × 10^6 tonnes·year^{-1} (Filizola and Guyot 2009; Martinez et al. 2009; Wittmann et al. 2011). In this Amazon-dominated coastal environment, one of the muddiest in the world, sandy beaches are rare, and form cheniers, and in French Guiana, headlound-bound bay beaches (Fig. 4.1). It has been suggested that the limited presence of sand bodies on this coast reflects the diluting influence of the enormous mud supply from the Amazon during the Quaternary and limited sediment yield from the local, well-forested drainage basins despite high rainfall (Anthony and Dolique 2004). Such blanketing of relict fluvial sand by the cover of Amazon mud on the inner shelf has been deemed by these authors to preclude shoreward sand reworking to form the beach-ridge barrier systems that are common along many sand-rich wave-dominated shorefaces such

Fig. 4.3 A four-phase model of sandy beach morphological change involving rotation in response to Amazon mud-bank activity in Cayenne, French Guiana. The cycle comprises a bank, an inter-bank and two transitional phases, as a typical mud bank attains and migrates past the Cayenne headland. The transitional phase between bank and inter-bank phases shows the most rapid (days to months) and most spectacular beach changes because the natural longshore drift (from southeast to northwest) generated by trade-wind waves on this coast is reinforced by longshore gradients in wave height due to inshore dissipation by mud trapped by northwestern headlands. This occurs as the trailing edge of a mud bank goes past each headland-bound beach in Cayenne (Modified, from Anthony and Dolique 2006)

as those of the southeast coast of Brazil (Dominguez et al. 1992) and the coast of West Africa (Anthony 1995). Seismic data off French Guiana show that inner shelf mud overlies sandy deposits of presumably fluvial origin that crop out on the middle shelf at depths beyond 20 m (Bouysse et al. 1977; Pujos et al. 1990). In this area, the coastal progradational sequence comprises over-consolidated mud on the inner shelf (0 to −20 m) that forms a relict Pleistocene to Holocene bed surface over which modern mud banks migrate (Allison et al. 2000), within a dynamic system of short-term to seasonal sedimentation and resuspension cycles. This dynamic system feeds the long-term inner shelf mud accumulation, which is characterised by offshore thinning of the mud wedge, a phenomenon typical of wave influence.

Beaches in French Guiana are characterised by relatively uniform coarse to fine quartz sand, a variable amount of heavy minerals and a very small fraction (<1 %) of shelly debris. Pujos et al. (2000) concluded from analyses of the heavy-mineral assemblages that these sands are not winnowed out from the migrating Amazon mud banks but are derived exclusively from local rivers west of the Amazon that drain the Quaternary coastal plain and adjacent crystalline Guiana Shield. The heavy-mineral suite is dominated by amphibolites, followed by staurolite, epidote, and pyroxenes. Sondag et al. (2010) have shown that some of these rivers have very low suspended loads, the Maroni, which forms the border between French Guiana and Surinam, having among the world's lowest values.

Sandy beaches are important both economically and ecologically on the muddy South American coast because these relatively rare deposits provide locations for human settlement and routes. The rare beaches on this part of the South American coast are fundamental for the ecology of protected marine turtles (*Lepidochelys olivacea*, *Chelonia mydas*, *Eretmochelys imbricata*, *Dermochelys coriacea*) which require mud-free beaches for successful nesting (Kelle et al. 2007; Caut et al. 2010).

ML beach is affected by trade winds from the northeast that are mainly active from January to April. Waves impinging on the beach have periods ranging from 6 to 12 s, indicating a mix of trade wind-waves and longer swell, while offshore modal heights are up to 1.5 m. The longer-period waves (>10 s) are large swell waves generated by North Atlantic depressions in autumn and winter (e.g., van Ledden et al. 2009) and by Central Atlantic cyclones in summer and autumn. The most energetic trade wind-waves are observed between January and April (Fig. 4.4) in response to peak wind activity while swell waves appear to be most frequent in autumn and winter, reinforcing the relatively high winter to early spring wave-energy regime induced by the trade winds. Tides are semi-diurnal and the spring tidal range is mesotidal (2.5–3.1 m).

The longshore migration of the mud banks, essentially under the influence of waves (Gardel and Gratiot 2005; Gratiot et al. 2007, 2008), results in marked space- and time-varying coastal geomorphic changes that can be summarized in terms of alongshore-alternating 'bank' and 'inter-bank' zones (Anthony and Dolique 2004; Anthony et al. 2010). Differences in migration rates also account in part for variations in the spacing between the banks, and possibly bank morphology as well, notably where mud banks are 'stretched' alongshore. Mud translation

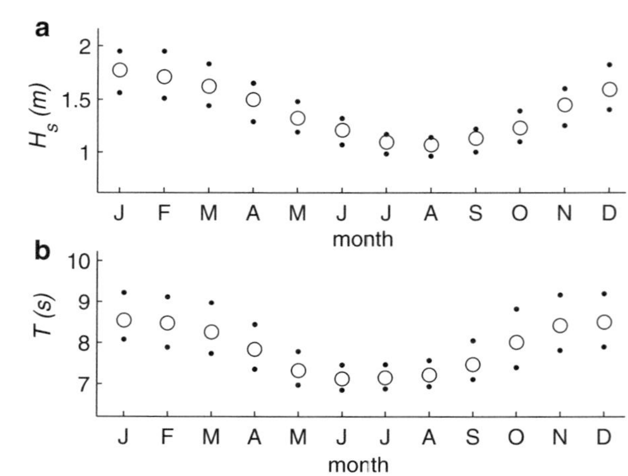

Fig. 4.4 Daily averages of wave-climate parameters offshore of French Guiana, H_s and T_s, derived from a 44-years record (1960–2004) of the ERA-40 (European ReAnalysis) wave dataset generated by the European Centre for Medium-Range Weather Forecasts (ECMWF) for the location 5° N, 52° W. Dots correspond to the first and third inter-quartiles, and circles to the median values (From Gratiot et al. 2007)

shoreward generally results in the formation and accretion of bars that favour rapid and large-scale mangrove colonization of the migrating mud bank (Anthony et al. 2008; Proisy et al. 2009; Gardel et al. 2011; Gensac et al. 2011). Banks and their mangrove vegetation dissipate wave energy (Wells 1983; Gratiot et al. 2007; Winterwerp et al. 2007), protecting the coast from wave attack. Inter-bank areas between the dissipative mud banks are associated with a deeper shoreface. They are either subject to rapid shoreline retreat (Anthony et al. 2011) over timescales corresponding to the inter-bank phases (order of years) where the coast has previously accreted through mud bank 'welding' onshore, or exhibit, where sandy beaches are present, typical beach morphodynamic behaviour.

Both mud-bank and muddy inter-bank areas show various stages of mud concentration and consolidation (Gratiot et al. 2007), depending on history, bed elevation within the tidal frame and liquefaction processes. In 'bank' areas, these range from very high-suspended sediment concentrations (1–10 $g{\cdot}l^{-1}$), through fluid mud, to settled mud, which, in turn, ranges from under-consolidated ($\leq$650 $g{\cdot}l^{-1}$) to consolidated sediment beds ($\geq$750 $g{\cdot}l^{-1}$). 'Inter-bank' zones are generally associated with 'clearer' waters (SSC of 1–5 $g{\cdot}l^{-1}$) but comprise consolidated beds. Inter-bank dynamics are essentially hinged on wave activity. The absence of a mud bank in inter-bank areas allows for significant wave energy incidence along the shore, but this effect is strongly modulated by the vertical tidal excursion. Notwithstanding the higher-energy status of inter-bank areas, inter-bank shorefaces are permanently muddy due to the pervasive influence of the Amazon muddy discharge, and as a result, the wave regime shows changes from spilling to solitary waves that are modulated by tides. Waves remain in the spilling domain up to the 'terrestrial' shore at high tide, while solitary wave behaviour expresses dissipation at low tide over the inner shoreface. Strong wave energy gradients occur in inter-bank areas during the course of the tidal excursion, with systematic wave-energy dampening by subtidal mud at low tide, and wave heights significantly increasing at high tide. High-tide hydrodynamic conditions are associated with a relatively narrow surf zone and energy concentration on the shore due to the marked sediment segregation between the flat muddy shoreface and the relatively steep sandy beach profile. In shoreline areas where only mud occurs, this high-tide wave energy incidence can lead to the rapid erosion of consolidated mud and large-scale mangrove removal.

4.3 Methodology

ML beach has been monitored using a multi-scale approach involving remote sensing, observations from low-flying aircraft and field measurements. Given the time frame of beach change under the influence of the large migrating mud banks (migration rates of the order of 1–5 km/year), we have had recourse to remote sensing at various timescales, based on the analysis of aerial photographs, aerial videographs, and satellite images. ML beach was surveyed topographically during two distinct periods (2000–2004, and 2011), using respectively, a total station and

GPS system. Field surveys were interrupted in 2004 due to logistical difficulties, and resumed in 2011. Both survey methods have yielded high-resolution data. Routine field observations of wave breaking heights were conducted during these surveys.

4.4 Results

Four SPOT images corresponding to the years 1986, 1995, 2003 and 2011 summarize the general medium-term dynamics of ML beach (Fig. 4.5). The situation in Fig. 4.5 a corresponds to a 'bank' phase in 1986. In this situation, mud has welded

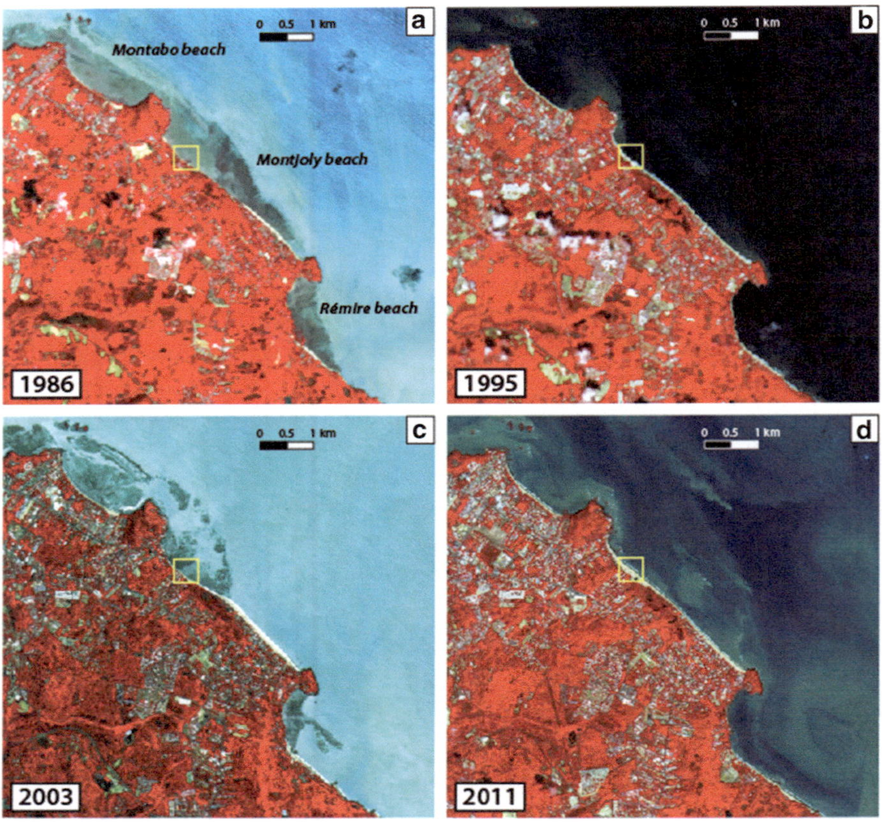

Fig. 4.5 Four SPOT images showing changes in ML beach sector (*yellow box*) associated with bank and inter-bank dynamics: (**a**) bank phase in 1986 resulting in completely mud-bound beaches; (**b**) inter-bank phase in 1996 and the instauration of 'normal' wave-beach interactions; (**c**) bank phase in 2003 but with only partial welding of mud on ML beach; (**d**) inter-bank phase in 2011

directly onshore, but the image does show the presence of a sandy beach only in the southeastern sector of Montjoly, thus suggesting erosion or fossilisation of ML beach by the important muddy foreshore which is up to 1 km-wide. The image follows at least 2 years of complete mud-bounding and mangrove colonization of the mud, and shows the inception of mud erosion, especially in the southeastern sector of Montjoly, and of the neighbouring Rémire beach (Fig. 4.1). Within the ten-year interval between the 1986 and 1995 images, the return to an inter-bank phase had resulted in complete erosion of the welded part of the mud bank and the instauration of 'normal' wave-beach interactions. The 1995 image (Fig. 4.5b) shows the recovery of ML beach and a fairly balanced beach width throughout Montjoly. The 2003 image (Fig. 4.5c) corresponds to a new bank phase. Unlike the 1986 situation where all the beaches of Cayenne were completely mud-bound (Fig. 4.5a), the 2003 situation was one of partial mud welding on the main Cayenne beaches, with welding becoming much more significant just west of the Cayenne promontory. The image shows an eroded ML beach bound by a significant patch of mud. The 2011 image shows a full inter-bank phase (Fig. 4.5d). The remarkable recovery of ML beach is clear in this image.

The foregoing remarks derived from analysis of the satellite images are corroborated by topographic survey data of ML beach for the period 2000–2004 and 2011 (Fig. 4.6). The successive profiles highlight the marked changes undergone by this sector of the beach in the course of: (a) the transitional (to bank) phase that prevailed from 1996 to at least 2002, (b) the partial bank phase shown in the 2003 image, and (c) the full inter-bank phase highlighted in the 2011 image. The profiles show a strongly eroded beach in 2000. The cliffed profiles of April 2000 and November 2000 started evolving in March 2002 into an accretional profile associated with a well-developed berm. This accretional phase was succeeded by an intermediate erosional phase between the profiles of May 2002 and February 2003. In just 8 months, between February 2003 and February 2004, the recovery was spectacular, resulting in a gain in beach width of over 60 m. Between February 2004 and March 2011, the gain in width continued, though at a much reduced pace. These successive changes are depicted in the ground photographs in Fig. 4.7. The progression goes from the erosive transitional (bank to inter-bank) phase in Fig. 4.7a, through the rapid sand recovery phase in Fig. 4.7b, to the strongly accreted phase that has prevailed from 2004 (Fig. 4.7c) to 2011 (Fig. 4.7d).

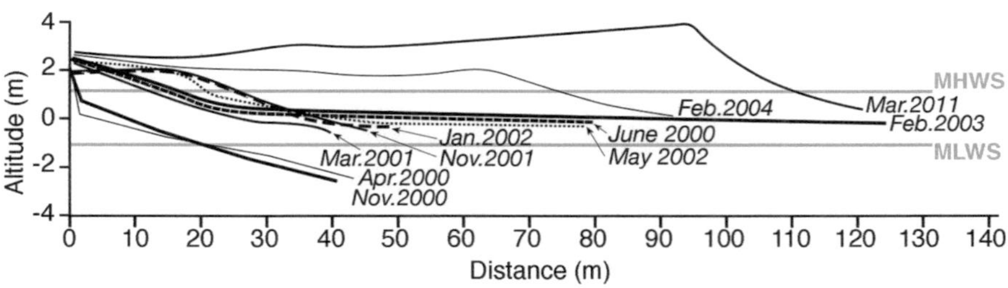

Fig. 4.6 Profiles of ML beach showing the extremely rapid accretion during the last transitional bank-to-inter-bank phase (2002–2004) and a still highly accreted beach in 2011 (inter-bank phase)

Fig. 4.7 Ground photographs showing successive stages of recovery of ML beach in the course of the last 12 years: (**a**) severe erosion during the transition from an inter-bank to an impending bank phase (June 2000); (**b**) onset of accretion (November 2001) during the march towards the bank phase; (**c**, **d**) full recovery during the inter-bank phase which has now lasted from around 2004 to 2012

Fig. 4.8 Aerial (**a**, January 2003) and ground photograph (**b**, March 2003) showing the migrating sand front that sourced the rapid accretion of the ML beach sector

Routine field observations showed that these changes were accompanied by sharp longshore gradients in sediment flux and wave breaking heights. During the 2000–2004 surveys, breaker heights generally decreased from maximum values of 0.5–1 m in the ML sector to no more than 0.5 m in the low-energy southeastern sector at high tide, where significant mud accumulations persisted below the mean neap tide level. The trend showed a complete reversal in the course of the surveys from 2003 to 2004, with low breaker heights in the ML sector and increasingly higher breakers to the southeast. The trend was accompanied by sand transfer from the latter sector to the ML sector, materialised by a migrating sand front (Fig. 4.8), updrift of which

Fig. 4.9 Ground photograph showing beach surface collapse features due to rapid and sustained sand flux over poorly consolidated mud inherited from the preceding bank phase (February, 2003). The collapse zone is preceded by a typical mud-erosion zone, the eroded mud accumulating further downdrift towards the ML beach sector in the background. The sand flux is associated with the migrating sand front shown in Fig. 4.8 under inter-bank conditions

occurred relatively high angles of breaker incidence (10–15°) followed by sharply refracted wave crests downdrift of the front. In the vicinity of the migrating sand front, the beach displayed unique bed deformation structures, essentially beach subsidence and collapse features (Fig. 4.9). These features appeared mainly in the mid-beach area, and were generally strictly limited to a zone ranging in length from a few tens of metres to over 100 m during each tide, and consisting of well-sorted and well-packed quartz sand. The dynamics of these features were very hard to monitor in the field using intrusive devices because of their instability and ephemeral nature. By the end of 2004, these features had completely disappeared as sand increasingly accumulated in the drift terminus sector of ML beach. In the course of field visits between 2004 and 2008, the southeastern sector of Montjoly, was seen to be undergoing strong erosion that necessitated the hasty emplacement of rock armouring to protect beach-front homes, in strong contrast to ML beach. A 2010 aerial photograph of Montjoly beach shows, in addition to the highly accreted ML sector, an eroded central sector and a moderately large beach in the southeast, indicating some recovery of the latter sector (Fig. 4.10).

4.5 Discussion and Conclusions

At the largest spatio-temporal scale, sediment flux on the French Guiana coast is essentially invested in massive mud banks that dissipate wave energy as they migrate alongshore at rates of a few kilometres a year. These banks are separated

Fig. 4.10 A 2010 aerial photograph of Montjoly beach showing the highly accreted ML sector, an eroded central sector and a moderately large beach in the southeast. The erosion of the central sector heralds the onset of a new cycle of sand flux towards the southeast under an impending bank phase that will ultimately lead to the erosion of the ML sector, as in 1998–2000

by relatively mud-deficient inter-bank zones characterized by much a less dissipative inner shoreface. Inter-bank zones (and inter-bank phases) are thus the loci of sand concentration within this predominantly muddy environment. In this study of beach sand flux on the muddy Amazon-influenced coast of French Guiana, the presence of mud has been shown to alter significantly the behavioural pattern of ML beach, which is normally influenced by seasonal changes in wave energy due to trade-wind activity. The results depicted in Figs. 4.5 and 4.6 highlight cycles of beach change that comprise two bank phases, a major one in 1986 (Fig. 4.5a) during which ML beach was completely mud-bound, and a minor one in 2003 (Fig. 4.5c) marked by the presence of a more patchy muddy foreshore. Between these two phases, the 1995 situation (Fig. 4.5c) corresponded to one of a classical inter-bank, just as the 2011 (Fig. 4.5d) situation. The images also highlight the inexistence of sand in the ML sector during both bank phases and significant beach recovery during inter-bank situations, thus underlining the intensity of beach changes during the transitional (bank-to-inter-bank and inter-bank-to-bank) phases, when the coexistence of mud and sand results in marked variability in sediment flux.

The changes shown by ML beach (Figs. 4.5, 4.6, and 4.7) are embedded in longshore variability. On this beach, mud bank phases are preceded by erosion of ML beach because mud is trapped during the inter-bank to bank transition in the updrift (towards the southeast) beach sector near Cape Montravel, resulting in differential wave energy dissipation. The strong gradient in incident wave energy provided by mud accumulation in the southeastern sector of Montjoly generates strong 'counteractive' longshore drift to this low-energy mud-bound sector (relative to the usual northwest drift direction towards ML during the 'normal' inter-bank phase), thus, resulting in the marked erosion of ML beach (Figs. 4.5a, c, 4.7a). In essence, understanding this cycle of beach changes implies that ML beach had been subjected to a phase of erosion during the inter-bank to bank phase preceding the 1986 image (Fig. 4.5a). In contrast, during the bank-to-inter-bank transition, as a mud bank migrates northwestward past Cayenne, mud is trapped downdrift in the lee of the headland, in the ML beach sector, which acts as a dissipative, low-energy zone. Changes are most marked during this bank-to-inter-bank transition. Beach erosion of the more exposed southeastern sector of Montjoly does not lead to offshore sand transfer, but rather to rapid longshore sand flux towards ML associated with a migrating sand front (Fig. 4.8) due to the sharp now inverted longshore gradient in wave energy. Longshore gradients in incident wave energy, due to differential refraction and dissipation, reinforce the 'usual' sand drift to the northwest generated by waves, thus leading to rapid and massive sand accumulation in the previously strongly eroded ML sector. The early phase of this accumulation showed an intermediate erosional phase between the profiles of May 2002 and February 2003 that appears to reflect embedded higher-order seasonal berm cut associated with either strong trade-wind wave activity in January (Fig. 4.4), or episodic swell in autumn.

The ensuing massive accumulation included a short-lived phase of sand loading over poorly consolidated mud marked by the development of rarely observed and spectacular but ephemeral beach deformation features (Fig. 4.9). The mechanism that appears to explain these features is hydraulically-driven adjustment of the underlying mud to sand loading (Anthony and Dolique 2006). Adjustment of the mud-rich beach profile to sand loading in the intertidal zone appeared to occur through a combination of dispersive flow of the upper fluid mud and further dewatering of in situ underlying under-consolidated mud. These two processes are deemed to generate accommodation space to which the overlying sand above the water exfiltration zone responded by forming subsiding packages of non-saturated sand delimited by cracks alongshore. The lower part of the deformation zone was affected by water exfiltration associated with sand piping and water undermining processes and with spatial differences in mud consolidation. The whole phase of collapse-feature formation ranged from 3 to 6 months, but the features at any one stage on the beach were ephemeral because they were formed in a zone of intense wave activity and were washed out by a tide-controlled succession of breaking waves (low tide) and surf-swash motions (rising tide) as the tide rises. Trenches cut in the beach during the formation of the features were very unstable, but showed that the vertical failure planes were not preserved and that mud was progressively buried under a thickening sand sheet.

The chief effect of the waxing and waning of mud-bank activity on the sediment flux of the drift-aligned headland-bound ML beach is, thus, periodic alternations in longshore drift that lead to a rare form of beach rotation that does not result from seasonal variations in deepwater wave approach directions, as is generally reported for non-mud bank-affected beaches (e.g., Thomas et al. 2012). These beach morphological changes correspond to the simple, four-stage conceptual model identified by Anthony and Dolique (2004), comprising bank, inter-bank and two transitional phases (Fig. 4.2). In the case of ML beach, rotation is a medium-term (>10 year < 15 years?) process due to changes in shallow shoreface bathymetry induced by the migrating subtidal to intertidal mud banks. These bathymetric changes affect wave refraction and dissipation patterns, resulting in marked longshore gradients in incident wave energy. These strong wave energy gradients along sections of the shore facing the leading or trailing edges of the mud banks generate longshores and flux in this headland-bound beach, resulting in alternations in erosion and accretion over time, without net sediment loss.

While the model of evolution of ML beach is inscribed in a cycle of rotation, there is presently no certainty as regards cycle duration. Each bank-to-bank cycle apparently involve periods of several years, certainly exceeding a decade. The SPOT image coverage suggests a mesoscale cycle of 17 years between the 1986 and 2003 bank phases. However, this periodicity involves several uncertainties and the two bank phases are quite dissimilar, the 2003 one being only partial, limited to ML beach and, thus, conducive to strong longshore gradients in sediment flux that may explain the impressive accumulation of sand in the ML beach sector. Apart from this condition of the degree of mud-bounding, the duration of this accumulation limb of the bank-to-inter-bank cycle is totally dependent on the rate at which the next bank intrudes on the southeastern sector of Montjoly. In the present cycle, this duration has now attained 10 years (2002–2012), and will be interrupted in the next 2 years given the proximity to Cape Montravel of the next mud bank. The situation illustrated in Fig. 4.10 may, thus, appear to herald the onset of a new cycle of sand flux towards the southeast under an impending bank phase. This phase appears to start with the erosion of the median sector of the beach where wave gradients are probably most marked, and will ultimately lead to the erosion of the ML sector, as in 1998–2000.

These considerations are important in terms of coastal zone management and ecology, the sandy beaches of Cayenne offering rare recreational space and egg-laying sites for marine turtles for over 300 km of muddy shore west of the mouth of the Amazon (Fig. 4.1). Gratiot et al. (2007) showed that notable phases of increased wave energy were accompanied by higher annual rates of longshore mud-bank migration, but these authors also noted a poor correlation between the wave forcing parameter combining wave height (H) and period (T), H_0^3/T^2, and migration rates because of the contribution of other mechanisms to bank migration, including wave incidence angle and wind stress. These other mechanisms include both regional meteorological-hydrodynamic forcing and distant Atlantic forcing. On a global scale, the role of storm tracks and storm intensity in the North Atlantic, such as those associated with the North Atlantic Oscillation and El Niño and La Niña events needs to be taken into account. These sources of hydrodynamic forcing provide scope for future studies (Anthony et al. 2013).

Acknowledgements The authors acknowledge various French research grants involving work on the Amazon-influenced coast of South America. These include funding by the Centre National d'Etudes Spatiales (CNES), by the Institut National des Sciences de l'Univers (INSU), and by the Université du Littoral Côte d'Opale (ULCO). Edward Anthony acknowledges a grant from the Institut Universitaire de France. Denis Marin and Patrick Pentsch are thanked for preparing the illustrations.

References

Allison MA, Lee MT, Ogston AS, Aller RC (2000) Origin of Amazon mudbanks along the northeastern coast of South America. Mar Geol 163:241–256

Anthony EJ (1995) Beach-ridge progradation in response to sediment supply: examples from West Africa. Mar Geol 129:175–186

Anthony EJ, Dolique F (2004) The influence of Amazon-derived mud banks on the morphology of sandy, headland-bound beaches in Cayenne, French Guiana: a short- to long-term perspective. Mar Geol 208:249–264

Anthony EJ, Dolique F (2006) Intertidal subsidence and collapse features on wave-exposed, drift-aligned sandy beaches subject to Amazon mud: Cayenne, French Guiana. Earth Surf Process Landf 31:1051–1057

Anthony EJ, Gardel A, Dolique F, Guiral D (2002) Short-term changes in the plan shape of a sandy beach in response to sheltering by a nearshore mud bank, Cayenne, French Guiana. Earth Surf Process Landf 27:857–866

Anthony EJ, Dolique F, Gardel A, Gratiot N, Proisy C, Polidori L (2008) Nearshore intertidal topography and topographic-forcing mechanisms of an Amazon-derived mud bank in French Guiana. Cont Shelf Res 28:813–822

Anthony EJ, Gardel A, Gratiot N, Proisy C, Allison MA, Dolique F, Fromard F (2010) The Amazon-influenced muddy coast of South America: a review of mud-bank-shoreline interactions. Earth-Sci Rev 103:99–121

Anthony EJ, Gardel A, Dolique F (2011) The Amazon-influenced mud-bank coast of South America: short- to long-term morphodynamics of 'inter-bank' areas and chenier development. J Coast Res SI 64:25–29

Anthony EJ, Gardel A, Proisy P, Fromard F, Gensac E, Peron C, Walcker R, Lesourd S (2013) The role of fluvial sediment supply and river-mouth hydrology in the dynamics of the muddy, Amazon-dominated Amapá-Guianas coast, South America: a 3-point research agenda. J South Am Earth Sci 44:18–24

Bouysse P, Kudrass HR, Le Lann F (1977) Reconnaissance sédimentologique du plateau continental de la Guyane française (mission Guyamer 1975). Bulletin du Bureau de Recherches Géologiques et Minières 4:141–179

Calliari LJ, Winterwerp JC, Fernandes E, Cuchiara D, Vinzon SB, Sperle M, Holland KT (2009) Fine grain sediment transport and deposition in the Patos Lagoon–Cassino beach sedimentary system. Cont Shelf Res 29:515–529

Caut S, Guirlet E, Girondot M (2010) Effect of tidal overwash on the embryonic development of leatherback turtles in French Guiana. Mar Environ Res 69:254–261

Dominguez JML, Bittencourt ACSP, Martin L (1992) Controls on quaternary coastal evolution of the east-northeastern coast of Brazil: roles of sea-level history, trade winds and climate. Sediment Geol 80:213–232

Filizola N, Guyot JL (2009) Suspended sediment yields in the Amazon basin: an assessment using the Brazilian national data set. Hydrol Process 23:3207–3215

Gardel A, Gratiot N (2005) A satellite image-based method for estimating rates of mud banks migration, French Guiana, South America. J Coast Res 21:720–728

Gardel A, Gensac E, Anthony EJ, Lesourd S, Loisel H (2011) Wave-formed mud bars: their morphodynamics and role in opportunistic mangrove colonization. J Coast Res SI 64:384–387

Gensac E, Gardel A, Lesourd S, Anthony EJ, Proisy C, Loisel H (2011) Short-term prediction of the evolution of mangrove surface areas: the example of the mud banks of Kourou and Sinnamary, French Guiana. J Coast Res SI 64:388–392

Gratiot N, Gardel A, Anthony EJ (2007) Trade-wind waves and mud dynamics on the French Guiana coast, South America: input from ERA-40 wave data and field investigations. Mar Geol 236:15–26

Gratiot N, Anthony EJ, Gardel A, Gaucherel C, Proisy C, Wells JT (2008) Significant contribution of the 18.6 year tidal cycle to regional coastal changes. Nat Geosci 1:169–172

Holland KT, Elmore PA (2008) A review of heterogeneous sediments in coastal environments. Earth-Sci Rev 89:116–134

Kelle L, Gratiot N, Nolibos L, Therese J, Wongsopawiro R, De Thoisy B (2007) Monitoring of nesting leatherback turtles (*Dermochelys coriacea*): contribution of remote-sensing for real time assessment of beach coverage in French Guiana. Chelonian Conserv Biol 6:142–149

Martinez JM, Guyot JL, Filizola N, Sondag F (2009) Increase in sediment discharge of the Amazon river assessed by monitoring network and satellite data. Catena 79:257

Masselink G, Short AD (1993) The effect of tide range on beach morphodynamics and morphology: a conceptual beach model. J Coast Res 9:785–800

Proisy C, Gratiot N, Anthony EJ, Gardel A, Fromard F, Heuret P (2009) Mud bank colonization by opportunistic mangroves: a case study from French Guiana using lidar data. Cont Shelf Res 29:632–641

Pujos M, Bouysse P, Pons JC (1990) Sources and distribution of heavy minerals in Late Quaternary sediments of the French Guiana continental shelf. Cont Shelf Res 10:59–79

Pujos M, Pons JC, Parra M (2000) Les minéraux lourds des sables du littoral de la Guyane française: bilan sur l'origine des dépôts de la plate-forme des Guyanes. Oceanol Acta 24 (Suppl):S27–S35

Sondag F, Guyot JL, Moquet JS, Laraque A, Adèle G, Cochonneau G, Doudou JC, Lagane C, Vauchel P (2010) Suspended sediment and dissolved load budgets of two Amazonian rivers from the Guiana Shield: Maroni river at Langa Tabaki and Oyapock river at Saut Maripa (French Guiana). Hydrol Process 24:1433–1445

Tamura T, Horaguchi K, Saito Y, Nguyen VL, Tateishi M, Ta TKO, Nanayama F, Watanabe K (2010) Monsoon-influenced variations in morphology and sediment of a mesotidal beach on the Mekong river delta coast. Geomorphology 116:11–23

Tatavarti R, Narayana AC (2006) Hydrodynamics in a mud bank regime during nonmonsoon and monsoon seasons. J Coast Res 22:1463–1473

Thomas T, Phillips MR, Williams AT, Jenkins RE (2012) Medium time-scale behaviour of adjacent embayed beaches: influence of low energy external forcing. Appl Geogr 32:265–280

van Ledden M, Vaughn G, Lansen J, Wiersma F, Amsterdam M (2009) Extreme waves along the Guyana coastline in October 2005. Cont Shelf Res 29:352–361

Wells JT (1983) Dynamics of coastal fluid muds in low-, moderate-, and high-tide-range environments. Can J Fish Aquat Sci 40:130–142

Winterwerp JC, de Graaff RF, Groeneweg J, Luijendijk AP (2007) Modelling of wave damping at Guyana mud coast. Coast Eng 54:249–261

Wittmann H, von Blackenberg F, Maurice L, Guyot JL, Filizola N, Kubik PW (2011) Sediment production and delivery in the Amazon river basin quantified by in-situ-produced cosmogenic nuclides and recent river loads. Geol Soc Am Bull 123:934–950

Chapter 5
The Coastal Sediment Provenance and Their Distribution in the Mediterranean Beaches of NW Morocco

Abdelmounim El Mrini, Driss Nachite, Giorgio Anfuso, Mohamed Maanan, Giuseppe Cultrone, Carmela Vaccaro, and Elena Marrocchino

Abstract This work deals with the granulometric and geochemical features of sediments collected at the foreshore of Tetouan beaches (NW Morocco) and at the mouth of the local five main watercourses in order to establish the links between the continental and coastal areas. The littoral, which underwent a great increase of human pressure in past decades, records great erosion rates that menace different human settlements and natural features of great environmental importance such as dune ridges, fossil cliffs and coastal lagoon. Specifically, the analysis of sediment samples collected along the Tetouan littoral made possible the characterization of the transport and depositional environments as well as the determination of sediment characteristics that are closely related to the geology and hydrology of adjacent basin areas and the relationship among long shore transport and the influence of human activities and natural coastal features that influence the geochemical composition of coastal sediments. The sedimentological studies support

A. El Mrini (✉)
Département de Géologie, Faculté des Sciences, Université Abdelmalek Essaâdi, Tétouan, Morocco
e-mail: aelmrini@gmail.com

D. Nachite
Faculté Polydisciplinaire, BP 745, 92004 Larache, Morocco

G. Anfuso
Dpto. de Ciencias de la Tierra, Facultad de Ciencias del Mar y Ambientales, Universidad de Cádiz, Polígono Río San Pedro s/n, 11510, Puerto Real Cádiz, Spain

M. Maanan
Institut de Géographie et d'Aménagement Régional de l'Université de Nantes, Géolittomer, LETG UMR 6554-CNRS, Nantes Cedex 3, France

G. Cultrone
Departamento de Mineralogía y Petrología, Universidad de Granada, Fuentenueva s/n, 18002 Granada, Spain

C. Vaccaro • E. Marrocchino
Department of Physics and Earth Sciences, University of Ferrara, via Saragat 1, 44100 Ferrara, Italy

M. Maanan, M. Robin (eds.), *Sediment Fluxes in Coastal Areas*, Coastal Research Library 10, DOI 10.1007/978-94-017-9260-8_5

coastal monitoring programs for suitable coastal protection and beach nourishment projects. Analyzed beach sediments are essentially composed by quartz-rich sand and can be clearly distinguished two different sectors: (i) the first one, between Ras Mazari and Cabo Negro headlands, is characterized by medium sand, from well to very well-sorted, main sedimentary supplies to the littoral being provided by Martil River; (ii) the second one, between Cabo Negro and Ceuta headlands, consists of coarse to very coarse sediments, poorly sorted, main sedimentary inputs being related to biogenic sources and to the erosion of metamorphic rocks from Cabo Negro headland.

5.1 Introduction

The Tetouan coast, in the Mediterranean littoral of Morocco, recorded in the past decades a progressive increase of human activities that induced deep changes in the functioning of the natural system (Nachite 2009). Along this area, sandy beaches, which had a great tourism value (Anfuso and Nachite 2011), recorded important erosion especially because of the diminution of river supplies that are captured in dams and because of the construction of ports that are barriers to the littoral transport (Anfuso et al. 2007; El Mrini 2011). Specifically, in the 1958–2003 period, the littoral of Tetouan recorded costal retreat rates of 2 myr^{-1} (Anfuso et al. 2007; Nachite 2007), and lost about 3,900,000 m^2 of beach surface (Niazi 2007); actually it presents a great vulnerability to coastal flooding and erosion processes especially under a scenario of sea level rise (Anfuso and Nachite 2011).

In this work granulometric and geochemical characteristics of sediments collected at Tetouan coast and along the main five watercourses were determined in order to establish the genetic links among river supplies and the characteristics and distribution of beach sediments as well as the modality of transport and the depositional environments which are closely related to the geology and hydrology of adjacent basin areas (Friedman 1967; Moiola and Weiser 1968; Rajamanickam and Gujar 1984; Anfuso et al. 1999; Frihy and Dewidar 2003). The sedimentological and geochemical features of surface sediments from beaches and rivers were compared using statistical methods to evaluate their characteristics and dispersal patterns and to identify potential risks associated with the diffusion of pollutants. This study defined coastal sectors with similar geochemical features and allowed an interpretation of the spatial variability of major elements and trace metals in the Tetouan coast – Mediterranean beaches of NW Morocco. The acquired information is basic for the understanding of the environmental status of the investigated area and for the development of a coastal monitoring and management program and constitutes the base for any suitable coastal protection and beach nourishment project (Nachite et al. 2005).

5.2 Study Area

The investigated area is located on the northwestern Mediterranean littoral of Morocco (Fig. 5.1). The coastline, broadly N-S oriented, is opened on the east side but restricted to the North and the South because of the headlands of Ceuta and Ras Mazari. It consists of low-lying coasts with small coastal plains in the northern part and mountainous areas in the southern part. Quartz rich beaches, dune ridges, fossil cliffs and, at places, rocky shore platforms are also present along the studied littoral (Nachite et al. 2004; Anfuso et al. 2004). Most important watercourses flowing into the northern area are the Rio Negro and Smir Rivers and Fnideq Stream (Table 5.1). South of Cabo Negro headland there are two main watercourses: Alila Stream, which presents a clear seasonal behavior and very limited sand inputs to the sea (LPEE 1994) and Martil River which is the most important of the region and shows a permanent regime with maximum flows generally recorded between October and April (Stitou 2002).

Concerning the physiographic characteristics of the continental shelf, north of Cabo Negro headland, it is quite narrow and composed by numerous rock outcrops (from the shoreline to the bathymetric line of 100 m) which give rise to relatively complex bathymetric patterns. South of Cabo Negro, the continental shelf is shallow and homogeneous and the bathymetric contours run parallel to the shoreline (Fig. 5.1).

The main urban centers are Martil, M'diq and Fnideq and, at aforementioned localities, are developed the main economic and touristic infrastructures (resorts, summer houses, fishing ports and marinas, etc.). Tourism is the main activity in this area and the development of human activities had important repercussions on geomorphologic features and natural environments. The construction of dams along the rivers (*wadis*) has reduced sediment inputs to littoral system. The construction of villages, summer residences and hotels on dune ridges has blocked the natural interchange of sediment between the dunes and the beach and affected two lagoons which are of great ecological interest (Castro et al. 2006). Finally, the three ports of this area, M'diq, Marina Smir and Kabila Marina, interrupted the longshore drift determining the formation of littoral cells (Anfuso et al. 2007; El Mrini 2011).

5.2.1 *Brief Geological Description of the Area*

The studied area is located at the northwestern end of the Rif Mountains, a tectonically and seismically active zone affected by a succession of "Horsts" and "Grabens". The chain is composed by a Paleozoic basement (metamorphic and plutonic rocks) and Mesozoic to Cenozoic covers of siliciclastic and carbonate rocks.

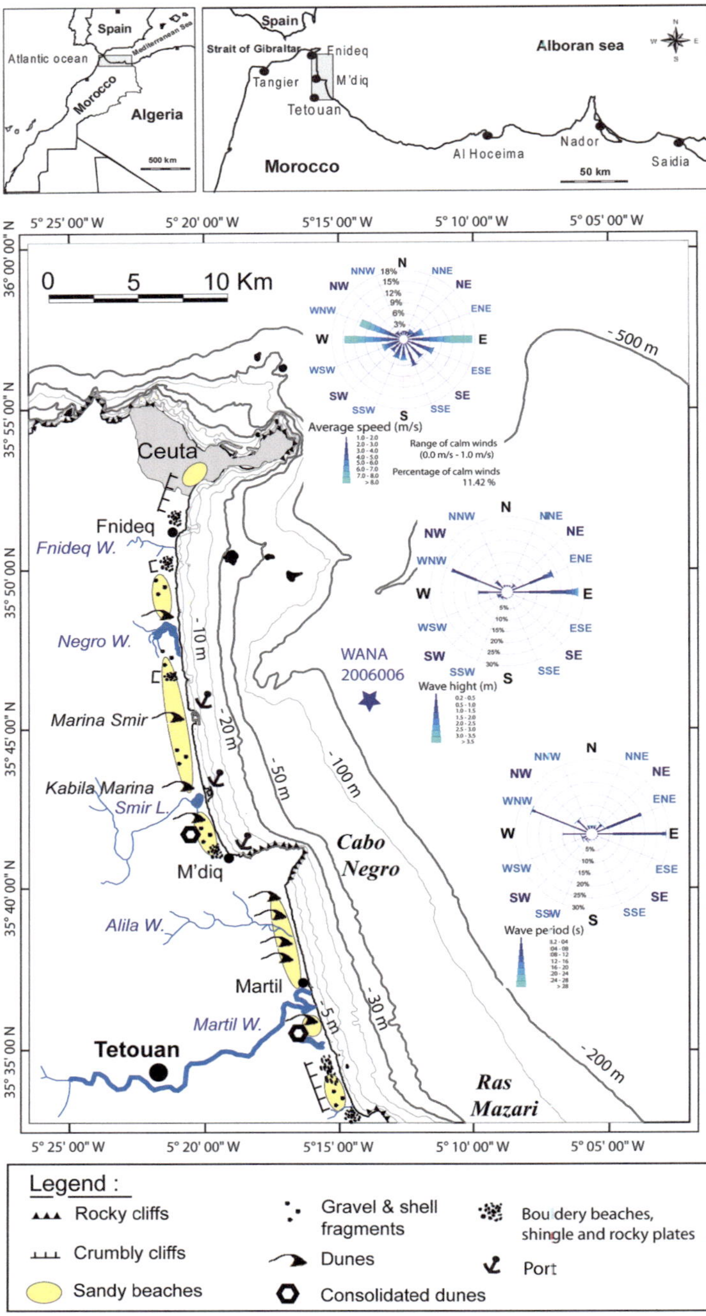

Fig. 5.1 Location map with main geomorphological features of the studied area

Table 5.1 Rivers draining into the Tetouan coast

River/ stream	Length of river/ stream (km)	Drainage basing (km^2)	River flow rate (m^3/s)	Transported sediment (ton/year)
Fnideq W.	10	10	0–10	n.a.
Negro W.	9	16	n.a.	10,000–30,000
Smir W.	13	74	0–154	10,000–30,000
Alila w.	10	13	0.5	n.a.
Martil W.	60	1,220	0.23–3,350	500,000

Compiled from L.P.E.E. (1994), Stitou (2002) and A.B.H.L. (2006)
n.a. not available

Stratigraphically, five main formations outcrop in the studied area (Fig. 5.2), which can be distinguished from the oldest to the most recent ones:

- **The Paleozoic domain** outcrops in the region as gneisses and micashists at metamorphic promontories. It can be divided into the Sebtides of Monte Hacho headland (orthogneisses) and the Devonian-Carboniferous and Permian-Triassic materials of Cabo Negro headland made up of micashists in its western part (Ghomarides), relatively soft and crumbly, and gneiss in the eastern side (Sebtides). The ultrabasic rocks (peridotites) and high-grade metamorphic rocks (kinzigites) outcrop north of Ceuta and their high content of heavy metals does not affect the composition of coastal sediments.
- **The Carbonate domain** is made up of a Liassic hard limestone and Triassic dolomites; their dissolution supplies calcareous clays and dolomite sands that accumulate on the relatively gentle slopes and in karstified areas.
- **The Flysch domain** involves several diverticulated sequences whose bedrock is formed by sandstones. Flyschs are mainly composed of bed load nappes of allochthonous terrains. The uppermost nappe is mainly made up of Late Oligocene–Aquitanian coarse siliciclastic turbidites (Numidian flysch, Michard et al. 2006) that locally form morphological heights (e.g. the Jbel ZemZem height).
- **The Pliocene** outcrops between Tetouan and Ceuta, along small alluvial plains and at the promontories. The most important Pliocene formations of Tetouan littoral are located south of Martil wadi, where it is possible to distinguish decimetric sandstone banks composed by very fossiliferous yellow sandy clays (Nachite 1993), and banks of 5 m of clear fine sand (Stitou 2002).
- **Quaternary formations** are essentially composed by marine sands and are especially abundant south of Martil River near Ras Mazari. Continental formations are mainly made up of unconsolidated fluvial deposits forming terraces on both sides of rivers and coastal plains consisting of pebbly formations, generally discontinuous, and silt-clay deposits (Taouil 2001).

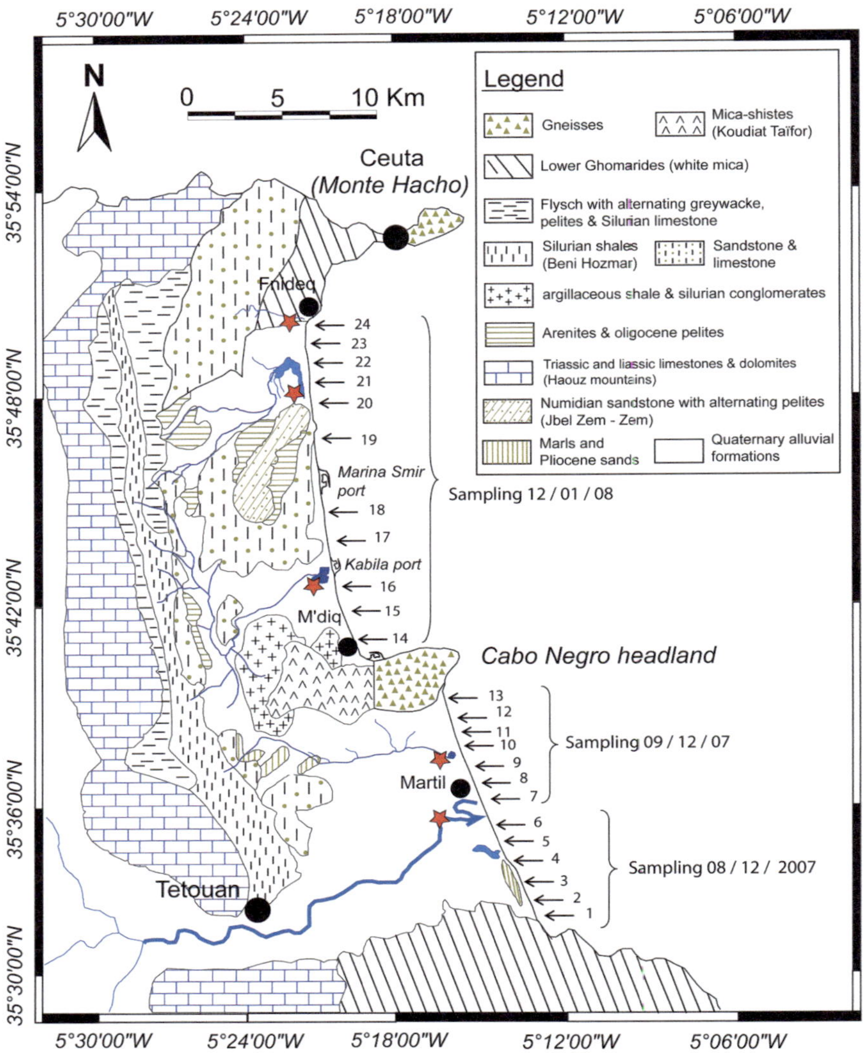

Fig. 5.2 Major stratigraphic units in the studied area (synthesis from various sources) and location of sampled points for sedimentological analysis: *arrows* indicate foreshore samples and *stars* indicate watercourses samples

5.2.2 River Drainage

Main rivers draining coastal hinterland and supplying terrigenous sediment to the beaches are listed in Table 5.1. The watercourses (except Martil wadi) are of ephemeral nature and flow unsteadily throughout the year with a low drainage during 4–5 months per year. This irregular hydrological regime is related to the high relief, the rainfall distribution – heavy rains are concentrated in winter and spring – and the predominance of impermeable facies.

Table 5.1 shows as most of the sediment load is carried by Martil wadi; the contribution of other streams is limited and made up essentially of fine sediments, in this sense their inputs are insignificant to coastal sedimentary budget. Lastly it is important to underlain that river supplies greatly decreased in last decades because of the construction of dams as the one on Smir River constructed in 1991 (Nachite et al. 2005) and on Nakhla (1961) and Ajras (1969), two effluent of Martil River. The water treatment plants are rare and the rivers serve as foul water conduits for the domestic and industrial waste; this means that nutrients and heavy metals waste waters can be trapped in river bottom sediments that arrive to the sea.

5.2.3 Marine Climate

The Mediterranean coast of the Alboran Sea is characterized by a Mediterranean-type climate: subtropical, moderate and hot. The Sea of Alboran is a very important area because of its ecosystems and it can be considered the dynamic motor of biodiversity in the western Mediterranean (Rodriguez el al. 2010). The studied area is a semidiurnal, microtidal environment, ranging tidal variations from a few centimeters in neap tides, to 80–100 cm in spring tides. The tidal wave, coming from the Atlantic Sea, penetrates into the Mediterranean and spreads out towards the east, progressively decreasing in intensity.

The Tetouan coast is exposed to wind and wave conditions typical of the Mediterranean North African climate (Fig. 5.1): the predominant easterly wind, the 'Chergui', prevails from May to October; the westerly 'Gharbi' wind essentially blows from October to February. Both winds achieve a great importance in terms of beach-dune dynamics because of coastal exposure and orientation.

Concerning wind characteristics at Smir, wind speeds are generally between 1.5 and 8 m/s. The northern part is more exposed to easterly winds meanwhile the southern part of the investigated littoral is more exposed to westerly winds.

The wave regime has been characterized using the data computed by the numerical model WANA 2006006 for a prediction point located offshore of the investigated area (Fig. 5.1). The re-analysis of wave data was carried out by the Spanish Network of Wave Measurements and Records run by the Spanish Port Authorities (http://www.puertos.es).

The offshore wave regime reflects the regional low pressure activity in the western Mediterranean associated with westerly winds in autumn, winter and spring (October to April) when maximum wave heights are recorded. Compilations of wave statistics covering the period 2005–2008 highlight a moderate wave energy regime in which significant wave heights less than 1.5 m represent more than 90 % of the spectrum. Significant heights exceeding 3 m represent only 5 % of the spectrum. The highest significant wave heights are observed in December and January and commonly exceed 4 m (El Mrini 2011). However, extreme wave height conditions can occur anytime within the high-energy season. As a result of the orientation of the coastline, waves approach the coast from the first and second quadrants. The main currents flow northwards and, during the summer season, toward the SSE, with a maximum velocity of 0.68 m/s (Lakhdar Idrissi et al. 2001).

5.3 Materials and Methods

Two sampling surveys were carried out in order to gather surface sediments, i.e. the upper 5 cm layer, at different locations along the investigated littoral. Beach foreshore samples were collected from 24 locations (Fig. 5.2) during December 2007 and January 2008 to determine grain size distribution along the littoral, the composition and mineralogical associations and in order to achieve a morphoscopic description of the investigated deposits. The second sampling campaign was carried out at the five main watercourses to a distance of less than 1 km from the shoreline to establish the linkage among sediment inputs, hinterland facies and coastal sediments.

5.3.1 Granulometry and Mineralogy

In laboratory, all samples were firstly thoroughly washed, oven dried and separated into subsamples using a mechanical splitter. For the determination of grain size, approximately 100 g of each sample were sieved in a Ro-tap machine through sieves with mesh sizes of 0.063, 0.08, 0.125, 0.2, 0.25, 0.315, 0.4, 0.5, 0.63, 0.8, 1, 1.25, 1.6 and 2 mm. The principal statistical parameters (mean, standard deviation, skewness and kurtosis; Folk 1980) were calculated according to the method of moments (logarithmic Φ) using the GRADISTAT program (Blott and Pye 2001).

The fraction below 0.063 mm was extracted by wet sieving and characterized using a computerized laser analyzer Galai CIS-1 which analyzes the fraction size comprised between 1 and 20 μm. The mineralogy of the samples was studied by X-ray diffraction (XRD), using a Philips PW 1710 diffractometer equipped with graphite monocromator, automatic slit and CuKα radiation ($\lambda = 1.5405$ Å). The data were collected in continuous scanning mode with 0.02° goniometer rate and 2θ from 3° to 60°. XRD goniometric calibration was performed using a silicon standard. The resulting data were interpreted using XPowder software (Martín 2004). The mineralogical characterization was performed moreover by in situ analyses of single grains with a Zeiss EVO 50 Scanning Electron Microscopy (SEM) coupled with an Oxford Instruments INCA microanalysis suite. The samples were washed in distilled water to remove the sodium chloride and then filtered to not lose the clay component; this procedure was necessary because all samples presented high concentrations of salt that not allowed quantitative analysis by means of X-ray fluorescence (XRF). The composition of samples was determined crushing them to a size of c. 40 μm in a low-blank agate mortar. After drying at 110 °C for 12 h, the bulk rock chemical composition was characterized by XRF on pressed powder pellets using a wavelength-dispersive automated ARL Advant'X spectrometer with accuracy and precision (based on the analysis of certified international standards) better than 3 % for Si, Ti, Fe, Ca, and K and 7 % for Mg, Al, Mn, and Na.

Loss on ignition (LOI) was carried out at 1,100 °C by standard gravimetric techniques for 12 h. The reported LOI values are the sum of LOI+ (representative of the structural H_2O and CO_2 contents).

5.3.2 Morphoscopy of Quartz

The analysis was carried out using a binocular microscope (× 40); the size of quartz grains ranged from 0.5 to 1 mm. The determination of the surface appearance of quartz sediments was performed according to the method defined by Cailleux (1943) who distinguished:

- Unworn grains (NU).
- Polished rounded grains (EL).
- Mat-rounded grains (RM).

5.4 Results

5.4.1 Grain Size Distribution and Morphoscopy of Quartz

Beach foreshore sediments are essentially composed by quartz-rich sand; the analysis of grain size distribution does not show any longshore trend but clearly distinguishes two sectors (Table 5.2 and Figs. 5.1 and 5.3a). The first one, between Ras Mazari and Cabo Negro headlands, is characterized by medium sand, well to very well-sorted. The two observed exceptions, i.e. samples 2 and 3, are due to the enrichment of gravel fraction linked to the local presence of shell fragments and gravel eroded from Ras Mazari headland. The second one, between Cabo Negro and Monte Hacho headlands, consists of coarse to very coarse sediments, poorly sorted and rich (at places) in shell debris. The sample 24 presented angular to sub-angular pebbles and gravel essentially showing flat grain morphologies associated with marine processes. Sediments that presented a bimodal curve were observed in beaches that showed high percentages of gravel and shell deposits, e.g. points 1–3, 14–17 and 20–24 (Table 5.2).

Sediment sorting (Fig. 5.3a) clearly reflected grain size trend, finer sediments presenting a better sorting and *vice versa*. In this sense, coarser sediments were

Table 5.2 Longitudinal variations of grain size indexes (Φ)

Samples	Textual group	Mode (phi)	D_{50} (phi)	Mean (phi)	Sorting (phi)	Skweness (phi)	Kurtosis (phi)	Morphoscopy
1	Gravelly sand	1.833	1.791	1.761	0.798	−0.041	3.202	EL (xxx) + NU (x)
2	Gravelly sand	0.494	0.572	0.535	0.675	−0.328	2.300	EL (xxx) + NU (x)
3	Sand	1.161 & 0.494	0.954	0.919	0.401	−0.035	0.844	EL (xxx) + NU (x)
4	Gravelly sand	2.161	2.020	1.903	0.933	−0.503	2.750	EL (xxx) + NU (x)
5	Sand	2.161	2.170	2.206	0.394	0.090	1.706	EL + RM
6	Sand	2.161	2.195	2.261	0.355	0.234	1.234	EL + RM
7	Sand	1.494	1.813	1.821	0.407	0.072	0.979	EL + RM
8	Sand	1.833	1.799	1.798	0.351	0.031	1.087	EL + RM
9	Sand	1.833	1.921	1.906	0.381	0.039	1.082	EL + RM
10	Sand	1.494	1.658	1.676	0.315	0.135	1.039	EL + RM (xxx)
11	Sand	1.833	1.745	1.758	0.307	0.120	0.915	EL + RM (xxx)
12	Sand	1.833	1.913	1.941	0.318	0.140	1.213	EL + RM (xxx)
13	Sand	2.161	2.044	2.028	0.280	0.078	1.083	EL + RM
14	Gravelly sand	0.833 & 2.161	1.087	1.192	1.033	−0.025	1.660	EL (xxx) + RM (x)
15	Slightly gravelly sand	1.161	1.150	1.126	0.320	−0.157	1.688	EL (xxx)
16	Slightly gravelly sand	0.833	0.716	0.725	0.428	−0.101	1.124	EL (xxx) + RM
17	Slightly gravelly sand	0.494	0.372	0.332	0.604	−0.070	1.898	EL (xxx)
18	Sand	1.161	1.210	1.244	0.309	−0.025	1.413	EL + RM
19	Gravelly sand	0.161	0.230	0.228	0.422	−0.264	1.765	EL (xxx)
20	Gravelly sand	0.161	0.015	−0.153	0.706	−0.526	2.095	EL (xxx)
21	Gravelly sand	0.161	−0.071	−0.132	0.468	−0.193	1.062	EL (xxx) + RM (x)
22	Slightly gravelly sand	0.494	0.576	0.612	0.450	−0.120	2.062	EL (xxx) + RM (x)
23	Gravelly sand	0.833 & −0.839	0.632	0.479	0.742	−0.388	1.187	EL (xxx) + RM (x)
24	Sandy gravel	1.833 & −2.000	0.606	0.057	1.729	−0.401	0.596	EL (xxx) + NU + RM (x)

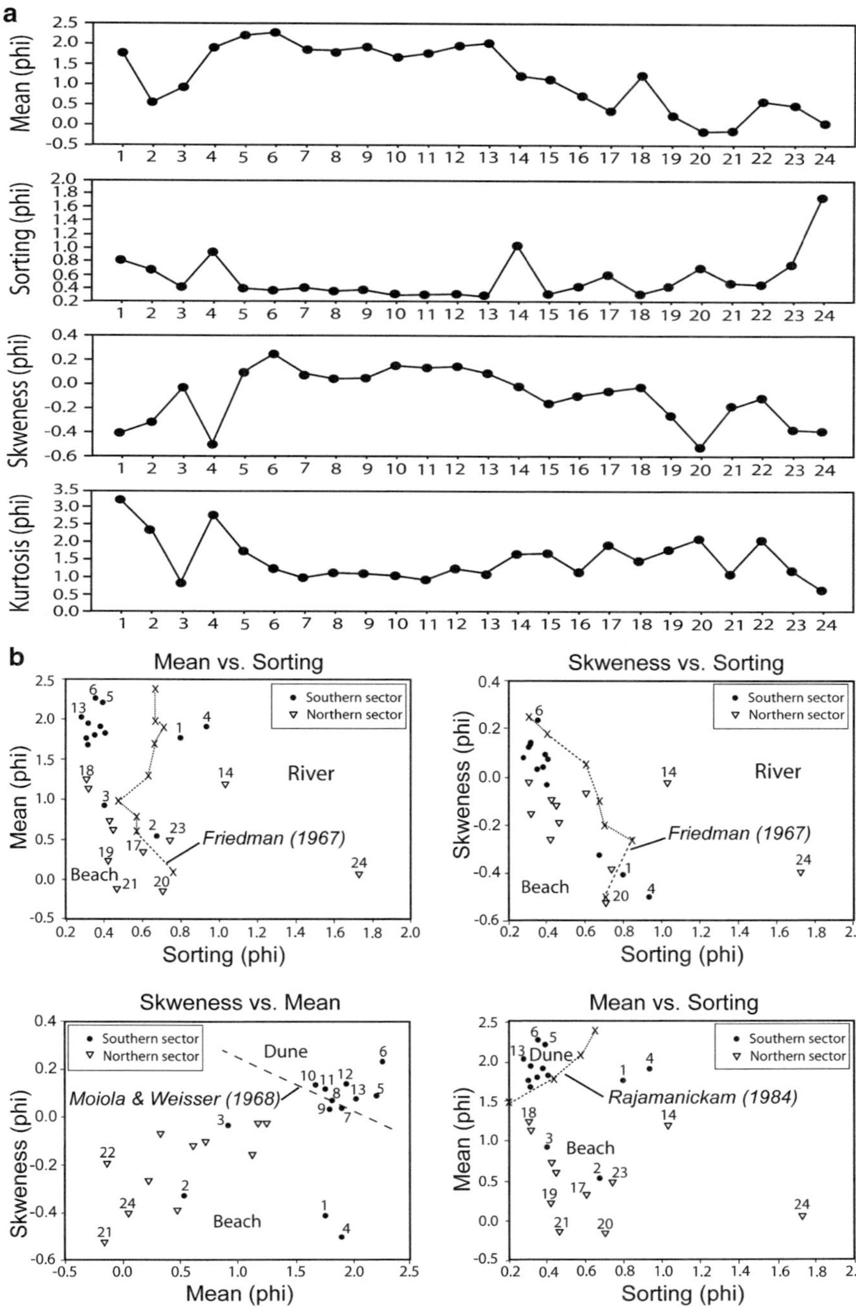

Fig. 5.3 (**a**) Longshore distribution of grain-size parameters and (**b**) representation of grain-size parameters and associated depositional environments

"moderately well sorted" and "moderately sorted", e.g. samples 1, 2 and 4 in the southern sector. This is quite evident in the northern sector too; samples 15–17 and 22–24 show a clear increase in grain size and a diminution of sorting (Fig. 5.3a). The skewness presented positive values in correspondence of well sorted sediments and negative values (coarser sediments) in correspondence of moderately sorted sediments, e.g. samples 1–4 (but 3) and 18–24 (Fig. 5.3a). The kurtosis presented mesokurtic and leptokurtic values, exceptions being recorded at samples 1–4 (but 3) and 18–24, which show very leptokurtic values.

Last, natural structures (headlands) and ports divide the littoral into morphological cells (Anfuso et al. 2007) and it is reflected by grain size distribution (Carter 1988; Anfuso et al. 2011). In this sense, grain size variations are observed around Cabo Negro headland (samples 13 and 14), Kabila port (samples 16 and 17) and Marina Smir port (samples 18 and 19).

The morphoscopy of quartz shows the omnipresence of EL grains, with enrichments by NU in the southern part which demonstrates the influence of water transport and the contribution of water-courses dynamics. The RM grains are present at beaches with dunes in conjunction with the EL and become dominant at the Cabo Negro beach showing the importance of wind transport. The last sample, gathered at the mouth of Fnideq wadi, shows the coexistence of the three forms of quartz grains indicating in this sense the presence of deposits linked to river supplies.

5.4.2 Origin of Materials and Depositional Environments

Since the fifties of last century, research has been focused on the statistical treatment of the different grain-size parameters, which has led to a rich literature on the subject. To determine the depositional environments of investigated sediments, binary representations between mean *vs.* sorting, skewness *vs.* mean and skewness *vs.* sorting were performed (Friedman 1967; Moiola and Weiser 1968; Rajamanickam and Gujar 1984) (Fig. 5.3b).

All samples showed a dominance of a beach environment in both northern and southern sectors with the exception of sample 24 collected at Fnideq wadi that reflects river deposits. The sample 6, collected south of Martil wadi reflects a facies of beach sand with enrichments of fluvial and dune inputs. As for sample 14, it shows a character of fluvial deposit, however, there is not any river at this site. Probably, beach sediments at this place record perturbations due to the presence of M'diq port and Cabo Negro headland.

At the southern sector, 64 % of the samples record the influence of wind inputs (samples 5–13); this highlights the important role of dunes in supplying investigated beaches. This is less evident in samples 7, 8 and 9 and in the northern sector because the complete absence of dune inputs, since they have been almost completely destroyed and urbanized in past decades.

5.4.3 Mode of Sediment Transport

Using grain-size results, several authors have developed graphical representations and have differentiated sediment populations according to their mode of transport. Among them, Passega (1964) proposed a simple method of interpretation of granulometric data using two parameters, the first percentile (Q99) on the ordinate and the median on the abscissa (Fig. 5.4).

This diagram shows two principal sediment groups; the first one, corresponding to the southern sector, mainly consists of sediment transported by gradual suspension with a few rolling elements; the second one, corresponding to the northern sector, consists of sediment essentially transported by rolling and secondarily in suspension.

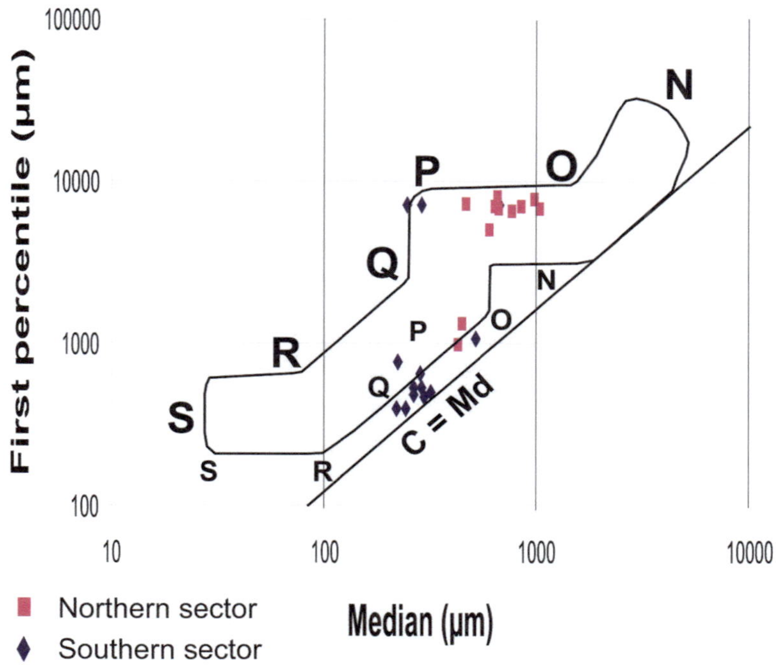

Fig. 5.4 The Passega diagram for foreshore samples: uniform suspension-SR, gradual suspension-RQ, suspension and rolling-QP, rolling and suspension-PO, rolling-ON

5.4.4 Geochemistry

5.4.4.1 Sector Ras Mazari – Cabo Negro

Six samples were selected for XRD in order to determine their origin and characterize their distribution:

Sample 1, located at the foot of Ras Mazari headland.
Samples 6 and 7, respectively located on the southern and northern part of Martil River mouth.
Samples 9 and 10, respectively located on the southern and northern part of Alila River mouth.
Sample 12, located at Cabo Negro beach.

Quartz is the main phase (40–80 %), followed by plagioclase, calcite and dolomite. The abundance of silicates (quartz and plagioclase) reflects the importance of continental inputs (Table 5.3) since carbonates are almost exclusively constituted by fragments of the shells of marine organisms of infauna and epifauna, essentially belonging to the following species: *Cardium edule, Callista chione* and *Glycimeris violacescens,* currently living in the nearshore area beaches and were identified by observation under optical microscope and the scanning electron microscope.

Most igneous and metamorphic rocks have high concentrations of quartz and feldspar (plagioclase in this case) and relatively low contents of other minerals. During weathering, feldspar rather rapidly alters into clays, while quartz, being unreactive, survives the weathering process and it is able to be accumulated along the beaches. Part of the clays that were formed by the alteration of feldspars are winnowed out from the surf zone and washed away to the open ocean to accumulate on the continental shelf. Quartz remains behind, travelling down the coastline because of longshore drift.

Finally, carbonates and quartz show an inverse linear relationship (Fig. 5.5), with the exception of samples gathered north of Fnideq wadi. Such deposits are probably linked to the drainage of the calcareous-dolomite mountains of Haouz.

Table 5.3 Mineral concentrations in beach sediments between Mazari and Negro headlands

	Quartz	Calcite	Dolomite	Plagioclase	Muscovite	Chlorite	Halite
1	67.3	5.8	14.2	6.8	3.1	1.9	–
6	60.1	14.3	2.4	22.5	Traces	Traces	0.5
7	40.4	29.5	9.5	19.7	Traces	–	0.7
9	65.6	6.5	2.6	24.6	Traces	Traces	0.6
10	68.7	6.8	10.8	12.9	Traces	–	0.6
12	76.4	7.6	3.0	11.5	–	–	1.3

Note: Percentages do not reach 100 % because of the loss of CO_2 (destruction of organic matter)

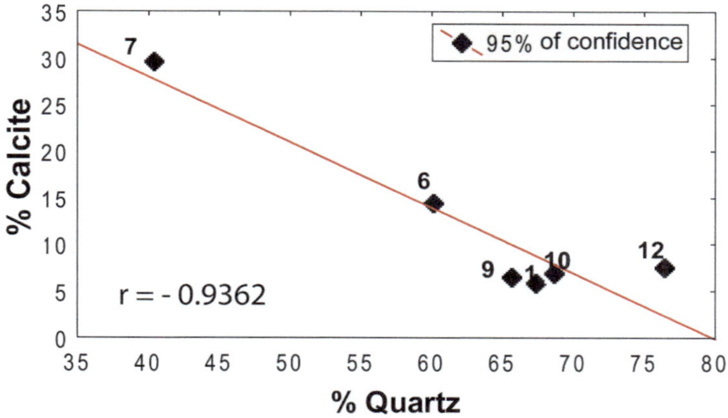

Fig. 5.5 Bivariate diagram of Quartz *vs*. Calcite for the sector Mazari – Cabo Negro headlands

The presence of dolomite is generally related to the abundance of red algae that during their growth fix this mineral; the cell walls of calcareous algae are in fact saturated with crystals of dolomite (Medaković et al. 1995; Alexandersson 1974).

Micas are mainly present in the sample gathered at Azla beach which lies near Ras Mazari headland; this last is partially constituted by schistose rocks. Therefore, this sample reflects immature and poorly evolved beach materials.

Despite the samples were washed with fresh water before the analysis, the residual presence of marine salt is reflected by the observed concentrations of halite.

5.4.4.2 Sector Cabo Negro – Ceuta

In order to investigate sediment characteristics in the northern sector, results presented by Nachite et al. (2005) were analyzed. Previous authors gathered 17 beach surface samples.

Concerning **major elements**, this coastal sector shows abundance of silica (SiO_2), followed by carbonates (CaO), with the existence of an inverse linear relationship. The sector between Kabila and Marina Smir ports presents the highest contents of carbonates which are associated with the presence of shell fragments. As for the other elements, contents are weak, only Al_2O_3 and MgO exceed 1 %. The low content of Al_2O_3 suggests the low contents in clay minerals and feldspars. The low concentrations of magnesium can be attributed to the absence of mafic rocks in the basins and to marine ecosystems were biomineralization processes are defined by organisms able to fix only calcium carbonate (Weiner and Dove 2003) (Table 5.4).

The Principal Component Analysis (PCA) (Fig. 5.6a) shows a very strong relationship among Al_2O_3, K_2O, and TiO_2, reflecting their common origin. M'diq beach (samples 1 and 2) and Fnideq beach (sample 17) show the highest concentrations of

Table 5.4 Distribution of major elements in sediments of the area between Cabo Negro and Ceuta headlands (Nachite et al. 2005)

	1	2	3	4	5	6	7	8	9	10	11	12	13	14	15	16	17
SiO_2	74.74	73.61	78.71	75.16	60.21	65.64	58.04	59.54	78.12	81.17	71.07	81.97	80.53	82.74	77.59	79.74	76.98
TiO_2	**0.13**	0.06	0.04	0.04	0.04	0.04	0.04	0.05	0.04	0.03	0.03	0.03	0.04	0.03	0.04	0.04	0.08
Al_2O_3	**3.53**	1.88	1.06	1.12	1.05	1.20	1.08	1.28	1.01	0.79	0.69	0.66	0.77	0.71	0.91	0.89	1.58
Fe_2O_3	**0.89**	0.42	0.22	0.30	0.42	0.48	0.47	0.58	0.23	0.17	0.17	0.16	0.20	0.18	0.32	0.30	0.62
MnO	**0.02**	0.01	0.01	0.01	0.01	0.01	0.01	0.01	0.01	–	–	0.01	0.01	0.01	0.01	0.01	0.01
MgO	1.29	1.32	1.04	1.29	**1.48**	**1.65**	**1.21**	**1.22**	1.05	0.86	0.89	0.80	0.87	0.95	1.19	0.91	1.09
CaO	11.15	13.49	11.37	13.25	**21.88**	**23.66**	**23.57**	**22.38**	11.74	10.12	16.55	9.95	10.64	9.24	12.10	10.99	11.51
Na_2O	0.60	0.52	0.44	0.47	0.51	0.47	0.44	0.52	0.42	0.37	0.42	0.34	0.34	0.35	0.38	0.39	0.40
K_2O	**0.57**	0.28	0.16	0.20	0.14	0.17	0.12	0.17	0.14	0.12	0.07	0.09	0.08	0.10	0.12	0.09	0.19
P_2O_5	0.04	0.04	0.03	0.03	0.03	0.04	0.03	0.03	0.03	0.02	0.03	0.03	0.03	0.03	0.03	0.03	0.04
LOI	7.04	8.38	6.94	8.13	14.23	6.65	14.99	14.21	7.22	6.33	10.08	5.98	6.50	5.66	7.31	6.61	7.51
Total	100	100	100	100	100	100	100	100	100	100	100	100	100	100	100	100	100

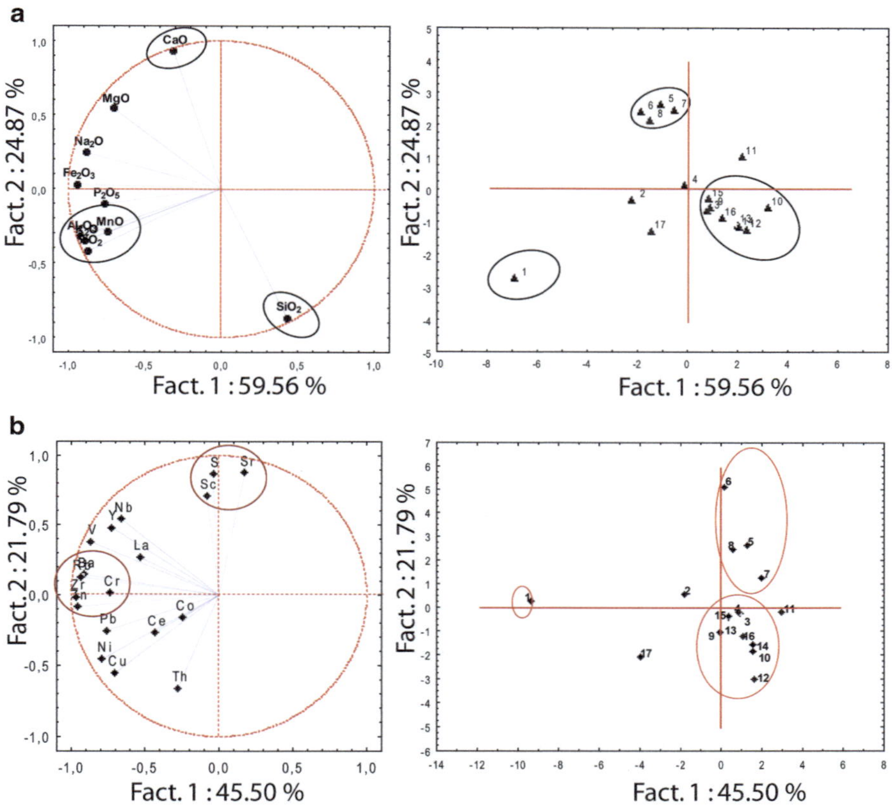

Fig. 5.6 Plot of principal component scores for the first two components in foreshore sediments between Cabo Negro and Ceuta headlands: (**a**) major elements content and (**b**) trace elements content. Trace elements (Pb, Zn, Ni, Co, Cr, V, Th in ppm)

aforementioned elements, certainly coming from the metamorphic complex of Cabo Negro and Monte Hacho headlands, which provide metamorphic materials. In these areas the sediment geochemistry reflects the outcropping of siliciclastic rocks. The concentrations of Zr and P indicate the presence of minerals such as zircon and apatite that for their hardness, extricate a strong geo-lithological control on the chemistry and mineralogy of beach sediments.

Table 5.5 shows as Sr and S are the most represented elements in this sector followed by Ba and Zr.

Zr and Rb can be attributed to contributions of the metamorphic formations of Cabo Negro headland. The concentrations of Zn and Cr at Fnideq beach (sample 17) is probably related to pollution processes due to the vicinity of the city.

PCA shows again the grouping of samples between Kabila and Marina Smir ports (5–8). They present elevated levels of Sr, S and Sc, this indicating a marine origin for Sc and S and a biogenic origin for Sr (Fig. 5.7). On the other hand, sample 1 shows the highest concentrations of Ba, Cr, La, Ni, Pb, Rb, V, Y, Zn, Zr and Cu.

Table 5.5 Distribution of trace elements in sediments between Cape Negro and Fnideq (Nachite et al. 2005)

	1	2	3	4	5	6	7	8	9	10	11	12	13	14	15	16	17
Ba	96.9	48.3	15.9	25.6	20.6	18.8	11.2	21.6	13.4	12.1	1.6	7.6	5.7	15.2	7.8	10.8	28.0
Ce	0.1	–	–	–	–	–	–	–	–	–	–	–	–	–	–	–	1.1
Co	–	2.0	–	–	–	–	–	2.0	–	–	–	1.7	–	–	–	–	2.7
Cr	15.3	5.3	3.5	1.9	1.8	2.3	0.2	2.0	6.0	0.4	0.4	0.8	11.5	0.3	1.1	4.5	2.5
La	12.2	4.0	7.3	3.6	6.9	4.9	6.9	5.1	–	7.4	3.6	1.0	8.4	2.9	2.1	1.8	6.0
Nb	2.5	2.5	1.6	1.1	1.9	2.6	1.4	2.3	1.4	0.9	0.8	1.2	1.3	1.1	1.8	1.0	2.5
Ni	5.3	2.0	1.5	–	0.1	–	–	–	3.1	.06	–	1.9	0.3	1.9	1.7	2.5	4.6
Pb	6.0	0.3	0.6	3.1	0.7	0.3	0.7	0.5	3.5	06	–	1.2	1.9	0.9	3.5	0.5	3.8
Rb	18.3	7.9	3.8	5.6	3.1	5.3	2.8	3.9	3.5	3.3	1.0	2.3	2	2.9	2.8	2.4	6.5
Sr	420.5	509.1	432.4	528.1	**802.4**	**826.5**	**801.1**	**760.7**	454.2	375.3	572.7	334.5	373.1	319.0	418.2	377.2	436.5
Th	1.5	1.6	0.7	1.1	0.5	–	0.6	0.9	1.1	2.0	1.0	1.4	0.2	1.3	0.7	1.3	1.4
V	20.3	11.3	7.5	8.5	9.8	11.6	10.8	10.5	8.7	4.5	6.1	5.9	6.4	6.1	6.9	7.7	12.8
Y	5.8	3.7	2.6	3.8	3.2	5.1	2.1	2.9	3.1	2.7	2.3	2.2	3.5	2.4	3.4	2.4	3.0
Zn	9.3	2.9	0.4	0.1	0.4	0.2	0.8	1.6	1.6	–	–	–	1.8	–	0.8	1.4	6.5
Zr	42.1	25.2	19.0	15.9	15.3	22.7	14.9	18.8	20.2	18.2	17.5	17.0	20.0	17.5	19.0	19.6	30.8
Cu	8.5	5.0	4.8	4.3	3.7	3.2	3.3	3.5	5.5	5.4	3.1	5.9	5.3	5.5	7.2	5.3	6.7
Ga	–	–	–	–	–	–	–	–	–	–	–	–	–	–	–	–	–
Nd	–	–	–	–	–	–	–	–	–	–	–	–	–	–	–	–	–
S	828.2	859.9	751.9	779.0	978.0	1,488.7	810.5	853.5	702.0	530.7	657.2	537.4	544.4	778.5	909.3	763.6	553.6
Sc	4.2	4.8	3.0	2.6	**5.7**	**6.4**	**3.0**	**7.9**	4.5	4.2	4.1	0.9	3.5	3.4	4.6	4.6	3.7

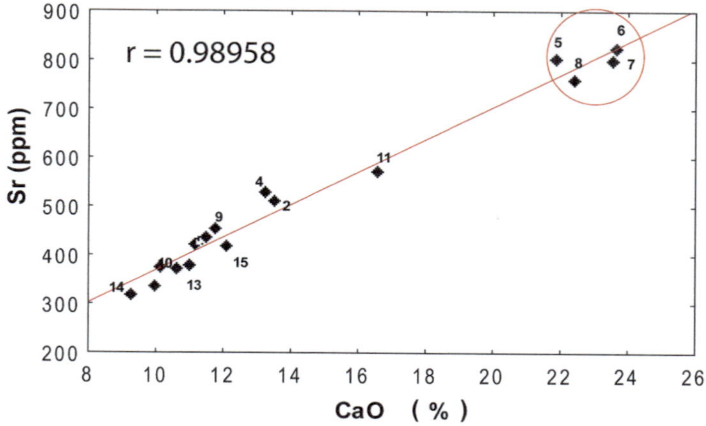

Fig. 5.7 Bivariate correlation between Sr and CaO

Table 5.6 List of fine fraction minerals of sediments collected at major watercourses in the studied area

Quartz		Calcitc	Dolomite	Muscovite	Chlorite		
Martil W.	XXX	X	–	tr	tr	XXX	Very abundant
Alila W.	XXX	tr	–	X	tr	XX	Abundant
Smir L.	XXX	XX	–	X	tr	X	Less abundant
Negro W.	XXX	X	–	tr	X	tr	Traces
Fnideq W.	XXX	X	tr	tr	–	–	Absent

5.4.4.3 Geochemical Analysis of Watercourses Sediments

Sediments collected at the edges of the five main rivers were analyzed by XRD and by the technique MultiRes-Vac34.

Analysing the results presented in Table 5.6, it is possible to state that investigated river sediments are mainly composed by silicates and, very secondarily by calcite and muscovite. Their mineralogical similitude with beach sediments evidences, by one way, the importance of river supplies to the littoral deposits and, by the other way, confirms the marine origin of carbonate inputs, essentially of biogenic origin.

The local enrichment in calcite observed in the sample gathered at Smir lagoon is due to a high percentage of shell fragments since the lagoon is emplaced on sandy sediments constituting a very important biological substrate (especially for bivalves). The presence of muscovite at Alila wadi and Smir lagoon is linked to the schistose and mica-schistose formations of Beni Hozmar and Koudiat Taïfour (see Fig. 5.2). Finally, the trace concentrations of dolomite observed at the mouth of Fnideq wadi are probably linked to the drainage of the calcareous-dolomite mountains of Haouz. It is not possible to exclude that the increased availability of

Table 5.7 Major elements distribution in sediments of principal watercourses

	Martil W.	Alila W.	Smir L.	Negro W.	Fnideq W.
SiO_2	50.00	40.16	42.74	46.20	42.65
TiO_2	0.88	0.95	0.82	1.07	0.93
Al_2O_3	16.77	18.81	16.48	18.38	15.91
Fe_2O_3	6.77	9.16	6.70	7.60	6.87
MnO	0.07	0.04	0.06	0.06	0.08
MgO	2.15	1.82	2.05	1.39	1.39
CaO	4.05	2.28	7.61	3.76	7.11
Na_20	0.70	1.33	1.27	0.15	0.59
K_2O	2.98	3.51	3.28	2.16	2.85
P_2O_5	–	0.32	0.26	–	0.56
SO_3	–	0.87	1.61	–	0.85
O (ppm)	−57	−3,126	−2,300	−28	−361

magnesium in water solution made possible the development of organisms with high content of magnesium in their carbonate shell.

Major elements in river sediments obtained by MultiRes-Vac34, are presented in Table 5.7. Specifically, SiO_2 is the most abundant element, especially at Martil wadi (>50 %), followed by Al_2O_3 and then Fe_2O_3. The correlation matrix (Table 5.8) shows that the strongest correlation is observed between Na_2O and K_2O ($r > 0.96$), the samples of Alila wadi and Smir lagoon showing the highest concentrations of the latter two elements that indicate towering rate of chemical weathering with removal of the elements with high mobility. Finally, recorded concentrations of CaO reflect results obtained by means of XRD analysis.

Dealing with the trace elements, the most represented are Ba, Cl, Cr, Rb, Sr, V, Zn and Zr and, secondarily Br, Cu, Ga, La, Ni, Pb and Pd (Table 5.9).

Atypical concentrations of some elements such as Ba, Cu, Pb, Zn and Zr are observed at Fnideq wadi. They are probably linked to the presence of pollutant elements, in particular waste oil since the sampling was gathered near a discharge point of a dump station. This hypothesis is validated by the low correlation with aluminium and iron and other elements that characterize the rock outcroppings.

Finally, the high levels of Sr observed at Smir lagoon confirm the importance of the biogenic origin of sediments.

The PCA analysis allowed subdividing watercourses into three groups (Fig. 5.8):

- the first, consisting of Martil and Río Negro rivers, shows similar facies even though mentioned rivers are geographically separated. These two rivers are the only ones that contain P and S; in addition, their salt (Cl and Br) and Pb contents are similar. These two rivers also carry contributions of wind sediment and the higher concentration of silica that is not correlated with aluminium allows to classify them as rocks with high maturity.

Table 5.8 Correlation matrix for major elements in watercourses sediments

	SiO_2	TiO_2	Al_2O_3	Fe_2O_3	MnO	MgO	CaO	Na_2O	K_2O	P_2O_5	SO_3
SiO_2	1,000										
TiO_2	0.046996	1.000									
Al_2O_3	−0.189147	0.632778	1.000								
Fe_2O_3	−0.538322	0.440609	**0.866753**	1.000							
MnO	0.370705	−0.154797	−**0.836846**	−0.760711	1.000						
MgO	0.268905	−0.765323	−0.130424	−0.148665	−0.263204	1.000					
CaO	−0.115454	−0.541976	−**0.868194**	−0.774575	0.606201	−0.033995	1.000				
Na_2O	−0.582748	−0.689166	0.028564	0.321382	−0.491554	0.622784	0.049800	1.000			
K_2O	0.510415	−0.721848	−0.064560	0.292329	−0.337806	0.630743	0.022741	**0.966386**	1.000		
P_2O_5	−0.749946	−0.246940	−0.398112	0.062751	0.310301	−0.340291	0.474956	0.351780	0.419381	1.000	
SO_3	−0.738639	−0.628179	−0.319084	−0.039830	−0.148761	0.201041	0.600936	0.750685	0.656006	0.642559	1.000

Table 5.9 Distribution of trace elements in watercourses sediments

	Martil W.	Alila W.	Smir L.	Negro W.	Fnideq W.
Ag	22	19	15	13	16
Ba	435	500	448	343	**740**
Bi	–	–	12	12	–
Br	28	**218**	**137**	30	17
Ce	–	207	415	313	175
Cl	242	**1.37 %**	**1.01 %**	112	0.16 %
Co	–	–	–	–	–
Cr	146	114	142	183	132
Cs	–	95	–	97	–
Cu	72	78	83	80	**124**
Eu	–	–	–	41	68
Ga	23	32	24	32	19
Gd	25	154	11	–	–
I	–	**123**	–	–	–
La	85	102	64	49	45
Lu	–	23	–	–	–
Mo	4	–	–	–	–
Nb	19	18	15	27	16
Nd	116	80	185	–	–
Ni	74	81	73	65	64
P	627	–	–	501	–
Pb	21	35	48	23	**86**
Pd	24	18	26	18	16
Pr	–	133	314	177	–
Rb	128	**181**	**140**	107	124
Ru	10	–	13	16	12
S	371	–	–	348	–
Sb	–	–	–	–	105
Sc	–	38	27	21	19
Sm	47	**106**	**176**	–	84
Sn	–	–	16	–	–
Sr	143	169	**265**	169	219
Tb	25	–	–	–	–
Te	–	–	–	29	–
Th	–	–	–	–	10
V	130	158	130	138	119
W	–	–	25	28	–
Y	22	18	17	23	24
Yb	24	–	–	–	27
Zn	167	204	228	147	**375**
Zr	232	137	246	286	**399**

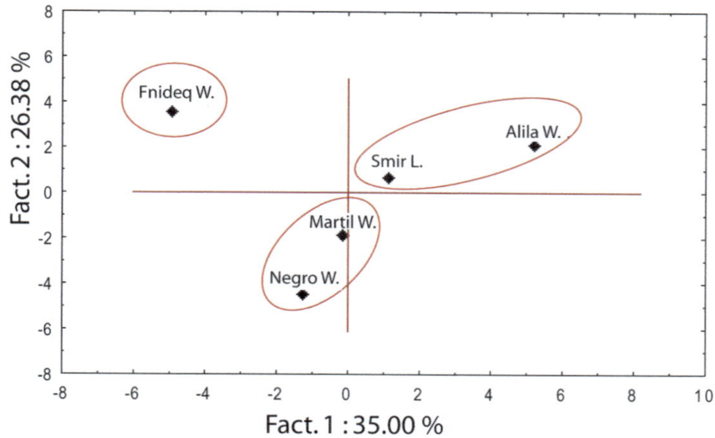

Fig. 5.8 Scores for the first two components of watercourses sediments according to their trace elements content

- the second group includes Alila wadi and Smir lagoon. These two water bodies contain the highest concentrations in Sm and Rb which is due to presence of mineral salts (resulting from evaporation processes) and muscovite (from schistose formations).
- Finally, Fnideq wadi is individualized by a particular facies characterized by high contents of elements which origin is probably linked to human contamination.

5.4.4.4 Regional Distribution of Studied Elements

The analyzed rocks present a variety of contaminants coming from different natural and anthropogenic pollution sources. Trace elements of mature sediments (rich in quartz) are relatively enriched in REE, Zr and P that are hosted in minerals with high hardness and chemical resistance (especially apatite and zircon). These elements characterize the metamorphic rocks which are also rich in K, Rb, Na, and other elements with a high degree of geochemical mobility. By the other way, Al and Fe are very poor in the previous types of sediment but are abundant in mature soils residually rich in oxides and hydroxides, which generally indicate low rate of wind erosion. Areas with large marine contributions are characterized by significant increases in Ca and only in specific environments an increase of magnesium is observed. Higher concentrations of Mg are linked to the outcrops of Mesozoic carbonate sediments and to the sedimentation of red algae (Rhodophyta) in marine areas investigated.

In order to obtain a scheme of heavy minerals distribution, the Factor Analysis method for the sector Cabo Negro – Ceuta was used. The validity of this method was tested, among others, by Hein et al. (1974) in studies with heavy minerals.

This method consists in projecting in the same diagram *variable-points*, corresponding to mineral species, and *observation-points*, corresponding to samples, in a way that it becomes possible to highlight the similarities according to the distances between the following points:

- Two observation-points are much nearer when the two samples have similar minerals content in all considered values.
- Two variable-points are much nearer when both variables (minerals) are more related in their variations among all considered samples.
- An observation-point and a variable-point are much nearer when the sample has for this mineral a high value.

In this study 19 variables were considered; nine major elements (SiO_2, TiO_2, Al_2O_3, Fe_2O_3, MnO, MgO, CaO, Na_2O, K_2O), ten trace elements (Ba, La, Nb, Rb, Sr, V, Y, Zn, Zr, Cu, Sc) and 20 observations (samples from 1 to 17 plus samples of watercourses: SMR = Smir lagoon, NGR = Río Negro wadi and FNQ = Fnideq wadi). The selection of variables was made taking into account the following conditions:

- Firstly, minerals that were widely present in all samples were taken into account. If exceptional rates of one mineral were observed in a very small number of samples, the consequence is that variable-points and associated observation-points will be eccentric while the rest of the distribution will appear concentrated on the opposite side of the diagram.
- Secondly, it is preferable to project a minimum number of points on the diagram for a better reading.
- Concerning the distribution of the **variable-points** (Fig. 5.9), following observations can be highlighted: Groups 1 (including SiO_2) and 2 (Sr-CaO) are located on the right side of the scatter plot and present an opposite position respect to the F1 axis; Group 3 (Na_2O and MgO) is located closely to aforementioned groups. Group 6 is located on the extreme left side and includes three elements (Zn, Cu and Ba); Group 4 (Sc, Y and MnO) is located in the central part of the scatter plot. According to the axis F2 there are two main sets of variables; Groups 1, 2 and 3 form a triangle and the others show a scatter distribution (Fig. 5.9). Therefore, the variable-points occupy approximately a tetrahedron whose vertexes are SiO_2-CaO-Zn-Nb.

More in detail, **Group 1** includes nine observation-points consisting of materials of continental origin and supplied by watercourses to the littoral – where they are redistributed by longshore drift.

Group 2 includes eight samples collected between Marina Smir and Kabila ports and consists of deposits rich in shell fragments. Samples 2 and 17 belong to an intermediate position between this group and the previous one.

Group 3 contains three samples, corteges *samples* are dominated by MgO and Na_2O and observation-points indicate that this corresponds to elements coming from the two metamorphic formations of the study area: Monte Hacho and Cabo Negro headlands.

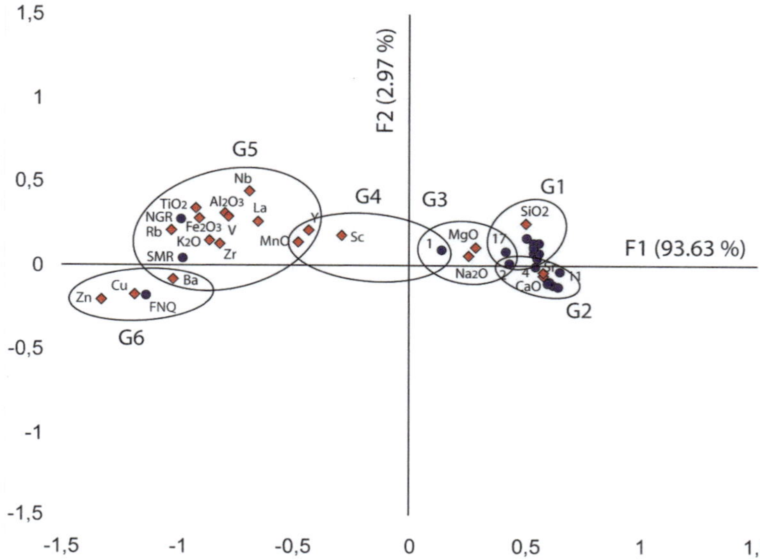

Fig. 5.9 Factor analysis diagram of variable-points (*in red*) and observation-points (*in blue*) according to factors 1 and 2

Group 4 is only represented by the sample gathered at M'diq beach just north of Cabo Negro headland. Both sets, G3 and G4 establish a transition between coastal and inland materials.

Group 5 includes samples gathered in correspondence of the two main rivers flowing in the coastal sector Cabo Negro – Ceuta. The group contains a great amount of elements, in this sense highlighting the importance of supplies of Rio Negro River and Smir Rivers. Within this data set, it is possible to identify two groups of minerals; the first contains MnO and Y, which arrive at the coast; the second comprises several elements (Al_2O_3, Fe_2O_3, TiO_2, K_2O, Zr, Nb, Rb, La, V), most of them record alteration processes or precipitate during the transport and do not arrive to the coast. Data show that concentrations of Mn O and Y in coastal and watercourses samples are quite similar; however, the concentrations of other components, such as Al and Fe, are much more important in watercourses sediments than at beaches (Rodríguez-Barroso et al. 2008; Tahri et al. 2005; Dominik et al. 2007).

Group 6 includes the sample of Fnideq wadi which presents the highest concentrations of Zn and Cu and, to a lesser degree, of Ba (probably linked to anthropogenic contamination).

The majority of components carried by the rivers remains upstream and do not supply the beaches, this being due to the characteristics of those minerals and the hydrological characteristics of rivers. Based on the analysis of presented data, it is possible to draw a map showing the source areas and way of distribution of the main mineralogical components of coastal sediments in Tetouan coast (Fig. 5.10).

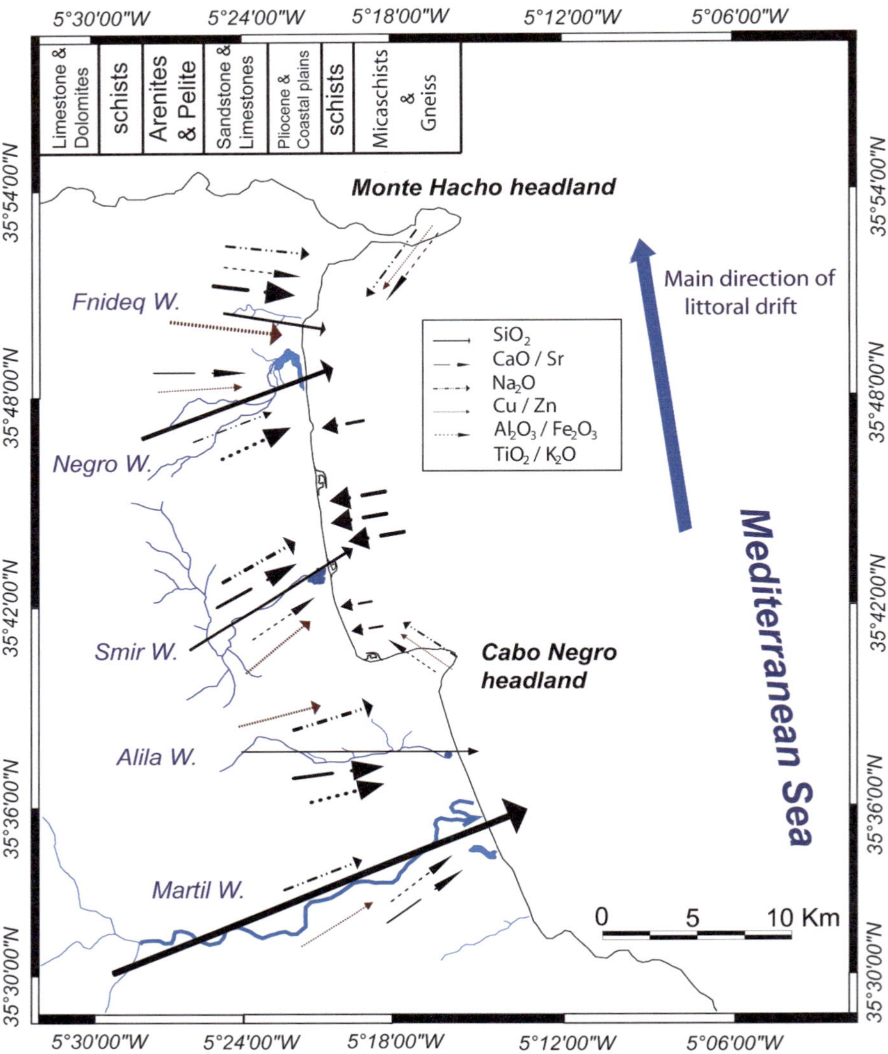

Fig. 5.10 Scheme showing the flow of studied elements in Tetouan watercourses and beaches; the size of the *arrows* indicates the importance of inputs

5.5 Synthesis and Conclusions

An amount of 46 surface samples of sediments were collected at the Tetouan coast and at major watercourses. Their textural and chemical features were analyzed in order to characterize their source areas, transport and spatial distribution.

Based on the sediment texture, Tetouan beaches can be subdivided into two main areas. The first one, south of Cabo Negro promontory, is mainly composed of medium, well to very well sorted sand. Morphoscopic analysis showed that beach sediments receive a significant percentage of aeolian inputs from dunes.

The second area, north of Cabo Negro promontory, is mainly composed of poorly sorted gravelly sand, with local enrichments of shell fragments and torrential inputs. The differences between the aforementioned sectors are controlled by coastal morphology, continental drainage system, hydrodynamic forcing and exposure to waves, as previously observed in other coastal regions (Komar 1998; Davis and Fitzgerald 2004; Ergin et al. 2007).

The hydrological regime of the investigated area is characterized by the presence of several short and steep-gradient ephemeral rivers and streams that flow from the mountainous hinterland to the coast. Martil wadi is the most important river of the area and the only one that shows a perennial water course.

Finally, human interventions had influenced sediments exchange by: retention of materials in dams, interruption of beach-dune exchanges because of dunes destruction and summerhouses construction at the backshore, and the disruption of longitudinal exchange due to the construction of leisure ports between Cabo Negro headland and Fnideq. Further, erosion processes have favoured the outcropping of older, coarser deposits (El Mrini 2011). Therefore, beach sediments from the northern sector of Tetouan littoral are coarser grained than those from the southern sector. The geochemical analysis of Tetouan littoral sediments reveals that they are composed by variable proportions of three main components (e.g. continental, biogenic and authigenic components).

5.5.1 Continental Component

All beaches and river samples of Tetouan littoral contain high concentrations of quartz and SiO_2 as a result of the hinterland rock weathering and the successive transport operated by rivers to the coastal area, the Martil wadi carrying the majority of siliciclastic sediments. The high content of Al_2O_3 and Fe_2O_3 in watercourses and the high positive correlation between these two elements reveal that they are predominantly linked to clay minerals. Summing up, in the study area, watercourses mainly carry sandy sediments, rich in SiO_2, that reach the coast and, secondarily, silt and clay deposits, rich in aluminium and iron, that are almost completely deposited in river bed before arriving at the coastline.

5.5.2 Biogenic Component

The highest concentrations of CaO are found in the coarse and very coarse sand deposits rich in shell fragments. The CaO contents present positive correlations with MgO and Sr because magnesium is easily incorporated in Mg-calcite and/or aragonite, Sr substitutes Ca in calcareous shells of marine organisms (mainly aragonite) (Martins et al. 2012).

5.5.3 Authigenic Component

The highest contents of K_2O and, to a lesser extent, Na_2O in beach sediments are observed in samples collected near rocky promontories of the area. During metamorphism processes, clays have been converted to muscovite. Thereby, metamorphic headlands constitute the third source of Tetouan beaches inputs; their contribution is of local character and it achieves certain importance only in close beaches, in fact K_2O contents decrease dramatically with distance from the promontories. The current sediments of the littoral could be ascribed mainly to the erosion of the outcropping rocks in the river basin (Aboumaria et al. 2009) while the carbonate components are due mainly to the current biotic and abiotic precipitation in coast environment. Finally, there is a facies locally important in the study area and linked to the contamination of anthropogenic origin. It is observed at Fnideq wadi mouth, which sediments are characterized by high levels of heavy metals contents, of oil origin.

Acknowledgements This work is a contribution to the Andalusia Research Group PAI RNM-328. The first author acknowledges a post-doctoral position funded by the Conseil Général des Pays de la Loire, France, within the framework of the project "Vulnérabilité des zones fragiles face aux changements locaux et globaux". Department of Mineralogy and Petrology, University of Granada (Spain) is acknowledged for technical assistance with the geochemical analyses. Further thanks to Renzo Tassinari of Department of Physics and Earth Sciences, University of Ferrara for XRF analyses support.

References

A.B.H.L. (Agence du Bassin Hydraulique de Loukkous) (2006) Les ressources en eau au niveau de la zone d'action de l'Agence du Bassin Hydraulique de Loukkos: Etat des lieux et perspectives de leur développement et leur sauvegarde. Débat national sur l'eau. Tetouan, Morocco, 29 p

Aboumaria K, Zaghloul MN, Battaglia M, Loiacono F, Puglisi D, Aberkand M (2009) Sedimentary processes and provenance of Quaternary marine formations from the Tangier Peninsula (Northern Rif, Morocco). J Afr Earth Sci 55(1–2):10–35

Alexandersson T (1974) Carbonate cementation in coralline algal nodules in the Skagerrak, North Sea; biochemical precipitation in undersaturated waters. J Sediment Res 44:7–26

Anfuso G, Nachite D (2011) Climate change and the Mediterranean southern coasts. In: Jones A, Phillips M (eds) Disappearing destinations: climate change and future challenges for coastal tourism. CABI International, Wallingford, UK, pp 99–110

Anfuso G, Achab M, Cultrone G, Lopez-Aguayo F (1999) Utility of heavy minerals distribution and granulometric analyses in the study of coastal dynamics: application to the littoral between Sanlucar de Barrameda and Rota (Cadiz, southwest Iberian Peninsula). Bol Inst Esp Oceanogr 15(1–4):243–250

Anfuso G, Benavente J, Nachite D, Bello E, Guiati R, Ghetti A, Meklach Y, Macias A (2004) Características morfodinámicas y variaciones estaciónales de las playas del tramo costero marroquí entre Ceuta y Cabo Negro. In: Benito G, Diez Herreo A (eds) Contribuciones Recientes sobre Geomorfología. SEG & CSIC, Madrid, pp 283–289

Anfuso G, Martinez del Pozo A, Nachite D, Benavente J, Macias A (2007) Morphological characteristics and medium-term evolution of the beaches between Ceuta and Cabo Negro (Morocco). Environ Geol 52:933–946

Anfuso G, Pranzini E, Vitale G (2011) An integrated approach to coastal erosion problems in northern Tuscany (Italy): littoral morphological evolution and cell distribution. Geomorphology 129:204–214

Blott SJ, Pye K (2001) GRADISTAT: a grain size distribution and statistics package for the analysis of unconsolidated sediments. Earth Surf Process Landf 26(11):1237–1248

Cailleux A (1943) Distinction entre sables marins et fluviatiles. Bulletin de la Société Géologique de France 13:125–138

Carter RWG (1988) Coastal environments. An introduction to the physical, ecological and cultural systems of coastlines. Academic, London

Castro M, Arroyo G, Bekkali R, Nachite D, Anfuso G (2006) Características ambientales del entorno de la laguna de Smir (Environmental characteristics of the Smir lagoon). Aula Universitaria del estrecho, University of Cadiz, Cadiz, 40 p

Davis RA Jr, Fitzgerald DM (2004) Beaches and coasts. Blackwell, Oxford, 419 pp

Dominik J, Vignati DAL, Koukal B, Pereira de Abreu MH, Kottelat R, Szalinska E, Bas B, Bobrowski A (2007) Speciation and environmental fate of chromium in rivers contaminated with tannery effluents. Eng Life Sci 7(2):155–169

El Mrini A (2011) Evolution morphodynamique et impact des aménagements sur le littoral tétounais entre Ras Mazari et Fnideq (Maroc nord occidental). PhD. thesis, University Abdelmalek Essaadi, Morocco and Université de Nantes, France. 303 p

Ergin M, Keskin S, Dogan AU, Kadioglu YK, Karakas Z (2007) Grain size and heavy mineral distribution as related to hinterland and environmental conditions for modern beach sediments from the Gulfs of Antalya and Finike, Eastern Mediterranean. Mar Geol 240:185–196

Folk RL (1980) Petrology of sedimentary rocks. Hemphill, Austin, 182 p

Friedman GM (1967) Dynamic processes and statistical parameters compared for size frequency distributions of beach and rivers sands. J Sediment Petrol 37:327–354

Frihy OE, Dewidar KM (2003) Patterns of erosion/sedimentation, heavy mineral concentration and grain size to interpret boundaries of littoral sub-cells of the Nile Delta, Egypt. Mar Geol 199:27–43

Hein JR, Allwardt AO, Griggs GB (1974) The occurrence of glauconite in Monterey Bay, California, diversity, origins, and sedimentary environmental significance. J Sediment Res 44:562–571

Komar PD (1998) Beach processes and sedimentation. Prentice Hall, Englewood Cliffs, 544 p

Lakhdar Idrissi J, Zidane F, Orbi A, Hilmi K, Sarf F, Rharbi N (2001) Etude d'impact des apports terrigènes sur l'activité aquacole dans la baie de M'diq. Art rev L'eau, l'industrie, les nuisances 243:61–67

L.P.E.E. (Laboratoire Publics d'Etudes et Essais) (1994) Le littoral de Cabo Negro. Données naturelles et évaluations de la dynamique hydrosédimentaire. Rapport pour la Société Africaine du Tourisme 97

Martín JD (2004) Using XPowder: a software package for Powder X-Ray diffraction analysis. www.xpowder.com. D.L. GR 1001/04.ISBN 84-609-1497-6. Spain, 105 p

Martins R, Azevedo MR, Mamede R, Sousa B, Freitas R, Rocha F, Quintino V, Rodrigues AM (2012) Sedimentary and geochemical characterization and provenance of the Portuguese continental shelf soft-bottom sediments. J Mar Syst 91:41–52

Medaković D, Popović S, Zavodnik N, Gržeta B, Plazonic M (1995) X-ray diffraction study of mineral components in calcareous algae (Corallinaceae, Rhodophyta). Mar Biol 122(3):479–485

Michard A, Negro F, Saddiqi O, Bouybaouene ML, Chalouan A, Montigny R, Goffé B (2006) Pressure–temperature–time constraints on the Maghrebide mountain building: evidence from the Rif–Betic transect (Morocco, Spain), Algerian correlations, and geodynamic implications. C R Geosci 338:92–114

Moiola RJ, Weiser D (1968) Textural parameters: an evaluation. J Sediment Petrol 38(1):45–53
Nachite D (1993) Los Ostracodos y la evolucion paleoambiental del Neogeno reciente del NO de Marruecos y del SE de España, PhD thesis, Univ. Granada, Spain, 310 p
Nachite D (2007) Le développement touristique du littoral de la Région-Tanger-Tétouan: une évolution vers des scenarios non désirables? Géologie et Géotourisme dans la rive sud du Détroit de Gibraltar. Aula Universitaria del Estrecho, Tétouan, Morocco, 13 p
Nachite D (2009) Le développement touristique du littoral de la Région Tanger-Tétouan: une évolution vers des scénarios non désirables? In: Dominguez Bella S, Maate A (eds) Geologia y geoturismo en la orilla sur del estrecho de Gibraltar. MCN-UCA, Cadiz, pp 59–78
Nachite D, El Moutchou B, Anfuso G, Benavente J, Bello E, Macias A (2004) Morfologíay evolución del litoral entre Fnideq y Mdiq. Geogaceta 35:43–46
Nachite D, Amri I, Anfuso G, Bello E, Marocchino E, Benavente J, Vaccaro C (2005) Geoquímica de los sedimentos de playas entre Fnideq y M'Diq (Tetuán, NO de Marruecos) (Geochemical characteristics of beach sediments between Fnideq and M'Diq, Tetuan, NW Morocco). Geogaceta 38:159–162
Niazi S (2007) Evaluation des impacts des changements climatiques et de l'élévation du niveau de la mer sur le littoral de Tétouan (Méditerranée occidentale du Maroc): Vulnérabilité et Adaptation., Thèse de Doctorat d'Etat. Faculté des Sciences, Université Mohammed V – Rabat. 230 p
Passega R (1964) Grain size representation by CM patterns as a geological tool. J Sediment Petrol 34(4):830–847
Rajamanickam GV, Gujar AR (1984) Sediment depositional environment in some bays in central west coast of India. Indian J Mar Sci 13:53–59
Rodríguez J, Nachite D, Berraho A, Najih M, Camiñas JA, Baro J, Alcántara A, Grissac AJ, Simard F, Fernández ILF, Bouillon FX (2010) Conservation and sustainable development of the Alboran Sea – strategic elements for its future management. IUCN, Gland/Malaga
Rodríguez-Barroso MR, Benhamou Y, El Moumni B, El Hatimi I, García-Morales JL (2008) Evaluation of metal contamination in sediments from north of Morocco: geochemical and statistical approaches. Environ Monit Assess 159:169–181
Stitou J (2002) Étude de la salinité des eaux souterraines des aquifères côtiers Martil-Alila et Smir : Intégrationdes méthodes hydrogéochimiques, géophysiques et isotopiques, Thèse de Doctorat d'etat. Univ. Abdelmalek Essaadi, 283 p
Tahri M, Benyaich F, Bounakhla M, Bilal E, Gruffat JJ, Moutte J, Garcia D (2005) Multivariate analysis of heavy metal contents in soils, sediments and water in the region of meknes (Central Morocco). Environ Monit Assess 102:405–417
Taouil A (2001) Milieu naturel et utilisation du sol dans le Haouz méditerranéen de Tetouan, Rif occidental, Maroc: facteurs physiques, système agro-sylvo-pastoral, production et évolution de l'espace. PhD Tesis, Universiteit van Amsterdam, 275 p
Weiner S, Dove PM (2003) An overview of biomineralization and the problem of the vital effect. In: Dove PM, Weiner S, De Yoreo JJ (eds) Biomineralization, vol 54. Mineralogical Society of America, Washington, DC, pp 1–31.7

Chapter 6
The Hydro-sedimentary System of the Upper-Normandy Coast: Synthesis

Stéphane Costa, Pauline Letortu, and Benoit Laignel

Abstract The aim of this paper is to examine the sediment budget along the coast of Upper-Normandy, including the gravel beach (stock, input and output). The cliff coast and pebble/gravel beach, such along Upper-Normandy coast, is also considered as a system because cliff retreat induces widening of shore platforms and supplies the pebble/gravel beach with flint. In return, shore platform and pebble/gravel beach contribute to reduce intensity and action time of the waves at the foot of chalk cliff, and therefore cliff instability. However, for this type of coast, sedimentary exchanges with shoreface and offshore are rarely taken into account because of the low crosshore mobility of pebbles/gravels. However, the internal structure of pebble beaches is very often composed of a fraction proportion which can exceed 50 %. The sand fraction, presents also on rock shore platform and creating a sandy low tide terrace, seems to participate in the adjustment of these gravel beaches with wave. Theses interactions between two domains (coarse grained beach/sandy foreshore and shoreface) require to extend seaward the limits of the hydro-sedimentary system coast of Upper-Normandy.

6.1 Introduction

To understand and manage coastal areas, they must be considered as an open system which dynamic equilibrium is governed by constant energy and sediments transfer. Variation of these flows in time and space determines the state of the sediment stock available, and therefore the rate of morphological evolution of the coastline. This morphodynamic approach, initiated in the early 1970s, requires defining the spatial boundaries of the system that have nothing in common with

S. Costa (✉) • P. Letortu
Lab. Géophen., UMR CNRS-LETG Caen Géophen 6554, University of Caen Basse-Normandie, BP 5186, 14032 Caen, Cedex, France
e-mail: stephane.costa@unicaen.fr

B. Laignel
Department of Geology, UMR 6143 CNRS M2C, University of Rouen, Place Emile Blondel, 76821 Mont-Saint-Aignan, France

M. Maanan, M. Robin (eds.), *Sediment Fluxes in Coastal Areas*, Coastal Research Library 10, DOI 10.1007/978-94-017-9260-8_6

too restrictive administrative boundaries. About shore deposit, especially sandy deposits, it is commonly admitted the existence of interrelations between the foreshore and shoreface, which affect the dynamic equilibrium of the shoreline (Morton et al. 1994; Héquette et al. 2001; McNinch 2004; Aagaard et al. 2004; Backstrom et al. 2009; Maspataud et al. 2009).

The cliff coast and gravel beach, such along Upper-Normandy coast, is also considered as a system because cliff retreat induces widening of shore platforms and supplies the gravel beach with flint. In return, shore platform and gravel beach contribute to reduce intensity and action time of the waves at the foot of chalk cliff, and therefore cliff instability. However, for this type of coast, sedimentary exchanges with shoreface and offshore are rarely taken into account because of the low crosshore mobility of gravels. Indeed, the morpho-sedimentary behaviour of these beaches is only considered as an upper foreshore deposit. Then, these gravel beach are only observe into consideration in their relations with cliff retreat or the mobility of their main components, especially the gravel class size (>2 cm). However, these gravel beaches may be also characterized by the existence of a significant sand fraction in volume and surface. The sand fraction is present in the gravel beach and on rock shore platform as a low tide terrace. Some rock shore platforms in Upper-Normandy have known since the early 1990s, a sudden and massive sandy up. The sandy up seems to influence the morpho-sedimentary behaviour of gravel beach (Costa 1997; Voulgaris et al. 1999; Van Wellen et al. 2000; Mason and Coates 2001; Buscombe and Masselink 2006; Allan et al. 2006; Ivamy and Kench 2006; Austin and Masselink 2006; Costa et al. 2008; Curtiss et al. 2009). This fact raises the question of origin, including shoreface origin, of these sandy materials whose granulometric characteristics are similar to sand observed in offshore zone.

The aim of this paper is to examine the sediment budget along the coast of Upper-Normandy, including the gravel beach (stock, input and output of gravel). This goal requires to also take into consideration the existence of an important sand fraction in the internal structure of gravel beach, and at its foot (low tide terrace), which seems to participate in the adjustment of these gravel beaches with wave.

6.2 Coast Influenced by Human Impacts and by Triple Association Coastal Chalk Cliff/Shore Platform/Gravel Beach

Coast of Upper-Normandy, which stretches from Cap d'Antifer to Le Tréport (Fig. 6.1) is made up of 120 km long coastal cliffs, mainly composed of chalk with flint. Cliff height average is about 70 m, but cliff height does not exceed 40 m at Cap d'Ailly. Cliff height decreases from south-west to north-east. In fact, their height is 105 m at Antifer and 35 m near Saint-Aubin-sur-Mer, and then increases again to reach 101 m at Le Tréport.

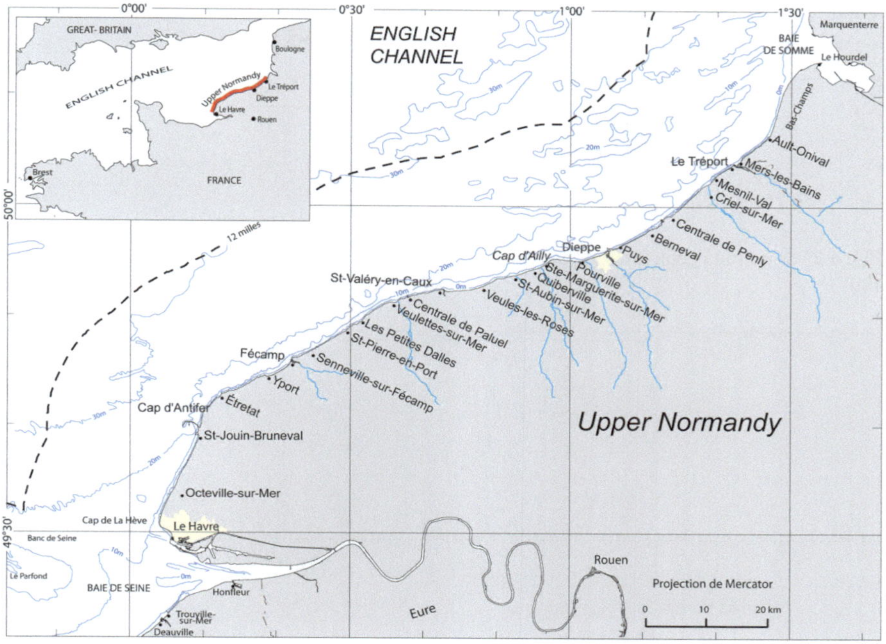

Fig. 6.1 Study area

6.2.1 Geology and Forms

Geologically, this area corresponds to the north-western termination of the Parisian Basin. Plateau of Haute-Normandy and Picardy, so its cliffs, is composed of Upper Cretaceous chalk (from Cenomanian to Campanian), which is more or less resistant to weathering, and influences the speed retreat. Residual formations with flint and Quaternary loess are also deposited on this karstified chalk (Quesnel et al. 1996; Laignel et al. 2004).

Main tectonic deformations in NW-SE directions result in the outcrop of various layers from the Upper Cretaceous (Fig. 6.2). Cliffs are mainly formed in Senonian (Coniacian, Santonian, and locally Campanian) white chalk, rich in flint. Even if, these chalks appear homogeneous, in fact, they hide more complex details (Juignet and Breton 1992; Laignel 1997).

Coniacian chalk is present between Antifer and Saint-Valéry-en-Caux, and also between Dieppe and Le Tréport. Santonian chalk is continuously located only in the central part of the cliff line from Saint-Valéry-en-Caux to Puys. Campanian chalk is locally present from Quiberville to Pourville. The grey-white Turonian chalk, containing clay and little or no flint, protrudes from Antifer to Etretat, from Fécamp to Eletot, and from Puys to Tréport. Its maximum extension is located in Penly. Locally, at the base of the cliffs in Antifer and Etretat, and to the east of Fécamp, Cenomanian chalk protrudes. These chalks are heterogeneous, sometimes rich in

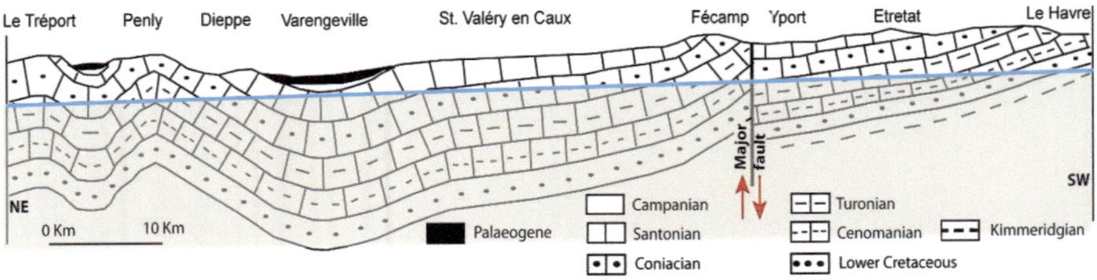

Fig. 6.2 Simplified geological cross-section of the coast between Le Havre and Le Tréport (Costa 1997)

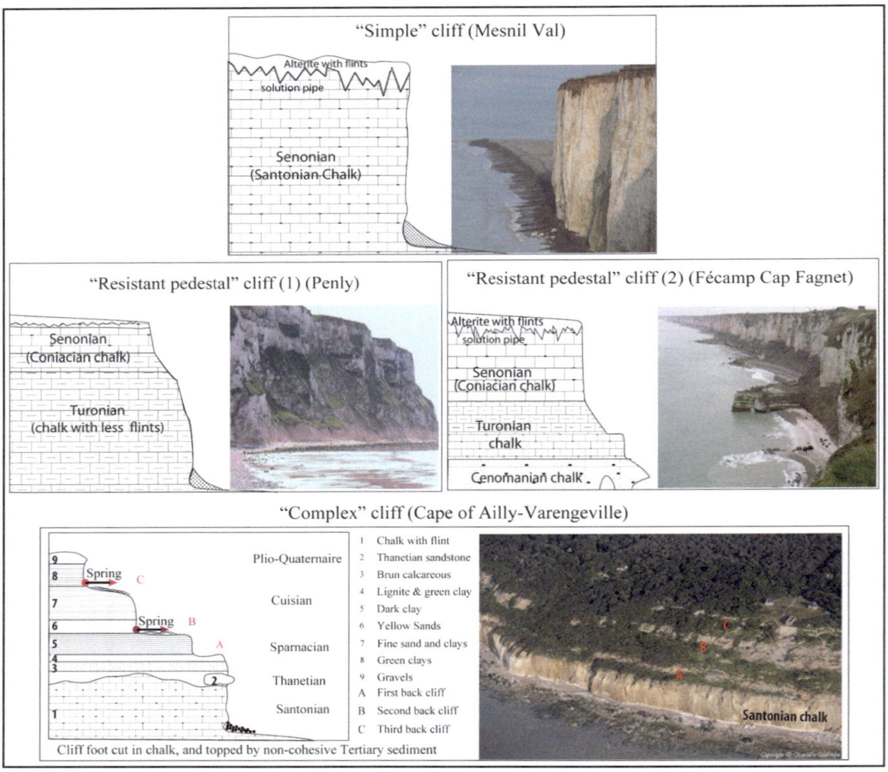

Fig. 6.3 Types of Upper-Normandy cliffs according to lithostratigraphy (Costa 1997)

detrital components (clay and quartz) and can be glauconitic or nodular. A cover approximately 10 m thick of sandy, clayish sediments of palaeogene origin can be found at the cliff top at Cap d'Ailly, Sotteville and at Bois de Cise. Because the different structural characteristics have differing susceptibilities to weathering, the various ages of chalk layers correspond to different types of cliff morphology with contrasting rates of evolution. Three main types of cliff are identified (Fig. 6.3): "Simply" cliffs are cut in Senonian chalk and stretch about 70 km along the coastline; “resistant pedestal” cliffs correspond to a resistant outcrop, generally the Turonian layer; “complex” cliffs have a cliff foot cut in the Santonian chalks, which are then covered by the non-cohesive Tertiary sediments. “Complex” cliffs, largely consisted of sand and clay layers, are mainly located around Cap d’Ailly.

6.2.2 *Shore Platform and Gravel Beach*

Shore platform, at the foot of cliff, is cut into chalk. The seaward slope is slight (a maximum of 2 % at Antifer). The width of these platforms increases from 100 m in SW (Antifer) to 250 m in NE. Maximum width of shore platform reaches 300 m between Saint-Valéry-en-Caux and Dieppe. Locally this platform is also characterized by a low tide cliff whose height is usually 1 or 3 m (Fig. 6.4).

The upper section of shore platform, in the intertidal zone and beyond, is hidden beneath a gravel accumulation which can take one of several shapes. The most common is a “composite gravel beach”, according to the classification of Jennings and Shulmeister (2002) that reaches up to the cliff base, or forms barriers close to valley exits. Beach is rather narrow in width (from 15 to 20 m), and approximately 2–2.5 m thick. Barrier usually has greater sediment volume in account of port jetties or major groynes, which decrease longshore drift close to river mouths. These beach accumulations are, on average, 40 m wide but near groynes, width can exceed 50–60 m (Fig. 6.5).

Fig. 6.4 Low tide cliff at Puys (Photo S. Costa)

Fig. 6.5 Pebble/Gravel beach at the foot of the cliff (**a**) and accumulated against the harbour jetty of Fécamp (**b**). (Photo S. Costa)

Fig. 6.6 Morphological and sedimentological characteristics of gravel beach of Upper-Normandy coast. Sand in gravel Beach (**a**) and Beach of Pourville (**b**)

Their bases are around +3 m (up to maximum spring low tide), and their ridges can reach +11 m. Along the study area, surface granulometric characteristics of gravel beach are simple and generally homogeneous (LCHF 1972; Costa 1997). Average size of gravel varies from 4 to 7.5 cm, rarely exceeding 14 cm. Gravels are rough-hewn, forming a slope of about 10 % but which varies in function of hydrodynamic conditions.

According to the classification of Jennings and Shulmeister (2002), gravel beaches in Upper-Normandy correspond to the "composite beaches". Indeed, they are characterized by an upper beach steep slope with a reflective aspect (~5 to 15 %), composed of a mixture of pebbles, gravels and sands. Nevertheless, in period of calm sea conditions, the surface is predominantly made up of gravel, becoming more refined in depth. At beach toe, a foreshore sand surface develops with a low slope (0.5–1.5 %), of about 200 m wide, giving a highly dissipative aspect to this segment of the beach profile (Fig. 6.6).

In the wake of the shore platform, the eastern English Channel sea floor is not characterized too by important shapes, and his depth rarely exceeds 50 m. The bottom is covered by a thin, discontinuous layer of clay, sand and gravel (Larsonneur 1971; Augris et al. 2004). These morpho-sedimentary characteristics are important for the question about the sedimentary relations/exchanges (sands) between upper shoreface and foreshore. In fact, the sands, which could come from shoreface, seem important for the behaviour of the gravel beach, influencing his permeability and porosity capacity (Van Wellen 1999, Van Wellen et al. 2000; Mason and Coates 2001; Voulgaris et al. 1999; Allan et al. 2006; Ivamy and Kench 2006; Austin and Masselink 2006; Costa et al. 2007; Ciavola and Castiglione 2009).

6.2.3 Hydrodynamic Conditions

Due to the shape of the eastern English Channel basin, even exposed to Westerly storms, study area is only subjected to the formation of moderated waves. The strongest and the most common waves (Hs) develop in the west, leading to a dominant longshore drift of beach gravels from south-west to north-east.

Any notable wave height is below 1 m 70 % of the time, to 2 m 95 % of the time, and exceeds 3 m 0.3 % of the time, i.e. 25 h/year (Augris et al. 2004). The wave period varies from 2 to 19 s, but the average is around 5–7 s. For stronger waves the period is around 7–10 s (Table 6.1).

In the English Channel, the tide is semi-diurnal. The tidal range is around 8.5 m in Dieppe (average spring tide), defining a megatidal environment. For an exceptional spring tide, the tidal range increases from the Havre (8.10 m) to Le Tréport, where it exceeds 10 m (Shom 2001). These tidal currents alternate. The flood current (5 h) moves in a north-easterly direction, then, the ebb current (7 h) moves to a south-west direction. Offshore currents can be strong (1–1.5 m/s), but decrease landwards. From 0.4 m/s at a depth of −6 m, they do not exceed 0.2 m/s on the foreshore and are able to transport only fine material such as sand.

These hydrodynamics condition and the direction of the coastline create a longshore drift from Cap Antifer to the Somme estuary. Nevertheless, at the end of the nineteenth century, jetties were built to prevent gravels from obstructing the port fairways. Whereas rockfalls can last from some months to some years, jetties interrupt the drift of gravel for good, by cutting the original hydro-sedimentary cell Antifer-baie de Somme into several cells delimited by harbour arms (Fig. 6.7).

Table 6.1 Significant wave (H1/3) along the Upper-Normandy coast (*in* Augris et al. 2004)

Location	Le Havre	Antifer	Paluel	Dieppe	Penly
Annual height (in m)	3.5	4.1	4.1	4.3	3.8
Decennial height (in m)	4.6	5.7	4.9	5.7	4.7

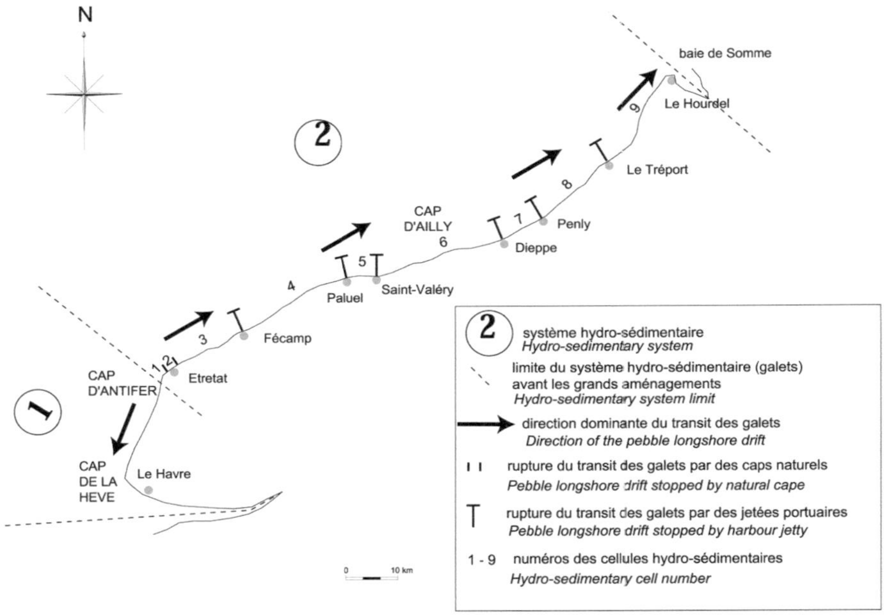

Fig. 6.7 Hydro-sedimentary cell and sub-cells of Upper-Normandy coast (Costa 1997)

Therefore, these obstacles cause an accumulation of sediment upstream, and a sedimentary crisis downstream. This deficit passes on in the direction of longshore drift, inducing an increase of the wave attack efficiency, and then, an exacerbation of the cliff retreat rate.

6.3 Supplies and Losses from the Hydro-sedimentary System of Upper-Normandy Coast

6.3.1 Supply of Flint Pebble from the Chalk Cliff Retreat: Currently the Only Source

To quantify the cliff erosion, a photogrammetric analysis was made. The 1966 (Mission FR-1191/100) and 1995 (Mission FR- 5049/100) vertical aerial photographic surveys from the French National Geographic Institute were used (1:10,000 scale). The flight path followed the coastline during low tide and geo-referenced markers, linked via planimetry and altimetry to the Lambert I projection system, was also located along the flight path to improve the accuracy of the analysis. Then, a stereo-preparation and an aero-triangulation of the shots were undertaken, allowing both a paper and numeric reconstruction on a scale of 1:2,000. So the cliff top from 1966 to 1995 was perfectly reproduced in planimetry in the Lambert I projection system. Altimetric points were collected on cliff top, on gravel beach (80 points per hectare), and on shore platform (5 points per hectare).

The advantage of the photogrammetric technique was to provide highly accurate results (margin of error in latitude, longitude and altitude is ±0.30 m), and cliff retreat is measured every 50 m (along the cliff line).

The flint content of the cliff was assessed for each chalk stratum by a section survey and by photographic analysis. For the section survey, flint content was calculated by measuring flintless chalk layers. For the photographic analysis, shots perpendicular to the cliff face were taken with a digital camera. Then, these photographs were processed in order to calculate a surface percentage of pixels equivalents to the flint quantity (Laignel 1997). Finally, these two methods were validated by granulometric analysis done by the aggregate industry (Laignel 1997; Costa et al. 2006; Laignel et al. 2008).

Photogrammetric analysis underlined that the mean retreat rate of the studied coastline (from Antifer to Le Tréport) was about 6 m between 1966 and 1995, so a rate of 0.21 m·year^{-1} (Costa et al. 2001). But this average rate hid a high spatial variability of cliff retreat (Fig. 6.8).

The analysis per hydro-sedimentary cell and sub-cell (Fig. 6.9) allowed the distinction of three areas: (i) an area of slow retreat rate (0.8–0.13 m·year^{-1}) between Antifer and Fécamp, (ii) an area of moderate retreat rate (approximately

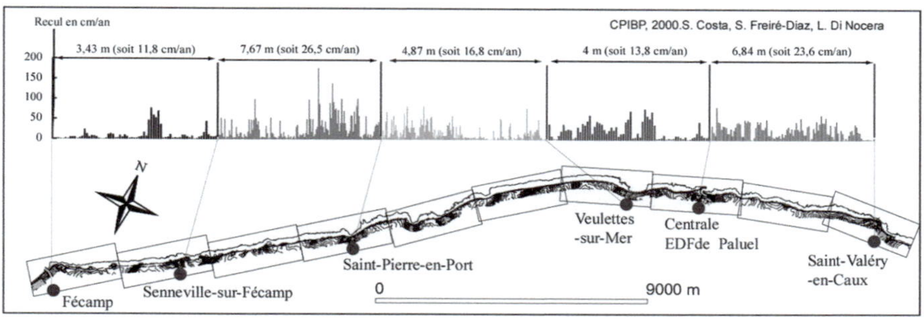

Fig. 6.8 Rate retreat of the chalk cliff between in Upper Normandy between 1966 and 1995 (Costa et al. 2001)

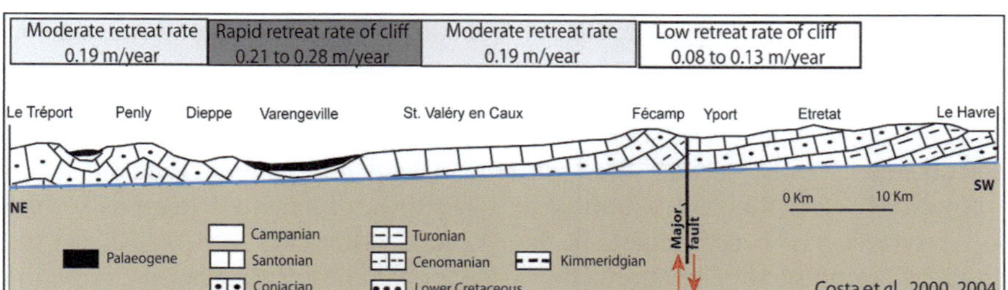

Fig. 6.9 Relationship between chalk rates cliff retreat and lithostratigraphy

0.19 m·year^{-1}) between Fécamp and Saint-Valéry-en-Caux, and between Dieppe and Le Tréport, (iii) an area of fast retreat (0.21–0.28 m·year^{-1}) between Saint-Valéry-en-Caux and Dieppe (Costa et al. 2001, 2004).

Even within each of these coastal sections important variations may exist. These sharp variations were linked to cliff falls influence and/or anthropogenic obstacles, such as harbour arms or major groynes, that disrupted the gravel transit from the south-west to the north-east.

The identification of three sectors with distinctive retreat rates raised questions about the causes of this spatial distribution of the cliff retreat rates, and especially, and its relations with the chalk outcrops (Costa 1997; Costa et al. 2001, 2004). On one hand, sectors with "slow" and "moderate" retreat, affected by rare but massive rockfalls, corresponded with Turonian, Cenomanian, and even Coniacian outcrops at cliff foot (Antifer/Fécamp ; Fécamp/Saint-Valéry-en-Caux ; Dieppe/Le Tréport). On the other hand, the rapidly retreating sector affected by frequent but less voluminous rockfalls, corresponded with Santonian and Campanian outcrops (Saint-Valéry-en-Caux/Dieppe).

The accuracy and reliability of cliff retreat results, coupled with the information about the flint content, enabled the measure of potential gravel production. This supply has effect on the sedimentary balance of beaches and their capacity to resist to wave attack. The flint content of coastal chalk cliffs in Upper-Normandy ranged from 4.5 to 15.7 % (Laignel 2003; Laignel et al. 2008). These values were quite homogeneous within a particular geological layer but changed from one layer to another. In the case of the Cenomanian Chalk, the flint content was about 15–18 % but can change vertically (16–17 % for the lower Cenomanian part, 17–20 % for the mid-upper Cenomanian part, and between 0.5 and 2 % for the upper-terminal Cenomanian part). Flint content in the Turonian layer is low: Between 0 and 1 % for the mid-lower Turonian part and between 3 and 5 % for the upper Turonian part. In the Coniacian chalk, the proportions were about 10 % and reach 10–15 % for the Santonian and the Campanian chalks. For the entire studied coastline, a progressive decrease of the flint content from south-west to north-east was noticed. Important variations, especially few decreases, are linked to intervals of flintless Turonian outcrops (Table 6.2).

For the studied coastline from 1966 to 1995, the potential supply of gravels due to cliff retreat (calculated from fallen volume and the flint content of the chalk) is 63,000 m^3·year^{-1} for the entire shoreline under study during the period 1966–1995 (i.e., an average of 720 m^3·year^{-1} per linear kilometre). This result estimates that flint loses 40 % of its volume in becoming gravel (LCHF 1972). For the sectors of Fécamp/Saint-Valéry-en-Caux and Saint-Valéry-en-Caux/Dieppe, the volume supplied is from 700 to 730 m^3·year^{-1} per linear kilometre. The lowest supply values are obtained for the sectors Antifer/Etretat, Dieppe/Le Tréport, Etretat/Fécamp (respectively 475, 500 and 620 m^3·year^{-1} per linear kilometre). Reasons for the low production of beach gravels in these sectors differ (Fig. 6.10). Cliffs in the Antifer/Fécamp sector contain relatively large quantities of flint but the retreat is very slow, whereas the more intense retreat rates of the Dieppe/Le Tréport sector are compensated by the low flint content of the cliffs due to significant Turonian outcrops.

Table 6.2 Physical and lithological characteristics of chalks of Upper-Normandy coast

Stratigraphic stage	Facies	Flint content (in %)	Porosity (in %)	Permeability millidarcy	Density
Cenomanian	Nodular chalk, clay more or less sandy, grey clayey chalk, glauconitic clayey chalk more or less sandy or clayey	0.5–20	15.4–41.3	0.1–13.1	1.6–2.1 (nodular chalk 1.8–2.4)
Turonian	Upper Turonian: grey chalk, lightly clayey and white	0–5 (T_{lower}: 3–5) ($T_{lower, middle, upper}$: 0–1)	26.3–47	0.1–4.1	1.7–2.1 (Ts: 1.7–1.9) (Ti, m: 1.9–2.1) (nodular chalk 1.9–2.4)
	Lower, Middle Turonian: grey clayey chalk Lower, Middle, Upper Turonian: nodule chalk				
Coniacian	White chalk (main facies) White chalk lightly clayey (at the cliff base) Nodular chalk (rare at the cliff base)	8–13.5	22.6–38.3	1.1–2.6	1.6–1.7
					1.8–1.9 (nodular chalk 1.9–2.4)
Santonian	White chalk	10–16	40.2–45.6	3.5–5.6	1.6–1.8 (nodular chalk 1.9–2.2)
All stages	Maximum	20	47	13.1	2.1 (nodular chalk 2.4)
	Minimum	0	15.4	0.1	1.6

Laignel (1997, 2003) and Laignel et al. (2006)

6.3.2 *Present Distribution of the Gravel Beaches and Losses of This System: A Mainly Human Origin*

Low rates of platform downwearing (LCHF 1972; Hénaff et al. 2002), and difficulty for flint to climb up the slope of the rocky shore (Costa 1997), make it difficult to quantify the gravels production resulting from the shore platform erosion. It is thought, however, that compared with the cliff retreat supply, that of the shore platform is negligible. In addition, a submarine origin of the gravels is excluded since it was proved that those situated beneath the level of wave action either do not move (LCHF 1972), or remain blocked by the low tide cliff (Costa 1997; Augris et al. 2004). In 1995, the gravel beach between Cap d'Antifer and Le Tréport had a volume of 7,500,000 m^3. In 1972, the French Central Hydraulic Laboratory stated

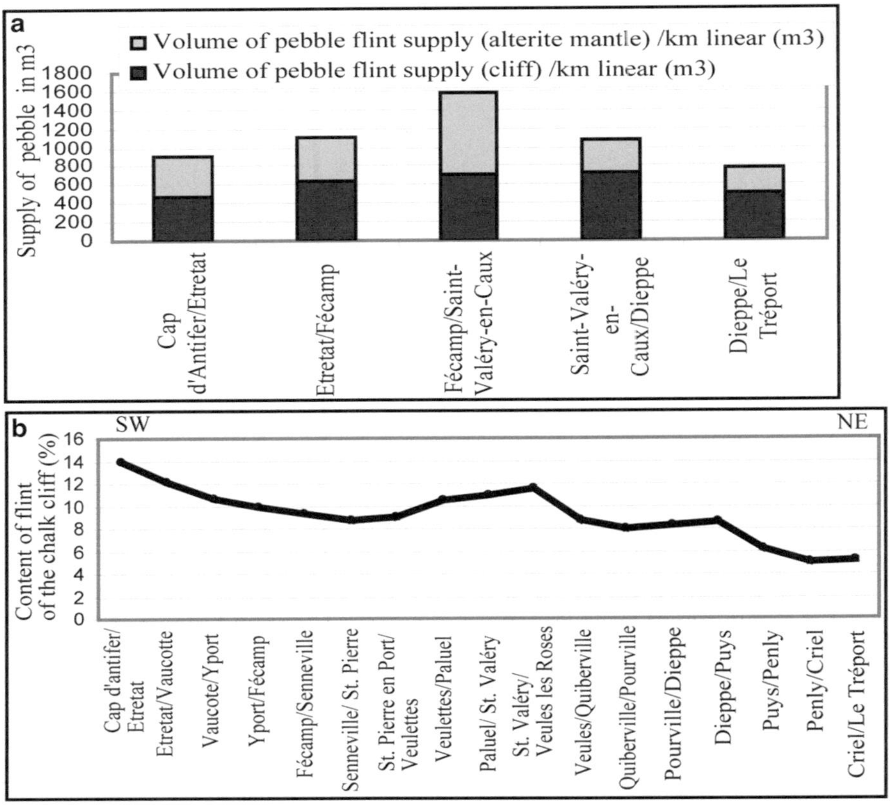

Fig. 6.10 Potential supply of flint gravel due to cliff and alterite with flints mantle retreat (**a**), and flint content of chalk cliff (**b**) (*In* Delahaye and Costa 2005)

there was "*a regular and homogeneous distribution of gravel volume at the foot of cliffs and on beaches*". No noticeably change seemed to occur for the coastline between Antifer and Saint-Valéry-en-Caux, but the sediment distribution greatly changed in the coastal area of Saint-Valéry-en-Caux/Dieppe and Dieppe/Le Tréport. Along this section, 61–67 % of the sedimentary stock is now concentrated along the beaches. At the scale of the study area, the gravel beaches distribution at the foot of the cliffs is not noticeably heterogeneous, except between Criel and Le Tréport (Fig. 6.11).

However, on a more precise scale, the study highlighted variations due to obstacles preventing gravel drift. These obstacles are from a natural and man-made origin. Obstacles include the deposit of cliff falls, and transversal man-made structure, such as port jetties and groynes. At the end of the nineteenth century, port jetties were built to prevent gravels from obstructing the port fairways. Rock falls can remain from some months to some years, but port jetties break off the

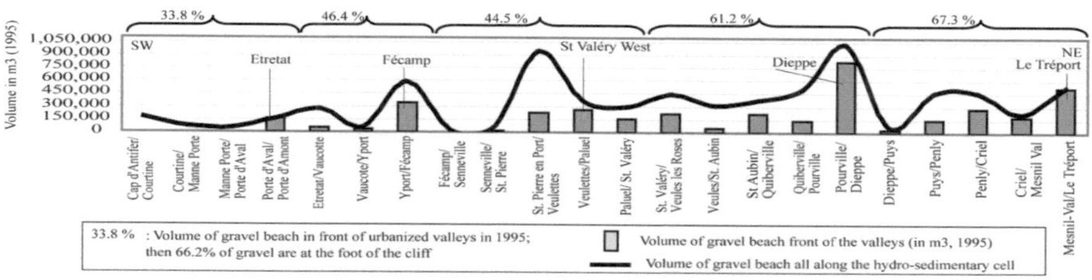

Fig. 6.11 Volume of gravel/pebble beach at the cliff foots and in front of the valleys in 1995 (*In* Delahaye and Costa 2005)

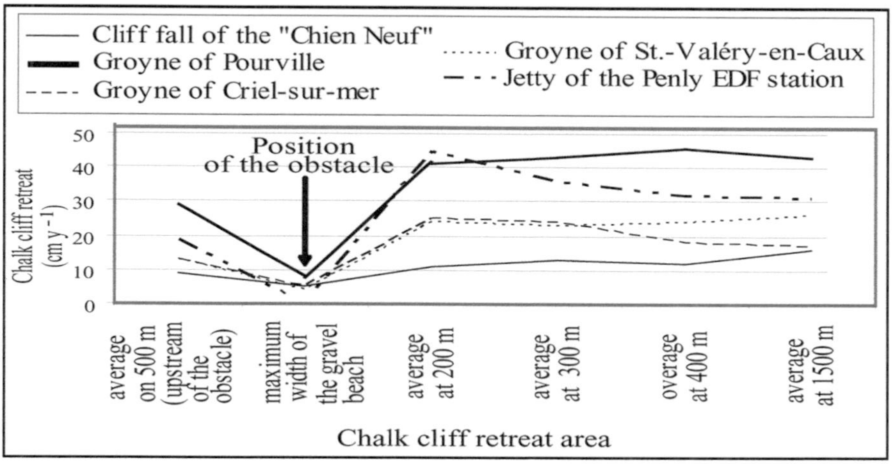

Fig. 6.12 Increase of the chalk cliff erosion rates downstream obstacles (cliff fall or jetty) for five cases along the Upper-Normandy Coast (Costa et al. 2004)

drift of gravel beaches by cutting the original hydro-sedimentary cell Antifer-baie de Somme into several cells delimited by harbour arms. Therefore, these obstacles have impacts on accumulation of sediment upstream, and end in a sedimentary crisis downstream.

This deficit passes on in the direction of longshore drift, ending in an increase of the wave attack efficiency, and then, an exacerbation of the cliff retreat rate (Fig. 6.12).

Other human interventions helped to alter distribution and volume of gravel beaches. Due to their high silica content and hardness, flint gravels have been highly exploited. According to available official figures, almost 3,000,000 m^3 have been extracted since the beginning of the last century, between Antifer and Le Tréport. This is roughly half the volume now present. Even though little information has been given on the extraction sites, this work had a significant impact on the thinning out of all the beaches. This is why extraction has been regulated in 1972.

Fig. 6.13 Pebbles/gravels entered in the port fairways (Photo, Costa 2012)

In addition, the high volumes of gravels that entered in the port fairways of Saint-Valéry-en-Caux and Dieppe, are then dredged and thrown out to sea (Fig. 6.13).

These sediments are not returned to the beaches, and so their removal drains the beach sedimentary system. This drain, halted in 1990 in Saint-Valéry-en-Caux, amounts to 150,000 m^3 (Fig. 6.14a) and to around 2,000 $m^3 \cdot year^{-1}$ for the port of Dieppe. Since 2 years, the authorities of the Dieppe Harbour and Seine Maritime Country organize a "bypass system". In fact, the gravels which are entered in the port fairways of Dieppe are now dredged and thrown out at the beach foot of Puys (7–8,000 $m^3 \cdot year^{-1}$). Then, with the help of wave, the gravels take place on initial the gravel beach (Fig. 6.14b).

6.3.3 A Sediment Budget Still Difficult to Quantify

Despite the quantification conducted during last years, it appears that the definition of Upper-Norman coastal sediment budget is not full. Indeed, the quantitative information is only a "state of zero" of knowledge, which, in the absence of new measurement surveys (especially sediment stocks) cannot clearly identify evolutionary trends. Moreover, among the unknowns, the volume of gravel transit is approximate. The only existing values concern the potential transit that was estimated at 20,000 or 30,000 $m^3 \cdot an^{-1}$ (LCHF 1972). Another uncertainty concerns the

Fig. 6.14 Bypass system use along the Upper-Normandy coast. Dredging of the port of Saint Valéry-en-Caux (**a**) (Photo, Costa 1990). After dredging pebbles in the port fairways of Dieppe (cf. Fig. 6.13), deposition on the beach of Puys (Downstream of Dieppe Harbor) (**b**) (Photo, Authorities of Dieppe Harbor 2011)

supply of gravels from the cliff erosion that is probably overestimated. Indeed, the calculation method suggests that fallen volumes are annually evacuated. However, the larger ones spend several years on the shore platform without releasing the flint they contain. In addition, measurement of flint content considered cliffs layers to be free of cragginess, whereas at North-East of Saint-Valery-en-Caux these consist essentially of flint nodules, called branching. These morphological characteristics of flint contained in the chalk are not without consequences for the gravel transit. Those resulting from massive plates provide big flat gravel hardly mobilized by waves (at least at the beginning). Flint nodules produce smaller gravel and especially strongly blunted because affected by rolling.

In view of the figures from the flint supply coming from the cliff retreat (110,000 $m^3 \cdot year^{-1}$, it's say, 63,000 m^3 from chalk cliff and 48,000 m^3 from the cover alterite with flint), supply should be able to compensate withdrawals made during the last century (3 million m^3 extracted before cessation of extraction in 1972). The state of current stocks, except for the beaches blocked by a port jetty, does not seem to highlight any trend.

Finally, another uncertainty is due to official figures of pebble extraction volume. These are probably much lower than reality. In 1984, a report of Y. Tual, engineer of the local government body responsible for public works, indicates that because of lack of supervision, effective extractions were locally two to three times higher than the allowed amount.

6.4 Evolution of Pebble Stocks in Front of Urbanized Valleys

Within the framework of two research programs, DGPS surveys were implemented in 2001 (BERM program; Delahaye and Costa 2002) and in 2003 (BAR program, Delahaye and Costa 2005) on twelve beaches sensitive to the risk of coastal flooding. These georeferenced data, compared to those provided by photogrammetric analysis (Costa et al. 2001), allow a diachronic study of changes between 1995 and 2003, and provide some answer elements about the future of these beaches (Fig. 6.15).

From this comparison, conclusions were:

- The volume of sediment increases for beaches bounded by a port jetty (Fécamp, East of Saint-Valery-en-Caux, Dieppe), except Le Tréport (because of contributions, and important loss in the port fairway). It is the same for beaches bounded by a major groyne (Quiberville, West of Saint-Valéry-en-Caux), except for Mesnil-Val and Criel which the "trap" constituted by the groyne is already saturated.
- The other beaches have a sediment budget in deficit or in balance.
- Two beaches have a singular behaviour because of their sediment deficits (Veules-les-Roses, and Veulettes-sur-Mer), even if this crisis seems to fade between 2001 and 2003.

In view of these results, it appears that the supply of flint from the cliff retreat feeds a very undernourished longshore drift, inevitably inducing rapid transfer of these gravels, and their accumulation toward the downstream end of

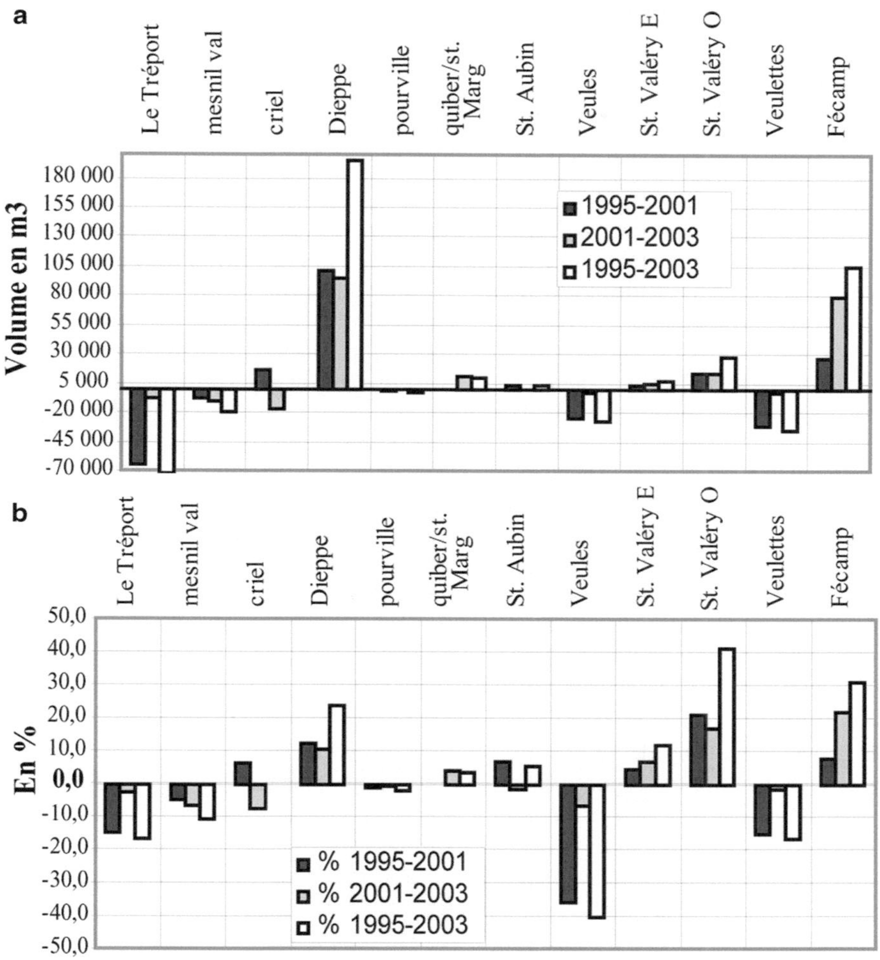

Fig. 6.15 Volume changes of 12 beaches of the Upper-Normandy coast (**a**) in m^3, (**b**) in %, between 1995 and 2003 (Delahaye and Costa 2005)

hydro-sedimentary cells, so against port jetty or major groyne. The relative stability of the other beaches, despite lateral supply, suggests that succession of groynes is already saturated. Occasional crises of some beaches can be explained either by a long period of wind action from North to North-East (reverse to dominant drift) leading to the displacement of large volumes of gravels to the cliffs or by the existence of debris falls upstream beaches, temporarily blocking the longshore drift. This reinforces the idea that the absence of reliable and regular information on volumes of gravels at the foot of the cliffs is highly damaging to the understanding and quantification of sediment budget system of the Upper-Normandy coast.

6.5 The Behaviour of the Gravel Beach: The Sandy Fraction Impact

6.5.1 The Gravel Beaches of Upper-Normandy: A "Composite Gravel Beach"

The gravel beaches of Upper-Normandy are characterized by an internal structure predominantly constituted by an interstitial sand fraction, and at their foot, a sandy foreshore with a soft slope (1 %) that is more dissipative.

The understanding of the behaviour of gravel beaches is still fragmented because it is a hostile environment due to strong agitation and abrasion from to the grain size. For these reasons the deployment of equipment of measure and tracer monitoring are very difficult. Nevertheless, these studies have more recently become the subject of new interest. The majority of scientific works on morpho-sedimentary behaviour of the coarse grained beaches envisaged these forms of accumulation only under the angle of the motion of the main essential elements (the grain size corresponding to the gravel class (>2 cm)). However, the internal structure of gravel beaches is very often composed of a sandy fraction proportion which can exceed 50 % (Kirk 1980; Carter et al. 1984; Powell 1988; Shulmeister and Kirk 1993; Quick and Dyksterhuis 1994; Costa 1997, 1999; Orford et al. 2002; Pontee et al. 2004; Costa et al. 2008; Ciavola and Castiglione 2009). The content of sand is not without influence on the adaptive reactions of the gravel beaches in relation with the conditions of agitation because it can vary the porosity and permeability, at least on the surface of the gravel accumulation (Masselink and Li 2001; Pontee et al. 2004). The sedimentary layout of coarse grained beaches is therefore very variable in time and space in reply to the evolution of agitation. This situation results from the different behaviours of various grain sizes in relation with hydrodynamic conditions, because sands undergo cross shore movements towards the offshore and the foreshore, by thrusting, saltation and suspension (under the influence of the tide and wave currents), while pebbles/gravels are subjected to predominant movements towards the coast, by sliding or rolling (and more seldom by saltation), under the unique effect of the swash (Van Wellen 1999; Van Wellen et al. 2000; Mason and Coates 2001; Voulgaris et al. 1999; Buscombe and Masselink 2006; Allan et al. 2006; Ivamy and Kench 2006; Austin and Masselink 2006; Curtiss et al. 2009; Williams et al. 2012). This significant agility of miscellaneous grain size sediments makes the grain size characterization particularly difficult for the accumulations of pebbles/gravels (Carter 1988; Orford and Carter 1993).

The gravel beaches distinguish themselves not only by the size of their composite elements, but also by their morpho-sedimentary adjustment to hydrodynamic conditions. Defined as being morphologically reflective (Short and Wright 1984; Nicholls and Wright 1991; Short 1999), these beaches are in general dominated by waves from which the breaking does not lead to an important zone of swash owing to the porosity and permeability of their surface (Carter 1988; Carter and Orford

1993; Mason and Coates 2001). The studies on the dynamic of these gravel accumulations, which especially concern barriers, highlight their evolution by "over-passing and over-topping", inducing an effect of rolling of this sedimentary feature on itself inwards from coasts in reply to strong agitation or a sea level rise (Carter and Orford 1980, 1988; Forbes et al. 1991, 1995; Orford et al. 1996, 2002; Williams et al. 2012).

Moreover, grain size layouts and morpho-dynamic adjustment of these gravel beaches to the agitation are generally completely different (slower) from the sand beaches (Carter and Orford 1980, 1984, 1993; Orford et al. 1991; Ivamy and Kench 2006). Nevertheless, the reactions of these accumulations of coarse material can be radically changed. On the one hand, by the presence of sea defence constructions, such as seawalls, on which the storm waves are reflected (Carter 1988; Costa 1997; Orford et al. 2001), and on the other hand, by the position of the ground water table (Horn and Holmes 2003; Isla and Bujalesky 2005). So, it proves to be that the saturation in water of the beach favours the displacement of materials, behaviour already published for sand beaches (Baird and Horn 1996).

According to this classification of Carter and Orford (1984, 1993), and Jennings and Shulmeister (2002), the gravel beaches in Upper Normandy correspond to "composites" beaches. Indeed, they constitute a steep slope upper beach with a reflective aspect (~5 to 15 %). At its toe, a foreshore sand surface with a low slope (0.5–1.5 %), of about 200 m wide develops, gives a highly dissipative aspect to this segment of the beach profile.

6.5.2 Distribution and Feature of the Sandy Foreshore and the Internal Sandy Structure of the Gravel Beach

The foreshore of the studied area is also characterized by the presence of a non-negligible volume of sand. On the rocky foreshore, first of all, there is a very mobile sand layer. It has an extension of some hundred square metres, and a thickness reaching 1.5 m at most. Other layers, more stable, and thicker, correspond to the infilling of the paleo-channels of the actual valleys again inscribed in the shore platform.

The grain size analysis and binocular shape observations of the sands from the foreshore show that they are principally constituted of blunted to sub-angular quartz grains, and by fine splintered shelves (5–10 %). The lower and the middle foreshore are made of fine sands well classified, disposed to a gradient of refinement going from the gravel beach toe to the bottom of the foreshore (Fig. 6.16).

So, during calm sea conditions, the sandy foreshore is composed, on average, of 88 % of fine-grained sand and 12 % of medium-grained sand. These characteristics are homogeneous in depth, on the first 50 centimetres of the sandy foreshore.

An abounding sand fraction is also present inside the gravel beaches. Indeed, they are composed at best of 50 % pebbles, the rest, its internal composition, being a

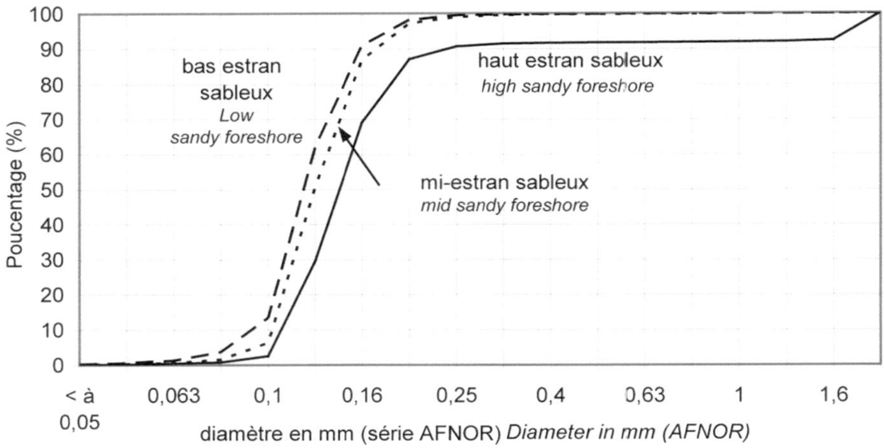

Fig. 6.16 Granulometric characteristics of the sand of the sandy foreshore at Pourville

Fig. 6.17 Pourville gravel beach before storm (**a**), and covered by a thin layer of sand after storm (**b**)

mixture of gravels and coarse grained sand in a proportion that can reach 70 %. Besides, during storm events, the middle and bottom of the mixed sediment beach, more seldom the summit, are often covered by a thin layer of sand (Costa 1997; Costa et al. 2008). This partial "capping" is particularly noticeable at the end of a storm and then quickly disappears (Fig. 6.17).

These observations suggest the possibility of vertical (from the internal gravel beach) or transversal sand exchanges that need to be specified. Sands from the internal structure of the shingle beach or those which cover it are rather badly classified (so comprised between 1.67 and 1.92), and heterogeneous. The sand fraction is almost principally made of quartz, but, it contains 15–20 % of siliceous splinters resulting from the pebbles' attrition. These characterise the sand of gravel beach. Or, find it at the bottom of the sandy foreshore after storm is the first evidence showing the existence of transverse sandy exchanges between gravel beach and sandy foreshore.

6.5.3 The Sandy Fraction: An Important Element in the Upper-Normandy Gravel Beach Behaviour

The placement into a prominent position of the sandy exchanges is based on two types of fieldwork measurements (Costa 2005; Costa et al. 2008). (1) The first one is the simultaneous realization of beach profiles with a DGPS (several profiles have been achieved in order to identify the longitudinal sandy transfers) and grain size analysis and binocular shape observations of the sands from the mixed sediment beach and the sandy foreshore. These surveys have been done, before, during, and after strong winds. (2) The second one is the follow-up of twenty fluorescent tracer injections during which entire topographic surveys and measurements of the hydro-dynamic conditions were done.

The simultaneous analysis of morphological and sedimentological parameters during various hydrodynamics conditions revealed the existence of sand transfers between a gravel beach and the lowest part of the sandy foreshore (Fig. 6.18). Thus, it seems that in periods of storm events, besides the morphological adaptation of the whole beach profile (toppling over of the profile corresponding to the erosion of the top part to the profit of the bottom part), a part of the interstitial sand seems also to

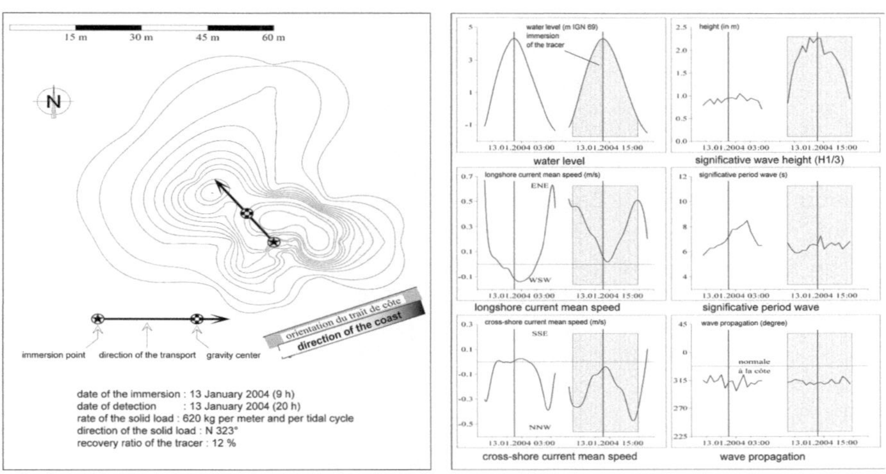

Fig. 6.18 Fluorescent tracers and hydrodynamic conditions survey during strong winds and neap or spring tides (Costa et al. 2008)

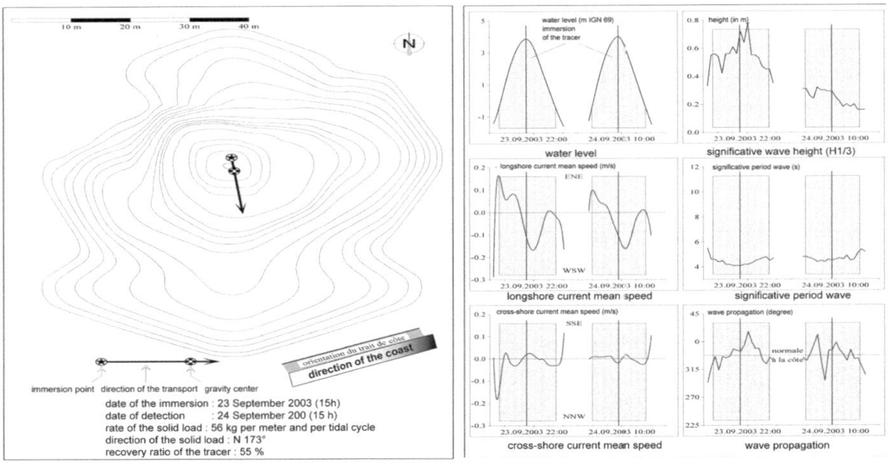

Fig. 6.19 Fluorescent tracers and hydrodynamic conditions survey during moderate winds (generally after storm) and during small or high tidal ranges (Costa et al. 2008)

migrate downwards to the foreshore to form a small ridge on which wave breaking occurs (Costa et al. 2008).

From a morphodynamic point of view, this migration confers to the low sandy foreshore a more reflecting character, whereas the gravel accumulation acquires a more dissipative aspect because of the grain size increase. It also induces a greater permeability that allows the absorption of the wave energy. The situation reverses itself after this storm event (Fig. 6.19).

This influence seems to be confirmed by various studies in scaled model or by fieldwork conducted on hydraulic conductivity (Mason et al. 1998; Mason and Coates 2001) and even, while using these two approaches (Pontee et al. 2004). These works based on permeability tests reveal that the hydraulic conductivity of the beaches mainly composed of sands and pebbles-shingle significantly decreases (of an order of magnitude 2) when the content of sand reaches close to 25 % (Mason et al. 1998). This determines the adjustment of the beach profile. However, according to the same author, above this figure of 25 %, a considerable increase of sand in the gravel beach does not seem to be sufficient to be seen on the speeds and the modes of the gravel beach profile evolution.

This conceptual model describing the behaviour of the composite beaches suggests that the sand fraction that constitutes the internal part of the gravel beach, and that sometimes covers the shore platform, is a part of the adaptation system to high energy events.

The morphodynamic evolution of the gravel part of a composite beach cannot therefore be studied solely through a longitudinal sedimentary mobility. Thus, the variable transverse sand exchanges in time and space need to be taken into account, implying an interdependence between the two domains (gravel beach/sandy

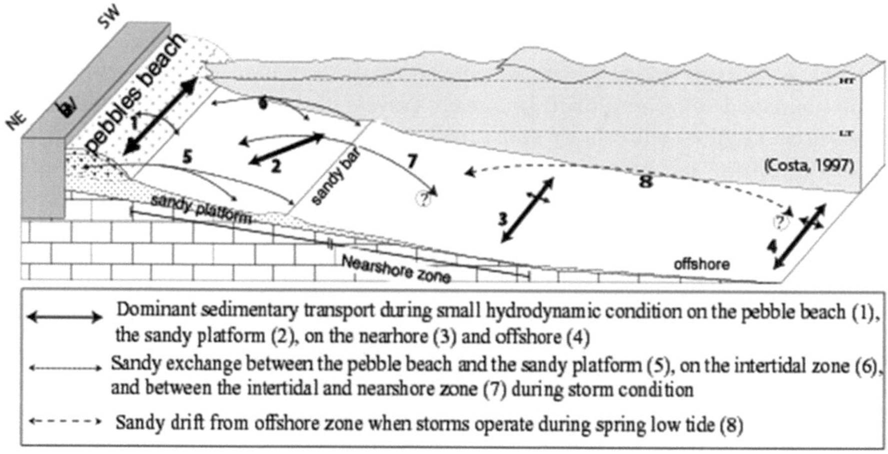

Fig. 6.20 Conceptual model of the Upper-Normandy gravel beach and sandy foreshore system (Costa 1997; Costa et al. 2008)

foreshore), or even with the shoreface area (Costa 1997, 1999; Augris et al. 2004; Costa et al. 2005, 2008). This phenomenon has already been recognized on sand beaches. Therefore, the understanding of the "composite beaches" behaviour requires extending seaward the limits of the hydro-sedimentary system (Fig. 6.20). However, this conceptual model maybe only applies to the Upper-Normandy beaches. Indeed, their specificities include many parameters: the presence of disruptive groynes, a significant sand content, the existence of a seaward gently sloping platform permitting cross-shore sand exchanges, moderate hydrodynamic conditions (epicontinental sea, and small fetch), and finally the proximity of a close and continuous source of coarse sediment (cliff erosion).

6.6 Conclusion

It is clear that the assessment of coastal sediment budget of coast of Upper-Normandy is still very incomplete because of the many unknowns and uncertainties. The data acquired after 1995 form the basis of the quantification, but will be relevant only if continuous surveys are implemented. However, it is necessary to exceed the extrapolations of measurements on too short time steps, even with a lot of instruments, which may not report, in the absence of old and reliable comparison data, evolutionary trends that are fundamentally nonlinear. Indeed, the definition of the sediment budget, and therefore the understanding of how the system cliff / shore platform / gravel beach needs to determine rhythms, thresholds and discontinuities of phenomena, but also combinations of factors and relay of processes variable in time and space, which govern the place.

In light of the first results, it appears that the contribution of flint from the cliff retreat does not seem to compensate the sediment crisis of the beaches sensitive to the risk of coastal flooding. Indeed, due to quasi-saturation groynes and a very undernourished longshore drift, produced gravels are quickly transported to the downstream hydro-sedimentary cells, particularly against the port jetty. From the point of view of the management of flooding risk, the vulnerability of sensitive current sites seems to not fade despite the cessation of extractions. In the absence of resizing works, and in this sedimentary context, implementation of defense against the sea policy called soft or environmental ("bypass" or beach nourishment), desired by some policy makers, would not be very effective.

The quantification of the annual flint supply still raises a question. Indeed, apart from the problems of spatial distribution, such volumes would be likely to renew all the current stock (7.5 million m^3) in a century! Although this quantification may suffer from some limitations, it remains that taking into account the minimalist contribution values (16,000 $m^3 \cdot year^{-1}$, LCHF 1972) suggests that the renewal of the stock could be a historical scale (~400 years). These results go against the commonly accepted idea that a significant volume of sediment is inherited from the last marine transgression. This applies perhaps to the gravel beach currently observable on the Upper-Normand coast. However, the rates of cliff retreat and gravel production are valuable only for a very recent period. Indeed, the position of the coastline has probably known very little change over the last five millennia. Marine action have initially evacuated the stocks found in the mouths of small coastal rivers and especially in Bay of the Somme, where they formed fossil gravel beaches, then the arrow of Bas-Champs (Cayeux-sur-Mer). It is only recently, perhaps even on a historical scale, that the intense regressive dynamic of chalk cliff, induced by marine action, occurs and accelerates due to the depletion sediments stock and human action.

Finally, there is the question of the influence of the sand fraction on the gravel beach volume, which sometimes constitutes more than 50 % of the internal structure of gravel accumulations. Recent studies (Delahaye and Costa 2002, 2005; Costa et al. 2008) demonstrated the existence of sand exchanges during strong marine agitation, between the lower foreshore (maybe to nearshore zone) and gravel beach. Such transfers could explain the rapid increase in the volume of certain gravel beaches observed by technicians of local government body responsible for public works, whose lateral contributions cannot report. These results also suggest, as sandy coasts, that understanding of morpho-sedimentary gravel beach requires extending seaward limits of the system.

References

Aagaard T, Davidson-Arnott R, Grenwood B, Nielsen J (2004) Sediment supply from shoreface to dunes: linking sediment transport measurements and long-term morphological evolution. Geomorphology 60:205–224

Allan JC, Hart R, Tranquili JV (2006) The use of Passive Integrated Transponder (PIT) tags to trace cobble transport in a mixed sand-and-gravel beach on the high-energy Oregon coast, USA. Mar Geol 232(1–2):63–86

Augris C, Clabaut P, Costa S, Gourmelon F, Latteux B (2004) Evolution morpho-sédimentaire du domaine littoral et marin de la Seine-Maritime (France). 158 p. Edition Ifremer, Conseil Général de la Seine-Maritime, EDF

Austin MJ, Masselink G (2006) Observations of morphological change and sediment transport on a steep gravel beach. Mar Geol 229(1–2):59–77

Backstrom JT, Jackson DWT, Cooper JAG (2009) Shoreface morphodynamics of a high-energy, steep and geologically constrained shoreline segment in Northern Ireland. Mar Geol 257:94–106

Baird AJ, Horn DP (1996) Monitoring and modeling groundwater behavior in sandy beaches. J Coast Res 12(3):630–640

Buscombe D, Masselink G (2006) Concepts in gravel beach dynamics. Earth Sci Rev 79:33–52

Carter RWG (1988) Coastal environments: an introduction to the physical, ecological and cultural systems of coastlines. Academic, London, 617 p

Carter RWG, Orford JD (1980) Gravel barrier genesis and management: a contrast. Coastal Zone 80. In: Proceedings of the 2nd symposium ocean management, 2. American Society of Civil Engineers, New York, USA, pp 1304–1320

Carter RWG, Orford JD (1984) Coarse clastic barrier beaches: a discussion of the distinctive dynamic and morphosedimentary characteristics. Mar Geol 60:377–389

Carter RWG, Orford JD (1988) Conceptual model of coarse clastic barrier formation from multiple sediment sources. Geogr Rev 78:221–239

Carter RWG, Orford JD (1993) The morphodynamics of coarse clastic beaches and barriers: a short-and long-term perspective. J Coast Res 15:158–179

Carter RWG, Johnston TW, Orford JD (1984) Stream outlets through mixed sand and gravel coastal barriers: examples from southeast Ireland. Zeitschrift für Geomorphologie, NF 28:427–442

Ciavola P, Castiglione E (2009) Sediment dynamics of mixed sand and gravel beaches at short time-scales. J Coast Res SI 56:1751–1755

Costa S (1997) Dynamique littorale et risques naturels: L'impact des aménagements, des variations du niveau marin et des modifications climatiques entre la Baie de Seine et la Baie de Somme. PhD thesis, 347 p, University of Paris I (Panthéon Sorbonne)

Costa S (1999) Sédimentologie des plages de galets des côtes françaises de la Manche: application à la défense contre la mer. Revue de Géographie de Lyon 74–1:35–43

Costa S (2005) Falaises à recul rapide et plages de galets: de la quantification des dynamiques d'un système complexe à la caractérisation des risques induits. Habilitation à Diriger des Recherches (Université de Bretagne Occidentale), 325p

Costa S, Freiré-Diaz S, Di-Nocera L (2001) Le littoral haut normand et picard: une gestion concertée. Annales de Géographie 618:117–135

Costa S, Delahaye D, Freiré-Diaz S, Davidson R, Di-Nocera L, Plessis E (2004) Quantification by photogrammetric analysis of the Normandy and Picardy rocky coast dynamic (Normandy, France). Ed by Mortimore et Duperret; Geological Society Engineering, Geology special publication, no 20: "Coastal chalk cliff instability", pp 139–148

Costa S, Gourmelon F, Augris C, Clabaut P, Latteux B (2005) Apport de l'approche systémique et pluridisciplinaire dans l'étude du domaine littoral et marin de la Seine-Maritime (France). Norois 196:91–108

Costa S, Henaff A, Lageat Y (2006) The gravel beaches of North-West France and their contribution to the dynamic of the coastal cliff-shore platform system. Zeitschrift für Geomorphology. Suppl-vol 144: 199–194

Costa S, Le Coeur C, Lageat Y (2007) Vers une quantification du budget sédimentaire des plages de galets du littoral haut normand. In ouvrage collectif en Hommage au Pr. Alain Godard: "Du continent au bassin versant. Théories et pratiques en géographie physique". *Presses Universitaires Blaise Pascal*, pp 457–468

Costa S, Levoy F, Monfort O, Curoy J, De Saint Léger E, Delahaye D (2008) ımpact of sand content and cross-shore transport on the morphodynamics of macrotidal gravel beaches (Haute-Normandie, English Channel). Zeitschrift für Geomorphology Suppl-vol 3(52): 41–62

Curtiss GM, Osborne PD, Horner-Devine AR (2009) Seasonal patterns of coarse sediment transport on a mixed sand and gravel beach due to vessel wakes, wind waves, and tidal currents. Mar Geol 259:73–85

Delahaye D, Costa S (2002) Pérennité des plages de galets de l'espace Rives-Manche (BERM). Rapport final. Préfecture de Haute-Normandie. Interreg II, 90 p

Delahaye D, Costa S (2005) Plages A Risques/Beaches At Risk (PAR/BAR). Rapport final. Conseil Régional de Haute-Normandie. Interreg IIIa, 175 p

Forbes DL, Taylor RB, Orford JD, Carter RWG, Shaw J (1991) Gravel-barrier migration and overstepping. Mar Geol 97:305–313

Forbes DL, Orford JD, Carter RWG, Shaw J, Jennings SC (1995) Morphodynamic evolution, self-organisation, and instability of coarse-clastic barriers on paraglacial coasts. Mar Geol 126:63–85

Hénaff A, Lageat Y, Costa S, Plessis E (2002) Le recul des falaises crayeuses du Pays de Caux: détermination des processus d'érosion et quantification des rythmes d'évolution. Géomorphologie 2:107–118

Héquette A, Desrosiers M, Hill PR, Forbes DL (2001) The influence of coastal morphology on shoreface sediment transport under storm-combined flows, Canadian Beaufort Sea. J Coast Res 17:507–516

Horn DP, Holmes P (2003) Measurement and modelling of gravel beach groundwater response to wave run-up. Coastal sediments 03. American Society of Civil Engineers, 11 p

Isla FI, Bujalesky GG (2005) Groundwater dynamics on macrotidal beaches of Tierra del Fuego, Argentina. J Coast Res 21(1):65–72

Ivamy MC, Kench PS (2006) Hydrodynamics and morphological adjustment of a mixed sand and gravel beach, Torere, Bay of Plenty, N.Z. Mar Geol 228:137–152

Jennings R, Shulmeister J (2002) A field based classification scheme for gravel beaches. Mar Geol 186:211–228

Juignet P, Breton G (1992) Mid-Cretaceous sequence stratigraphy and sedimentary cyclicity in the western Paris Basin. Paleogeogr Paleoclimatol Paleoecol 91:197–218

Kirk RM (1980) Mixed sand and gravel beaches: morphology, process and sediments. Prog Phys Geogr 4:189–210

L.C.H.F. (Laboratoire Central d'Hydraulique de France) (1972) Etude de la production des galets sur le littoral haut-normand. Rapport général, 63 p

Laignel B (1997) Les altérites à silex de l'ouest du Bassin de Paris: caractérisation lithologique, genèse et utilisation potentielle comme granulats. Thèse, Univ. Rouen, Edit. BRGM, Orléans, 264, 219 p

Laignel B (2003) Caractérisation et dynamique érosive de systèmes géomorphologiques continentaux sur substrat crayeux. Exemple de l'Ouest du Bassin de Paris dans le contexte nord-ouest européen. Habilitation à Diriger des Recherches. Université de Rouen, 138 p

Laignel B, Dupuis E, Rodet J, Lacroix M, Massei N (2004) An example of sedimentary filling in the chalk karst of the Western Paris Basin: characterization, origins and hydrosedimentary behaviour. Z F Geomorphol 48(2):219–243

Laignel B, Dupuis E, Durand A, Dupont JP, Hauchard E, Massei N (2006) Erosion balance in the loamy watersheds of the Western Paris Basin from the continuous measurement in the surface water. C R Geosci 338:556–564

Laignel B, Costa S, Lequien A, Massei N, Durand A, Dupont JP, Le Bot S (2008) Apports sédimentaires continentaux aux plages et à la mer de la Manche. Exemple des falaises et des rivières littorales de l'Ouest du Bassin de Paris. Zeitschrift für Geomorphology Suppl-vol 3(52): 21–40

Larsonneur C (1971) Manche centrale et Baie de Seine: géologie du substratum et des dépôts meubles. Thèse, Université de Caen, 394 p

Mason T, Coates T (2001) Sediment transport processes on mixed beaches; a review for shoreline management. J Coast Res 17(3):645–657
Mason T, Voulgaris G, Simmonds DJ, Collins MB (1998) Hydrodynamics and sediment transport on composite (mixed sand/shingle) and sand beaches: a comparison. Coastal Dynamics, American Society of Civil Engineers, pp 48–57
Maspataud A, Ruz MH, Héquette A (2009) Spatial variability in post-storm beach recovery along a macrotidal barred beach, southern North Sea. J Coast Res SI 56:88–92
Masselink G, Li L (2001) The role of swash infiltration in determining the beachface gradient: a numerical study. Mar Geol 176:139–156
Mc Ninch JE (2004) Geologic control in the nearshore: shore-oblique sandbars and shoreline erosional hotspots, Mid-Atlantic Bight, USA. Mar Geol 211:121–141
Morton RA, Gibeaut JC, Paine JG (1994) Stages and duration of post-storm beach recovery, south-eastern Texas coast, USA. J Coast Res 10:884–908
Nicholls RJ, Wright TP (1991) Longshore transport of pebbles. Experimental estimates of K. In: Proceedings of the costal sediments 99. American Society of Civil Engineers, pp 920–933
Orford JD, Carter RWG (1993) The morphodynamics of coarse clastic beaches and barriers: a short and long term perspective. J Coast Res Special Issue 15:158–179
Orford JD, Carter RWG, Forbes DL (1991) Gravel barrier migration and sea level rise: some observations from Story Head, Nova Scotia, Canada. J Coast Res 7:477–488
Orford JD, Carter RWG, Jennings SC (1996) Control domains and morphological phases in gravel dominated coastal barriers of Nova Scotia. J Coast Res 12:589–604
Orford JD, Jennings SC, Forbes DL (2001) Origin, development, reworking and breakdown of gravel-dominated coastal barriers in Atlantic Canada: future scenarios for the British coast. In: Packham JR (ed) British shingles. Westbury, Otley, pp 23–55
Orford JD, Forbes DL, Jennings SC (2002) Organisational controls, typologies and time scales of paraglacial gravel-dominated coastal systems. Geomorphology 48:51–85
Pontee NI, Pye K, Blott SJ (2004) Morphodynamic behaviour and sedimentary variation of mixed sand and gravel beaches, Suffolk, UK. J Coast Res 20:256–276
Powell KA (1988) The dynamic response of shingle beaches to random waves. In: Proceedings of the 21st international conference on coastal engineering. (American Society of Civil Engineers), pp 1763–1773
Quesnel F, Maurizot P, Laigniel B, Lebret P, Meyer R (1996) S.I.G., géomorphologie et formations superficielles. Exemple des résidus à silex de l'Ouest du bassin de Paris. Colloque Formations superficielles et géomorphologie. Rouen, 19–20 Mars 1996. *Doc.B.R.G.M.* 248. 49 p
Quick MC, Dyksterhuis P (1994) Cross shore transport for beaches of mixed sand and gravel. International symposium: waves – physical and numerical modelling. Canadian Society of Civil Engineers, pp 1443–1452
SHOM (2001) Les instructions nautiques C2-1. France (côte Nord). De la frontière belge aux Casquets, 241 p
Short AD (1999) Handbook of beach and shoreface morphodynamics. Wiley, Chichester, 379 p
Short AD, Wright LD (1984) Morphodynamics of high energy beaches: an Australian perspective. In: Thom BG (ed) Coastal geomorphology in Australia. Academic, Sydney, pp 43–68
Shulmeister J, Kirk RM (1993) Evolution of a mixed sand and gravel barrier system in North Canterbury, New Zealand, during Holocene sea-level rise and still-stand. Sediment Geol 87(3–4):215–235
Van Wellen E (1999) Modeling of swash zone sediment transport on coarse grained beaches. PhD thesis, Department of Civil Engineering, University of Plymouth
Van Wellen E, Chadwick AJ, Mason T (2000) A review of assessment of longshore sediment transport equations for coarse-grained beaches. Coast Eng 40:243–275
Voulgaris G, Workman M, Collins MB (1999) Measurement techniques of shingle transport in the nearshore zone. J Coast Res 15:1030–1039
Williams JJ, Alegría-Arzaburu AR, McCall RT, Van Dongeren A (2012) Modelling gravel barrier profile response to combined waves and tides using XBeach: laboratory and field results. Coast Eng 63:62–80

Part III
The Use of Modelling Approaches of Sediment Fluxes at a Higher Spatial and Temporal Scale

Chapter 7
Tidal Prism Variation in Venice Lagoon and Inlet Response over the Last 70 Years

Georg Umgiesser, Rachel Helsby, Carl L. Amos, and Christian Ferrarin

Abstract The Venice lagoon inlets have undergone extensive modification during the past, responding in their evolution to the changing physical forcings and human intervention. In order to quantify the adaptation to these forcings the northernmost inlet (Lido) has been studied in detail through numerical modeling and high-resolution bathymetry data collected during three consecutive years.

Eleven sections have been chosen in these channels where the cross-sectional area has been determined. The discharges and with it the tidal prism through these sections have been computed through numerical simulations of an existing, calibrated hydrodynamic model (Shyfem). The obtained results have been compared to empirical relationships between the tidal prism and the cross-sectional area of tidal channels (O'Brien relation and Jarrett formula).

The computations have been repeated with available data from bathymetry charts for the years 1990, 1970 and 1930 to detect any temporal variation of the cross-sectional areas of the channels and their tidal prism and to evaluate the stability of the Lido inlet. Results from all inlets indicate a relative stability of the tidal prism entering Venice Lagoon, though some changes were detected for the year 1970.

7.1 Introduction

Coastal lagoons depend crucially on the exchange with the open sea through their inlets. These inlets govern the volume of water that enters and exits on each tidal cycle, which controls the water quality. However, there is also a feedback from the flow passing through the inlets and the cross-sectional area of that inlet. This

G. Umgiesser (✉) • C. Ferrarin
Institute of Marine Sciences, ISMAR-CNR, Arsenale Tesa 104, Castello 2737/F, 30122 Venezia, Italia
e-mail: georg.umgiesser@ismar.cnr.it

R. Helsby • C.L. Amos
School of Ocean and Earth Science, National Oceanography Centre, Empress Dock, Southampton, Hampshire, UK

M. Maanan, M. Robin (eds.), *Sediment Fluxes in Coastal Areas*, Coastal Research Library 10, DOI 10.1007/978-94-017-9260-8_7

relationship has been investigated by many authors (LeConte 1905; O'Brien 1931, 1969; Escoffier 1940; Jarett 1976; Hume and Herdendorf 1988). To summarize, there is a well-defined cross section that is in equilibrium with a given volume of water that passes through it over a tidal cycle. This flow is characterised by the tidal prism, which is the volume of water that passes through the cross section in a half tidal spring cycle.

In a recent paper Townend (2005) investigated 79 estuaries in the UK, and the relevance of the relationships proposed by O'Brien (1931) and Jarrett (1976). He also evaluated the relationship proposed by Renger and Partenscky (1974), which incorporates the surface area, volume and tidal prism of an estuary. Fontolan et al. (2007) studied the sand storage of Venice lagoon in relation to the tidal prism. He produced a relationship of the O'Brien type, using data only from the North Adriatic inlets.

This purpose of this paper is to investigate the theory of the tidal inlet stability using the tidal channels in the northern Venice Lagoon, i.e., Lido inlet, Treporti channel, and Burano channel and the other two inlets of the lagoon (Malamocco and Chioggia). We also aim to determine whether the tidal prism has changed significantly over the 70 year period between 1930 and 2000. The supply of sand to the inlets is controversial and appears to have increased in recent times. This period incorporates the onset of sand influx from Cavallino Beach (Helsby et al. 2006) via the tip of the Lido inlet's northern jetty into Lido inlet thus deepening the cross section of the mouth of Lido inlet. There has been a continual downcutting of Treporti channel by 2–3 cm/year (Umgiesser et al. 2006; Helsby et al. 2006), a change in tidal dominance from flood to ebb (Helsby et al. 2008) and the resulting formation of a sub-aqueous ebb spit (in Lido inlet), and the development of an offshore ebb tidal delta (Amos et al. 2004, 2005). Thus, there have been continuous changes in the morphology and geometry of Lido inlet and its tidal channels.

This work uses a hydrodynamic model to compute the tidal prism. Whereas the cross section is a geometric entity that is readily available, the tidal prism is normally not measured but estimated by multiplying the area of the estuary with the tidal excursion. This method does not always give reliable data, especially in areas that exhibit a strong deformation of the tidal wave inside its basin.

7.2 Methods

7.2.1 The Relationship Between the Tidal Prism and Cross-Sectional Area of an Inlet

The stability of a tidal inlet can be evaluated by application of a cross-sectional area/tidal prism relationship. In theory, inlets with a smaller cross section or larger tidal prism than the predicted relationship should increase its cross-sectional area in order to accommodate the tidal prism or vice versa. However, as the inlet cross-sectional area increases with erosion or decreases with deposition, the discharge and velocity is also affected, which has a feed back on the tidal prism.

The relationship between the cross-sectional area (*A*) of an inlet and its tidal prism (*P*) has been investigated by numerous authors (LeConte 1905; O'Brien 1931, 1969; Escoffier 1940; Jarett 1976; Hume and Herdendorf 1988). These authors have all concluded that the relationship can be expressed by a variation of the general formula

$$A = xP^n \tag{7.1}$$

where *A* is the cross-sectional area of the inlet, *P* is the tidal prism, and *x* and *n* are constants. If an inlet follows this relationship, then it is regarded as stable in terms of its equilibrium with the tidal prism.

Le Conte (1905), O'Brien (1931, 1969) and Nayak (1971) used data collected from inlets along the Pacific coast of North America to define a standard relationship of inlet stability. In addition, O'Brien (1969) distinguished between natural inlets and jettied inlets. For natural inlets, he used the constants $x = 6.56 \cdot 10^{-5}$ and $n = 1$, whereas for jettied inlets he determined $x = 9.02 \cdot 10^{-4}$ and $n = 0.85$. (All constants are in metric units, as discussed later.) He found a slightly larger cross-sectional area in the jettied inlets.

Jarrett (1976) published a summary of cross-sectional area/tidal prism relationships using data on inlets along the Pacific, Atlantic, and Gulf coasts of N. America. He was able to demonstrate differences in the relationship between Pacific and Atlantic coast inlets, with the constants in Eq. 7.1 for the Atlantic inlets given by $x = 1.58 \cdot 10^{-4}$ and $n = 0.95$. A summary of all the formulas can be found in Table 7.1.

Pacific and Atlantic coasts are subject to different tidal conditions as the former has a pronounced diurnal inequality, the latter does not. Jarrett (ibid), however, concluded that the wave climate and ratio of the inlet width to the hydraulic radius were significant in creating the differences in the relationship. The mean wave height in the Pacific is greater than in the Atlantic by over a metre; this influences the magnitude of the littoral drift of sand and hence the hydraulic radius (the ratio between the cross-sectional area and the wetted perimeter). The greater the

Table 7.1 Summary of constants used by various authors for the relationship between cross-sectional area *A* and tidal prism *P* (Eq. 7.1): $A = xP^n$

Author	Notes	n	x [feet]	x [m]
LeConte (1905)	Inner harbor	1.00	$4.3 \cdot 10^{-5}$	$1.41 \cdot 10^{-4}$
O'Brien (1931)	Pacific, jettied inlets	0.85	$46.9 \cdot 10^{-5}$	$9.02 \cdot 10^{-4}$
O'Brien (1969)	Pacific, natural inlets	1.00	$2.0 \cdot 10^{-5}$	$0.656 \cdot 10^{-4}$
Jarrett (1976)	All inlets	0.95	$5.74 \cdot 10^{-5}$	$1.58 \cdot 10^{-4}$
Jarrett (1976)	Atlantic, 2 jetties	0.95	$5.77 \cdot 10^{-5}$	$1.58 \cdot 10^{-4}$
Fontolan (2007)	Northern Adriatic	0.7439	n.a.	$68. \cdot 10^{-4}$

The values for x are given in both systems of reference, using either feet (originally) or metric units magnitude of littoral drift, the smaller the hydraulic radius becomes (for a given cross-sectional area).

Other authors have found that the O'Brien (1969) relationship is not always suitable and have thus formulated new relationships. Examples are Shigemura (1981) in Japan and Hume and Herdendorf (1993) in New Zealand.

The relationships mentioned above are all based upon the smallest cross-sectional area measured at low water. Also, the tidal prism is calculated for a spring tide, which is the greatest volume of water that enters the inlet during flood conditions. Also it may be that the relationship is valid anywhere along a tidal channel as long as the tidal prism is calculated for each specific cross section.

7.2.2 The Hydrodynamic Model

The hydrodynamic data used in the simulations have been derived from the numerical model Shyfem, developed at ISMAR-CNR of Venice. Shyfem is a finite element program that can be used to resolve the hydrodynamic equations in shallow water. The program uses finite elements for the spatial resolution of the equations and an effective semi-implicit time resolution algorithm, which makes this program especially suitable for the application to complicate geometry and bathymetry (Umgiesser et al. 2004).

The subdivision of the system into triangles, varying in form and size, enables the simulation of shallow water flats and tidal marshes that may be covered during high tide and then fall dry during ebb tide.

The equations used in the model are the well-known vertically integrated shallow water equations in their formulation with water levels and transports:

$$\frac{\partial U}{\partial t} - fV + gH\frac{\partial \varsigma}{\partial x} + RU + X = 0 \tag{7.2}$$

$$\frac{\partial V}{\partial t} + fU + gH\frac{\partial \varsigma}{\partial y} + RV + Y = 0 \tag{7.3}$$

$$\frac{\partial \varsigma}{\partial t} + \frac{\partial U}{\partial x} + \frac{\partial V}{\partial y} = 0 \tag{7.4}$$

where ζ is the water level, u, v the velocities in x and y directions, U, V the vertical integrated velocities (transports)

$$U = \int_{-h}^{\varsigma} udz \qquad V = \int_{-h}^{\varsigma} vdz \tag{7.5}$$

g the gravitational acceleration, $H = h + \zeta$ the total water depth, h the undisturbed water depth, t the time and R the friction coefficient. The terms X, Y contain all other terms that may be treated explicitly by the semi-implicit algorithm as the wind stress or the non-linear terms. (Umgiesser et al. 2004).

The grid of the Venice lagoon model is constructed by a subdivision of the area into 4,000 nodes and almost 8,000 triangular elements to describe the lagoon's geometry and bathymetry. The flexible size of the elements enables a higher spatial resolution for the three inlets and the small channels, which is impossible with a fixed grid. The model has been calibrated and validated thoroughly. Details can be found in Umgiesser et al. (2004).

7.2.3 Conversion of Equations

Over the course of this study we found large differences in the equations in literature governing the relationship between tidal prism and cross-sectional area of an inlet. It appears that these differences are due to erroneous application of conversion formulas. In order to convert Eq. 7.1 from units of feet to the metric system, we begin with (7.1)

$$A' = xP'^n \tag{7.1a}$$

where A' and P' are the cross-sectional area and tidal prism (volume) measured in square feet and cubic feet respectively. If $\alpha = 0.3048$ is the factor to convert feet to metres (1 foot $= 0.3048$ m), we may express A' and P' in meters by $A = \alpha^2 A'$ and $P = \alpha^3 P'$. We now solve for A' and P' and insert into (7.1a) to yield

$$\frac{A}{\alpha^2} = x\left(\frac{P}{\alpha^3}\right)^n. \tag{7.6}$$

Rearranging, we finally have

$$A = \frac{\alpha^2}{(\alpha^3)^n} xP^n. \tag{7.7}$$

Equation 7.7, expressed in units of metres, has the same structure and exponent as Eq. 7.1, but the coefficient x has to be multiplied by a factor $\alpha^2/(\alpha^3)^n$ in order to convert from units in feet to metres. In Table 7.1 the original factors together with the converted factors are presented for comparison.

7.2.4 Computation of the Tidal Prism

In order to apply Eq. 7.1 to the Venetian inlets, eleven minimum cross-sectional areas were chosen across Lido inlet, Treporti channel and Burano channel (Fig. 7.1) using a dataset of bathymetry from 1990. The positions of the sections were close to

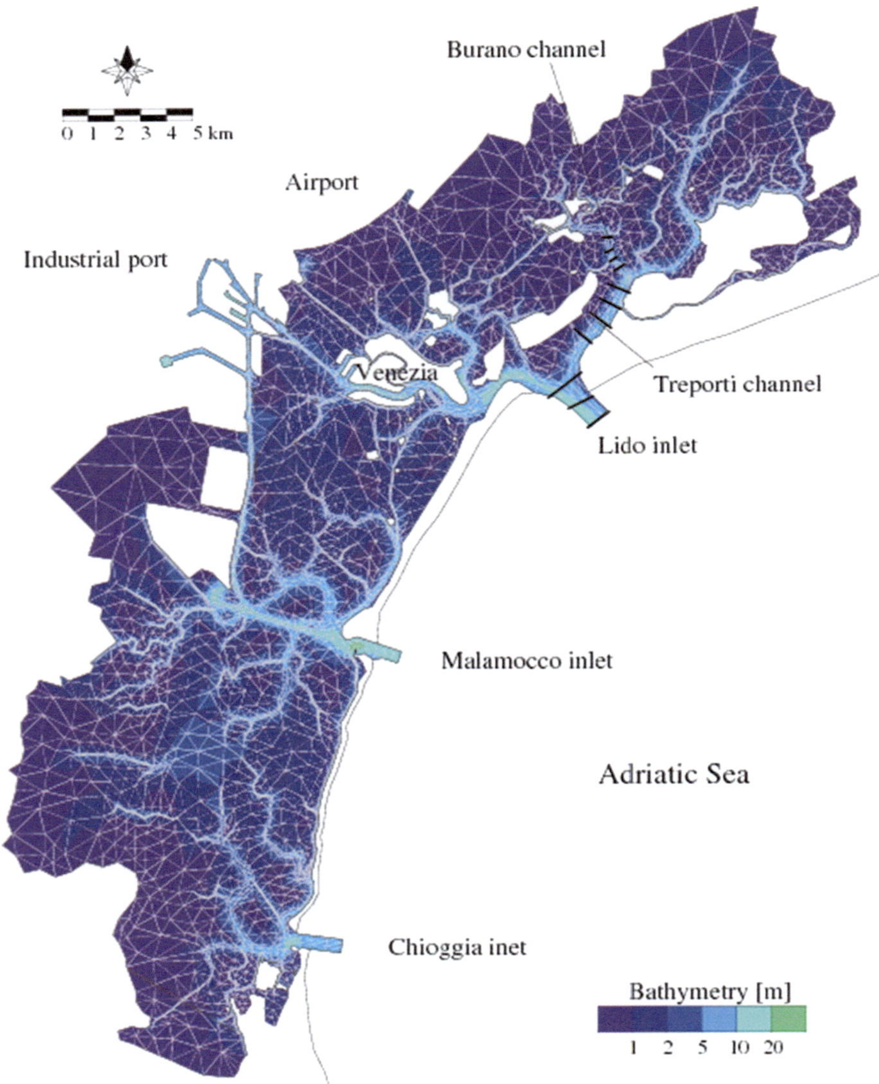

Fig. 7.1 Overview of the Venice lagoon and northern channel system. The sections where the cross-sectional area and the tidal prism has been computed are shown. The figure also shows the bathymetry of the lagoon in 1990 and the computational grid of the finite-element model

nodes of the numerical grid in order to facilitate the extraction of data and comparison of results. A typical spring tide in Venice Lagoon (±50 cm, using the bathymetry of 1990) has been simulated to calculate the tidal prism. Discharge, tidal elevation and current velocity data were estimated across each cross-section every time-step (300 s) of a tidal cycle at a point along each profile, so the tidal prism could be calculated using different methods. The first method is that of O'Brien (1931, 1969):

$$P = \frac{AV_{\max}T}{\pi} \tag{7.8}$$

where $V_{\max}$ is the maximum velocity and T is the tidal period. A second method has been tested which was proposed by the U.S Army Corps. of Engineers (Shore Protection Manual 1984):

$$P = \frac{Q_{\max}T}{\pi} \tag{7.9}$$

where $Q_{\max}$ is the maximum discharge during the flood tide.

As simulated discharge data were produced at every time step of the tidal cycle, instead of using a sinusoidal approximation to the discharge (which has been applied in Eq. 7.9) the discharge can be integrated directly summing the single values of discharge $Q(t)$ entering the profile during a flood tide and multiplying with the time step $\Delta t = 300$ s:

$$P = \sum Q(t)\Delta t \tag{7.10}$$

All three formulas have been used for the computation of the tidal prism and have been compared against each other. The results of the inter-comparison are shown in Fig. 7.2.

To calculate the cross-sectional area, the bathymetry of the lagoon from 1990 was re-gridded. Generic Mapping Tools (GMT, Wessel and Smith 1991) was then used to extract the low water depth at equal distances along each profile. The depth was assumed to be uniform for each of the parts (dividing the cross-section into rectangles of equal width) so that a trapezoidal calculation could be performed.

Once both the tidal prism and cross-sectional areas have been calculated for the profiles, a plot of the results was prepared for comparison with the regression line of the O'Brien's equation for inlets with two jetties (line 2, Table 7.1). This process was repeated using the bathymetry from 1930, 1970 and 2000. Also, other cross-sectional area/tidal prism relationships were plotted as a comparison to O'Brien's relationship, for example, Jarrett's Atlantic inlet relationship (line 5, Table 7.1).

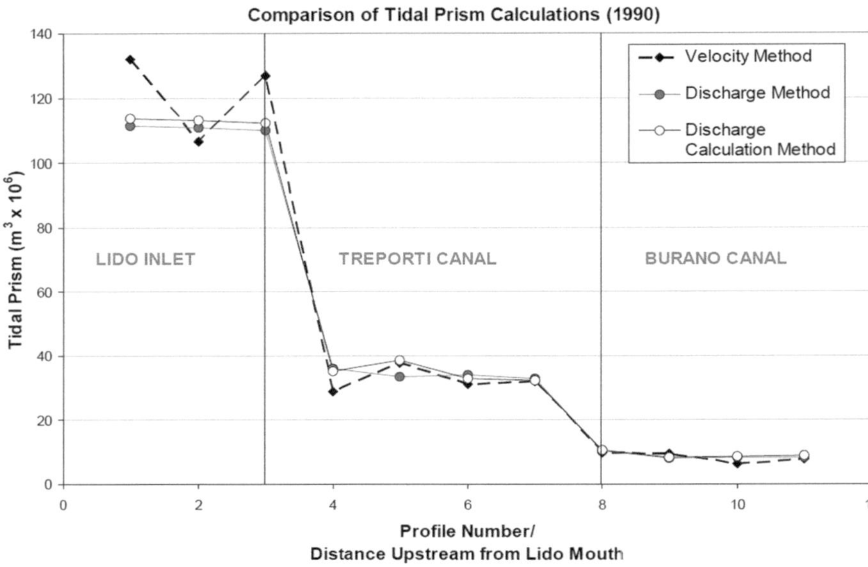

Fig. 7.2 A comparison of the different methods of computing the tidal prism along the northern Venice lagoon channel system. The method using discharges (either maximum or directly computed) are similar, whereas the velocity method appears more error prone

7.3 Results

7.3.1 Comparison of Tidal Prism Computation

The various formulas for computing the tidal prism have been compared. As can be seen in Fig. 7.2, the discharge equation (Eq. 7.9) compared favorably with the numerical discharge calculation of the tidal prism (Eq. 7.10). The results from the velocity Eq. 7.8 differ by over 10 % when compared to the direct discharge calculation in Lido inlet despite being similar to the results for the Treporti and Burano channel profiles. Also, it seems unlikely that the tidal prism would change by as much as $2 \cdot 10^7$ m^3 from where Lido inlet separates into Treporti channel and Lido channel. For this reason, the discharge method (Eq. 7.9) was used to calculate tidal prism as it seemed to provide a better fit than the velocity method and its application was simpler to apply than the equivalent numerical discharge calculation.

7.3.2 *The Northern Channel System*

The ratios of the tidal prism and cross-sectional area in 1990 (Fig. 7.3) reveal that the cross-sections of Lido were, on average, larger than predicted by the O'Brien and Jarrett formulae. This would suggest that the Lido inlet should infill in order to reach equilibrium with the tidal prism. However, Treporti and Burano channels are in equilibrium with the tidal prism relationship of both O'Brien or Jarrett.

O'Brien's work on the tidal prism/cross-sectional area relationship was predominantly based on stabilized tidal inlets on the Pacific coast (O'Brien 1931, 1969). However, the study was expanded by Jarrett (1976) in order to determine whether this relationship was valid for inlets along the Atlantic and Gulf coasts. He concluded that inlets on the Atlantic coast followed a different relationship than the inlets on the Pacific coast; that they had a larger cross-sectional area to a given tidal prism (see Table 7.1 for the formulas)

A comparison of the Venice lagoon data to the relationships of O'Brien and Jarrett is shown in Fig. 7.3. It is clear that the data from Venice lagoon fits the relationship for the Atlantic coast of Jarrett (1976) and O'Briens relationship for

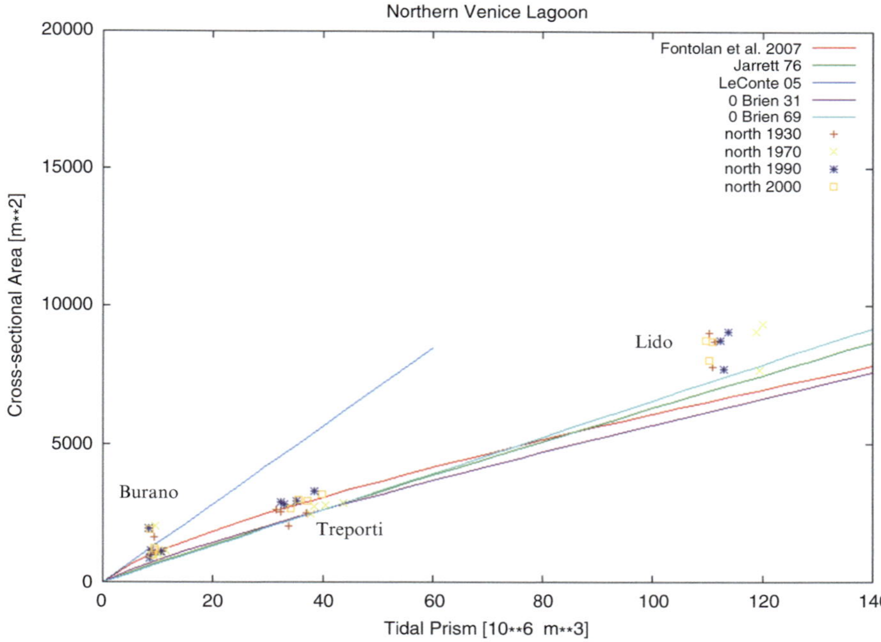

Fig. 7.3 The tidal prism relationship for the channels in northern Venice lagoon. The model data are compared with the O'Brien and Jarrett relationships. Also the relationships of LeConte (1905) and a recent fit of North Adriatic data by Fontolan et al. (2007) have been plotted. The data are from the Lido inlet (highest values), Treporti channel (medium values) and Burano channel (smallest values)

natural inlets (1969) slightly better than the relationship of O'Brien (1931) with jetties. Burano channel has a relatively large cross-sectional area for the tidal prism. However, it does fit slightly better a relationship for inner harbour entrances formulated by Le Conte (1905).

The data for other years where bathymetry was available has been plotted in Fig. 7.3. In the 70 years from 1930 to 2000 the inlet relationship appeared stable, with little variation. Lido inlet remained relatively stable between 1990 and 2000 despite the apparent need to reduce its cross-sectional area (to be stable according to the O'Brien relationship). This is supported by results in Fig. 7.4, where both the average tidal prism and the cross-sectional area are plotted. Data have been combined to one value for each of the channel systems of Lido, Treporti and Burano. The smallest channel (Burano) is the most stable, whereas Lido first shows a increasing, then a decreasing trend. Finally, Treporti shows an increasing cross-sectional area and tidal prism, which varies through the years, though the tendency of Treporti channel is erosional over the years.

7.3.3 *Evolution of the Three Inlets*

The same computations as those described above have been applied to the other two inlets of the Venice lagoon. Results of the comparison are shown in Fig. 7.5. It can be seen that the results for Malamocco and Lido are very different. Whereas Lido (with respect to O'Brien and Jarrett relationships) seems too large, the cross sectional area of Malamocco seems too small for its tidal prism. Malamocco shows an outlier during 1930. After that it seems that Malamocco become stable over the last 30 years.

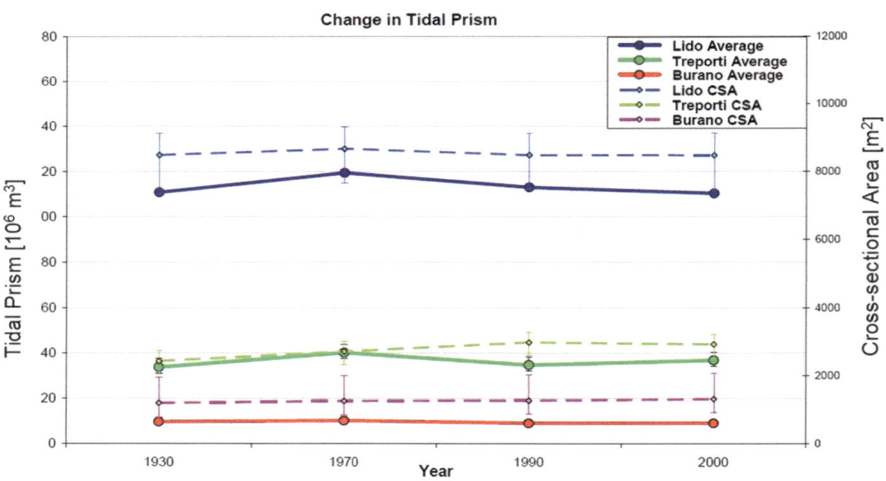

Fig. 7.4 Changes in tidal prism and cross-sectional area (CSA) over the last 70 years for channels in northern Venice lagoon

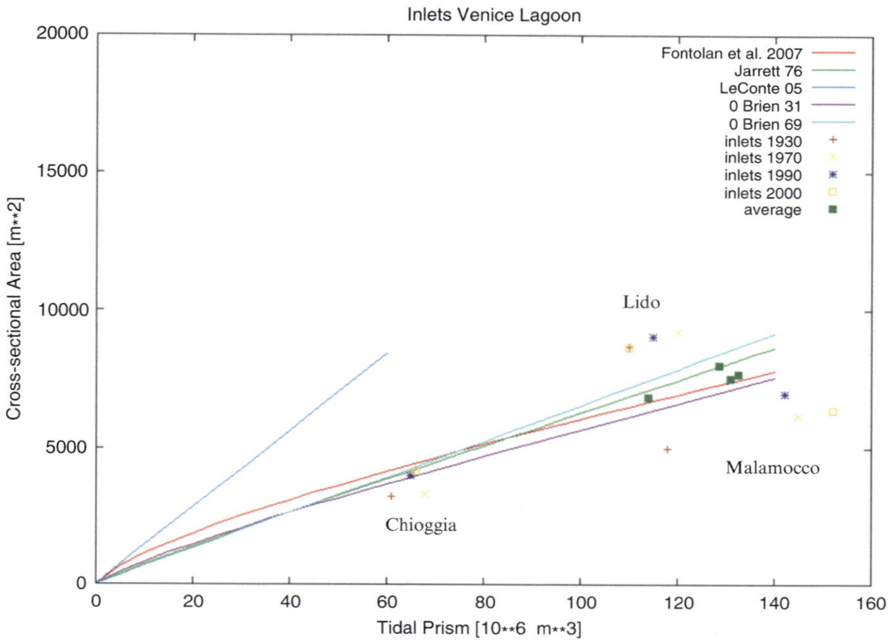

Fig. 7.5 The tidal prism relationship for the inlets of Venice lagoon. The data for Lido can be seen lying above the O'Brien and Jarrett curves, and Malamocco data below the curves. Chioggia data show tidal prism values only about half of the other two inlets ($60–70 \cdot 10^6$ m^3). Finally, average values ("average") between Lido and Malamocco have been computed. They fall in the middle of the tidal prism relationships

Chioggia inlet appears more stable than Malamocco and is in line with the O'Brien relationship. The figure also confirms that the northern and central inlets (Lido and Malamocco) accommodate about twice the discharge of the southern inlet (Chioggia).

7.4 Discussion and Conclusions

7.4.1 Northern Channel System

The channels of the northern Venice Lagoon fit the O'Brien relationship. Only the Lido inlet shows deviations from the tidal prism relationship. If we were to assume that the O'Brien relationship is valid, then the Lido inlet should be infilling. However, the area of each cross-section between 1930 and 2000 has increased in size (i.e. erosion has occurred) by a total average of 9 % between 1930 and 2000.

Lido inlet was depositional between 1970 and 2000, which reduced the average cross-sectional area by 2 %. However, the average cross-sectional area should have decreased by an average of 7 % to become stable according to O'Brien's relationship. As the cross-sectional areas of Lido inlet have also altered by around 7 % between 1930 and 2000, it would appear that the inlet is presently relatively stable. This is confirmed by the relative good correspondence to the relationship. Profile 1, at the mouth of Lido inlet, has remained close to the relationship line at all times, altering its cross-sectional area to the changing tidal prism. Interestingly, the cross-sectional area and tidal prism at this point are now the same as they were in 1930, despite fluctuations in 1970 and 1990. Profile 2 passes through both the ebb scour channel (erosional) and ebb spit (depositional), and is the least stable section of Lido inlet when compared to the Atlantic relationship. It appears too small for the tidal prism and hence should erode as indeed it has, by 3 % between 1930 and 2000.

Lido inlet, before the construction of its jetties, consisted of two inlets that gave access to the northern and central lagoon. After the construction of the jetties, these two inlets were confined to a single inlet. However, inside the lagoon, the main channel forks both north- and southward into the old tidal channels. As a result, Lido inlet is the widest inlet of the Venice lagoon (1,000 m), whereas the other two inlets are only 500 m wide.

Treporti channel was erosional between 1930 and 2000, although there was a period of slight accretion between 1990 and 2000 (see Fig. 7.4). However, Treporti channel fits the tidal prism relationship well and therefore appears relatively stable. Since Treporti channel has deepened 2–3 cm/year over the last 70 years, as also confirmed by Umgiesser et al. (2006), it is unstable in the long-term.

Burano channel also fits O'Brien's Atlantic relationship. However from Fig. 7.4 it seems that a slightly better fit is the relationship of Le Conte (1905) or even Fontolan et al. (2007). This is not unexpected as Burano channel is sheltered from the waves and a relationship that takes into account the wave climate of the Pacific or the Atlantic would be inappropriate to the Venetian situation. Le Conte (1905) created a formula for inner harbour entrances, which accounts for the differences of a channel further away from the sea. The data from Burano appears to fit this relationship. Profile 9 extends across a triple junction scour hole, and therefore has a much larger cross-section as a result. It can be seen as an outlier in all years considered in Fig. 7.4. If we discount this outlier, the rest of the Burano data falls between the Atlantic relationship and the Le Conte inner harbour relationship. Between 1930 and 1970, when Burano channel was depositional and flood dominant (Amos et al. 2005, table 1), it appeared to move towards the Atlantic relationship line by depositing sediment whilst the tidal prism increased. The channel began to move away from the Atlantic relationship and towards that of Le Conte. This trend continued despite an increase in the tidal prism between 1990 and 2000. Profile 11 became stable according to the Le Conte relationship in 1990, and responded to the change in tidal prism by the removal of a proportionate amount of sediment to remain that way. Therefore, it seems likely that, for the last 30 years, Burano channel has been responsive to the Le Conte inner harbour relationship and was slightly erosional in order to maintain stability.

Apart from the Burano channel, which is well inside the lagoon, the Lido and Treporti channels show relative large changes before and after 1970. During the end of the 1960s a new artificial channel was build inside the lagoon, starting from the central Malamocco inlet. It is generally referred to as the *Petroli* channel, as it is the channel that is used by the big commercial ships and oil tankers to reach the industrial harbor at the main land inside the lagoon. This channel is the deepest in the lagoon with depths up to 15 m.

The construction of the Petroli channel marked a change in hydrodynamics in the Venice lagoon (Molinaroli et al. 2009). It also deviated part of the water transiting originally through Lido to Malamocco inlet. This trend in the tidal prism is still ongoing, as can be seen in Fig. 7.4. For a short time the Treporti channel also responded to this shift. However, after 1990 Treporti channel seems to have continued its former trend of slight erosion and increasing tidal prism.

7.4.2 Evolution of the Three Inlets

Figure 7.5 shows the tidal prism/cross-sectional area of the three inlets in Venice Lagoon. Chioggia inlet appears to fit the O'Brien relationship, and therefore should be more wave influenced than Lido inlet. Therefore, it should be comparable to the Pacific coast relationship of O'Brien (1969) with high littoral drift (partly from the rivers Adige and Brenta) reducing the relative cross-sectional area. Malamocco inlet, however, appears to be similar to the offset of Lido inlet from the O'Brien relationship.

Malamocco shows one outlier in 1930, where the tidal prism of the inlet was much smaller. The Petroli channel has profoundly changed the hydrodynamics of this inlet. This can be seen by the tidal prism of Malamocco, which has increased from $118 \cdot 10^6\ m^3$ in 1930 to over $145 \cdot 10^6\ m^3$ in 1970. In the same period, the tidal prism of Lido increased slightly from $111 \cdot 10^6\ m^3$ in 1930 to over $120 \cdot 10^6\ m^3$ in 1970. This shows that the two inlets are not compensating their flow (Malamocco increases – Lido decreases) but the tidal propagation inside the lagoon has changed such that the whole tidal prism of the lagoon has increased. All three inlets show this increase, including Chioggia; the total tidal prism has grown from $289 \cdot 10^6\ m^3$ in 1930 to over $333 \cdot 10^6\ m^3$ in 1970. This corresponds to a 15 % increase in volume.

It is interesting to note that Malamocco has a tidal prism consistently too big for its cross-sectional area, whereas Lido's tidal prism is too small. All data points from Malamocco lie below the curve describing the relationships, and the data points of Lido lie above the curves. Malamocco inlet is constrained in its width by the jetties, and is already the deepest inlet of the lagoon. At about 13–14 m the bottom of the inlet is very compact and there is little sand to be transported. This might reduce the potential for scour.

However, if we take averages of the tidal prism and cross-sectional area between Lido and Malamocco, the data fall onto the tidal prism relationships of O'Brien or Jarrett (points labeled "aver" in Fig. 7.5). This could be an indication that, in

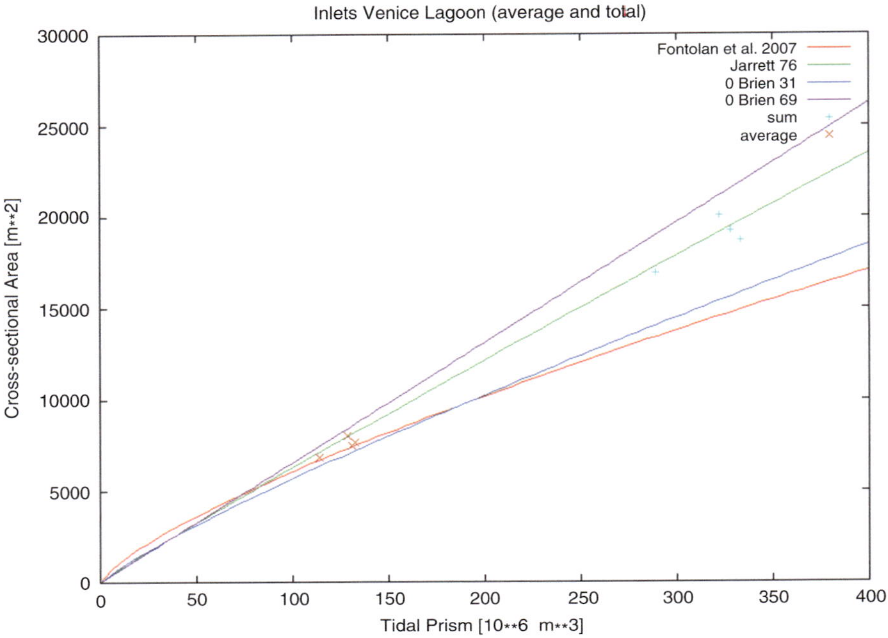

Fig. 7.6 The tidal prism relationship for the sum of the inlets of Venice lagoon. The total tidal prism and cross-sectional area have been computed for the lagoon as a whole ("sum"), as well as the average value for Lido and Malamocco ("average"). The data fit the Jarrett relationship, and to a certain degree the O'Brien relationship (1931)

situations of multiple inlets that serve the same basin, the relationships of O'Brien may not be valid in any of the inlets, but the average of all should be in equilibrium.

To further investigate this point the tidal prism of all three inlets has been summed and compared to the total cross-sectional area of all inlets. In this case the tidal prism is the total volume that is exchanged during one tidal cycle between the lagoon and the Adriatic Sea. Results are shown in Fig. 7.6. The data points of all years fall very close to the Jarrett curve (and also to the relationship of O'Brien 1931).

In conclusion, the inlets of the Venice lagoon, and also its northern channel system, seem to have been very stable over the last 70 years. Judging only from the fit of Lido and Malamocco with the tidal prism relationship, this might seem a little surprising. Interpreting these data alone it seems that Malamocco should still erode and Lido should be depositional. However, in the last 40 years this tendency has not been observed. It may be that lagoons with multiple inlets have a compensating mechanism. It is surprising that the lagoon as a whole does fit both the O'Brien and Jarrett relationship very well, and this fact hints at the importance of the compensating mechanism.

Acknowledgements This work has been carried out with the partial support of the Corila project 3.2 (Idrodinamica e morfologia della laguna di Venezia). The authors also want to thank the VECTOR project for partial funding.

References

Amos CL, Umgiesser G, Helsby RA, Friend PL (2004) Final report – CORILA 3.2 – Idrodinamica e morfologia della laguna di Venezia (VELMA). In: Scientific Research and Safeguarding of Venice, vol II, Corila, Venice, pp 189–202

Amos CL, Helsby R, Umgiesser G, Mazzoldi A, Tosi L (2005) Sand transport in northern Venice lagoon. CORILA 3.2 – Idrodinamica e morfologia della laguna di Venezia (VELMA). In Scientific Research and Safeguarding of Venice, vol III, Corila, Venice, pp 369–383

Escoffier FF (1940) The stability of tidal inlets. Shore Beach 8(4):114–115

Fontolan G, Pillon S, Delli Quadri F, Bezzi A (2007) Sediment storage at tidal inlets in northern Adriatic lagoons: Ebb-tidal delta morphodynamics, conservation and sand use strategies. Estuar Coast Shelf Sci 75:261–277

Helsby R, Amos CL, Umgiesser G (2006) Morphological evolution and sand pathways in northern Venice Lagoon, Italy. In: Campostrini P (ed) Scientific research and safeguarding of Venice, Proceedings of Corila Research programme 2004–2006, vol IV. Corila, Venezia, pp 388–402

Helsby R, Amos CL, Umgiesser G (2008) Tidal prism variation and associated channel stability in N. Venice lagoon. In: Campostrini P (ed) Scientific research and safeguarding of Venice, Proceedings of Corila Research programme 2004–2006, vol VI. Corila, Venezia, pp 453–466

Hume TM, Herdendorf CE (1988) A geomorphic classification of estuaries and its application to coastal resource management. J Ocean Shoreline Manag 11:249–274

Hume TM, Herdendorf CE (1993) On the use of empirical stability relationships for characterising estuaries. J Coast Res 9(2):413–422

Jarett JT (1976) Tidal prism-inlet area relationship. CERC-WES General Investigation of Tidal Inlets, Department of the Army, U.S Corps of Engineering, report 3, pp 1–32

LeConte LJ (1905) Notes on the improvement of river and harbour outlets in the United States. Transactions, American Society of Civil Engineers, LV(Dec), pp 306–308

Molinaroli E, Guerzoni S, Sarretta A, Masiol M, Pistolato M (2009) Thirty-year changes (1970 to 2000) in bathymetry and sediment texture recorded in the Lagoon of Venice sub-basins, Italy. Mar Geol 258:115–125

Nayak IV (1971) Tidal Prism-Area Relationship in a Model Inlet, University of California, Hydraulic Engineering Laboratory, Report HEL-24-1, Berkeley, CA, 72 pp

O'Brien MP (1931) Estuary tidal prism related to entrance areas. Civil Eng 1(8):738–739

O'Brien MP (1969) Equilibrium flow areas of inlets on sandy coasts. J Waterway Harbour Div ASCE 95(WW1):43–52

Renger E, Partenscky HW (1974) Stability criteria for tidal basins. In: 14th international coastal engineering conference, Copenhagen, Denmark, ASCE, pp 1605–1618

Shigemura T (1981) Tidal prism-throat width relationships of the bays of Japan. Shore Beach 49 (3):34–39

Shore Protection Manual (1984) 4th ed, vol 2, U.S. Army Engineer Waterways Experiment Station, U.S. Government Printing Office, Washington, DC

Townend I (2005) An examination of empirical stability relationships for UK estuaries. J Coast Res 21(5):1042–1053

Umgiesser G, Melaku Canu D, Cucco A, Solidoro C (2004) A finite element model for the Venice Lagoon. Development, set up, calibration and validation. J Mar Syst 51:123–145

Umgiesser G, De Pascalis F, Ferrarin C, Amos CL (2006) A model of sand transport in Treporti channel: northern Venice lagoon. Ocean Dyn 56:339–351

Wessel P, Smith WHF (1991) Free software helps map and display data. EOS Trans AGU 72:441

Chapter 8
Tidal Inlet Dynamics and Relocation in Response to Artificial Breaching

Bendahhou Zourarah, César Andrade, Mohamed Maanan, Maria da Conceição Freitas, Asmae Mhamdi Alaoui, Rui Taborda, Khalid Mehdi, and Marc Robin

Abstract This chapter addresses the relations between inlet dynamics and nearshore wave regime at a coastal lagoon in the Atlantic coast of Morocco. The study of wave climate indicates a southward trend for the net annual longshore sediment transport, which modifies previously reported conclusions fundamented upon limited series of observations on waves and interpretation of the inlet geomorphology. The snapshot images used here to characterize the morphodynamic behavior of the inlet indicate that its mobility is driven essentially by the northward component of the wave-borne longshore energy flux and transport, thus bearing no direct relation with the net annual residue of longshore energy flux and sediment transport; we interpret this as a result of contrasting effectiveness in early wave energy dissipation induced by shoal fields populating the nearshore north and south of the inlet. Moulay Bousselham inlet illustrates a case where geomorphological interpretation of coastal features may be insufficient to support inferences on coastal hydrodynamics.

B. Zourarah (✉) • A. Mhamdi Alaoui • K. Mehdi
Environment – Integrated Coastal Zone Management, Department of Geology, Faculty of Sciences, UFR: ST/18/05, El Jadida, Morocco

Faculté des Sciences, Laboratoire des Geosciences Marines et Sciences du Sol (Unité associée CNRST-URAC 45), El Jadida, Morocco
e-mail: zourarah@gmail.com

C. Andrade • M.C. Freitas
Centro e Departamento de Geologia, Faculdade de Ciências, Universidade de Lisboa, Lisboa, Portugal

M. Maanan • M. Robin
Institut de Géographie et d'Aménagement Régional de l'Université de Nantes, Géolittomer, LETG UMR 6554-CNRS, Nantes Cedex 3, France

R. Taborda
LATTEX/IDL, Departamento de Geologia, Faculdade de Ciências, Universidade de Lisboa, Lisboa, Portugal

M. Maanan, M. Robin (eds.), *Sediment Fluxes in Coastal Areas*, Coastal Research Library 10, DOI 10.1007/978-94-017-9260-8_8

8.1 Introduction

Coastal lagoons are shallow water bodies usually found on low lying coasts, separated from the ocean by a barrier, connected at least intermittently to the ocean by one or more restricted tidal inlets and receiving small contributions of freshwater. They were formed as a result of rising sea level mostly during the Holocene and sheltered by coastal barriers, which usually developed 6,000–5,000 years ago by marine processes related to the deceleration of sea level rise.

They are sensitive areas and often highly productive systems but at the same time, may be extremely stressed by anthropogenic inputs and human activities, which disturb their natural functioning, leading to use conflicts that are difficult to resolve. The management of these areas in view of spatial planning, optimizing habitat conservation, environmental protection, resource exploitation and economic/recreational uses, is urgently needed.

Barriers are dynamic systems and this is closely related to the tidal inlets, which may be stable, stabilized or drifting, ephemeral (whenever temporarily closed off by sediment deposition as a result of wave action) or permanent features. Several authors have focused their attention on the study of these relations, namely on tidal inlet evolution and behavior (e.g. O'Brien 1969; Jarrett 1976; Boon and Byrne 1981; Fitzgerald and Nummedal 1983; Aubrey and Speer 1984; FitzGerald 1984; FitzGerald et al. 1984; FitzGerald 1988; Oertel 1988; Davis et al. 1989; Fitzgerald 1996; Vila-Concejo et al. 2002; Andrade et al. 2004; Castelle et al. 2007). Besides their natural and environmental importance in ensuring mass exchanges between the lagoon and the ocean, tidal inlets provide access to harbors or coastal communities. Natural and anthropogenic factors such as sea level rise, storm events, dune occupation or coastal engineering works, often produce changes in tidal inlet conditions. Background knowledge of tidal inlet behavior and evolution is therefore needed to understand and predict consequences of engineering actions or extreme natural events.

This study focuses on the seasonal to mesoscale (70 year) morphodynamics of Moulay Bousselham inlet in order to characterize and understand its functioning and relations with hydrodynamic forcing and contribute to provide scientific background to the design of management solutions aiming the best possible compromise between conservation of natural values and use.

8.2 Study Area

Moulay Bousselham (MYB) is the northernmost (34°47′N–6°13′W and 34°52′N–6°14′W) and widest lagoon of the Atlantic coast of Morocco (Fig. 8.1) located about 120 km north of Rabat. The lagoonal depression is part of the subsiding Rharb basin that experienced silting up since the Miocene. It is limited southwards by the Mio-Pliocene anticline structure of Lalla Zohra, which trends east–west and

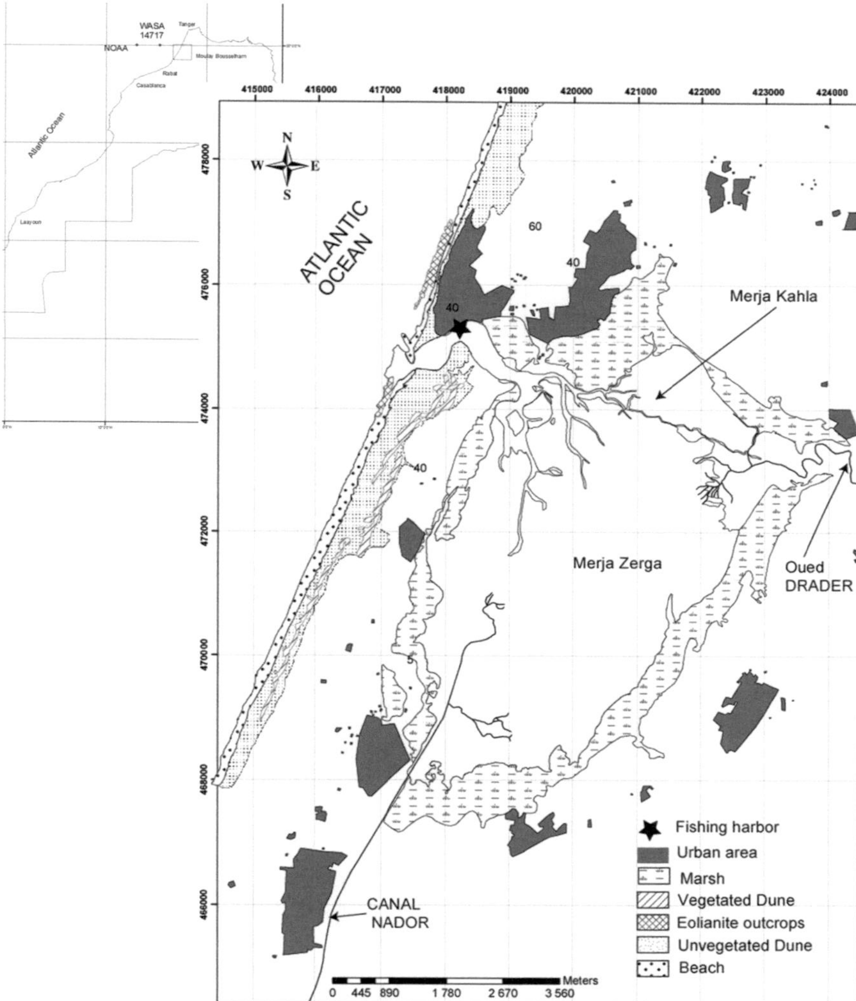

Fig. 8.1 Location of Moulay Bousselham lagoon in the Atlantic coast of Morocco and location of NOAA and WASA grid points

culminates at 100 m high (Le Coz 1964; Cirac 1985; Benmohammadi et al. 2007), eastwards by the Lalla Mimouna depression, north and northeastwards by the Mio-Pliocene higher Khlot terranes. The western boundary consists of a NE-SW elongated ridge of Quaternary consolidated dunes (eolianites), in which four growth episodes have been recognized (Le Coz 1964) and generally control the present-day coastline, which trends N23°E. Seaward, the bathymetric lines develop roughly parallel to the coastline, suggesting a simple morphology for the inner shelf.

The lagoon is 9 km long, 5 km wide and extends across 30 km^2. It is separated from the ocean by a sandy barrier, which shows a simple cross shore morphology with no dunes and consisting of a beach face and berms. The barrier is artificially breached since at least the early twentieth century to allow navigation and renewal of the lagoonal water, preventing eutrophication. Both the barrier and the inlet are quite dynamic features and the inlet commonly remains active for several years before silting up naturally. The inlet may drift within a 730 m-wide strip contained between Pleistocene eolianite outcrops that emerge well above sea level in this location. Seaward, these rocks form a discontinuous line of shoals located at a distance of 50–200 m from the high water line (SOGREAH 1961). North of Moulay Bousselham this feature is wide and completely emerges in low tide and confines with the sandy foreshore; here, its elevation is enough to provide an efficient sheltering regarding the incoming waves. To the south, the rocky alignment is narrow and despite emerging in low tide, a flooded runnel persists, separating the shoal from the adjacent beach; here, its summit elevation is lower and its sheltering efficiency is diminished. In between, the rocky shoals are absent and this may be related with an east–west fracture controlling the linear shape and emplacement of the Drader river in its downstream section, which aligns with the inlet area.

According to our data, an ebb delta develops only exceptionally, in contrast with the flood tidal delta, which is persistent and made of (usually) three major imbricate sand lobes. A persistent northern channel meanders between these lobes and a second (southern) channel may develop and in times become dominant.

The Drader river divides the lagoon in two sub-basins (Fig. 8.1): Merja Kahla, to the north, with 3 km^2 and average depth of 0.3–0.5 m, and Merja Zerga, to the south, the main lagoonal body with 27 km^2 and 1–1.5 m deep. Three channel systems developed in Merja Zerga: (1) one main linear channel with 3.8 km connecting the inlet with the linear terminal section of the Drader river; (2) a smaller set of bifurcated channels that dissect the tidal flats close to the barrier and convey the discharge of the (dredged) Nador channel, and (3) a small, poorly bifurcated and barely incised system located further east, bearing no apparent connection with neither the Drader nor the Nador. The maximum incision of the channels, about 4–5 m, is attained some distance away from the inlet.

The annual average rainfall is about 525 mm according to Benbekhta (1994) and 599 mm according to Carruesco (1989), estimated for the 1983–1992 and 1933–1963 periods, respectively; the maximum values are registered in December and virtually no rain falls during the dry season (May to September).

Moulay Bousselham lagoon is an important area for wildlife, including a rich variety of birds (that use the lowland as a winter stopover from Europe to the south – Benhoussa 2000), fishes and plants, justifying the status of Natural Park. Despite being a biological reserve with an international interest for avifauna since 1978 and a Ramsar site, the abundance and diversity of flora and fauna are threatened by human activities (El Agbani et al. 1998). In fact, inhabitants of Moulay Bousselham and surroundings are about 154,000. Their main activities are agriculture and cattle raising, complemented by traditional catch of both fish and mollusks (Benhoussa 2000) and more recently, summer tourism, a growing source of income. Agro-chemicals are largely used in the majority of the cultivated area around the lagoon and no waste water treatment is implemented (Mhamdi et al. 2010; Zourarah et al. 2007, 2008). Two major hydraulic works for irrigation purposes impacted the lagoonal space: the construction of the Nador channel (1953) and the damming of the Drader River in 1979. The biological and ecological state of the lagoon is strongly dependent on the efficiency of water exchanges with the ocean and in this respect the closure of the inlet has negative effects previously mentioned by several authors (e.g. Carruesco 1989; Ameur et al. 2003); moreover, the absence of the tidal channel prevents the use of the lagoon as a harbor for the local fishing community.

Tides along the North Atlantic coast of Morocco are semidiurnal and range between 3.34 (2.45) and 0.35 (1.28) m elevation in spring (neap) conditions offshore Larache, the highest (lowest) high (low) water reaching 3.79 (0.10) m above local chart datum (ZH – Hydrograpic Zero, which stands 1.92 m below local mean sea level – msl) (Charouff 1989, quoting results from field surveys in 1970). Accordingly, the coast is high-mesotidal in the modified classification of Hayes (1979) – mean annual tidal range 2.08 m. The currents offshore are moderately persistent and weak throughout the year (ASD 2006). The tide experiences distortion when propagating landwards of the Moulay Bousselham inlet; according to Carruesco (1989) the lagoonal tide is delayed in phase with respect to the ocean and the time lag is higher in spring conditions (2 h in low tide and few minutes in high tide); in neap water the lag between lagoonal and ocean tide is about 1 h. Measurements by the same author indicate that the lagoonal tide is also significantly reduced in amplitude and asymmetrical in duration of flow, indicating flood dominance. The Moulay Bousselham spring tidal prism was estimated in some 32×10^6 m^3 in the summer, reducing to about 20×10^6 m^3 in winter (Carruesco 1989) due to fresh water retention in the lagoonal space.

According to Jaaidi (1993), waves affecting the Morocco Atlantic coast are mostly far-generated in the North Atlantic. They essentially propagate from west and northwest and travel for 2–4 days before reaching the shore. Reported periods range between 7 and 18 s and heights may reach 7–9 m. No systematic instrumental records of wave characteristics exist along the coast (or offshore) the North Atlantic Morocco and the scarce information provided in the literature is discontinuous. The only instrumental data the authors are aware of correspond to 4 months-long buoy observations taken during winter 1969/70 in the Larache area (LHCF 1972). Also, Charouf (1989) compiled wave information from the British Ocean Wave Statistics Atlas (OWSA) and U.S. Oceanographic Atlas of the North Atlantic Ocean (OANAO) (containing several years of visual ship-borne observations) but remarked that both atlases yield different wave statistics (Table 8.1). The information quoted above is

Table 8.1 Directional distribution of waves according to data sources mentioned in text

	OWSA[a]		OANAO[a]	
Sector	260–280° (W)	290–310° (WNW)	247.5–292.5° (W)	202.5–247.5° (SW)
%	9.6	10.5	26.9	6.9

[a]*OANAO* Oceanographic Atlas of the North Atlantic Ocean, *OWSA* Ocean Wave Statistics Atlas

insufficient to allow processing of wave data with the accuracy needed for sediment transport calculations; accordingly, wave data used and processed in this study consist of hindcasts of sea surface.

8.3 Methods

The nearshore wave climate of Moulay Bousselham was reconstructed using a simple shoaling-refraction procedure based upon Airy wave theory, considering bathymetric lines parallel to the shore and excluding occurrences making an angle >90° with the normal to the shoreline. The parameters of waves at breaking were calculated after shoaling and refraction of each deep-water condition in WASA and NOAA databases (see below), using successive iterations for the depth variable until a breaking criterion (Hb/Db = 0.78) was met.

Analysis of morphological changes of the Moulay Bousselham inlet area was carried out using vertical aerial photographs taken in 1949, 1963, 1972, 1988, 2000 and 2003, SPOT images of 1987, 1994, 1997 and 2005, complemented by topographic maps (Moulay Bousselham at 1/50,000 published in 1974) and a cartographic sketch (dated 1937) (Table 8.2).

All documents were scanned at 200–400 DPI resolution and calibrated according to the resolution (DPI) and the number of pixels on the horizontal and the vertical axes.

Table 8.2 Images referred in text

Type	Date	Source	Scale
Cartographic sketch	1937	Gruvel (1937)	1: 10,000
Aerial photographs	1949	Ministères d'Energie et des Mines (Meknes)	1: 50,000
	1963	Direction de la Conservation Foncière et des Travaux Topographiques, Ministère de l'Agriculture et de la Réforme Agraire, Maroc	1: 30,000
	1972		
Topographic map	1974		1:50,000
SPOT Satellite	1987 ISI SPOT	Faculté des Sciences El Jadida (PAI101/MA/04)	
Aerial photographs	1988	Direction de la Conservation Foncière et des Travaux Topographiques, Ministère de l'Agriculture et de la Réforme Agraire, Maroc	1: 20,000
SPOT Satellite	1994		
	1997		
Aerial photographs	2000		1: 5,000
	2003		1: 10,000
SPOT Satellite	2005 ISI SPOT	Faculté des Sciences El Jadida (PAI101/MA/04)	

Shoreline data was extracted from scanned aerial photographs and digitized from the original (topographic 1:50,000) map using the ArcGIS software. The geometric correction of the images has been performed using the Erdas software, the topographic 1/50,000 map and retaining the local geodesic system (Merchich reference ellipsoid).

The maximum error of corrected images was of 20 m (horizontal) and 1 m (vertical) for documents prior to 1963, and 2 m and 0.1 m, respectively, after 1972. The reliability of measurements was checked using stable features (rocky outcrops) common to all images.

8.4 Results and Discussion

8.4.1 Deep Water Waves

Data available to study the deep-water wave climate offshore Morocco consist of two series (significant wave height – Hs, peak period – Tp and mean direction), generated by numerical models and departing from wind fields. One set (1997–2007) was made available by NOAA (Program WAVEWATCH-III, cf. Tolman 1997) and refers to a grid point located at 08° 45′W 35° 00′ N (Fig. 8.1). A second data set referring to a grid point WASA 14717 at 7° 30′W 35° 00′N (Fig. 8.1) and to 1970–1994 was supplied by Puertos de Estado (Spain). Comparison of scalar and directional statistics of the wave climate yielded by both models suggest that results are not much different (Table 8.3), major discrepancies being found in N and NW frequencies.

Comparisons of modeled and buoy wave height data in Las Palmas and Gulf of Cadiz yields correlation of 0.7 and indicates that the WASA model overestimates wave height by a factor of about 1.7 in those regions of the Atlantic (http://www.puertos.es).

An additional limitation in both data sets results from the large dimensions of the grid cells (1.25° long. 1° lat.-NOAA; 1.5° long. 1.5° lat.-WASA) used in both wave models. The plan shape of the coast developing from southern Portugal to Morocco forms a pronounced gulf and the northern section of the Atlantic Moroccan coast is markedly offset in longitude in relation to the SW Portuguese coast. This suggests that the study area benefits from significant sheltering regarding deep water waves travelling from NW to N and the spatial resolution of the grids used by both wave models is too low to retain and accurately represent these effects, thus accounting for the discrepancies referred above.

Table 8.3 Direction of waves (%) and mean values of Hs (m) and Tp (s)

	N	NE	E	SE	S	SW	W	NW	Hs	Tp
WASA	11.9	1.7	1.2	0.3	0.4	0.9	15.9	67.7	1.9	11.9
NOAA	4.4	1.4	0.0	0.0	0.0	0.3	13.7	80.2	1.7	10.2

Table 8.4 Wave direction and energy offshore Loukkos estuary (Larache) between October 1969 and January 1970 (LHCF 1972)

	South					North						
Direction	250	260	270	280	290	300	310	320	330	340	350	360
Number of days	5	6	5	9	19	16	10	4	1	0	1	1
%	7	7	7	12	25	21	13	5	1	0	1	1
Energy descriptor (H^2T)	244	612	246	428	580	601	341	43	23	0	2	18

Table 8.5 Distribution of wave direction (%) in January 1970 according to WASA

Sector	N	NE	E	SE	S	SW	W	NW
%	0	0	0	0	0	7	72	20

The buoy observations quoted in LHCF (1972) are shown in Table 8.4. These results show 7 % occurrences from SW, a figure higher than the annual average yielded by the longer-term NOAA and WASA datasets and of the same order of magnitude of observations reported in OANAO (Table 8.1). Wave data for the months of October to January in the NOAA and WASA series indicate an average 0.5 % frequency for southwesterlies. However, the computation of the wave data for the month of January 1970 in the WASA series (the only time period common to the instrumental data reported in Table 8.4) yields the results in Table 8.5 and suggests that observations in this month (and eventually the winter 1969/70) were strongly influenced by southwesterlies and therefore do not represent an annual climate.

In agreement with the previous discussion, we will use the modeled WASA and NOAA wave climate for further description of coastal hydrodynamics of the study area. The values of accumulated frequencies of deep water wave height plot along straight lines in Fig. 8.2, suggesting a lognormal distribution for both series. The derived statistics indicate mean annual Hs of 1.9 m (σHs 1.10 m) and mean Tp of 12 s (σTp 4 s) and Hs of 1.7 m (σHs 0.91 m) and mean Tp of 10 s (σTp 2.6 s) for WASA and NOAA series, respectively – Table 8.3. The maximum wave height and period were 18 m and 22 s (WASA) and 8 m and 21 s (NOAA). These figures correspond to annual wave power density of 68 kWm^{-1} (WASA) and 44 kWm^{-1} (NOAA), using Hs and peak period, and 30 kWm^{-1} (WASA) and 21 kWm-1 (NOAA) using Hs and estimates of zerocrossing mean period according to correspondences proposed by Soulsby (1997). These values apparently exceed the ones reported by Pires and Pessanha (1986) and Pires et al. (1989) for the Atlantic offshore the Portuguese western coast (16–25 kWm^{-1}) but the latter were calculating using zero-crossing mean period and Hrms (root mean square), an estimate of wave height that roughly halves the associated energy. Thus, our results are congruent with the latitudinal decrease in wave power along the North Atlantic and the derived magnitude of annual wave power compares with values reported in WERATLAS (1997) for the Moroccan sea sheltered by Cape S. Vicente (20–30 kWm^{-1}), suggesting that our datasets may to some extent overestimate wave energy. Wave directions strongly

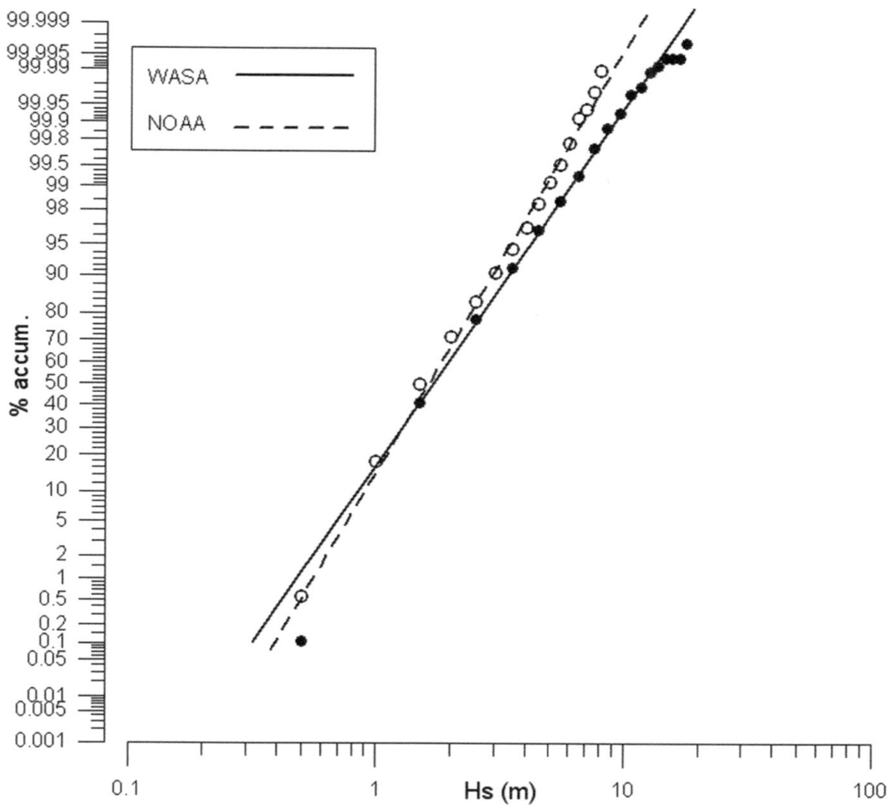

Fig. 8.2 Cumulative distribution of WASA and NOAA wave height data; y axis in probability scale

concentrate in the NW quadrant (Fig. 8.3) and the mean annual wave direction is 313° in both WASA and NOAA data sets, whereas the mean power vector trends 304° (WASA) and 310° (NOAA) – Fig. 8.4. The more energetic (storm) waves approach rotated (2–7°) westward (Figs. 8.3 and 8.4). Westerlies and southwesterlies, though rare in both datasets, associate in general with high energy. The normal to the general shoreline elongation makes a large angle with the deep water mean annual wave power vector (11° WASA and 17° NOAA, Fig. 8.4), implying a net longshore energy flux directed south, though 20 % (WASA) and 13 % (NOAA) occurrences reverse that direction.

The study of time series of wave characteristics indicates important inter-annual to decadal variability (Fig. 8.5). The 1970 decade shows higher wave height and period, essentially during winter, and the directions are more rotated westward. Wave period shows a decrease trough time in both winter and summer seasons. The winter semester is characterized by higher wave height and period and by more frequent westerlies, though the differences to the summer semester vary trough time.

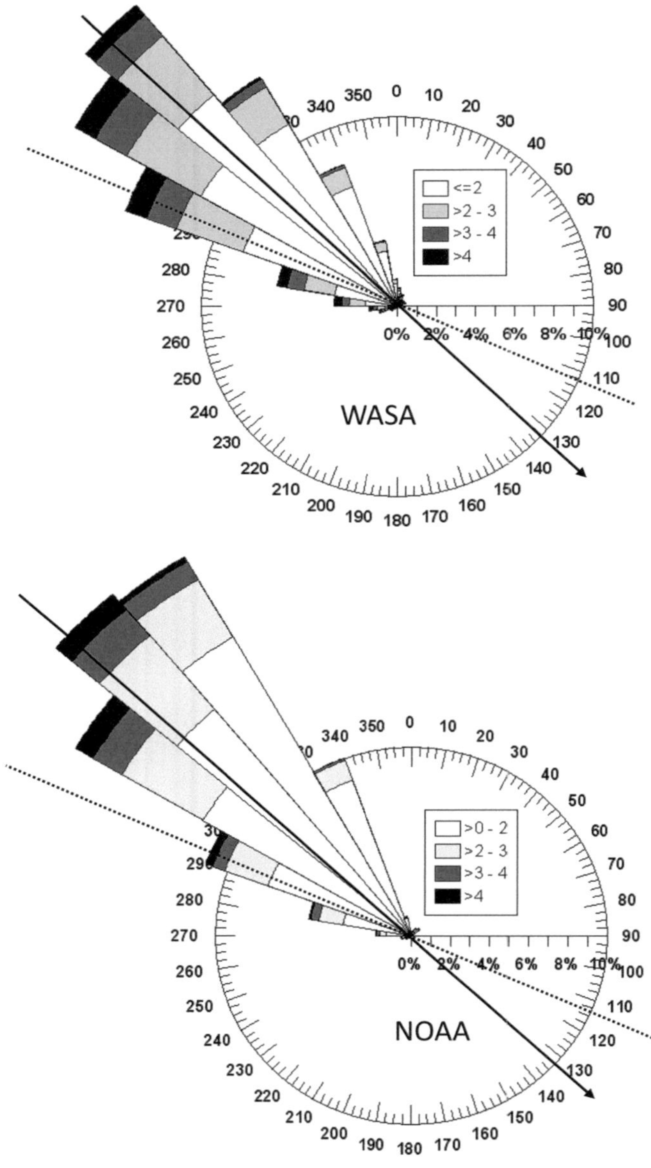

Fig. 8.3 Joint distribution of deep water wave height (m) and direction offshore Moulay Bousselham. *Arrow*: mean wave direction; *dotted line*: normal to coastline.

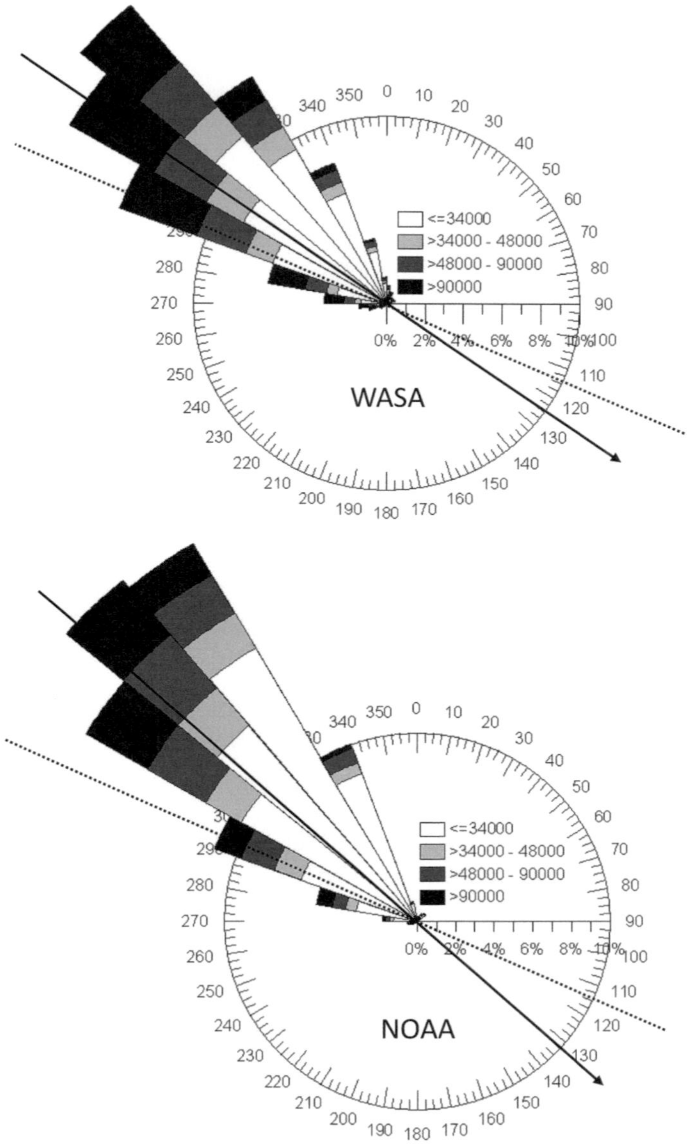

Fig. 8.4 Joint distribution of deep water wave power (Wm^{-1}) and direction offshore Moulay Bousselham. *Arrow*: mean power vector; *dotted line*: normal to coastline

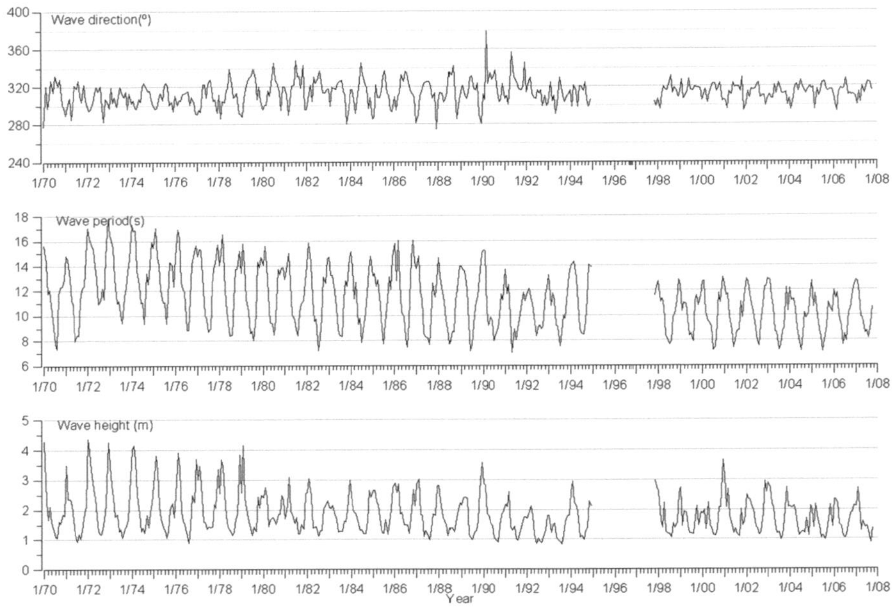

Fig. 8.5 Time series of deep water wave height, period and direction (monthly averages)

8.4.2 Nearshore Waves and Longshore Sediment Transport

Given the relatively simple submarine morphology, the shoaling effects largely predominate in wave transformation and mean wave height at breaking increases to 2.4 m (WASA) and 2.1 m (NOAA), which should be taken as overestimates. The plot of wave and tidal data in Hayes (1979) diagram indicates this coast as mixed energy and wave dominated (Fig. 8.6).

Refraction reduces directional dispersion focusing waves in the NW sector and the correspondent mean power vectors at breaking trend 296° (WASA) and 298° (NOAA), thus decreasing obliquity of breaking to 3° (WASA) and 5° (NOAA). The coupling of breaking wave data with the empirical formulation of USACE (2002) yielded computations of longshore sediment transport rate (see below):

$$Q_l = k\left[\frac{\rho\sqrt{g}}{16k_b^{1/2}(\rho_s-\rho)(1-n)}\right]H_b^{5/2}\sin\left(2\alpha_b\right)$$

where:

Ql – volumetric sand transport rate ($m^3\ day^{-1}$)
ρ – mass volume of marine water (1,025 kgm^{-3}),
ρs – mass volume of sediment (2,650 kgm^{-3}),
n – porosity (0.4),
g – gravitational acceleration (9.81 $m.s^{-2}$),
kb – breaking criterion (0.78),

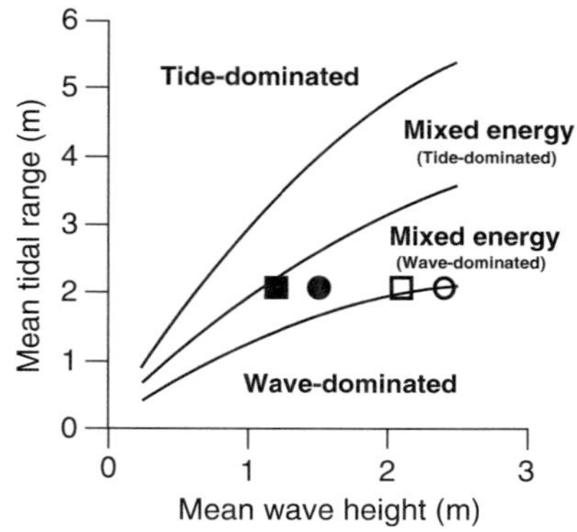

Fig. 8.6 Plot of wave and tide data for Moulay Bousselham on Hayes (1979) diagram; *squares* – NOAA; *circles* – WASA. Shift from *open* to *solid symbols* represent shift in wave energy related with coastal sheltering (see text for explanation)

Hb – wave height at breaking (m),
αb – wave angle at breaking (°),
k – empirical adimensional coefficient.

In this formula, the value assigned to the proportionality coefficient k strongly influences the magnitude of predicted transport rates. A default value of $k = 0.39$ is frequently used (energy parameterized with Hs) but this may lead to unrealistic results. Bertin et al. (2008) discussed this problem and stressed the need of casuistic calibration, noting that the use of non-calibrated empirical transport formulas coupled with numerical models of wave propagation often results in very large errors, the predicted and measured transport rates differing as much as orders of magnitude. In fact, a preliminary assessment of the littoral drift magnitude at Moulay Bousselham with $k = 0.39$ and the breaking conditions described above produced results of about $1 \times 10^7\ m^3\ year^{-1}$. This estimate is clearly unrealistic, as shown by comparison with the exposed high-energy wave-dominated NW Portuguese sand coast, where measured values of net annual drift are of some $1 \times 10^6\ m^3\ year^{-1}$ (cf. Coelho 2005 for a revision of published estimates). Similarly exaggerated predictions of littoral drift have been obtained in the NNE-SSW drift-aligned and fully exposed Portuguese sand coast of Aveiro, departing from modeled wave data (the same wave model used in this study) and $k = 0.39$; in the case of Aveiro, the calibration of the proportionality coefficient with independent morphological information resulted in $k = 0.04$ (e.g. Silva 2008); further use of this calibrated value in the coastal sections of Nazaré and Sintra (west Portugal) yielded predictions of potential longshore drift in broad agreement with independent estimates (Silva 2008; Andrade et al. 2009).

An additional source of error is related with the overestimation of northerly components of the wave spectrum due to inaccurate representation of sheltering effects in the wave generation model. A first approach to address this problem consisted in reprocessing modeled wave data using a directional filter: all deep water waves travelling from directions >314° (the alignment between Moulay Bousselham inlet and Cape São Vicente) were removed from the deep water data bases and the wave climate at breaking recomputed. This resulted in a significant reduction of mean annual values of wave height and energy (Hs 1.5 m, power 48 $kW\ m^{-1}$ – WASA; Hs 1.2 m, power 27 $kW\ m^{-1}$ – NOAA) and the angles between the normal to the shoreline and the mean annual power vector decreased to

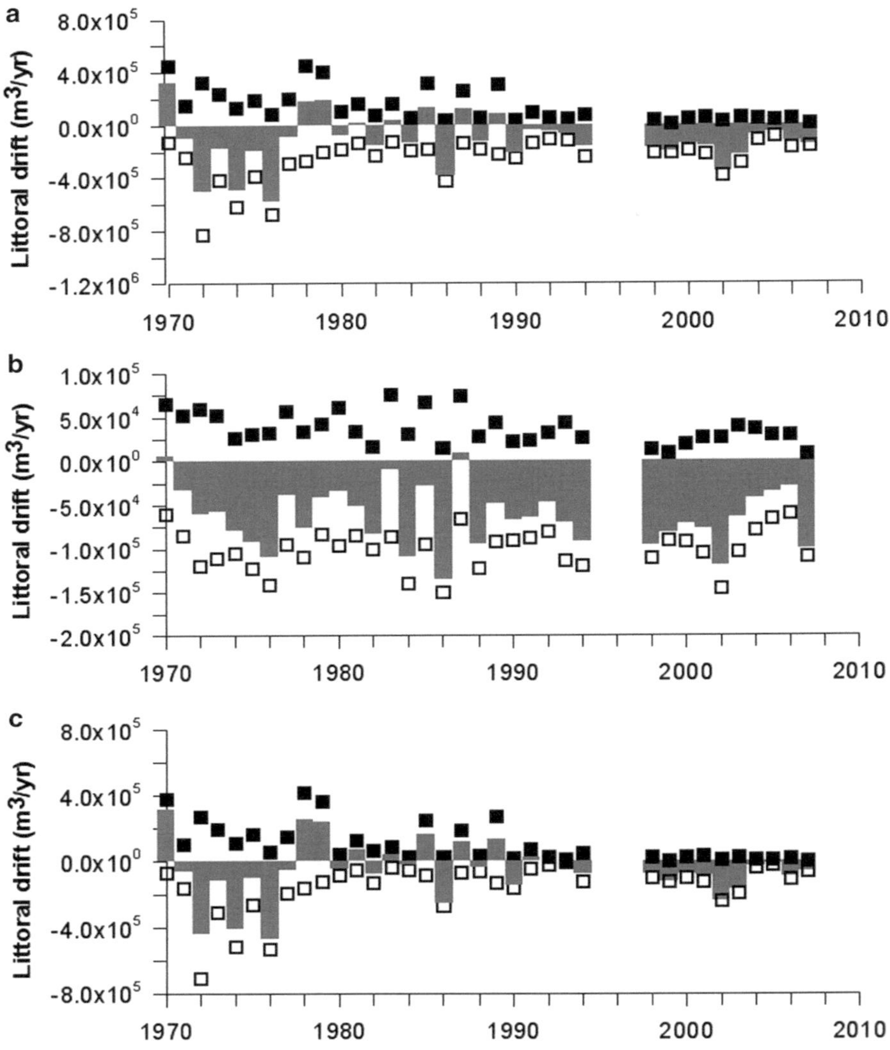

Fig. 8.7 Time series of littoral drift magnitude in Moulay Bousselham ($k = 0.04$, directional filter set at 314°). *Open symbols* southward component; *solid symbols* northward component; *grey bars* annual residue. (**a**) All waves, (**b**) Contribution of waves with $Hs \leq 3$ m. (**c**) contribution of waves with $Hs > 3$ m

1° (WASA) and 2° (NOAA), still indicating southward prevalence but lower persistency in direction, and reduced magnitude of net annual littoral drift (Fig. 8.7). In the Hayes (1979) diagram, this coast still comes out as mixed energy and wave-dominated with a decrease in the relative influence of wave energy, as expected (Fig. 8.6). The near match found between wave power direction and coastline trend suggests that small interannual to decadal latitudinal variations in the location of generation areas may have significant impacts in the net direction of longshore transport.

Computations of longshore transport rates in Moulay Bousselham by the energyflux method using k = 0.04 and the filtered wave data indicate dominance of the southward component (Fig. 8.7), which varies typically between 9×10^4 and 8×10^5 m^3 $year^{-1}$, whereas the northward transport, less important, varies between 3×10^4 and 4×10^5 m^3 $year^{-1}$. The net residue shows pronounced interannual variation in magnitude (less important after 1998) of 1 to 2×10^5 m^3 $year^{-1}$ (either north or south) and increasing to 3–4 × 10^5 m^3 $year^{-1}$ in stormy years; 4 years in the studied series show virtually null residual drift. The magnitude and direction of net drift is essentially controlled by modal to low-energy waves in some years, while in others storms are dominating.

The southward direction of the prevailing net annual longshore drift reported here conflicts with previously published material. SOGREAH (1961), Mathieu (1986) and Carruesco (1989) refer an opposite (northward) direction for this transport based upon observations of geomorphological changes in coastal forms or analyses of wave data sets, but in both cases the time window used was very short, making these observations unrepresentative of the longer-term coastal dynamics.

8.5 Morphodynamical Evolution of the Tidal Inlet

The comparison of documents depicting the inlet area of Moulay Bousselham and adjacent coast between 1937 and 2005, illustrated in Fig. 8.8, shows that three different major morphodynamic configurations may occur: updrift, overlapping and negligible offset, suggesting significant changes in the relative magnitude of northward longshore transport (CERC 1984).

The earliest document is dated from 1937 and consists of a cartographic sketch by Gruvel (1937), which shows strong similarities with the earliest (1949) photo; both images show two spits elongated NE-SW with negligible offset, the northern one more developed (circa 660 m) than the southern one (circa 260 m). Detailed observation of the 1949 photo reveals the scars of the last artificial breaching of the inlet, indicating a maximum width of about 90 m for the tidal channel shortly after that opening, and a subsequent evolution essentially characterized by the growth of low-tide bars at each margin, narrowing the channel section. Despite the exact date of this breaching being unknown, its location was in the southern half of the barrier – where it was usually performed before 1950, according to SOGREAH (1961).

SOGREAH (1961) reports the channel was re-opened artificially in 1950 in a northern location (indicating that the narrowing observed in 1949 rapidly lead to complete silting up of the inlet) and that until the early 1960s the artificial breaching was displaced towards the northern half of the barrier, aiming to increase the life span of the inlet. Indeed, the same report indicates that between 1950 and 1961 the inlet remained active.

The image of 1963 shows a shorter channel, placed in a more northern location and leaning against the northern cliff boundary; the northern spit does not exist and a general fattening of the southern sand banks margining the southern cliff occurred; both tips of the inlet remain with negligible to slight offset. In addition,

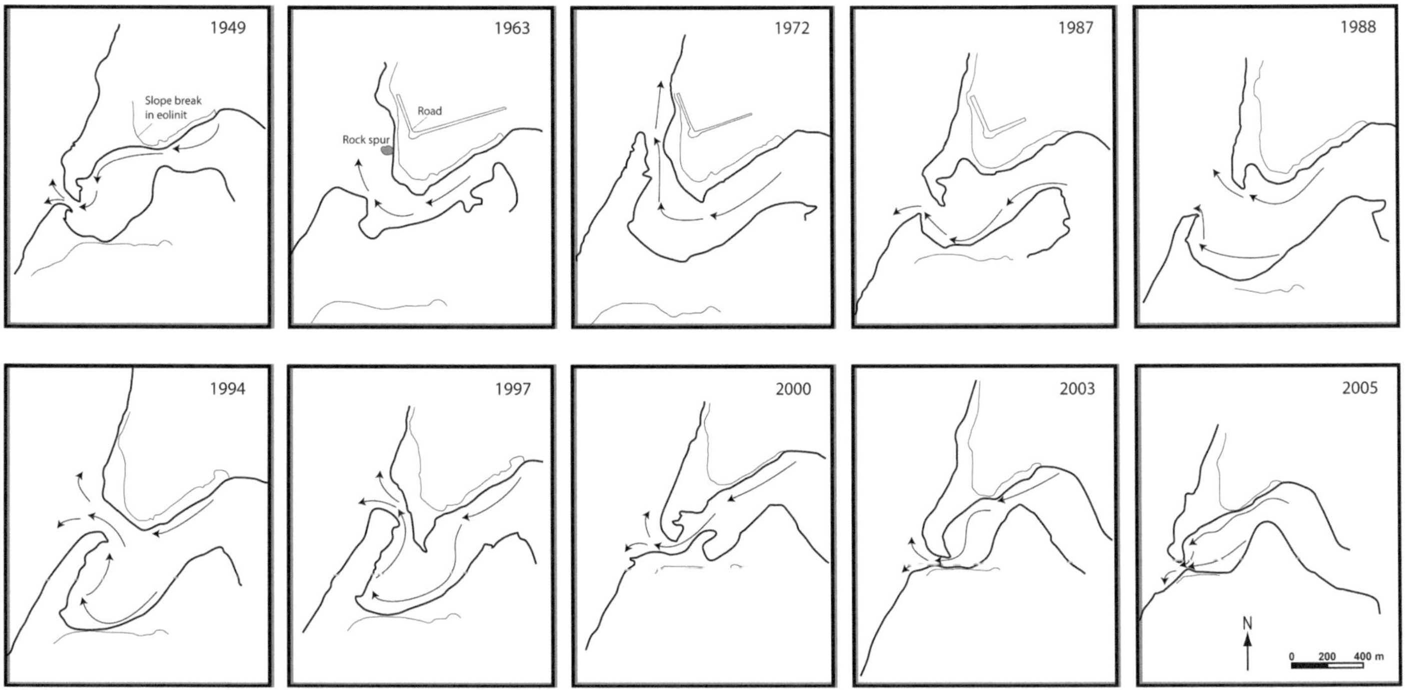

Fig. 8.8 Morphological sketches of Moulay Bousselham inlet. *Arrows* indicate proeminent channels

the beach of Moulay Bousselham village shows significant retreat (200 m at reference latitude of 475400 Fig. 8.8) in comparison with the 1949 situation, exposing a Pleistocene eolianitic bedrock spur, which extends perpendicular to the general trend of the coast. The exposure of this and other rocky shoals was also noted and depicted by SOGREAH in 1961. The 1972 photo shows an overlapping southern spit that grew northwards for 250 m; this considerably increased the length of the inlet channel, which remains very close to the northern cliff boundary; the northern spit still does not exist and the beach sheltered by the spit enlarged 60 m at the same reference latitude. Carruesco (1989) depicted for the year of 1969 an intermediate situation between the morphologies observed in the aerial photos of 1963 and 1972. The sketches he presented for the years of 1974, 1979 and 1980 are very similar to the 1972 situation. Beaubrun (1976, quoted in Carruesco, 1989) indicates that after 1928 this inlet silted up three times. The next available image is a SPOT satellite image dated from 1987, showing the inlet channel in a more southern location than in 1980 and this reflects another (southward) relocation of the artificial breaching in February 1983, following the natural closure of the inlet in its former northern location, in the same year (Carruesco 1989). The inlet is confined between two spits, in an arrangement similar to 1949, although the beach at the reference latitude is narrower than in 1949, and the main inlet channel now leans against the southern margin. The 1988 aerial photo shows intense reworking, eastward migration and shortening of the northern spit, whereas the southern spit increased its length; the width of the inlet mouth increased in relation to the previous year, reaching about 240 m and two tidal channels are present in the inlet gorge, with the southern channel clearly dominating; the inlet displays a small updrift offset. Carruesco (1989) reports a continuous northward growth of the southern spit since 1983 and according to Ameur (1994) and Bazaïri (1999) the inlet barely closed in 1990, again in a northward location; this is confirmed by the LANDSAT image of 1990 and suggests that for about 7 years northward littoral drift controlled an episode of rapid spit growth leading to almost complete closure of the inlet.

According to Bazaïri (1999) the inlet completely closed in 1991 and Ameur (1994) reports that the barrier was again artificially breached in that year though its location could not be precised. In the aerial photo of 1994 the southern spit shows a scar indicating a southern location for the artificial breach and this feature is consistent with the deactivation of the southern inlet channel, which is shown completely blocked by the root of the well-developed southern barrier. Morphological similarity in the southern channel geometry between images of 1987, 1988 and 1994, together with the scar of a former breaching (probably 1983), indicates these two features as inherited from the previous years (1983–1988). The northern spit is absent, the inlet shows negligible offset and the main tidal channel again migrated towards the north. Altogether, this information suggests that the 1991 breaching was located north.

The aerial photo of 1997 shares similarities with the previous one in the absence of a northern spit and negligible offset, but the main inlet channel was forced into a tight meander, leaving a point bar attached to the northern bank. The 1997 image is the only photo showing the presence of a well-developed ebb-delta with numerous short swash bars. Further south, numerous linear shore-parallel swash bars margin the beach, suggesting that this picture was taken during a period of beach recovery following a storm.

Between 1997 and 2000 the inlet closed in a northern position and was reopened southward. The aerial photos dated 2000, 2003 and 2005 show only one well developed northern spit and between 2000 and 2003 the inlet channel reached its southernmost location, leaning against the cliffed southern boundary, which makes an unsurpassable obstacle to further drifting. In the period 2000–2005 there are no significant morphological changes: the inlet apparently remained stable in its present day (southern) location.

Both the information collected from the documentary record and aerial photographs examined in this study indicate an average time interval for the lifespan of the inlet of 10^1 years.

In summary, the descriptions above and available data indicate that between 1937 and 2009 the inlet of Moulay Bousselham relocated and evolved differently in four time intervals. Within each time-interval, the inlet channel remained essentially stable or relocated northward and only minor changes in the morphological features (e.g. location of swash bars, channel bends, point bars) populating the inlet area and extension or shortening of barrier tips occurred. Between successive periods, major changes in the behaviour of the drifting pattern are noticeable and significant reorganization of the morphological contents of the inlet area took place. We found no evidence of southward drift of neither the inlet, with concomitant rearrangement of the confining barrier tips, nor of the main inlet channel within an essentially invariant inlet gap.

The first period extends until 1983, when the inlet silted naturally and no oceanographic data exist to compare with the earliest documentary descriptions (1937–1970). After 1950 all documents depict a persistent northward location of the inlet, with every artificial reopening also located north. In 1963 a slight overlap between barrier tips is observed and the large abundance in sand south of the inlet channel contrasts with sediment starvation of the beach adjacent to Moulay Bousselham village, with extensive exposure of the intertidal bedrock and eventual reactivation of the cliff toe.

This situation is documented since at least 1961. In 1972 the overlapping pattern came to an extreme (and both the southern barrier tip and terminal stretch of the inlet channel reached maximum length) whereas a sand beach had accumulated against the cliff toe, benefiting from sheltering offered by the growing barrier and simultaneously constraining the (now elongated) channel. The four sketches covering 1972–1980 are in broad agreement with the above description. This is compatible with a pattern of shortage in longshore sand supply to the coastal cell northward of the inlet, sediment being preferably retained by the southern barrier until episodic bypassing was allowed.

Significantly, 1970, 1978 and 1979 were characterized by the largest intensity of northward net drift produced by waves in the time-series studied; in 1970, both west and southwest storm and low-energy wave regimes contributed to this result, while in the latter the storm-generated drift reversed the general N-S direction of longshore transport imposed by low-energy waves. In between, pronounced inter-annual changes in the magnitude of net drift occurred (though it remained directed south, on yearly average), essentially associated to high storm intensity from both NW and W to SW. Coupling wave data with longshore sediment transport and independent morphological information indicates that in the interval 1963–1983, southwesterlies and westerlies were predominant in determining northward drift to the inlet of Moulay Bousselham or imposing its permanency at an uttermost north location, determined by bedrock constrains. Storms of comparable intensity and reversing the direction of longshore transport were apparently unable to change the morphodynamic arrangement of the inlet. This may be due to contrast in energy dissipation ability of the rocky shoal lines extending north and south of the inlet, the northern shoals inducing early breaking and offering larger protection to any sand accumulation resting landward and reducing the erosion potential of south moving wave-induced currents.

A second period extends between 1983 and 1991, when another natural closure occurred. This period is characterized by significant intensity of W to SW storms and low energy waves and by frequent reversal of the net annual residue of littoral drift; the year of 1986 is exceptional in determining high intensity of southward transport in association with both high and low energy waves. Migration of the inlet towards north is documented after 1987, compatible with predominance of W to SW waves in triggering northward drift. The general decrease in energy observed between the 1970s and the 1980s, probably explains the minor volume of sediment captured within the inlet area and the lack of overlapping configurations.

The third period extends between 1991 and 2000 and corresponds to a northern breaching and permanency of the inlet. This is compatible with the minimum magnitude of the net annual drift and infrequent and moderate storms regardless their direction.

The last time interval extends from 2000 onwards. It initiates with a south breaching of the inlet and its permanency in the same location until present. The net drift is slightly higher than in the previous period and W and SW storms were almost absent. The Google images 2009 to 2013 and field observations indicate an extremely silted inlet area and a long and sinuous, poorly efficient, channel. This suggests impending closure of the inlet and this should be followed by artificial re-opening in a significantly northward location; this would diminish the length and reduce the curvature of the inlet channel, therefore increasing the efficiency of water exchange within the lagoon and the lifespan of the inlet, although at the cost of reducing carrying capacity of Moulay Bousselham beach.

Our results indicate that within the time window studied, there is not a simple relationship between the directional preference of inlet relocation and the direction of net annual drift. A northward preference for inlet (re)location and drift seem to occur in periods with frequent activity of the northward component of longshore transport in either high or low energy conditions, regardless the intensity and frequency of the opposite component or the magnitude and direction of the yearly resultant. A southern inlet location is preferred or more stable only when the northward component of littoral drift is significantly reduced. We suggest that this may be an effect of geomorphology resulting from contrasting effectiveness of the shoal fields extending north and south of the inlet area in dissipating wave energy. A large fraction of the longshore wave power propagating north will translate into actual sediment movement upon and in the vicinity of the beach face in any wave condition, given the permeability offered by a lower, discontinuous and thinner shoal field extending seaward and south of the inlet. In contrast, the southward propagation of longshore energy flux will be modulated by a more robust shoal field, determining that a variable fraction of the associated transport will be dissipated away from the beach line or remain in essence as potential in the vicinity of the beach face; this dumping effect will be minimized in low-energy conditions (waves breaking upon the beach face) whereas high waves breaking farther from the shore may induce a sediment bypassing corridor that does not significantly interfere with the beach line in the vicinity of the inlet and associated spit, thus failing to trigger an immediate geomorphological response of relocation or drift of the inlet. In this case, it is not possible to infer a long term directional trend for the net drift departing from macroscale morphological features.

Moreover, given the quasi-equilibrium directional relation between shore development and wave power, we hypothesize that previous periods of decadal dimension and characterized by shift of the directional spectrum of waves (related, for example, with NAO and expressed by increase of the westerly components of the wave climate) may have increased both the energy level at the coast (by reducing sheltering effects) and the northward drift trend of the inlet.

8.6 Conclusions

The approach used in this study links the analysis of the nearshore wave climate at Moulay Bousselham with independent information on the morphodynamics and mobility of its tidal inlet. Results show that this coast is high-mesotidal and mixed energy, but dominated by wave energy, which is strongly attenuated at this latitude by sheltering offered by the Iberian coast. The analyses of the offshore and breaking wave climates indicate a significant reduction of the directional spectrum, though shoaling effects prevail over refraction in modulating littoral waves. The mean annual wave power direction is slightly rotated in relation to the coastline trend, indicating a southward annual residue of longshore energy flux and drift (magnitude estimated in 1×10^5 m^3 $year^{-1}$) though pronounced interannual and interdecadal variations exist. This result conflicts with previous studies indicating a northward residue of littoral transport based upon limited wave measurements and morphological interpretation of the inlet.

The study of maps and vertical photographs illustrating the inlet morphodynamic arrangement and variation through time suggests that there is no simple relationship between inlet drift or relocation preference, and the balance between both components of longshore sediment transport. Indeed, the preferred drift trend and location of a (meta) stable inlet depends essentially on the frequency and magnitude of only the northward components of the longshore energy flux and transport existing during several years. Directional reversal of the energy flux comes out as less efficient in determining southward sediment transport and significant morphological changes in the barrier or a south stable location of the inlet, despite the dominancy of the promoting waves. This asymmetry is imputed to contrast in sheltering conditions offered by a field of rocky shoals in the nearshore, making it impossible to derive a dominant directional pattern for littoral drift departing from geomorphological interpretation. This highlights the utility of combining independent methods of analysis of coastal hydrodynamics to extract long term patterns of coastal behavior.

Acknowledgements This work was supported by Cooperation GRICES-Portugal/CNRST-Maroc and LAGMAR Programme (REMER). The authors are grateful to Bruno Castelle (Bordeaux 1 University) and Hakkou Rachid (Kenitra, Ibnou Tofail University) for information on the NOAA dataset and to Puertos de Estado (España) for making available the WASA wave data offshore Morocco.

References

Ameur B (1994) Aspects biologique et dynamique de la population de Mugil cephalus L. 1758 (Poissons, Mugilidés) de la lagune de Moulay Bousselham (Maroc). Thèse DES, Université Mohammed V, Rabat, 93 pp

Ameur B, Bayed B, Benazzou T (2003) Rôle de la communication de la lagune de Merja Zerga avec l'océan Atlantique dans la reproduction d'une population de Mugil cephalus L. (Poisson Mugilidae). Bullet. de l'Institut Scientifique, Rabat, section Sciences de la Vie 25, pp 55–62

Andrade C, Freitas MC, Moreno J, Craveiro SC (2004) Stratigraphical evidence of Late Holocene barrier breaching and extreme storms in lagoonal sediments of Ria Formosa, Algarve, Portugal. Mar Geol 210:339–362

Andrade C, Taborda R, Marques F, Freitas MC, Antunes C, Mendes T, Carreira D (2009) Zonas Costeiras. In: Santos FD, Aguiar ER (eds) PECSAC. Alterações Climáticas – Sintra. Plano Estratégico do Concelho de Sintra face às Alterações Climáticas. Relatório Executivo e Integrador. Câmara Municipal de Sintra, Sintra, 48 p

ASD (2006) Admiralty sailing directions. Admiralty Charts and Publications, Taunton, UK, 395 p

Aubrey D, Speer P (1984) Updrift migration of tidal inlets. J Geol 92:531–545

Bazaïri B (1999) La faune macrobenthique de la lagune de Moulay Bousselham, structure des peuplement et succession spatio-temporelle. Thèse de Doctorat, Fac Sci Rabat, Université Mohammed V, 199 p

Beaubrun PC (1976) La lagune de Moulay Bousselham: Etude Hydrologique et sédimentologique. Bull Inst Sci Rabat 1:5–35

Benbakhta B (1994) Structure et dynamique du zooplancton de la lagune de Moulay Bou Selham (Maroc). Thèse d'Etude Supérieure de 3° cycle, Fac Sci Rabat, Université Mohamed V

Benhoussa A (2000) Caractérisation des habitats et microdistribution de l'avifaune de la zone humide de Merja Zerga (Maroc). Thèse Doc. d'État, Université Mohamed V, Rabat, 256 p

Benmohammadi A, Griboulard R, Zourarah B, Carruesco C, Mehdi K, Mridekh A, El Moussaoui A, Mhamdi Alaoui A, Carbonel P, Londeix L (2007) Hyperactive neotectonics near the South Rifian front. Lifted Late Quaternary lagoonal deposits (Atlantic Morocco). Comp Rend Geosci 339:831–839

Bertin X, Castelle B, Chaumillon E, Butel R, Quique R (2008) Longshore transport estimation and inter-annual variability at a high-energy dissipative beach: St. Trojan beach, SW Oléron Island, France. Cont Shelf Res 28(10):1316–1332

Boon JD, Byrne RJ (1981) On basin hypsometry and the morphodynamic response of coastal inlet systems. Mar Geol 40:27–48

Carruesco (1989) Genèse et évolution de trois lagunes du littoral atlantique depuis l'Holocène: Oualidia, Moulay Bou Salham (Maroc) et Arcachon (France). Thèse d'État, Université Bordeaux-1, 485 p

Castelle B, Bourget J, Molnar N, Strauss D, Deschamps S, Tomlinson R (2007) Dynamics of wave-dominated tidal inlet and influence on adjacent beaches, Currumbin Creek, Gold Coast, Austrália. Coast Eng 54:77–90

CERC (1984) Shore protection manual, vol 1. Coastal Engineering Research Center, US Army Corps of Engineers, Vicksburg

Charouff L (1989) Les problemes d'ensablement des ports Maroccains sur la façade Atlantique. Le impact sédimentologique sur le littoral. Thèse Doctorat, Université Paris-Sud, 302 p

Cirac P (1985) Le bassin Sudrifain au Néogène supérieur. Évolution de la dynamique sédimentaire et de la paléogeogaphie au cours d'une phase de comblement. Thèse de Doctorat es Sciences, Univer. Bordeaux 1. Mem. Inst. Géol. du Bassin d'Aquitaine 21, Bordeaux, 287 p

Coelho CDB (2005) Riscos de exposição de frentes urbanas para diferentes intervenções de defesa costeira. PhD dissertation, Universidade de Aveiro, Aveiro, Portugal, 404 p

Davis RA, Andronaco M, Gibeaut JC (1989) Formation and development of a tidal inlet from a washover fan, west-central Florida coast, U.S.A. Sediment Geol 65:87–94

El Agbani MA, Dakki M, Bayed A (1998) Elaboration d'un programme de suivi écologique de Merja Zerga. Report AEFCS/MedWet 2, 35 p

FitzGerald DM (1984) Interactions between the ebb-tidal delta and landward shoreline: price inlet, South Carolina. J Sediment Petrol 54(4):1303–1318

FitzGerald DM (1988) Shoreline erosional-depositional processes associated with tidal inlets. In: Aubrey DG, Weishar L (eds) Hydrodynamics and sediment dynamics of tidal inlets, vol 29, Lectures notes on coastal and estuarine studies. Springer, New York, pp 186–225

Fitzgerald DM (1996) Geomorphic variability and morphologic and sedimentologic controls on tidal inlets. J Coast Res SI23:47–71

FitzGerald DM, Nummedal D (1983) Response characteristics of an ebb-dominated tidal inlet channel. J Sediment Petrol 53(3):833–845

FitzGerald DM, Penland S, Nummedal D (1984) Control of barrier island shape by inlet sediment bypassing: east Frisian Islands, West Germany. Mar Geol 60(1–4):355–376

Gruvel A (1937) Études sur les lagunes da la côte occidentale du Maroc. Faune des Colonies françaises, t. IV, fasc 6:559–596

Hayes MO (1979) Barrier island morphology as a function of tidal and wave regime. In: Leatherman S (ed) Barrier islands. Academic, New York, pp 1–28

Jaaidi EB (1993) La couverture sédimentaire post-glaciare de la plateforme continentale atlantique ouest rifaine (Maroc nord occidental): Exemple d'une séquence transgressive. Thèse de doctorat es Sc. Université Mohamed V, Rabat, Maroc, 238 p

Jarrett JT (1976) Tidal prism – inlet area relationships. U.S. Army Coastal Engineering Research Center, Fort Belvoir, Virginia, 32 p

LCHF (1972) Campagne d'etude 1970–1972. Rapport Gènérale de Synthèse. Rapport technique, Laboratoire Central d'Hydraulique de France, Trav. Publiques, Larache, Maroc

Le Coz J (1964) Le Rharb, Fellahs et colons. Étude de géographie régionale, vol 1, Les cadres de la nature et de l'Histoire. Thèse d'État, Rabat, Maroc

Mathieu R (1986) Sédiments et foraminifères actuels du marge Atlantique du Maroc. Thèse Doctorat d'État ès Sciences Naturelles, Université Pierre et Mariée Curie, Paris, 420 p

Mhamdi Alaoui A, Choura M, Maanan M, Zourarah B, Robin M, Freitas Conceição M, Andrade C, Khalid M, Carruesco C (2010) Metal fluxes to the sediments of the Moulay Bousselham lagoon, Morocco. Environ Earth Sci 61(2):275–286

O'Brien MP (1969) Equilibrium flow areas of inlets on sandy coasts. J Waterways Harbor Div 95 (1):43–52

Oertel GF (1988) Processes of sediment exchange between tidal inlets, ebb deltas and barrier islands. In: Aubrey DG, Weishar L (eds) Hydrodynamics and sediment dynamics of tidal inlets, vol 29, Lectures notes on coastal and estuarine studies. Springer, New York, pp 297–318

Pires H, Pessanha L (1986) Wave power climate of Portugal. In: Evans D, Falcão A (eds) Hydrodynamics of ocean wave-energy utilization. Springer, Berlin, pp 157–167

Pires H, Carvalho F, Rodrigues A (1989) Comparação dos resultados do modelo MAR 211 com observações. Unpublished technical report, Instituto Nacional de Meteorologia e Geofísica, Lisboa, 10 p

Silva A (2008) Deriva litoral na zona costeira adjacente à Nazaré. Unpublished report of PhD Advanced Training Seminar, Department of Geology, University of Lisbon, 34 p (in Portuguese)

SOGREAH (1961) Le problème de l'érosion littorale à Moulay Bousselham. Unpublished technical report R771, Travaux Publics du Maroc, 12 p

Soulsby R (1997) Dynamics of marine sands: a manual for practical applications. Thomas Telford, London, 249 p

Tolman HL (1997) User manual and system documentation of Wavewatch-III version 1.15. NOAA/NWS/NCEP/OMB Tech. Note 151, 97 p

USACE (2002) Coastal Engineering Manual. Engineer Manual 1110-2-1100, U.S. Army Corps of Engineers. Washington, DC (in 6 volumes)

Vila-Concejo A, Matias A, Ferreira O, Duarte C, Dias JMA (2002) Recent evolution of the natural inlets of a barrier island system in Southern Portugal. J Coast Res SI 36:741–752

WERATLAS (1997) European wave energy atlas. INETI – Instituto Nacional de Engenharia, Tecnologia e Inovação I.P, Portugal

Zourarah B, Maanan M, Carruesco C, Aajjane A, Mehdi K, Freitas M (2007) Fifty-year sedimentary record of heavy metal pollution in the lagoon of Oualidia (Moroccan Atlantic coast). Estuar Coast Shelf Sci 72(1–2):359–369

Zourarah B, Maanan M, Robin M, Carruesco C (2008) Sedimentary records of anthropogenic contribution to heavy metal content in Oum Er Bia estuary (Morocco). Environ Chem Lett 7(1):67–78

Chapter 9
Sediment Transport Formulae for Coastal Morphodynamic Simulation: Calculated Sediment Flux Against In Situ Data

Philippe Larroudé, Mehdi Daou, Adrien Cartier, and Arnaud Hequette

Abstract The aim of this chapter is to show the influence of the choice of sediment transport formulae in morphodynamic simulations. These simulations were conducted in the nearshore zone for time scales on the order of individual storm events. In a part of the chapter, we also compare directly the sediment flux calculated in the sediment code with different formulae with in-situ sediment transport measurements obtained on several beaches of the north coast of France.

9.1 Introduction

The work consisted in setting up the methodology of calculation based on the work of De Vriend (1987), De Vriend and Stive (1987) and Smit et al. 2008. The principle is to make an external coupling of three codes. This coupling consists in enchained Artemis for swells, Telemac2d for the currents and Sisyphe for the morphodynamic evolution (Hervouet 2007). The basic principle of this external coupling is to make this loop on the codes with a step of morphodynamic time depending essentially on weather conditions and on the environment hydrodynamics of the studied beach. These models were used in the framework of a simulated meteorological cycle describing the seasonal evolution of hydrodynamic factors.

This paper discusses the abilities of numerical models to predict the morphodynamics over sandy and rigid beds. In the first part of the paper, the sediment transport model is presented which solves the bed evolution equation in conjunction with sediment transport formulas. The flow field and the water depth are calculated using the depth-averaged hydrodynamic model TELEMAC-2D and a

P. Larroudé (✉) • M. Daou
UMR 5519, LEGI, Université de Grenoble, Saint-Martin-d'Hères, France
e-mail: Philippe.Larroude@legi.grenoble-inp.fr

A. Cartier • A. Hequette
Laboratoire D'Océanologie et des Géosciences, UMR 8187 LOG, Université du Littoral Côte d'Opale, Wimeureux, France

M. Maanan, M. Robin (eds.), *Sediment Fluxes in Coastal Areas*,
Coastal Research Library 10, DOI 10.1007/978-94-017-9260-8_9

simplified model called Multi1dh. This model was already used and tested in Camenen and Larroudé (2003b).

This study had multiple objectives, the first being aimed at setting up a procedure for linking the three codes to be able to simulate realistic climate regimes. This procedure was validated in terms of hydrodynamics and morphodynamic evolution (Larroudé 2008). This technique of simulation was then used to compare and to study the contribution of various sediment transport formulae as in Camenen 2002 on the site of Sète during two specific storm events (see Robin et al. 2010).

In the present contribution, we improve this methodology to simulate the Rising-Apex-Waning of a Storm event. We also look at the comparison of the current during these different periods of the storm. To calibrate all these sediment formulae, we also compare our simulations with in-situ data of longshore and cross-shore sediment transport measured on several beaches of the North sea and of the English Channel (Cartier and Héquette 2011a, b).

9.2 Description of the Study Sites

Site 1: The "Plage de la Corniche", located near Sète on the Mediterranean coast, France, was selected as the first study area (Fig. 9.1). Located in a microtidal, swell-dominated coastal environment, the "Plage de la Corniche" is a linear beach of about 2.5 km length. The mean near shore bed slope is 0.04, while the median grain size in the surf zone is 0.25 mm.

The mean significant offshore wave height is about 1.5 m increasing to 3–6 m during storms, while the predominant wave direction is from SSE with occasional SE swells. There is no significant seasonal variation in the offshore wave climate.

Certain and Barusseau (2006) showed that the morphodynamic evolution of offshore bars in a microtidal environment and bimodal moderate wave regime follows two different conceptual models, the main one being a seasonal pattern in line with the observed cycle of hydrodynamic conditions (see also Certain 2002).

Site 2: The second study area consists of three intertidal sandy beaches on the coast of Nord-Pas-de-Calais (northern France) located at Zuydcoote, Wissant and Hardelot Plage (Fig. 9.2). The Zuydcoote site, located east of Dunkirk, is characterized by a beach of fine sand ($D_{50} = 0.2$ mm), 350–400 m wide, with an average slope of about 0.014. The tidal range varies from 3.4 m during neap tide to 5.2 m during spring tides on average, and this site can therefore be considered as meso-to macrotidal. The coast, oriented NE-SW, facing the North Sea, is characterized by fetch-limited short waves.

The Wissant site is located in a bay that extends over 6 km, bordered on the south by the Cap Gris Nez and the north by the Cap Blanc Nez. The hydrodynamics is more powerful due to the exchange of water mass between the North Sea and The English Channel which is particularly intense. The test site is located in the eastern part of the bay, characterized by a beach of fine sand ($D50 = 0.22$ mm) and an

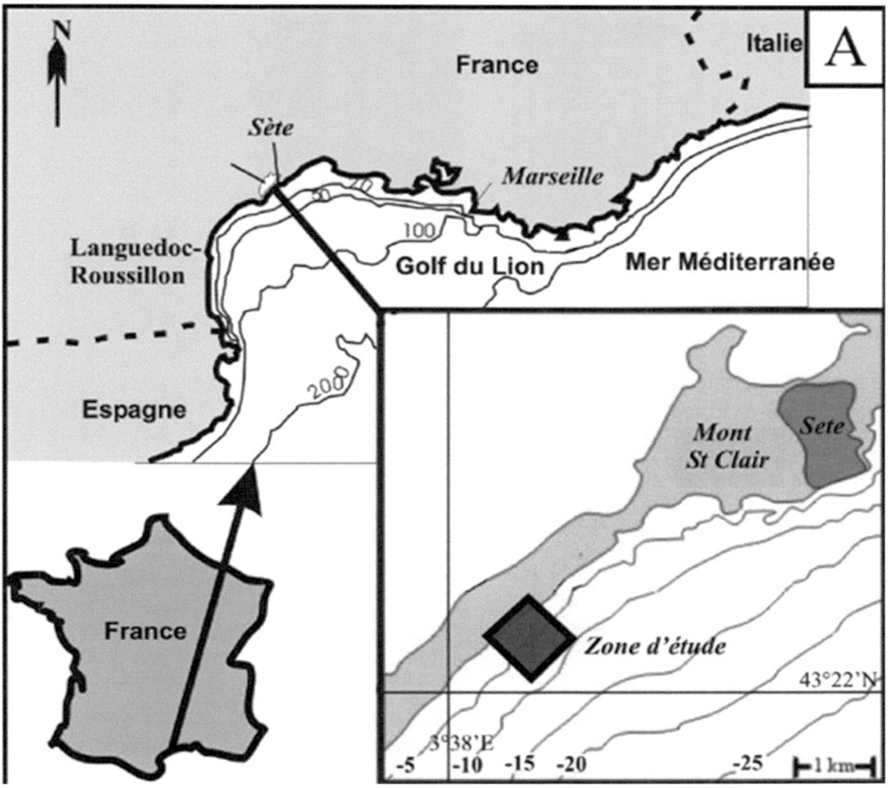

Fig. 9.1 Location of the "plage de la Corniche" at Sète, Mediterranean Sea

average slope of 0.012. The coast is subject to a tidal range from 4.2 to 6.7 m for neap and spring tides.

The third site is located at Hardelot beach, at the Dune du Mont St-Frieux. The beach consists of fine sand (D50 = 0.23 mm) and has an average slope of 0.026. The tidal range reaches 4.8 m at neap tide on average and 8.0 m in times of great water. Oriented N-S, the coast is facing the English Channel.

Tidal currents on the three beaches flow parallel to the shore and are characterized by a flood-dominated asymmetry. This dominance of flood currents, combined with a system of winds and swells from the SW, generates a hydrodynamic circulation and sediment transport directed eastward on the coast of the North Sea and northward on the shores of the Channel (Sipka and Anthony 1999).

The purpose of the field experiments carried out on the beaches of northern France was to estimate the longshore flow and sediment transport in the surf zone (and sometimes in the shoaling zone). Sediment transport rates were estimated using streamer traps following the method proposed by Kraus (1987), allowing to measure suspended and near bed transport.

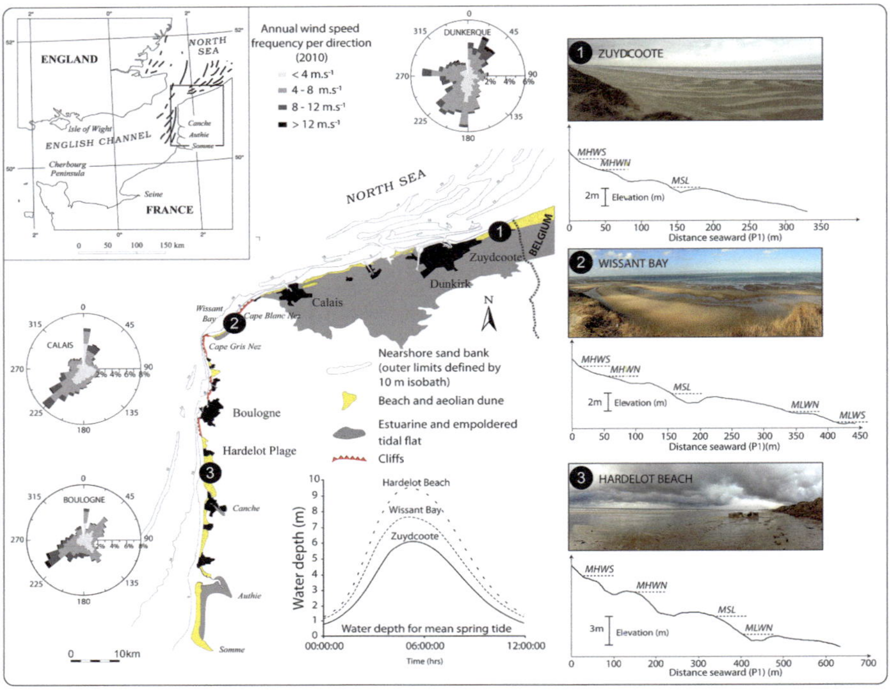

Fig. 9.2 Location of the three study sites along the coast of Northern France: (*1*) Zuydcoote; (*2*) Wissant Bay; (*3*) Hardelot Beach as well as shore perpendicular beach profiles, panoramic and aerial vertical photographs (©Orthophoto, 2005) of each study site

Kraus structures capture the sediment in suspension over a depth range of about 1 m. They are composed of five nets with a mesh size of 63 μm to trap sediment at 0.05, 0.26, 0.46, 0.66 and 0.86 m above the bed. During high wave energy conditions, the sediment trap had to be deployed in shallower water and the two upper nets (0.66 and 0.86 m) were then removed. The structures were placed for 10 min, facing the mainstream, which is determined visually by the operator. The sampling time was generally 10 min, but may varied between 5 and 10 min depending on the conditions of agitation and/or the rate of tide-induced water level variations during sampling.

Current meters were also deployed on the foreshore. The instruments were routinely placed on the outer side of intertidal bars. Three instruments were used, ADCP, S4 and ADW Valeport (electromagnetic current meter). These instruments were programmed to measure wave and current parameters at a frequency of 2 Hz during 9 min bursts every 15 min, yielding values of significant wave height (H_s), period and direction, and mean near-bottom current speed and direction.

Morphological monitoring of each studied zone was carried out every sampling day using a high precision DGPS (for detail see Cartier and Héquette 2011b) (Fig. 9.3).

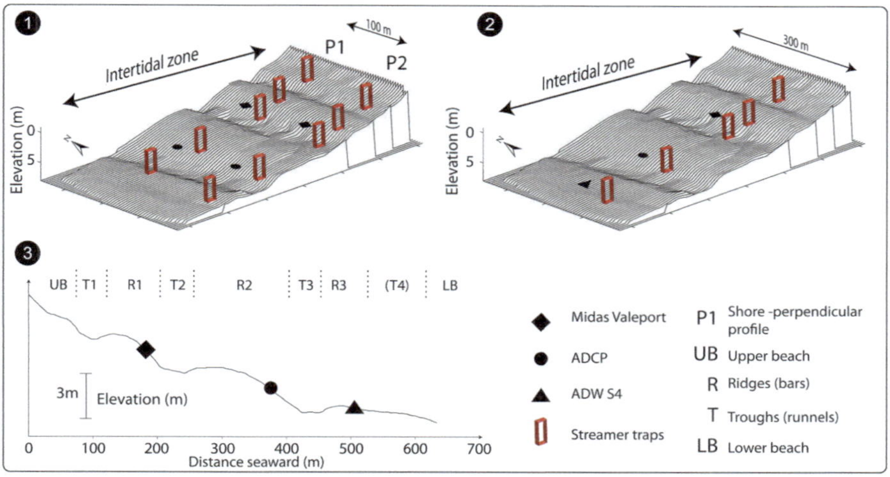

Fig. 9.3 Field methodology. (*1*) Field methodology during ZY08, WI09 and HA09, the sediment traps were deployed along two shore-perpendiculars transects with a spacing of about 100 m. (*2*) Field methodology during ZY09, WI10 and HA10. (*3*) Shore-perpendicular profile, hydrographic instruments are deployed on the stoss side on the intertidal bars. Codes refer to beach morphology where *UB* and *LB* are Upper and Lower Beach respectively; *R* and *T* correspond to ridges and troughs. Elevations are relative to French topographic datum (IGN69)

Each sediment flux measurement was obtained at a given point in the littoral zone and at a given time of a tidal cycle. The flux is integrated over the water column and expressed in $\mathrm{kg} \cdot \mathrm{s}^{-1} \cdot \mathrm{m}^{-1}$. Trapping was carried out in different directions in order to measure longshore, onshore and offshore sediment flux.

9.3 Model and Methodology

The sedimentary evolution is modeled under the action of the oblique incident waves and is coupled with different numerical tools dedicated to the other process involved in the near shore zone. We can mention the following modules:

The wave module takes into account the surge energy dissipation (hyperbolic equation of extended Berkhoff). The Artemis code (Agitation and Refraction with Telemac2d on a MIld Slope) solves the Berkhoff equation taken from Navier-Stokes equations with some other hypotheses (small wave steepness of the surface wave, small slope. . .).

The main results are, for every node of the mesh, the height, the phase and the incidence of the waves. Artemis can take into account the reflection and the refraction of waves on an obstacle, the bottom friction and the breakers. One of the difficulties with Artemis is that a fine mesh must be used to have good results whereas Telemac2d does not need such a fine mesh.

The hydrodynamic module calculates currents induced by means of the surge of the waves, from the concept of radiation constraints obtained according to the

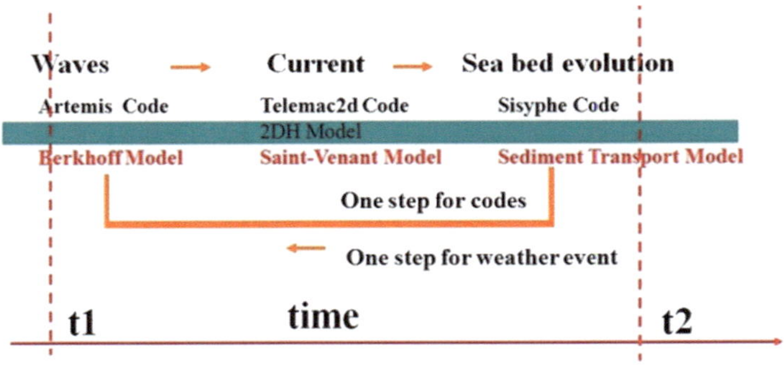

Fig. 9.4 Diagram of the model ATS (Artemis-Telemac-Sisyphe) loop over one weather event time step (between t1 and t2) used for our simulations

module of waves. Telemac2d is designed to simulate the free surface flow of water in coastal areas or in rivers. This code solves Barré Saint-Venant equations taken from Navier-Stokes equations vertically averaged.

Then, the main results are, for every node of the mesh, the water depth and the velocity averaged over the depth. Telemac2d is able to represent the following physical phenomena: propagation of long periodic waves, including non-linear effects, wetting and drying of intertidal zone, bed friction, turbulence,...

The sedimentary module integrates the combined actions of the waves and the wave currents (2D or 3D) on the transport of sediment Hervouet (2007).

The Sisyphe code solves the bottom evolution equation which expresses the mass conservation by directly using a current field result file given by Telemac2d (Fig. 9.4). Several of the most currently empirical or semi-empirical formulas are already integrated in Sisyphe. In this paper we show only the simulations with the Bijker formulas. The main results are, for every node of the mesh, the bottom evolution and the solid transport. The equations of the three modules are detailed in Hervouet (2007).

A hydrodynamic simplified model (called Multi1DH) uses the following assumptions: a random wave approach and a 1DH (cross-shore) direction. An offshore wave model (shoaling + bottom friction + wave asymmetry) is used with the break point estimation. The waves in the surf zone are modeled with the classic model of Svendsen (1984) with an undertow model (roller effect, Svendsen 1984; Dally et al. 1984). The longshore current model is the Longuet-Higgins's model (1970). The model is included in the Sysiphe code to calculate the sea bed evolution with several sediment transport formulas.

9.4 Results

We set up a procedure to use the coupled codes Artemis-Telemac2d-Sisyphe and more particularly we improved the treatment of the boundary conditions in order to be able to work on fields of calculations close to the coastal zone and equivalents in dimension for the three codes. The wave module grid is the same as the flow and morphodynamic grid. The waves are incidents on both the lateral and seaward boundaries of the grid. The lateral boundaries of the flow model are defined as zero water levels.

The morphological evolution in the near shore region, including its large-scale features, was first investigated using a combination of a commercial 2DH model (Camenen and Larroudé 2003a, b). Simulation of the wave-driven currents was carried out with Telemac, a finite elements model, and the Sisyphe sand transport module served to compute sediment transport rates and bed evolution. This methodology of morphodynamic modeling for sandy beaches was already improved in terms of mesh, time step and convergence in Camenen (2002), Larroudé and Camenen (2004) and in Falquès et al. (2008) and Larroudé (2008).

We first present results for Site 1 ("Plage de la Corniche"), focusing on the month of December 2008 and February 2009 for the validation and the first test of the different sediment transport formulas. During these months, we had two similar storms in term of significant wave height and period, but in December the outer bar moved offshore and during the storm of February this outer bar moved onshore (see Fig. 9.5a, b).

In the case of the February storm, the Multi1dh model reproduces very well the onshore migration of the bar with all the sediment transport formulas (Fig. 9.5b, d). On the opposite, the offshore migration that took place during the December storm is not so well simulated, but the results seem to be acceptable (Fig. 9.5a, c). For the

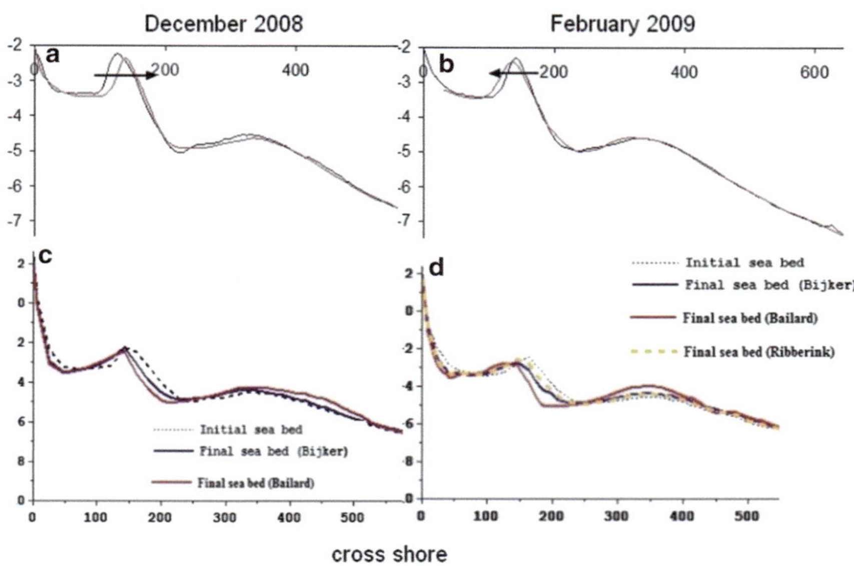

Fig. 9.5 Morphodynamic evolution at site 1 in December 2008 based on: (**a**) in situ measurements (initial bathymetry in *black*) and (**c**) simplified model Multi1DH and several sediment transport formulas, and in February 2009: (**b**) in situ measurements (initial bathymetry in *black*) and (**d**) simplified model Multi1DH and several sediment transport formulas

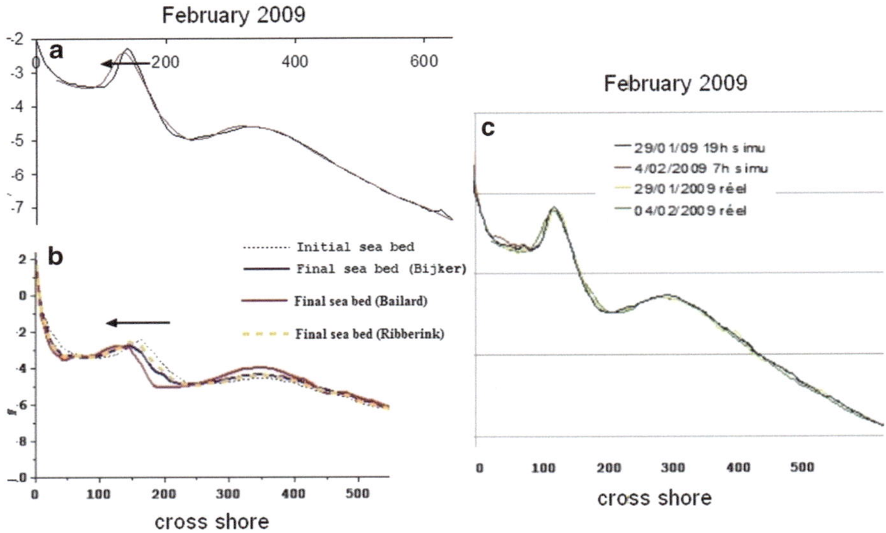

Fig. 9.6 Morphodynamic evolution at site 1 from the 29/01/09 to the 04/02/09, based on (**a**) in situ measurements (initial bathymetry in *black*), (**b**) simplified model Multi1DH and several sediment transport formulas, and (**c**) the 2DH model ATS

2DH model ATS, the modeling of the cross shore current (undertow) is missing. The results for both storms are thus not well representative as the model failed in simulating the cross-shore migration of these sand bars (Fig. 9.6).

Our results show that the different formulas of transport did not correctly reproduce what was observed in reality. During the storm of February, the onshore displacement of the inner bar was not represented by the majority of formulas. We can see through this case that the Bijker formula and Soulsby-Van Rijn overestimates sediment transport, while the other formulas underestimate it. The modeling of the December storm, however, shows that some formulas are more robust than others, the formulas of Ribberink, of Soulsby-Van Rijn and Egelund Hansen being the least robust. For the same storm, the Bijker formula seems to overestimate the sediment transport, while the Watanabe & Dibajnia formulae coded in the Sisyphe code has a tendency to overestimate the sediment flux when there are strong velocities (Fig. 9.7).

The purpose of the second part of the study is to compare the solution obtained with different sediment transport formulas directly with in situ measurements of sediment transport. We use a set of data obtain on the North Sea and the English Channel beaches.

There are three calculations per site with the formulas of Bijker, Einstein and Van Rijn with the first approach of simulation and there are two calculations per site with the formulas of Bijker and Dibajnia-Watanabe for the second numerical approach.

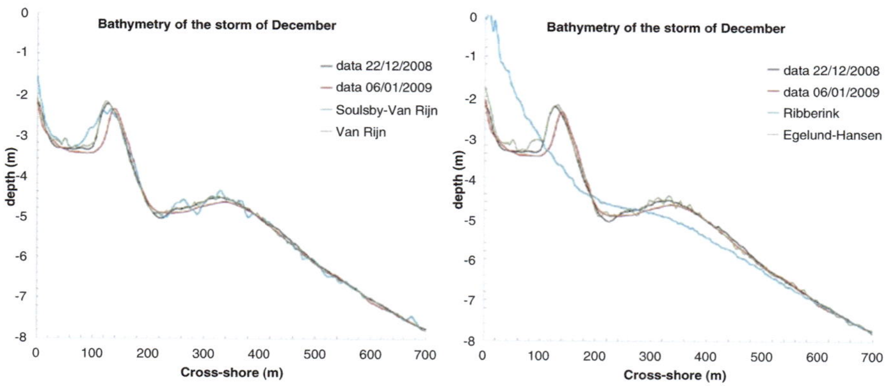

Fig. 9.7 Comparison of a cross shore profile evolution during the December storm at site 1 using different sediment transport formulae

Table 9.1 In-situ data (Zuydcoote) and simulated (second approach) longshore sediment fluxes

Date	Longshore Flux measured ($kg \cdot s^{-1} \cdot m^{-1}$)	Longshore Flux calculated ($kg \cdot s^{-1} \cdot m^{-1}$)
13/11/2008 15:50	4,25E-04	3,26E-03
14/11/2008 10:45	4,88E-04	1,11E-03
17/11/2008 13:17	9,99E-04	1,33E-03
24/11/2009 14:22	7,18E-02	2,74E-02
27/11/2009 12:07	8,22E-04	6,93E-04
30/11/2009 14:37	4,12E-04	5,17E-03
03/12/2009 11:22	6,60E-04	9,44E-04
06/12/2009 13:07	2,07E-03	3,79E-03

The difference between the first and second numerical approach is the way of taking into account the boundary conditions in term of velocity in the telemac2d code and using wave simulation results directly into some sediment transport formulae in Sisyphe code.

For the Hardelot and Wissant data, the comparison between measured and simulated sediment fluxes show that the first approach gives better results, but for Zuydcoote it seems that the second approach is more appropriate, (see Table 9.1 and Fig. 9.8).

The results obtained with the other formulas show that there is often an order of magnitude between in-situ and computed data which demonstrate that although these early tests are interesting further work is still needed to improve sediment transport modeling in these macrotidal environments (see Figs. 9.9 and 9.10).

All the numerical results are taken in the middle of the simulation domain between the beach and the offshore boundary. Our results show that there is no

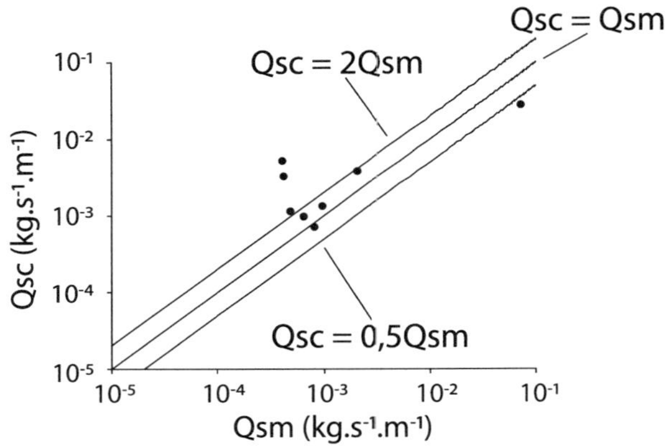

Fig. 9.8 In-situ data Qsm (Zuydcoote) and simulated Qsc (second approach) longshore sediment fluxes (Data from Table 9.1)

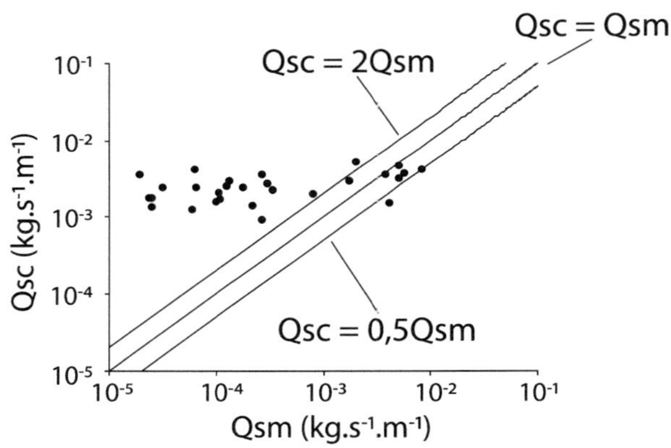

Fig. 9.9 In -situ data Qsm (Hardelot) and simulated Qsc (first approach, with Bijker) longshore sediment fluxes (depth = 1 m)

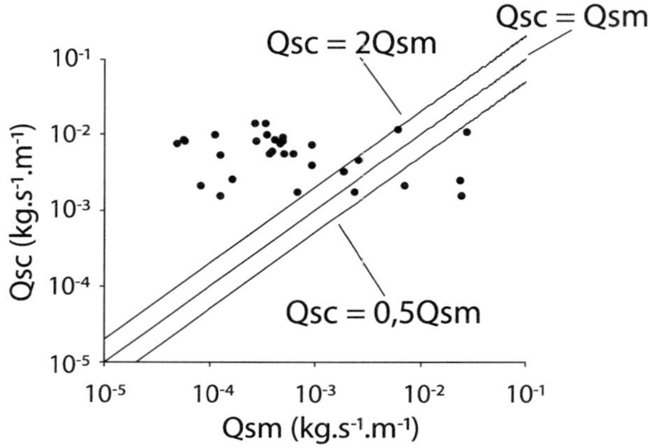

Fig. 9.10 In-situ data Qsm (Wissant) and simulated Qsc (first approach, with Van Rijn) longshore sediment fluxes

variation in the calculated flux with Bijker or Van Rijn on respectively Hardelot and Wissant beaches, while the measured sediment flux varies greatly (see Figs. 9.9 and 9.10).

The sediment traps mainly collecting sediments transported in suspension, the next step of this study will be to de-couple the suspended and bed load transport calculation in the different sediments transport formulas to compare only the suspended fluxes in the North Sea and English Channel beaches data. The second improvement will be to reach a better precision on the velocity field.

Measured sediment fluxes (Qsm) have been compared with calculated fluxes (Qsc) using the formulas of Bijker (1968), Soulsby (1997) and Van Rijn (1993) (noted SVR97). It is generally accepted that the estimate is acceptable when the flux is between 0.5 and 2 times the in situ measurement (Camenen and Larroudé 2003a, b). Thus, in the following figures (Figs. 9.11 and 9.12), three lines symbolize the extent of data that are significant at 0.5 Qsm < Qsc <2 Qsm. The standard error (S_{rms}) was also calculated using the following equation (Eq. 9.1) to characterize the dispersion of data, where the higher the values, the higher the data are scattered.

$$S_{rms} = \sqrt{\frac{\sum_{i=1}^{N} [Log(Qsc) - Log(Qsm)]^2}{N-2}} \tag{9.1}$$

where Qsc is the flux calculated, Qsm the measured flux and N the number value.

Sediment flux measurements were performed in a water depth between 1 and 1.5 m, and because of the excursion of the tide, these measurements were made at several locations on the foreshore. The calculation of sediment load in the same place in the field and in the field requires a lot of computer manipulations. So initially, the sediment loads are modeled fluxes in the middle of the digital domain. The water level in the middle of the simulated field rarely matches the water level measured during sampling. A test was therefore carried out to assess the potential effects of water depth on computed sediment flux using the data measured during the two field experiments at Hardelot beach (2009 and 2010). For the numerical simulations, we assumed that the bathymetry was stable during and between the two field campaigns.

The following graphs show the control of the water level on the accuracy of modeled flux (Fig. 9.11). The example is based on calculations based on the expression of Bijker (1968), similar observations having been observed for the other formulations. The results show that sediment fluxes tend to be better estimated with decreasing water depth, which is consistent with the depths at which measurements were made. The correlations are even better in a layer of water just below the water level of the in situ measurement (<1 m).

In a water depth between 2.70 and 1.74 m, the values seem to line up around $1 \times 10^{-3}\ \mathrm{kg \cdot s^{-1} \cdot m^{-1}}$. There is very little change in calculated flux in comparison with those measured in situ. As soon as the water level is similar to that of measurement at the time of trapping (1.51 m), the distribution of points tends to align the right Qsc = Qsm. However when the water column is much lower than

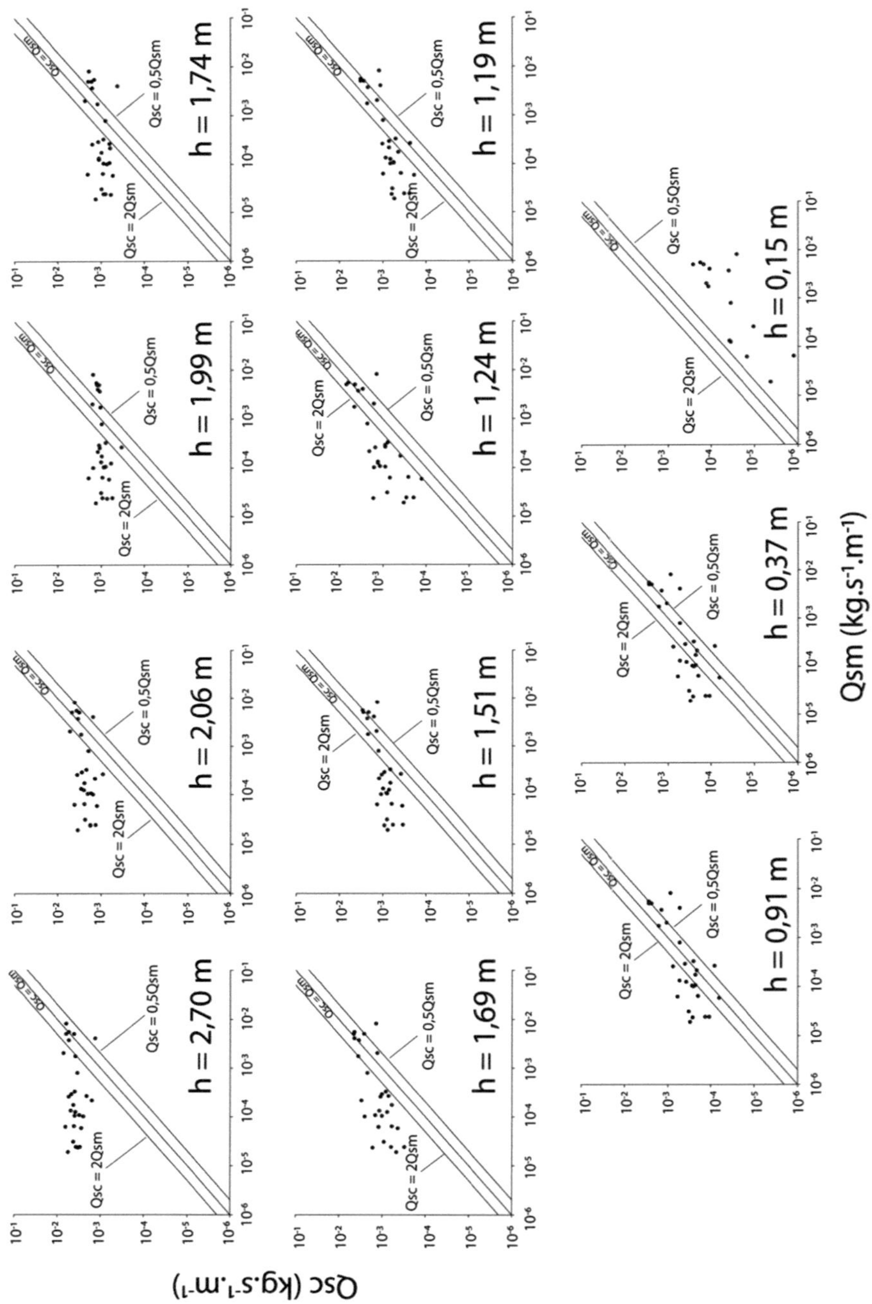

Fig. 9.11 Comparison between measured (Q_{sm}) and computed (Qsc) transport rates using Bijker's formula (1968) for different water depths

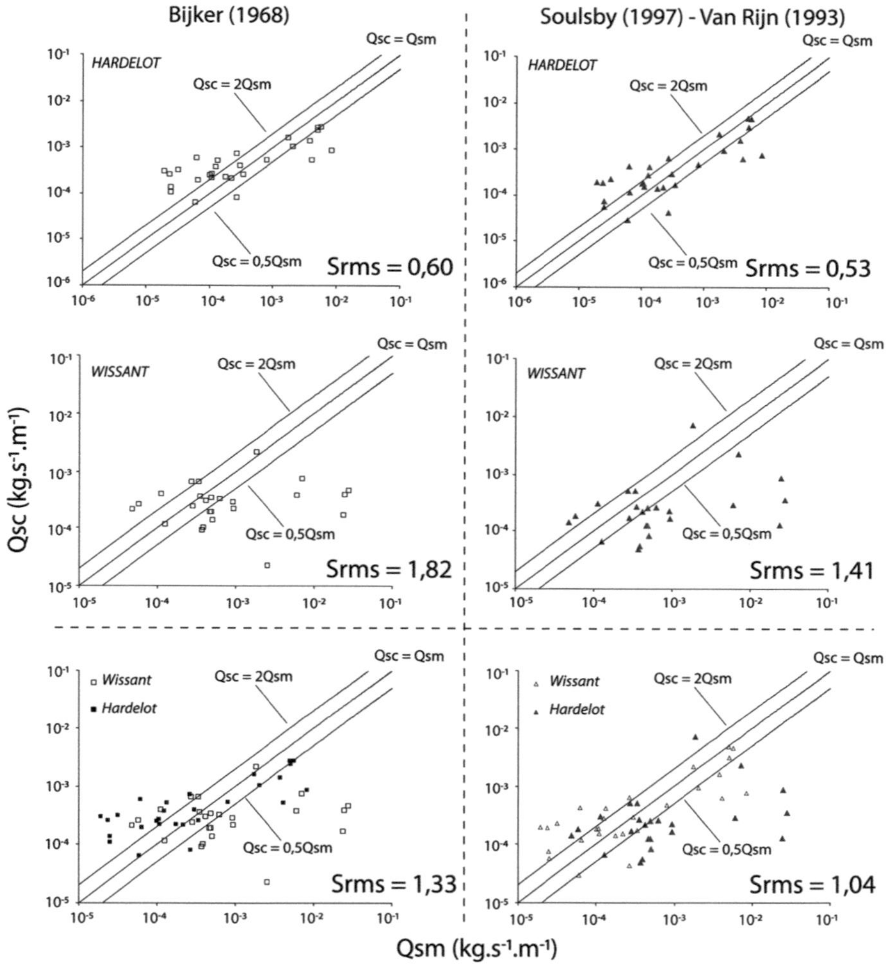

Fig. 9.12 Comparisons between in situ (Q_{sm}) sand transport rate measured during HA09, HA10, WI09 and WI10, with calculated sediment fluxes(Q_{sc}) following Bijker and Soulsby – Van Rijn's formulae

reality, many errors appear in the calculation and the estimation of sediment flux becomes completely false. In fact, the RMS errors are quite high when the water level is far from the actual water depth (Fig. 9.11). It should be emphasized, however with all the initial approximations, the mere fact of positioning the water level at the same level as during the sampling resulted in relatively better results. In particular, when h = 0.91 m, which resulted in a percentage of acceptable values of 32 %. Overall calculated sediment fluxes are nevertheless generally overestimated.

The water level acts directly on the current profile and associated sediment transport mechanisms. Thus, when the water column is higher than that at the time of measurement, the transport in suspension is favored in the modeling, leading to an overestimation of the integrated flux in the water column. In contrast, a shallower water column could lead to higher sediment fluxes due to increased bed shear. However, it appears that the formulas are struggling to express sediment transport in very shallow water. Despite very simplified initial conditions, the results obtained in this study show that the coupling of these three codes is not so far from reality when we take into account the water level measured in situ. More precise calibrations will likely improve the accuracy of the results in the future.

Using the water levels measured during the field experiments, the calculations of sediment transport were calibrated for each case to be as close as possible to the in situ measurement. Sediment transport modeling was carried out on the beaches of Wissant and Hardelot, and sediment loads calculated by some formulas have been extracted and compared to field data. The calculations concerning the location Zuydcoote are not presented because of problems related to the computational domain. Indeed, the bathymetry input is not broad enough, and the waves spread by the code Artemis then undergo many artifacts and measurement errors do not allow for the time being, sediment transport calculation.

Sediment fluxes were then compared with the expressions of Bijker (1968), Soulsby (1997) and Van Rijn (1993) (noted SVR97) (Fig. 9.12). The results were analyzed according to the study site and the mathematical expression used. The results are better on the site of Hardelot for both formulas, the error Srms being indeed less than 1.0 with a minimum of 0.53 with SVR97. Moreover, the percentage of significant values reaches 32 and 46 % for SVR97 and BI68, respectively. On the site of Wissant, it does not exceed 30 % whatever the formula. RMS errors also result in a greater dispersion of data readily observable in the graphs (Fig. 9.12). When considering all the data, the formula for SVR97 is the expression that is most satisfactory with a Srms of only 1.04 and 36 % of acceptable values. The formula of van Rijn (1993) in the first parametric analysis had already appeared most appropriate to calculate the sediment discharge.

The proportion of sediment flux of low intensities ($<1 \times 10^{-3}\ \mathrm{kg \cdot s^{-1} \cdot m^{-1}}$) is higher during the campaigns carried out in Hardelot than those held in Wissant. Conversely, the flux measurements acquired during the field investigations in the Bay of Wissant proved to be higher. Morphological changes were also more significant in Wissant than during the campaigns conducted in Hardelot.

The Bijker formula generally tends to underestimate the sediment transport when there is interaction of waves and current (Camenen and Larroudé 2000), which is generally the case in the coastal zone. This formula takes into account only the swell as a term of suspended sediment. Therefore, when the swell is important, and if the average current is low, the sediment load will remain insignificant. Even if the current is usually related to the conditions of agitation, it may sometimes be forced by the wind or induced by the combination of tidal currents and those generated by the incident swell. The suspended particles are then provided by currents and waves. The results show, however, that the higher sediment fluxes ($>1 \times 10^{-3}\ \mathrm{kg \cdot s^{-1} \cdot m^{-1}}$) are underestimated, which may be due to low wave height and mean current that are powerful enough to induce a strong transport, which cannot be modeled by this expression. Conversely, the lowest sediment transport rates occur when the swell and the mean current are of low intensity. The direction of tidal currents is also directly involved in the magnitude of the sediment flux since it can easily reduce or conversely increase, the currents induced by waves depending on the phase of the tidal cycle and the direction of the longshore current. Such types of case are not considered in the model, however, which may explain a part of the variability observed between measured and computed sediment fluxes.

The formula of Soulsby-Van Rijn comes from the coupling of the Van Rijn (1993) formula with an expression modeling the transport in suspension. It takes into account many physical parameters for estimating the bed load and suspension. Although the calculations are more complicated and time consuming, the estimate is generally better, but significant errors may occur when the wave direction is opposite to that of the current (Camenen and Larroudé 2000). In this study, the results are particularly satisfactory for the data obtained during the fields campaigns at Hardelot (Fig. 9.12). When taking into account all values, it clearly appears that the most significant fluxes can be largely underestimated since some values may be up to four times lower than the measured transport rates. During conditions of high agitation, the morphology and roughness of the bottom change rapidly due to an increase in bed load sediment transport. The impact of these bed changes on the distribution of sediment in the water column is crucial and plays an important role in the mechanisms of suspended sediment transport. Because bed roughness is variable, largely depending on the local morphology of the beach, it is necessary to incorporate changes in beach morphology in the process of calculation which has not been done yet in this first approach.

9.5 Conclusions

We used a 2DH morphodynamic model to simulate the evolution of linear sandy beaches, these investigations being aimed to better define the response of these coastal landforms to storm event. We have calibrated our numerical methodology of simulation against in situ measurements. The first results are good in terms of comparison with in-situ data regarding the hydrodynamic and morphodynamic parameters. This work was based on different scenarios of wave classes, storm occurrence frequency, etc... We have had to simulate all these configurations to identify the sensitivity of rising-apex-waning of the storm. Our methodology of simulation and the complementarily of both models allowed us to test the various configuration of storms to understand the results derived from the in-situ data.

Acknowledgements This work has been supported by French Research National Agency (ANR) through the Vulnerability Milieu and Climate program (project VULSACO, n° ANR-06-VMC-009), RELIEF MICROLIT and the CNRS PLAMAR project. We highly appreciate the constructive discussions with D. Idier, (BRGM, Orléans, France), Raphaël Certain and Nicolas Robin from the University of Perpignan.

References

Bijker E (1968) Littoral drift as function of waves and current. In: 11th coastal engineering conference proceedings, ASCE, London, UK, pp 415–435
Camenen B (2002) Modélisation numérique du transport sédimentaire sur une plage sableuse. PhD thesis, Université Joseph Fourier, Grenoble, 298 p
Camenen B, Larroude´ P (2000) Numerical comparison of sediment transport formulae. In: Sandwave dynamics workshop, Lille, France, pp 37–42
Camenen B, Larroudé P (2003a) Comparison of sediment transport formulae for a coastal environment. J Coast Eng 48:111–132
Camenen B, Larroudé P (2003b) Un modèle morphologique côtier pour la création de barres rythmiques, Revue française de génie civil. Génie côtier 7:1099–1116
Cartier A, Héquette A (2011a) Estimation of longshore and cross-shore sediment transport on sandy macrotidal beaches of northern France. Proceedings coastal sediment 11', 7th international symposium of coastal engineering, Miami, Etats-Unis, 2–6 mai 2011, pp 2130–2143
Cartier A, Héquette A (2011b) Variation in longshore sediment transport under low to moderate conditions on barred macrotidal beaches. J Coast Res SI64:45–49
Certain R (2002) Morphodynamique d'une côte sableuse microtidale à barres: le golfe du Lion (Languedoc-Roussillon). PhD thesis, University of Perpignan, 199 pp
Certain R, Barusseau JP (2006) Conceptual modelling of straight sand bars morphodynamics for a microtidal beach (Gulf of Lions, France), ICCE 2006, San Diego
Dally WR, Dean RG, Dalrymple RA (1984) A model for breaker decay on beaches. In: 19th coastal engineering conference proceedings. ASCE, New York, pp 82–88
De Vriend HJ (1987) 2DH mathematical modelling of morphological evolutions in shallow water. Coast Eng 11:1–27
De Vriend HJ, Stive MJF (1987) Quasi-3D modelling of nearshore currents. Coast Eng 11:565–601
Falques A, Dodd N, Garnier R, Ribas F, MacHardy LC, Sancho F, Larroudé P, Calvete D (2008) Rhythmic surf zone bars and morphodynamic self-organization. Coast Eng 55:622–641
Hervouet JM (2007) Hydrodynamics of free surface flows: modelling with the finite element method. Wiley, Chichester, 360 p
Kraus NC (1987) Application of portable traps for obtaining point measurements of sediment transport rates in the surf zone. J Coast Res 3:139–152
Larroudé P (2008) Methodology of seasonal morphological modelisation for nourishment strategies on a Mediterranean beach. Mar Pollut Bull 57:45–52
Larroudé Ph, Camenen B (2004) 2DH and multi1DH morphological model for medium term evolution of large scale features and nourishment in the nearshore region: application to TrucVert and Corniche beach (France) and la Barrosa beach (Spain). In: 29th international conference on coastal engineering, ASCE, Lisbon
Longuet Higgins MS (1970) Longshore currents generated by obliquely incident sea waves. J Geophys Res 75(33):60778–60801
Robin N, Certain R, Godon C, Aleman N, Gervais M, Bouchette F, Meule S, Jean-Paul Barusseau JP, Ferrer P, Balouin Y, Brambila E (2010) Caractérisation des profils de courants pendant des événements de tempête sur une plage à barre rectiligne en milieu microtidal, doi:10.5150/jngcgc.2010.014-R, pp 113–120
Sipka V, Anthony EJ (1999) Morphology and hydrodynamics of a macrotidal ridge and runnel beach under modal low conditions. Journal de Recherche Océanographique 24:25–31
Smit MWJ, Reniers AJHM, Ruessink BG, Roelvink JA (2008) The morphological response of a nearshore double sandbar system to constant wave forcing. Coast Eng 55:761–770
Soulsby R (1997) Dynamics of marine sands, a manual for practical applications. Thomas Telford/H.R. Wallingford, London/Wallingford. ISBN 0-7277-2584X
Svendsen IA (1984) Mass flux and undertow in the surf zone. Coast Eng 8:347–365
Van Rijn L (1993) Principles of sediment transport in rivers, estuaries and coastal seas. Aqua Publications, Amsterdam

Part IV
Extremes, Events and Sediment Fluxes: The Case of Tsunamis

Chapter 10
Tsunami Deposits and Their Morphological Effects: A Regional Scale Approach

Hervé Regnauld and Giuseppe Mastronuzzi

Abstract Tsunami are high energy events which have heavy morphological impacts on the shore lines. A review of the literature shows that these impacts are very difficult to differentiate from large storms impacts in most of the cases. This paper begins with a description of tsunami impacts, at a local scale, in terms of erosion and of accumulation. It studies cases where tsunami accelerate "normal" behaviour of the coast or, on the other hand go against expected normal behaviour. In order to better understand the relative roles of tsunamis and storms, the local forms are replaced within a regional scale/context and some important regions (Mediterranean Sea, New Zealand, the Antilles) are taken as examples of the interrelation between storm-forced evolution and tsunami – controlled behaviour.

10.1 Introduction

Tsunami deposits, both ancient and modern, have been widely studied all over the world and the literature concerning them is now somewhat extensive. Some of the most comprehensive recent review papers are those of Bourgeois (2009) and Goff et al. (2012). They explain the unusual imprint of tsunami deposits caused by their unique flow characteristics and interactions with the nearshore and coastal environment. While some tsunamis can have extreme run-up heights, such as the 1958 Lituya Bay tsunami that reached over 520 masl (Miller 1960), others affect coastlines in ways similar to that of extreme storms.

Whatever the features of the deposits may be, from mud and organics, to thin sandy-layers interbedded in muddy lagoons, to the largest megaboulders – many

H. Regnauld (✉)
Laboratoire Costel UMR 6554 LETG et IFR Caren, Université de Rennes 2, Rennes, France

UMR CNRS 6554 LETG, Université de Rennes 2, Rennes, France
e-mail: herve.regnauld@uhb.fr

G. Mastronuzzi
Dipartimento di Scienze della Terra e Geoambientali, Università degli Studi "Aldo Moro", Bari, Italy

M. Maanan, M. Robin (eds.), *Sediment Fluxes in Coastal Areas*,
Coastal Research Library 10, DOI 10.1007/978-94-017-9260-8_10

papers have focussed on the identification of tsunamis deposits, in order not to confuse them with those of severe storms or hurricanes (e.g. Dawson 1994; Goff et al. 2001, 2004, 2010a, b, 2012; Tuttle et al. 2004; Williams and Hall 2004; Mastronuzzi et al. 2006; Bourrouilh-Le Jan et al. 2007; Kortekaas and Dawson 2007; Perez-Torrado et al. 2006; De Martini et al. 2003, 2010; Goto et al. 2009a, b; Chagué-Goff et al. 2011).

Some deposits are easier than others to identify as having been laid down by tsunamis. Gravel pavements on top of high sand dunes (Nichol et al. 2003a, b, 2004; Regnauld et al. 2004, 2008a, b) for instance, are excellent indicators of a tsunami wave which collects coarse beach material and lays it down well above storm wave height on top of back barrier dunes. These deposits are easily distinguished from storm fans, which are found at lower elevations and indicate reworking by successive waves. Many other deposits are on the other hand difficult to assign unequivocally to either a storm or a tsunami.

Large blocks or mega clasts have long been used as tsunami proxies but several recent studies indicate the ambiguity of this line of evidence. In many cases such clasts have been reworked by storms, indicating that they could also have been deposited by such events in the first place (e.g. Mastronuzzi and Sansò 2004; Switzer and Burston 2010; Regnauld et al. 2010; Barbano et al. 2010; Goto et al. 2010a). They may be said to be polygenic. In order to try and determine whether they are storm or tsunami boulders many authors have used a series of equations which take into account the difference in energy regime between the two processes (Noji et al. 1985; Nott 1997, 2003, 2004; Noormets et al. 2002, 2004; Imamura et al. 2008). These approaches are based on a physical model which describes how the wave lifts and drags clasts landwards. These equations have been further developed (Pignatelli et al. 2009; Piscitelli et al. 2009; Engel and May 2012) and have reached a point where they may well be able to separate storm and tsunami boulders, but they are not fool-proof (Regnauld et al. 2010). Some storm deposits comprise blocks that are similar to those laid down by tsunamis (Hall et al. 2006; Hansom et al. 2008). This is simply because some extreme storms have waves which can be more than 18 m high (Cariolet et al. 2010), may displace blocks up to 42 tons (Fichaut and Suanez 2010) and build cliff top deposits with mega clasts (cliff-top storm deposit(s) = CTSDs; Hansom et al. 2008).

In the case of coarse grained layers interbedded into back barrier marshes, tsunamis and storms are not always easy to differentiate either (Bruzzi and Prone 2000; Haslett and Bryant 2007; Paris et al. 2009; Wassmer and Gomez 2011; Shiki et al. 2008). Goff et al. (2012) highlight that in the case of geomorphological features "*there is room for confusion in areas of low accommodation space (e.g. in a small pocket beach, there may be insufficient longshore and landward space for more than one lobate fan and two pedestals)*". Equally however, Goff et al. (2012) stress that "*Integration of geological proxies with biological, chemical, geomorphological, archaeological, anthropological and contextual data, as well as with numerical modelling offers greater scope for not only identifying older events, but also assessing their magnitude.*" The point being that used together, multiple proxies can not only differentiate between storms and tsunamis, but can also go beyond that to determine the magnitude of events. Some of the most interesting developments are therefore being made in multi-proxy studies.

Accepting this state of the science, some authors have tackled the problem of tsunami deposits from another point of view. They do not focus on one single deposit but study a whole region where tsunamis occur and try to determine how the regional setting controls the type of tsunami impacts and deposits. They do not think there is a typical type of tsunami signature *per se* but that tsunamis deposit a large range of sediments and sediment patterns which depend mainly on the regional context and sediment sources (e.g. Goff et al. 2011). This context-based approach seems to be the most satisfactory one at the moment. This way of studying the sedimentological and morphological imprint of past tsunami allows: (i) – the identification of the full extent of an inundated coastline, (ii) – the reconstruction of the sequence of tsunami waves; (iii) – the evaluation of the inland extent of inundation. Understanding these types of data is useful for assessing local tsunami hazard and vulnerability and adds underpinning information for coastal planning. Knowing these points (i, ii and iii) is vital for the development of site specific hydrodynamic models capable of predicting the limit of future inundations. All these data are important for determining an integrated coastal zone management (ICZM) plan, for post-tsunami disaster management, and for general emergency management plans.

This paper discusses morphological effects due to unambiguous tsunamis and later focuses on regional scale issues. In some regions, tsunamis occur but play almost no role in coastal evolution, in others coastal evolution is forced by tsunamis.

10.2 Tsunamis as Local Events Shaping Local Features

The main morphological effects of tsunamis are three-fold. First, tsunamis tend to erode parts of the coastline. Second, they tend to deposit new material and build new features. These two actions are linked as the building up of a new form often occurs with the material that has just been eroded. Third, in some cases, tsunamis halt morphological evolution. They do not erode, they do not actually build a new form, but rather they lay down deposits which act as non-depositional surfaces or by- passing sites (e.g. Morton et al. 2008a).

10.2.1 Erosive Effects

There are numerous erosive effects. A tsunami may affect the nearshore area destroying coral reefs or platforms (Moore et al. 2006). In this case the waves act first by destroying the front of the reef and second by dragging debris onto the top of the reef platform, creating furrows or trenches orientated towards the coast. These processes have been recognised as one of the main impacts of the Indian Ocean Tsunami (IOT) 2004 at Pakarang Cape, Thailand (Goto et al. 2007). Similar evidence of this type was noted on Ishigaki Island (Ryukyu Islands, Japan) and ascribed to the Meiwa (1771 AD) and Melija (1836 AD) tsunamis (Goto et al. 2010b). In the latter case for example, a 200 ton coralline boulder was deposited about 20 masl. These processes continue landward as the water column inundating the coast contains much coarse and fine debris, which act on the beach/ dune system as sand paper on a block of wood. In the marshes the impacts are less important as the bottom on which the tsunami waves move is flat and more plastic.

The erosion phase continues when the tsunami water returns seaward. This can often lead to the formation of notable erosional features, normally associated with topographic lows where the water is preferentially channelled. Recent work by Bujalesky (2012) describes how two different tsunamis eroded a large paraglacial gravel beach at La Colonia Bay, Tierra del Fuego, Argentina. The beach consists of a large gravel ridge fed by longshore drift from the neighbouring headlands. At one point on the ridge a huge wash-over fan has been emplaced by waves that exceeded the height on all known storm fans in the region. Ground Penetrating Radar profiles taken across this part of the ridge show deep erosive scars buried below the huge fan. Bujalesky (2012) states:

> "*In this setting, a tsunami backwash could generate megavortexes in the nearshore zone of the bay linked to the depressed areas of the abrasion platform. The combined action of large seepage, tsunami backwash currents, and tangential currents of the vortex applied on saturated gravel beaches would cause carving of the lower section of the beach and instability of the entire profile. Then collapses of relevant volumes of gravel and sand would lead to the formation of semicircular erosive scarps.*" In this site the tsunami is a very possible cause for these scars even if big storms cannot be absolutely rules out.

While the nature of the physical processes involved is conjectural, this type of erosion of soft sediment coastal features has been reported for both palaeotsunamis and historical events from several sandy coastlines (e.g. New Zealand: Goff et al. 2008, 2011; Sri Lanka: Morton et al. 2008a).

Other workers (e.g. Mastronuzzi and Sansò 2000, 2004; Mastronuzzi et al. 2006) describe different types of erosive processes. These relate to the tsunami-impacted limestone coastal platforms of southern Italy. Large isolated or clustered groups of boulders, sometimes stacked, are reported up to 4 m asl (present sea level). The sources for these boulders have been traced back to the edge of the platform and from this information, coupled with the weight and shape of the displaced blocks, researchers have attempted to determine the magnitude of the tsunami waves required to erode and entrain the clasts (Mastronuzzi and Sansò 2000, 2004; Mastronuzzi et al. 2006).

Figure 10.1 shows some of these blocks on the coast of Puglia, close to Torre Santa Sabina (Carovigno, Brindisi) ascribed to the impact of two different tsunamis; the first in 1676 was generated by the Dubrovnik (today Croatia) earthquake, whereas the second relates to the Otranto Channel earthquakes of the winter

Fig. 10.1 Boulder accumulation at Torre Santa Sabina, near Brindisi (Puglia, Italy)

of 1743. Others boulders have been scattered inland by more recent exceptional storms like those that occurred in the winter of 2003 (Mastronuzzi and Sansò 2004).

These limestone blocks were initially below sea level (submerged) and have been eroded from the front of the coastal platform and entrained inland by probable tsunami waves. As they originate from a limestone layer fractured by tectonics, they tend to be shaped as long, narrow and flat blocks and may be moved more easily than rounded boulders. Because of this morphology, in the equations describing the physical forces that lift and drag the block inland, Pignatelli et al. (2009) have highlighted the importance of the lift as opposed to the drag coefficient. This shows that physical models must be developed to take into account the local morphological characteristics of the eroded site as opposed to being applied generically to any situation. It is also not enough to reduce the lithology to a simple density value. The shape of the site and of the local clasts is an important control for fine tuning the general model. High resolution digital surveys can provide such information and be used to improve the application of the appropriate hydrodynamic models (Pignatelli et al. 2009, 2010; Piscitelli et al. 2009).

10.2.2 Tsunamis Building New Landforms

Tsunamis are also able to build new landforms especially by re-depositing landward the material they have eroded from the intertidal zone or coastal fringe

Fig. 10.2 Marsh filled by the 1883 Krakatau tsunami, with an isolated boulder (2 m high) in the middle (Carita, West Java Island)

(e.g. Fig. 10.2). The simplest forms are layers of debris and sediment deposited out of the water column. Wassmer and Gomez (2011) used the anisotropy of magnetic susceptibility to show that waves from the 2004 Indian Ocean Tsunami deposited five different layers of sediment. The first wave deposited a sheet of sand in the back barrier marshes. This sand was sourced mainly from the coastal dunes. Overlying this material was a fining upward sequence of sediment that had settled out of the water column as the tsunami moved inland and then returned to the sea as backwash. Two further incoming waves laid down distinct sediment layers. Wassmer and Gomez (2011) calculated that the sediment laid down by the first wave amounted to about 45 % of the total deposit. This input did not really create a new landform *per se* but it contributed significantly to the infilling of a pre-existing wetland system. In a similar context, Moore et al. (2011) developed a model that links the settling velocity of the largest grain in the water column with tsunami inundation distance. The model is used to calculate the thickness of the water column and the speed of the first incoming wave. Thickness values of 3–5 m coupled with speeds of about 5–6 m/s are common for tsunami deposits.

Most interesting are forms which differ markedly from the pre-existing topography. Some of the most spectacular are large washover forms resembling a tidal delta flowing into a lagoon. Such forms have been studied by Mastronuzzi and

Fig. 10.3 Tsunami-laid delta into a lagoon, north of Lefkada Island, Adriatic Sea

Sanso (2012) along the Adriatic coast of Puglia (south Italia) and are also reported from Greece (Vött et al. 2006) (Fig. 10.3). The basic process is similar to that described by Wassmer and Gomez (2011) but with deposition taking place into a lagoon as opposed to a marsh. The first wave erodes the dune barrier and deposits the sand in a form of an elongated, landward tidal delta. The main difference is that there is no recognisable backwash as the excess water may be ponded in the lagoon, or exit through the lagoon entrance. There is therefore, no seaward erosional scar with any subsequent waves continuing to rework the delta and extend it inland.

One of the best known forms of tsunami construction are block fields or boulder barriers. Tsunamis detach blocks from the submarine zone or from the emerged platform and pile them inland in groups, ramparts or clusters. Some of the best example have been found where a tsunami struck an archaeological site, with written sources detailing block displacements. In Algeria, Maouche et al. (2009) studied large blocks displaced inland from the coast and were able to identify two possible tsunamis. ^{14}C ages of the blocks indicate two possible events dated to about 400 AD and 1700 AD. There were three historical tsunamis around 1700 AD that are likely candidates, but there are no known tsunamis for the 400 AD event.

A similar coastal landform has been recognised along the southernmost coasts of Puglia close to Otranto (Lecce). There a ~2.5 km long boulder berm has been ascribed to the tsunami generated by the 1743 AD earthquake on ^{14}C age determinations on marine bioclasts, shell and archaeological remains, with the epicentre localized in the Otranto Channel near the Ionian Islands (Mastronuzzi et al. 2007).

When boulders fields are located in a site where no archaeological proxy or archival documents are available the only way to differentiate between storm blocks and tsunami blocks is to apply one of the available models. The most famous one by Nott (2003) is ambiguous and needs to be locally tuned (see above in the

Fig. 10.4 A storm on the Island of Ushant (24 Feb 2010, waves of about 7–10 m –significant height- between 12 PM and 14 PM, surge estimated to about 1 m above high tide level) with an up rush moving blocks landward, some over one ton heavy

Puglian case in Italy). Therefore there is always a large discussion about the real ability of a model to decide between a storm deposit and a tsunami deposit (Fig. 10.4). In the Island of Ushant (western France) two storms in 2008 and 2010 are known to have moved blocks that according to models, should be thought of as tsunami blocks, may be the Lisboa one (1765) (Regnauld et al. 2010).

10.2.3 Non Deposition Topographies

The third type of tsunami features are bypassing surfaces. They freeze the morphological evolution. They have been described in New Zealand (Nichol et al. 2003a, b, 2004) and in the Falkland Islands (Regnauld et al. 2008a, b). They are sheet deposits one gravel thick (Figs. 10.5 and 10.6)

These types of deposits are very curious because they top eolian dunes with gravel, transported from the submarine beach offshore. The tsunami probably acts as a sheet flood incorporating the gravels and when this thin layer of water flows over the dune, the water seeps into the sand and the gravels are laid with a clear fining landward sorting. Once this gravel pavement is laid, the sand blown from the shore to the dune does not accumulate on it and the dune doesn't pile up any sand any more. The gravel create a real non deposition surface or a by passing surface

Fig. 10.5 Top of a dune barrier covered by a sheet of rounded gravel (Falkland, Pebble Island)

Fig. 10.6 Close up on the gravel layer. There are never two gravels on top of each other and the sheet is uniformly one gravel thick, although not all gravels are alike. On this photo the largest ones are about 10 cm long whereas the small ones are about 2–4 cm

and they fossilize the topography at the height it had on the day of the event. Of course as the sand by-passes the pavement a new set of dune piles up landward and ^{14}C dates show they are post tsunami constructions.

These elementary tsunami forms are relatively easy to understand if they are recent or present. As soon as they are discovered in cores or cross sections, ambiguity arises. In their review paper Goff et al. (2012) declare namely that

> However, defining whether a deposit relates to a palaeotsunami as opposed to palaeostorm is far more complex and can only be achieved convincingly through a multidisciplinary approach using a suite of proxies

This clearly begs for a multi-disciplinary approach in which tectonics, archaeology and other sciences are inter fingering in order to study the tsunami risks in a definite area.

10.3 Tsunami as "Forming Forces" at a Regional Scale

Tsunami imprints and deposits have to be understood in a regional context. This new phase in tsunami studies is not equally developed everywhere. It was first discussed by Goff and McFagden (2001, 2002), who stated that tsunamis were part of a series of processes "forcing" or driving coastal evolution. This was intended as a way to stress the importance of solitary and extreme events on coastal evolution instead of the usually accepted theory according to which coasts were in equilibrium with average weather conditions. The best known regions for testing this interesting hypothesis are the Antilles, the Mediterranean Sea and the coasts of New Zealand. In the Mediterranean Sea the context is relatively simpler than in the other places as tsunamis and earthquakes are, by far, more efficient than storms (Mastronuzzi et al. 2006), although human pressures are highly important. In the Antilles tsunami deposits may be mistaken with hurricane deposits and the local context is more ambiguous. At least in New Zealand, no hurricanes occur but extreme storms cannot be ruled out.

10.3.1 The Mediterranean Sea: Anthropogenic Pressures, Tsunamis and Earthquakes as Forming Forces?

A recent multi-proxy study by De Martini et al. (2010) found evidence for at least six tsunamis that hit the SE coast of Sicily in the last 4,000 years, including the ca. 3600 BP Santorini, 365 AD Crete and other paleo- and historical events. Using a similar multi-proxy approach with an emphasis on foraminifera assemblages, Smedile et al. (2011) were then able to identify up to 12 tsunami deposits in offshore sedimentary sequences, including some that were probably not preserved on land, such as the Messina and Reggio event of December 28, 1908, and other historical and palaeo-tsunamis. Both studies provided new information about the recurrence interval of tsunamis in that region.

Moreover, Mastronuzzi and Sansò (2012) have summarized more than one decade of field work and studies in a paper that deals with the coastal evolution of a large part of the Adriatic coasts of Puglia. Significant stretches of this coast are similar to that shown in Fig. 10.7.

The coast itself is a limestone platform which leads inland to limestone hills making headlands and limestone karstic valleys creating embayments. Figure 10.7 shows in the foreground the limestone hill being dissected by karstic processes (lappiaz in this precise case). In the middle ground a set of two little embayments with low cliffs (about 3 m) are made of the same material. It is easy to understand that such rocks are easily detached from the low cliff by strong waves (storm or tsunami waves). The dark zone along the coast is the zone where storms usually hit and where vegetation growth is sparse. The white blocks just inland of this storm-dominated zone are tsunami blocks (some of them with shells in living position and ^{14}C datations) and they are so numerous that they form a tsunami-controlled zone which is a dominant part of the landscape.

About 200 km north, in the Lesina lake region Mastronuzzi and Sansò (2000) have shown that as few as four large earthquakes with their related co seismic tsunamis can explain the present morphology of the coast. The first one was during the fifth century BC. It uplifted part of the coast and created a large washover fan. After this event the coast was prograding, especially because of deforestation in the

Fig. 10.7 The coast of Puglia, south of Ostuni, with tsunami blocks inland of the storm-dominated part of the coastal fringe

nearby hills, providing high amounts of sediments to the local rivers. The second earthquake (Fifth century AD) resulted first in a large erosional scarp on the newly prograded coast and in the building of a second washover fan. The third earthquake (probably less intense) is not well documented (about 1087 AD) but resulted in a significant local uplift. However this uplift was followed by subsidence and progradation of the coast due to terrestrial inputs and soil erosion. The last earthquake, on June 30 1627 triggered a new uplift and the building of two larges new fans.

The general pattern along this coast is that long periods of progradation forced by human land use practises are counterbalanced by intense and rare events that erode large section of the coastline, transporting the material inland as large washover fans. As Goff et al. (2012) stated, there is a need to merge archaeological, historical and sedimentological data to be able to better understand the main trends in coastal evolution. In this region, competition between human-forced progradation and tsunami-controlled erosion is the key forcing mechanism of coastal evolution. This model may certainly be applied to other parts of the Mediterranean Sea where tsunamis and coseismic movements are, at present, the only forces which are able to counter balance human-induced sedimentation.

10.3.2 The Antilles Basins, Tsunamis and Hurricanes: A Debate

The leeward Netherlands Antilles islands in the West Indies are a very interesting region where different teams of scientists have studied the same sites and have reached different conclusions. Sheffers and Kelletat (2003) have proposed that tsunami effects should be assessed at the regional scale. They use the term "forming force" to stress the importance of tsunamis as main forcing agent on the morphology of these islands. Their field evidences are three-fold. They first studied extensively boulder fields and ramparts and calculated that more than one million tons of blocks had been moved inland by tsunamis during the late Holocene. These blocks are piled in ridges parallel to the coast and separate the coastal fringe from the local hinterland. They are comprised of 0.2–1.2 m blocks with a few isolated mega clasts (3–4 m) and are located between 5 and 10 masl, at a distance of several hundred meters of the coast.

The second evidence is found in local "calanquen", or "boka" which are karstic valleys infilled by the sea water and which are deprived of coral platform at their contact with the open sea. They are asymmetric with an almost vertical east facing flank and a gently sloping west facing flank. According to Sheffers and Kelletat (2003) this is an indication of more energy coming from the east, i.e. from where the tsunamis are originating.

The third evidence is the absence of fringing reefs on the eastern side of the islands. Sheffers and Kelletat (2003) explain that this lack of reefs is not just a recent feature but that it was true during the entire late Holocene. No Holocene reef is found in the ramparts even in those which have been dated up to 3,000 BP.

From this set of three types of field evidences Sheffers and Kelletat (2003) propose the hypothesis that the coasts of these islands are mainly controlled by tsunamis. They forbid the building of reef platforms, they excavate previous karstic valleys and they pile up material inland. These authors calculate that a 30 s long event may erode as much limestone than a 1,000 years long "normal" erosive sequence.

Morton et al. (2008b) have scrutinized the ramparts and demonstrated that they were built by a repetition of events which are too frequent to be tsunamis. They studied aerial photos taken before and after the main recent hurricanes and show how the ridges are fed by these tropical storm waves. They also note that the morphology of the ramparts or ridges is more consistent with storm waves than tsunamis, stating that:

> Pre-mining aerial photographs of southwestern Bonaire show landward margins of the ridge complexes molded into bedforms that in planform were asymmetrical to the north. The asymmetry is consistent with shallow-water reworking by strong currents driven by hurricane-force winds at the time of backridge deposition. These back- ridge morphological features are not consistent with ridge overtopping by a tsunami.

Engel et al. (2010) have been working in the same area (and adjacent ones) and reached similar conclusions to those of Morton et al. (2008b). Although they see a regional logic to the distribution of tsunami imprints they do not speak of tsunami-only forces but of "extreme wave events" which may be, or not tsunamis. They write:

> the application of tsunami signatures which are based on investigations on sedimentary characteristics of recent onshore tsunami deposits worldwide reveals certain difficulties, since they strongly depend on local topographic settings as well as sedimentary environments and thus vary considerably.

The local setting has to be taken into account as shown by Engel and May (2012) who demonstrate that many boulders fields are linked to hurricanes and not to tsunamis but that the larger blocks are probably related to tsunamis. In this region where much work still needs to be carried out, it seems that coastal evolution is under the control of (first) extreme meteorological events and (second) tsunamis.

10.3.3 New Zealand and the Seismic Staircase

The coast of New Zealand is one part of the world where tsunami research has been ongoing since the mid-1990s. De Lange (2003) recognised 40 historical tsunamis since 1820, two of them with a wave height of ten (and more) meters, in 1931 and 1947. These historical tsunamis had many different origins. Most were from distant sources in and around the Pacific Ocean (Chile, Japan, Kermadec Islands) but some were locally generated. The Tonga Kermadec Trench (TKT), a subduction zone

ENE of New Zealand, is characterised by numerous earthquakes which can also generate submarine landslides and related tsunamis (e.g. Walters et al. 2006; Power et al. 2012). Their wave heights can easily exceed 10 m and there is only a matter of 10's of minutes to an hour or so between the detection of the quake and the arrival of the tsunami. To the SW of the South Island of New Zealand the Puysegur subduction zone (PSZ) can also generate tsunamis, although these are not considered to be as large as those produced by the TKT. The geomorphology of the coastline in the South Island of New Zealand sees tsunamis generated in the SW primarily inundating the SE coast as wave wrap around the southern end of the country (Goff et al. 2009). Ruptures of the predominant strike-slip Alpine Fault, in the South Island of New Zealand can trigger landslide-generated local tsunamis, although these are generally less powerful than those from the TKT or PSZ. The last notable source of local tsunamis is from subaerial landslides in Fiordland (SW coast) which are not always linked with earthquakes. From this short list it is clear that the entire New Zealand coast is threatened in some way by numerous locally and distantly generated tsunamis and paleotsunami research carried out along the coasts New Zealand over the last two decades has added much to the understanding of tsunami sources and recurrence intervals affecting New Zealand (e.g. Goff et al. 2001, 2010a, b; Chagué-Goff et al. 2002; Nichol et al. 2003b, 2007).

The importance of tsunamis as "forming forces" must be understood within the context of a complete "earth system" (Mc Fagden and Goff 2005) which comprises tectonic events, erosive processes, tsunamis as well as human-controlled land use changes. The term "earth system" or "seismic staircase" is a direct reference to a complex set of different inter fingering events which occur in a logical process chain of events one after the other but linked together in time and space. A short, simplified description may be done as follows. The mountains of the Southern Island are being eroded by rain and frost during several decades and slope deposits are formed. A local earthquake on the Alpine Fault displaces two blocks and the entire slope geometry between them is anew. Therefore the slope debris are not any more in a stable position and begin to flow, or fall down-stream where they are transported by a river and delivered to the sea. Locally, within the down drift area of the estuary the coast becomes sediment rich. The problem is that the earthquake has also triggered a tsunami which has hit the coast and depleted large parts of it. It is possible that the tsunami-hit area is exactly the one where sediment will be brought later by the slope/river/longshore drift chain of processes. It is also possible that the tsunami hit area is not compensated by the drift (Goff and McFagden 2002; Mc Fagden and Goff 2005; Goff et al. 2008, 2009).

The same "earth system" may obey to the same laws and processes but the earthquake may just happen at a moment when the slope deposits have not yet been able to accumulate. This is frequent when two quakes follow each other. In this case there is no large delivery of sediment to the coast and the associated tsunami cannot be compensated for. Any scenario is possible as long as it takes together the earthquakes and its effect on land to sea sediment delivery and the tsunami with its localised impacts (Regnauld et al. 2008a, b). Complications arise when volcanic eruptions occur and when deforestation by local people increases the rates of soil erosion.

The idea behind the concept of earth system is to find a coherent model that would link volcanism, earthquakes and tsunamis as regional forcings and surficial erosion and longshore drift as local controls.

10.4 Conclusion

Tsunami deposits may present many different facies, some of them being very similar to storm or hurricane deposits. Many elaborated techniques are helpful to sort out between the two origins but in many places the deposits cannot clearly be identified as having been laid by one or the other of these two events. Furthermore, tsunami deposits may be reworked by violent storms. A deposit in itself is not sufficient to understand the role and the impact a tsunami has on coastal morphology and coastal evolution. Present research tends to see tsunami as part of a large set of events, some very violent, some more average-conditions looking like. These must be understood and assessed within the regional morphodynamics context, i.e. in relation with the climate and the storm patterns and have to be possibly linked with societal impacts on sediment delivery.

Tsunami science is progressively turning into an integrated model of tectonic/climatic and historical intermingling; this is absolutely important for a correct Integrated Coastal Zone Management that comprise all the human activities from the residential one to the commercial and the strategic ones. The last decades will be remembered because of the impact of the most dramatic tsunamis in the human history. This not only for the intrinsic tsunami features, but as a consequence of the rapid and uncontrolled rise of the human settlements along the coast in highly vulnerable areas. The recent occurrence of the Indian Ocean Tsunami on December 26, 2004 and resulting 230,000 victims or more, dramatically underlined the necessity to manage human activities in coastal areas and to improve the knowledge of the regional effects of a tsunami. More recently events of September 30, 2009 around Samoa Islands, of February 28, 2010 in Chile and finally of March 11, 2011 (Tohoku Ohi tsunami and nearly 19,000 fatalities) underline the necessity to consider these events as majors forcing and controlling elements. They are responsible for instantaneous regional changes and must be assessed before any management plan of coastal areas is designed for the safety of human life.

Acknowledgements The authors express their greatest thanks to James Goff and Catherine Chagué-Goff for their help during the writing phase of this paper.

References

Barbano MS, Pirrotta C, Gerardi F (2010) Large boulders along the south-eastern Ionian coast of Sicily: storm or tsunami deposits? Mar Geol 275:140–154

Bourgeois J (2009) Geological effects and records of tsunamis. In: Robinson A, Bernard E (eds) The sea, vol 15. Harvard University Press, Cambridge, MA/London, pp 53–91

Bourrouilh-Le Jan FG, Beck C, Gorsline DS (2007) Catastrophic events (hurricanes, tsunami and others) and their sedimentary records: introductory notes and new concepts for shallow water deposits. Sediment Geol 199(1–2):1–11

Bruzzi C, Prone A (2000) Une méthode d'identification sédimentologique des dépôts de tempête et de tsunami: l'exoscopie des quartz, résultats préliminaires. Quaternaire 11(3–4):167–177

Bujalesky G (2012) Tsunami overtopping fan and erosive scarps at Atlantic Coast of Tierra Del Fuego. J Coast Res 28:442–446

Cariolet JM, Costa S, Caspar R, Ardhuin F, Magne R, Goasgen G (2010) Aspects météo marins de la tempête du 10 mars 2008 en Atlantique et en Manche. Norois 215:11–31

Chagué-Goff C, Dawson S, Goff J, Zachariasen J, Berryman K, Garnett D, Waldron H, Mildenhall D (2002) A tsunami (ca. 6300 years BP) and other Holocene environmental changes, northern Hawke's Bay, New Zealand. Sediment Geol 150:89–102

Chagué-Goff C, Schneider J-L, Goff JR, Dominey-Howes D, Strotz L (2011) Expanding the proxy toolkit to help identify past events – lessons from the 2004 Indian Ocean Tsunami and the 2009 South Pacific Tsunami. Earth-Sci Rev 107:107–122

Dawson AG (1994) Geomorphological effects of tsunami run-up and backwash. Geomorphology 10:83–94

De Lange W (2003) Tsunamis and storm surges in New Zealand. In: Goff J, Nichol S, Rouse H (eds) The New Zealand coast. Dunmore Press, Wellington, pp 79–96

De Martini PM, Burrato P, Pantosti D, Maramai A, Graziani L, Abramson H (2003) Identification of tsunami deposits and liquefaction features in the Gargano area (Italy): paleosismological implication. Ann Geophys 46(5):883–902

De Martini PM, Barbano MS, Smedile A, Gerardi F, Pantosti D, Del Carlo P, Pirrotta C (2010) A unique 4000 year long geological record of multiple tsunami inundations in the Augusta Bay (eastern Sicily, Italy). Mar Geol 276(1–4):42–57

Engel M, May SM (2012) Bonaire's boulder fields revisited: evidence for Holocene tsunami impact on the Leeward Antilles. Quat Sci Rev. doi:10.1016/j.quascirev.2011.12.011

Engel M, Brückner H, Wennrich V, Scheffers A, Kelletat D, Vött A, Frank Schäbitz F, Daut G, Willershäuser T, May SM (2010) Coastal stratigraphies of eastern Bonaire (Netherlands Antilles): new insights into the palaeo-tsunami history of the southern Caribbean. Sediment Geol 231:14–30

Fichaut B, Suanez S (2010) Dynamique d'arrachement de transport et de dépôt de blocs cyclopéens par les tempêtes: le cas de la tempête du 10 Mars 2008 sur l'Ile de Banneg (Archipel de Molene, Finistère). Norois 215:33–58

Goff J (2011) Evidence of a previously unrecorded local tsunami, 13 April 2010, Cook Islands: implications for Pacific Island countries. Nat Hazards Earth Syst Sci 11:1371–1379

Goff JR, McFadgen BG (2001) Catastrophic seismic-related events and their impact on prehistoric human occupation in coastal New Zealand. Antiquity 74:155–162

Goff JR, McFagden BG (2002) Seismic driving of nationwide changes in geomorphology and prehistoric settlement – a 15th century New Zealand example. Quat Sci Rev 21:2229–2236

Goff JR, Chagué-Goff C, Nichol SL (2001) Palaeotsunami deposits: a New Zealand perspective. Sediment Geol 143:1–6

Goff JR, Lane E, Arnlod J (2009) The tsunami geomorphology of coastal dunes. Nat Hazard Earth Syst Sci 9:847–854

Goff JR, McFadgen BG, Chagué-Goff C (2004) Sedimentary differences between the 2002 Easter storm and the 15th-century Okoropunga tsunami, southeastern North Island, New Zealand. Mar Geol 204:235–250

Goff J, McFadgen BG, Wells A, Hicks M (2008) Seismic signals in coastal dune systems. Earth Sci Rev 89:73–77

Goff J, Pearce S, Nichol S, Chagué-Goff C, Horrocks M, Strotz L (2010a) Multi-proxy records of regionally-sourced tsunamis, New Zealand. Geomorphology 118:369–382

Goff J, Nichol S, Chagué-Goff C, Horrocks M, McFadgen B, Cisternas M (2010b) Predecessor to New Zealand's largest historic trans-South Pacific tsunami of 1868 AD. Mar Geol 275:155–165

Goff J, Chagué-Goff C, Dominey-Howes D, McAdoo B, Cronin S, Bonté-Grapetin M, Nichol S, Horrocks M, Cisternas M, Lamarche G, Pelletier B, Jaffe B, Dudley W (2011) Palaeotsunamis in the Pacific. Earth-Sci Rev 107:141–146

Goff J, Chagué-Goff C, Nichol S, Jaffe B, Dominey-Howes D (2012) Progress in palaeotsunami research. Sediment Geol 243–244:70–88

Goto K, Chavanich SA, Imamura F, Kunthasap P, Matsui T, Minoura K, Sugawara D, Yanagisawa H (2007) Distribution, origin and transport process of boulders deposited by the 2004 Indian Ocean tsunami at Pakarang Cape, Thailand. Sediment Geol 202:821–837

Goto K, Okada K, Imamura F (2009a) Importance of the initial waveform and coastal profile for the tsunami transport of boulders. Polish J Environ Stud 18:53–61

Goto K, Okada K, Imamura F (2009b) Characteristics and hydrodynamics of boulders transported by storm wave at Kudaka Island, Japan. Mar Geol 262:14–24

Goto K, Miyagi K, Kawamata H, Imamura F (2010a) Discrimination of boulders deposited by tsunamis and storm waves at Ishigaki Island, Japan. Mar Geol 269:34–45

Goto K, Kawana T, Imamura F (2010b) Historical and geological evidence of boulders deposited by tsunamis, southern Ryukyu Island, Japan. Earth-Sci Rev 102:77–99

Hall AM, Hansom JD, Williams DM, Jarvis J (2006) Distribution, geomorphology and lithofacies of cliff-top storm deposits: examples from the high-energy coasts of Scotland and Ireland. Mar Geol 232:131–155

Hansom JD, Barltrop NDP, Hall AM (2008) Modelling the processes of cliff-top erosion and deposition under extreme storm waves. Mar Geol 253:36–50

Haslett SK, Bryant EA (2007) Reconnaissance of historic (post-AD 1000) high energy deposits along the Atlantic coasts of southwest Britain, Ireland and Brittany, France. Mar Geol 242:207–220

Imamura F, Goto K, Ohkubo S (2008) A numerical model for the transport of a boulder by tsunami. J Geophys Res 113:C01008. doi:10.1029/2007JC004170

Kortekaas S, Dawson AG (2007) Distinguishing tsunami and storm deposits: an example from Martinhal, SW Portugal. Sediment Geol 200:208–221

Maouche S, Morhange C, Meghraoui M (2009) Large boulder accumulation on the Algerian coast evidence tsunami events in the western Mediterranean. Mar Geol 262:96–104

Mastronuzzi G, Sansò P (2000) Boulders transport by catastrophic waves along the Ionian coast of Apulia (Southern Italy). Mar Geol 170:93–103

Mastronuzzi G, Sansò P (2004) Large boulder accumulations by extreme waves along the Adriatic Coast of southern Apulia (Italy). Quat Int 120:173–184

Mastronuzzi G, Sansò P (2012) The role of large earthquakes and tsunami in the Late Holocene evolution of Fortore River coastal plain (Apulia, Italy): a synthesis. Geomorphology 138:89–99. doi:10.1016/j.geomorph.2011.08.027

Mastronuzzi G, Pignatelli C, Sansò P (2006) Boulder fields: a valuable morphological indicator of Paleotsunami in the Mediterranean Sea. Zeitschrift für Geomorphologie, NF Suppl-Bd 146: 173–194

Mastronuzzi G, Pignatelli C, Sansò P, Selleri G (2007) Boulder accumulations produced by the 20th February 1743 tsunami along the coast of southeastern Salento (Apulia region, Italy). Mar Geol 242(1):191–205

Mc Fagden BG, Goff JR (2005) An earth systems approach to understanding the tectonic and cultural landscapes of linked marine embayments: Avon-Heathcote Estuary (Ihutai) and Lake Ellesmere (Waihora), New Zealand. J Quat Sci 20(3):227–237

Miller DJ (1960) Giant waves in Lituya Bay, Alaska. U.S. Geological Survey, Professional Paper 354C, pp 51–83

Moore A, Nishimura Y, Gelfenbaum G, Kamataki T, Triyono R (2006) Sedimentary deposits of the 26 December 2004 tsunami on the northwest coast of Aceh, Indonesia. Earth Planets Space 58:253–258

Moore A, Goff J, McAdoo BG, Fritz HM, Gusman A, Kalligeris N, Kalsum K, Susanto A, Suteja D, Synolakis CE (2011) Sedimentary deposits from the 17 July 2006 Western Java tsunami, Indonesia: use of grain size analyses to assess tsunami flow depth, speed, and traction carpet characteristics. Pure Appl Geophys. doi:10.1007/s00024-011-0280-8

Morton RA, Goff J, Nichol S (2008a) Hydrodynamic implications of textural trends in sand deposits of the 2004 tsunami in Sri Lanka. Sediment Geol 207:56–64

Morton RA, Richmond BM, Jaffe BE, Guelfenbaum G (2008b) Coarse-clast ridge complexes of the Caribbean: a preliminary basis for distinguishing tsunamis and storm-wave origin. J Sediment Res 78:624–637

Nichol SL, Goff JR, Regnauld H (2003a) From cobbles to diatoms: facies variability in a paleo tsunami deposit. In: Proceedings of the 5th international symposium coastal engineering, Florida Press, pp 1–11

Nichol SL, Lian OB, Carter CH (2003b) Sheet-gravel evidence for a late Holocene tsunami run-up on beach dunes, Great Barrier Island, New Zealand. Sediment Geol 155:129–145

Nichol SL, Regnauld H, Goff JR (2004) Sedimentary evidence for tsunami on the NE coast of New Zealand. Geomorphologie 1:35–44

Nichol S, Goff J, Devoy R, Chagué-Goff C, Hayward B, James I (2007) Lagoon subsidence and tsunami on the West Coast of New Zealand. Sediment Geol 200:248–262

Noji M, Imamura F, Shuto N (1985) Numerical simulation of movement of large rocks transported by tsunamis. In: Proceedings of IUG/IOC international tsunami symposium, pp 189–197

Noormets R, Felton EA, Crook KAW (2002) Sedimentology of rocky shorelines: 2. Shoreline megaclasts on the north shore of Oahu, Hawaii – origins and history. Sediment Geol 150:31–45

Noormets R, Crook KAW, Felton EA (2004) Sedimentology of rocky shorelines: 3. Hydrodynamics of megaclast emplacement and transport on a shore platform, Oahu, Hawaii. Sediment Geol 172:41–65

Nott J (1997) Extremely high wave deposits inside the Great Barrier Reef, Australia: determining the cause-tsunami or tropical cyclone. Mar Geol 141:193–207

Nott J (2003) Waves, coastal boulder deposits and the importance of the pre-transport setting. Earth Planet Sci Lett 210:269–276

Nott J (2004) The tsunami hypothesis – comparisons of the field evidences against the effects, on the Western Australian coast, of some of the most powerful storms on Earth. Mar Geol 208:1–12

Paris R, Wassmer P, Sartohadi J, Lavigne F, Barthomeuf B, Desgages É, Grancher D, Baumert P, Vautier F, Brunstein D, Gomez C (2009) Tsunamis as geomorphic crisis: lessons from the December 26, 2004 tsunami in Lhok Nga, west Banda Aceh (Sumatra, Indonesia). Geomorphology 104:59–72

Perez-Torrado FJ, Paris R, Cabrera MC, Schneider JL, Wassmer P, Carracedo JC, Rodrigues Santana A, Santana F (2006) Tsunami deposits related to flank collapse in oceanic volcanoes: the Agaete Valley evidence, Gran Canaria. Canary Islands Mar Geol 227:135–149

Pignatelli C, Sansò P, Mastronuzzi G (2009) Evaluation of tsunami flooding using geomorphologic evidence. Mar Geol 260:6–18

Pignatelli C, Piscitelli A, Damato B, Mastronuzzi G (2010) Estimation of the value of Manning's coefficient using Terrestrial Laser Scanner techniques for the assessment of extreme waves flooding. Zeitschrift für Geomorphologie 54(3):317–336

Piscitelli A, Pignatelli C, Mastronuzzi G (2009) Hydrodynamic equations to evaluate the impact of extreme storms on the Adriatic coast of Apulia (Southern Italy). In: Damiani L, Mossa M (eds) Coastlab 08 – Bari, Application of physical modelling to port and coastal protection. University of Bari, pp 351–358, ISBN:978-90-78046-07-3

Power W, Wallace L, Wang X, Reyners R (2012) Tsunami hazard posed to New Zealand by the Kermadec and Southern New Hebrides subduction margins: an assessment based on plate boundary kinematics, interseismic coupling, and historical seismicity. Pure Appl Geophys 169:1–36

Regnauld H, Nichol SL, Goff JR, Fontugne M (2004) Maoris, middens and dune front accretion rate on the N E coast of New Zealand: resilience of a sedimentary system after a tsunami. Géomorphologie 1:45–54

Regnauld H, Planchon O, Goff J (2008a) Relative roles of structure, climate, and of a tsunami event on coastal evolution of the Falkland Archipelago. Géomorphologie Reliefs Processus Environnement 1:33–44

Regnauld H, Goff JR, Nichol SL, Chagué-Goff et Jean-Noël Proust C (2008b) Littoraux et volcanisme en Nouvelle-Zélande: du forçage direct au contrôle en relais. In: Etienne S, Paris R (éditeurs) Les littoraux des îles volcaniques : une approche environnementale. Presses Universitaires de Clermont Ferrand, pp 57–71

Regnauld H, Oszwald J, Planchon O, Pignatelli C, Piscitelli A, Mastronuzzi G, Audevard A (2010) Polygenic (tsunami and storm) deposits? A case study in Ushant island, western France. Zeitschrift für Geomorphologie 54:197–217

Scheffers A, Kelletat D (2003) Sedimentologic and geomorphologic tsunami imprints worldwide – review. Earth-Sci Rev 63:83–92

Shiki T, Tsuji Y, Yamazaki T, Minoura K (eds) (2008) Tsunamiites, features and implications. Elsevier, Amsterdam, 411 pp

Smedile A, De Martini PM, Pantosti D, Bellucci L, Del Carlo P, Gasperini L, Pirrotta C, Polonia A, Boschi E (2011) Possible tsunami signatures from an integrated study in the Augusta Bay offshore (Eastern Sicily–Italy). Mar Geol 281:1–13

Switzer AD, Burston JM (2010) Competing mechanisms for boulder deposition on the southeast Australian coast. Geomorphology 114(1–2):42–54

Tuttle MP, Ruffman A, Anderson T, Hewitt J (2004) Distinguishing tsunami from storm deposits in eastern North America. The 1929 Grand Banks tsunami versus the 1991 Halloween storm. Seismol Res Lett 75:117–131

Vött A, May M, Brückner H, Brockenmüller S (2006) Sedimentary evidence of Late Holocene tsunami in Lefkada Island (NW Greece). Zeitschrift für Geomorphologie NF 146(Suppl):139–172

Walters RA, Goff J, Wang K (2006) Tsunamigenic sources in the Bay of Plenty, New Zealand. Sci Tsunami Haz 24:339–357

Wassmer P, Gomez C (2011) Development of the AMS method for unconsolidated sediment. Application to tsunami deposits. Géomorphologie 3:279–290

Williams DM, Hall AM (2004) Cliff-top megaclasts deposits of Ireland, a record of extreme waves in the North Atlantic – storms or tsunamis? Mar Geol 206:101–117

MIX
Papier aus verantwortungsvollen Quellen
Paper from responsible sources
FSC® C105338

If you have any concerns about our products,
you can contact us on
ProductSafety@springernature.com

In case Publisher is established outside the EU,
the EU authorized representative is:
Springer Nature Customer Service Center GmbH
Europaplatz 3, 69115 Heidelberg, Germany

Printed by Libri Plureos GmbH
in Hamburg, Germany